PREVENTION'S®

Health
Guaranteed
Cookbook

- ◆ Customized Eating Plans for Men, Women & Dieters
- ◆ Maximum Nutrients & Minimum Fat
- ◆ The Ultimate in Taste!

By the Food Editors of Prevention Health Books™
& University Hospitals Synergy Culinary School

Edited by David Joachim

Foreword by Adam Drewnowski, Ph.D., Director, Program in Human Nutrition,
University of Michigan School of Public Health

Photographs by Angelo Caggiano

Interior Illustrations by Robbin Gourley

Rodale Press, Inc.
Emmaus, Pennsylvania

Library of Congress Cataloging-in-Publication Data

Prevention's health guaranteed cookbook : customized eating plans for
    men, women, and dieters; maximum nutrients and minimum fat; the
    ultimate in taste! / by the food editors of Prevention Health Books
    and University Hospitals Synergy Culinary School ; edited by David
    Joachim ; photographs by Angelo Caggiano ; illustrations by Robbin
    Gourley.
        p.   cm.
    Includes index.
    ISBN 0–87596–537–7 hardcover
    1. Cookery, American.   2. Low-fat diet—Recipes.   3. Nutrition.
I. Joachim, David.   II. Prevention Health Books.
TX715.P9313   1998
641.5'63—DC21   97–27739

Distributed in the book trade by St. Martin's Press

2 4 6 8 10 9 7 5 3 1   hardcover

─── OUR PURPOSE ───

*"We inspire and enable people to improve
their lives and the world around them."*

Prevention's Health Guaranteed Cookbook

Editorial Staff

Editor: David Joachim
Managing Editors: Anne Egan, Jean Rogers
Contributing Writer: Kristine Napier, R.D., L.D.
Book Concept: Carol Petrakovich
Assistant Research Manager: Anita C. Small
Editorial Researchers: Lori Davis, Teresa A. Yeykal
Rodale Test Kitchen Manager: JoAnn Brader
Senior Copy Editor: Kathy D. Everleth
Art Director: Darlene Schneck
Interior and Cover Designer: Kristen Morgan Downey
Layout Designer: Thomas P. Aczel
Food Stylist: William Smith
Prop Stylist: Sherry Younis
Manufacturing Coordinator: Patrick T. Smith
Office Manager: Roberta Mulliner
Office Staff: Julie Kehs, Bernadette Sauerwine

University Hospitals Synergy Staff

Medical Director: Barry A. Effron, M.D.
Project Coordinator: Chavanne B. Hanson, R.D., L.D.
Recipe and Menu Development: Michelle Gavin, C.C.P.
Nutritional Analyses and Menu Development: Shannon Stovsky, R.D., L.D.
Nutritional Consultant: Barrie K. Rosencrans, R.D., L.D.
Exercise Consultant: Michelle Innocenzi
Support Staff: Rose Viskovic

Rodale Health and Fitness Books

Vice-President and Editorial Director: Debora T. Yost
Executive Editor: Neil Wertheimer
Design and Production Director: Michael Ward
Research Manager: Ann Gossy Yermish
Copy Manager: Lisa D. Andruscavage
Book Manufacturing Director: Helen Clogston

In all Rodale Press cookbooks, our mission is to provide delicious and nutritious low-fat recipes. Our recipes also meet the standards of the Rodale Test Kitchen for dependability, ease, practicality and, most of all, great taste. To give us your comments, call 1-800-848-4735.

Contents

Recipes

Here's a look at the nutritional profile of every recipe in this book. The recipes are organized by food category so that you can quickly find what you're looking for. Recipes are listed from lowest to highest based on calories, and figures are based on one serving. Use this list to plan meals that meet your nutritional needs. For a complete nutritional analysis, turn to the actual recipe page.

Breakfasts	Calories	Fat g.
Fluted Egg Cups (p. 80)	54	1.1
Blueberry-Cornmeal Flapjacks (p. 194)	109	2.2
Smoked Salmon Tart (p. 418)	111	3.6
Banana-Pecan Pancakes (p. 42)	124	3.5
Gingerbread Pancakes (p. 458)	124	2
Apple Pancakes (p. 415)	126	2.8
Sunrise Smoothies (p. 334)	132	0.9
Buttermilk Pancakes with Fruit Compote (p. 152)	139	1.9
Country-Style Blueberry Muffins (p. 180)	147	2.9
Bacon-Cheddar Muffins (p. 399)	149	5.2
Morning Tea Cakes (p. 376)	151	3.2
Cherry-Oatmeal Bread (p. 434)	156	3.7
Dried Apricot and Currant Scones (p. 230)	162	3.4
Sour Cream Waffles (p. 220)	162	2.6
Homestyle Hash Browns (p. 293)	163	2.5
Potatoes Peperonata (p. 438)	165	2.9
Glorious Morning Muffins (p. 58)	167	4.6
Oatmeal with Dried Cherries (p. 360)	171	1.3
Strawberry Scones (p. 76)	171	4.3
Cheese Blintzes (p. 448)	175	3.6
Herbed Asparagus Omelets (p. 103)	177	8.8
Breakfast Bread Pudding (p. 389)	189	0.3
Chocolate Chip–Banana Muffins (p. 318)	204	7.2
Italian Frittata (p. 68)	204	7.1
Salmon-Artichoke Hash (p. 48)	216	5.8
Stewed Winter Fruits (p. 392)	221	2.2
Stuffed French Toast (p. 96)	231	6.4
Orange Bran Muffins (p. 280)	233	7.1
Lone Star Omelets (p. 428)	235	10.6
Cheesy Grits Casserole (p. 350)	261	5.4
Pecan Cinnamon Rolls (p. 268)	268	9.3
Garden Bounty Omelets (p. 162)	271	13.7
Fruit and Nut Cereal (p. 288)	305	11.9
Cranberry Coffee Cake (p. 423)	305	8.7
Star-Spangled Popover Pancake (p. 247)	307	5.1
Synergy Eggs Benedict (p. 198)	317	5.1
Texas Breakfast Burritos (p. 276)	317	11.6
Sausage Melt Sandwiches (p. 335)	318	2.9
Mediterranean Breakfast Bake (p. 328)	331	10.4
Breakfast Parfaits (p. 168)	333	3.6

	Calories	Fat g.
Oat-Berry Pancakes with Vanilla-Ricotta Cream (p. 250)	387	3.6
Lemon Poppy Seed Bread with Lemon Glaze (p. 84)	396	6.5
Citrus French Toast (p. 366)	400	4

Condiments, Dressings, and Sauces

	Calories	Fat g.
Triple-Berry Cream Cheese (p. 185)	20	1
Country Cider Vinaigrette (p. 93)	32	2
Very Veggie Cream Cheese (p. 258)	38	3.1
Guiltless Guacamole (p. 190)	42	1.4
Strawberry-Orange Marmalade (p. 65)	43	0
Dill Sauce (p. 60)	45	0.3
Turkish White-Bean Dip (p. 212)	55	2.1
Cucumber Chutney (p. 158)	53	0.3
Pear and Cranberry Sauce (p. 354)	141	1.5
Pear and Apple Sauce (p. 306)	146	0.7

Sandwiches

	Calories	Fat g.
Eggless Egg Salad Sandwiches (p. 272)	184	2.4
Grilled Mediterranean Sandwiches (p. 188)	185	5.6
Southwest Bean Burgers with Lime Cream (p. 183)	190	1.2
Turkey Barbecue Sandwiches (p. 90)	233	1.8
Canadian Bacon and Roasted-Pepper Sandwiches (p. 145)	262	8.6
Seafood Salad Sandwiches (p. 341)	267	3.6
Barbecued Fish Tacos (p. 159)	302	8.1
Roast Beef Sandwiches (p. 164)	309	5.3
Home-Run Hamburgers (p. 217)	312	7.1
Hungry Man's Hoagies (p. 64)	334	4
Ham and Cheese Melt Sandwiches (p. 302)	340	11.1
Salmon Burgers (p. 86)	345	12.2
Portobello Burgers with Shoestring Fries (p. 221)	348	2.9
Oh-So-Sloppy Joes (p. 106)	353	7.9
Grilled Chicken Burgers with Caramelized Onions (p. 253)	361	9.3
Rolled Garden Sandwiches (p. 43)	372	5.4
Pesto Chicken Picnic (p. 210)	374	12.5
Eggplant Parmesan Sandwiches (p. 455)	388	7.2

Poultry, Seafood, and Meats—Continued

	Calories	Fat g.
Apricot-Mango Barbecued Chicken (p. 245)	307	6.4
Stuffed Sole with Saffron Sauce (p. 44)	314	5.5
Seafood Gratin (p. 81)	317	5.2
Thai Chicken Stir-Sizzle (p. 98)	328	7.4
Italian Veal Torta (p. 397)	331	8.7
Roasted Leg of Lamb (p. 464)	336	15.7
Herbed Chicken Pinwheels (p. 111)	366	9.5
Chicken Tacos with Charred Salsa (p. 312)	371	6.4
Chicken Potpie (p. 70)	372	5.9
Lamb Kabobs (p. 157)	375	8.8
Old-Fashioned Beef Stew (p. 419)	384	13.7
Poached Salmon with Creamy Spinach Fettuccine (p. 433)	418	11.2
Apricot-Stuffed Pork Loin (p. 408)	421	14
Fish Sticks with Banana Chutney (p. 277)	435	7.2
Wrap and Roll Cabbage (p. 440)	436	5.4
Chinese Pepper Steak (p. 402)	449	7.2
Cornish Hens with Wild Mushroom Dressing (p. 270)	453	13.9
Baked Halibut Curry with Basmati Rice (p. 453)	484	9.6
Parmesan Chicken Strips (p. 73)	531	8.4
Baked Chicken and Vegetable Couscous (p. 308)	588	5.3
Cornish Hens with Orange-Rosemary Sauce (p. 122)	597	14.3

Pasta, Pizza, and Vegetarian Dishes

	Calories	Fat g.
Wild Mushroom Pizza (p. 296)	155	4.6
Spaghetti Squash with Salsa (p. 259)	159	4.8
Garden Salad Pizza (p. 216)	161	4.4
Southern Barbecue Pizza (p. 367)	185	4
Mediterranean Pizza with Shrimp and Feta (p. 124)	205	6.5
Vegetable Pancakes (p. 232)	229	1.1
Lasagna Bundles (p. 101)	230	3.5
Goat Cheese Quesadillas (p. 134)	250	14.7
Black-Bean Ragoût (p. 465)	253	6.2
Gnocchi Florentine (p. 345)	264	2.5
Black-Bean Burritos with Verde Sauce (p. 74)	280	8.3
Tuna-Pasta Bake (p. 410)	291	6.5
Aegean Sea Pasta (p. 240)	292	5
Asian Sesame Noodles (p. 202)	293	4.6
Fennel and Swiss Quiche (p. 178)	293	12.7
Isle of Capri Pasta (p. 49)	294	6.7
Salsa Pizza (p. 359)	300	11.6
Scallion Noodles (p. 292)	304	5.4
Sweet-Potato Gnocchi with Sage Sauce (p. 425)	308	3.4

	Calories	Fat g.
Five-Star Vegetable Chili (p. 383)	309	2.8
Spinach Spaetzle (p. 372)	310	4.1
Harvest Shepherd's Pie (p. 275)	357	2.2
Old-Fashioned Macaroni and Cheese (p. 285)	358	10.3
Fiery Fusilli (p. 63)	420	7.4
Baked Ziti (p. 211)	428	7.6
Rotini with Roasted Vegetable Sauce (p. 301)	437	6.2
Pasta with Shrimp and Sun-Dried Tomato Pesto (p. 449)	480	91
Pasta Carbonara (p. 340)	486	12.2
Spaghetti and Meatballs with Garlic Bread (p. 378)	489	6.5
Beef and Spinach Lasagna (p. 264)	595	12.5

Desserts, Snacks, and Cookies

	Calories	Fat g.
Peanut Butter Sandies (p. 404)	68	2.4
Apricot Kisses (p. 420)	73	2.1
Fruitti Biscotti (p. 450)	74	0.8
Strawberry-Kiwi Smoothies (p. 50)	75	0.3
Chewy Oatmeal Cookies (p. 303)	76	1.7
Triple Chocolate Drops (p. 133)	85	2.3
Pear Sorbet (p. 265)	87	0.3
Gold Rush Lemon Bars (p. 407)	93	2.6
Berry Soufflés (p. 207)	111	0.4
Caribbean Fruit Frappé (p. 226)	115	1.4
Apricot Soufflé (p. 445)	143	0.2
Raspberry Swirl Brownies (p. 225)	149	5.2
Chocolate Mousse (p. 315)	164	4.6
Italian Parfaits (p. 114)	186	1.3
Peach-Blueberry Crisp (p. 215)	200	4.8
Summer Fruit Turnovers (p. 242)	204	2
Kiwifruit Shakes (p. 129)	214	0.5
Strawberry-Rhubarb Cobbler (p. 130)	235	4.6
Spice Cake with Maple Glaze (p. 260)	241	5.7
Key Lime Pie (p. 298)	246	7.8
Plum Strudel (p. 351)	246	4
English Trifle (p. 331)	252	1.6
Peppermint Patty Cake (p. 346)	254	4.4
Pear and Cranberry Crisp (p. 373)	255	3.5
Chocolate-Cinnamon Flan (p. 368)	258	5.6
Summer Dessert Pizza (p. 200)	266	8.6
Baked Apples (p. 339)	275	5.3
Crêpes Julia (p. 146)	328	6.3
Breezy Chocolate Chip Milk Shakes (p. 206)	338	5.4
Carrot Cake (p. 430)	343	7.6
Mile-High Apple Pie (p. 356)	352	12.6
Tiramisu (p. 108)	357	11.4
Lemon Cheesecake (p. 117)	388	10.4
Banana Bread Pudding with Caramel Sauce (p. 286)	459	2.9

Foreword

Bringing health and pleasure to the table is a rare gift. It requires both knowledge and talent. This book combines sound health guidelines with recipes developed by professional chefs and nutritionists from University Hospitals Synergy, a preeminent healthy-lifestyle clinic in Cleveland. On the principle that a successful diet should satisfy both body and mind, the emphasis here is on taste, eating pleasure, satisfaction, and enjoyment.

We all know what a healthy diet is. An ideal diet is low in fat and sugar yet rich in grains, vegetables, and fruits. This cookbook translates these basic principles of good eating into a wide range of dishes with extraordinary richness, diversity, and variety. If you associate healthy eating with choosing the same two or three "healthy" foods, you'll be pleasantly surprised. Here, no foods are excluded, and no food taboos exist. All foods, in moderation, have a place in this healthy eating plan.

The essential components of good eating are balance, moderation, and variety. Balance is a matter of making wise choices among plant-based foods, dairy products, and meats. Moderation means cutting down on—but not totally eliminating—dietary sources of sugar and fat. Variety, perhaps the most important of the three, means being adventurous, making novel food choices, and adding to the diversity of your core diet. Expanding, not restricting, food choices is the secret of healthy eating.

Two more basic principles apply here. First, pleasure and enjoyment should be the main rewards of healthy eating. This cookbook's celebrity chefs and expert recipe developers have made sure that every dish delivers maximum satisfaction as well as optimal nutrients. And, finally, this book emphasizes healthy lifestyles, not crash diets. Increased energy and vitality—and not merely "pounds off"—are the true measure of a diet's success. If healthy eating leads to greater physical activity, so much the better.

Health experts, nutritionists, and chefs have much to learn from each other. Their combined artistry, knowledge, and skills are what bring health and pleasure to the table. Their efforts have rarely been showcased to better effect than in this well-coordinated, easy-to-follow, and, above all, delicious, eating plan. As Julia Child says, bon appétit.

Adam Drewnowski, Ph.D.
Director, Program in Human Nutrition
University of Michigan School of Public Health

Your Health Plan for Life

Keeping up with the latest health and nutrition news is almost impossible. Every day, new research hits the headlines, telling us what's in, what's out, what's good, and what's bad. And more often than not, today's news contradicts yesterday's. (Remember when margarine was recommended instead of butter? Now, many experts say that butter and margarine are just about equal from a health standpoint because they both have the potential to raise blood cholesterol levels.) Even when nutrition advice sticks around for a while, it can be so complex that you need a degree in nutrition just to interpret the lingo—let alone turn it into some kind of action plan.

What you really need is someone to sort out all this health and nutrition information, then translate it into a simple eating plan. A plan that provides all the nutrients you need. A plan that minimizes those things that aren't good for you. A plan that accommodates individual food preferences and individual lifestyles. A plan that takes into account what's available in the supermarket at different times of the year. A plan that's easy. Most of all, a plan with food that tastes good. That would be a dream come true.

Stop dreaming and keep reading. This book makes all this possible. If you follow its 80 full-day meal plans, it *guarantees* a healthy diet. For *anyone*. Whether you're a woman or a man, in your twenties or beyond, trying to lose weight or prevent disease, this book is for you. It's a total package for total health. And it's easy, so it's a plan you can live with—for life.

How did we do it? This book required the scientific knowledge of a registered dietitian to meet *Prevention* magazine's stringent health guidelines for fat, calories, and important nutrients. It also demanded the culinary skill and artistry of a trained chef so that the recipes would taste good. After all, if you don't like the food, you won't stick with any eating plan.

Fortunately, we found the perfect combination in University Hospitals Synergy, one of the nation's most prominent healthy-

What's Your BMI?

Body mass index (BMI) is a measurement used by the National Institutes of Health to gauge your weight-related risk of developing high blood pressure, diabetes, and heart disease. So if you've put on a few extra pounds, calculate your BMI to determine if you're overweight or at risk for illness. Here's how.

Multiply your weight in pounds by 705. Divide that number by your height in inches. Then divide by your height again. The result is your BMI.

For example, if you weigh 175 pounds and are 5'7" tall (67"), your BMI is 27.5. (Here's the math: $175 \times 705 = 123,375 \div 67 = 1,841.4 \div 67 = 27.5$.) If you weigh 140 pounds and are 5'4" tall (64"), your BMI is 24.1.

Generally, a BMI under 25 is considered very low risk, 25 to 29 is low risk, 30 to 39 is moderate to high risk, and 40 or above is very high risk.

lifestyle clinics. Affiliated with the University Hospitals of Cleveland and Case Western Reserve University in Cleveland, Synergy has excellent credentials among health professionals. They also have a nationally renowned cooking school that specializes in healthy, high-flavor cooking. We teamed up with Synergy's talented staff of nutritionists and chefs to create 240 delicious recipes and a foolproof diet plan that you can use all year long.

A Healthy Diet—Guaranteed

The eating plan is simple. This book's recipes are organized into 80 seasonal menus. Every menu provides a full day's meals, including breakfast, lunch, dinner, and a snack. Many menus include dessert. And here's what makes the plan unique: Every menu is broken out into three different calorie levels. This means that the menus are tailor-made to meet your individual health needs. All you have to do is pick the appropriate calorie level. That's it. No guesswork. No calorie counting. No fat budgeting. Every menu guarantees that your diet is high in important nutrients and low in fat and calories. This is the easiest, healthiest eating plan you'll find anywhere. To see just what we're talking about, take a peek at the menu on page 40.

And the best part? These recipes are not diet food. All 240 recipes were developed and tested by trained chefs. Synergy's well-respected school offers more than 140 healthy-cooking classes a year, which are attended by thousands of students. Even famous chefs like Graham Kerr and Wolfgang Puck teach classes at its state-of-the-art facilities. But just to make sure that you'd like the food, we did further testing at the Rodale Test Kitchen. We're happy to report that the recipes are easy to follow, reliable, and terrific tasting.

Of course, the book's recipes and eating plan aren't the whole picture. Good health comes from a lifestyle that promotes super well-being. Here's where the folks at Synergy really excel. Their staff of registered dietitians and exercise physiologists is devoted to teaching people how to reach peak health. "Our ultimate mission is to help people learn to improve their health and reduce the risk factors for heart disease, diabetes, and other chronic illnesses," says licensed dietitian Chavanne B. Hanson, R.D., director of nutrition services.

In addition to the pros at Synergy, we consulted with other top health specialists across the country to get the latest, most reliable healthy-living information. Then we put their expert advice into a format that you can understand and use easily. This book brings the expertise of these health specialists right into your home.

The next few pages are packed with easy-to-use information

on how to achieve a healthy lifestyle. You'll learn the basic building blocks of a healthy diet, plus how to eat smart in restaurants, how to lose weight safely and effectively, how to grocery shop for maximum health, how to cook low-fat without sacrificing flavor, and much more. We also pinpoint the one thing that reduces stress, increases energy, helps you think more clearly, and lowers the risk of heart attack. What is it? Exercise. And since most Americans don't exercise regularly, we offer supereasy ways to get moving again.

If there's one thing that nutrition research has shown for sure, it's this: What you eat plays a major role in your health. Foods contain dozens of substances that affect your body in various ways. Eat too many calories and you'll put on pounds that could lead to serious ills like arthritis, diabetes, and certain types of cancer. Overindulge in fatty foods and your blood cholesterol levels could go up, putting you at risk for heart disease. Skimp on fruits and vegetables and you'll be shortchanged on vitamins and minerals, which could make you feel run-down. But you can avoid these pitfalls with smart food choices.

Calorie Control and Weight Loss

You've read the headlines about fat, and you know how much emphasis has been placed on limiting its intake. But let's get this straight: Calories count, too. Calories are found in every food you eat, whether that food is primarily carbohydrates, protein, or fat. And if you take in more than you need or more than you work off, those extra calories are likely to be stored as body fat.

Americans should pay particular attention to calorie intake. According to statistics, a solid one-third of the U.S. population is considered obese (weighing at least 20 percent more than ideal). That makes obesity an urgent problem in this country. Carrying around too much weight is more than a cosmetic issue. Obesity is linked with several serious health problems, including high blood pressure, arthritis, diabetes, heart disease, and cancer. The good news is that weight loss doesn't have to be dramatic to be effective. Studies show that obese people who lose just 5 to 10 percent of their body weight lower their blood pressure and cholesterol levels.

More good news: Dieting is dead! The simple reason is that traditional diets don't work. It's true that you can shed pounds on most of the countless weight-loss programs available in this country. But very few people—if any—keep the weight off. Studies show that most dieters regain all of the weight they lose within two to five years.

There are three main reasons that diets fail, says nutrition consultant and weight-management expert Dayle Hayes, R.D., of

6 Steps to Safe Weight Loss

Here is one of the most simple, safe, and effective ways to lose weight. It all comes down to balancing your intake against your outflow for fat and calories.

1. Pick a calorie level that's right for you, then stick with it.

2. Focus on weekly weight loss. To lose one pound of fat, you need to burn an extra 3,500 calories. Losing that much in a day is impossible because most people eat only about 1,500 to 2,000 calories a day. But if you stretch that loss over a week, that's only 500 calories each day.

3. Eat smart. Your goal is to burn or lose 500 calories a day. You can eliminate the first 250 calories by eating smart. Pass up that candy bar or that small bag of chips and a soda. Don't think that because a food is fat-free you can have unlimited amounts—it still might be loaded with calories. These extra calories are generally what keep the weight hanging on.

(continued)

Billings, Montana. "Most important, going on a diet to lose weight implies that you'll go *off* the diet at some point. For most people, that means resuming their former eating habits—the ones that may have caused them to gain weight in the first place." In addition, says Hayes, the whole psychology of dieting is unhealthy. "Severely restricting food intake, as many dieters do, generally leads to feelings of deprivation and eventually to bingeing, or at least overeating." And here's the kicker: According to Hayes, repeated research shows that chronic dieters develop a preference for foods that are high in fat and sugar. So dieting can actually make things worse—it can make you eat less healthfully and sometimes even gain weight.

What's more, some weight-loss programs are downright dangerous. "Restricting calories to less than 1,200 makes it almost impossible to get enough essential nutrients," says Hayes, "which often results in fatigue and other subtle signs of nutrient deficiency."

And, adds Hanson, "some programs severely limit calories to 800 or 1,000 calories, which is considered starvation by the World Health Organization."

Calorie control is important, but it's pretty clear that when it comes to long-term weight control and optimal health, cutting calories alone just isn't the answer. So what is? "Quite distinct from dieting routines is making long-term, healthy changes in your eating style. Simple changes can lead to slow but steady weight loss," says Hayes. "Enjoying the food you eat and feeling satisfied is critical to this overall scheme. Avoiding deprivation is the only way you'll succeed in adopting healthier eating habits to last a lifetime."

That's exactly what this book helps you do—stay healthy without feeling deprived. Take a peek at the recipes throughout the book. You'll find things like London Broil and Raspberry Swirl Brownies. You can enjoy foods like this when they're prepared in a low-fat way and eaten in the overall context of a good-for-you eating plan. That's why it's important to choose your daily calorie level first. The key is putting the focus on your daily eating plan as a whole, rather than on every food you eat. Pick a daily calorie level that works for you, whether you want to lose, gain, or maintain weight—then stick with it by eating from the menus in this book. Or create your own menus with the mix-and-match section on page 29.

Fend Off Fat

Americans consume 839 billion fat calories each year, which means that 34 to 36 percent of all the calories we eat come from fat. In the 1970s, the United States Senate's Select Committee on Nutrition and Human Needs urged all Americans over the age of

two to limit fat calories to 30 percent. Now, many health experts recommend limiting fat to 20 to 25 percent of total calories.

Too much fat is dangerous for many reasons—beyond the fact that it quickly leads to weight gain. For instance, researchers know from studying large groups of people that those who eat more fat are more likely to get cancer than those who eat less fat. High fat intake is also a risk factor for gallbladder disease. And fat's relationship to clogged arteries, or coronary artery disease, is well-known. Consuming too much saturated fat is the single most important dietary culprit in raising blood cholesterol and increasing your risk of heart disease, according to Henry N. Ginsberg, M.D., professor of medicine at Columbia University College of Physicians and Surgeons in New York City.

Why do we eat so much fat? After all, we say that we're genuinely concerned about dietary fat and how it affects our health. Fat has been the key nutritional concern among Americans since the early 1990s, according to the Food Marketing Institute's *FMI Trends* survey. But the simple truth is that taste is more important than nutrition when making our food choices.

We've simply grown to love the taste of fatty foods. The more difficult question is: Which came first? A love for some intrinsic flavor in fat itself? Or a preference for fatty foods because that's what we're used to?

Experts can't agree on this chicken/egg question, but they can explain our overconsumption of fats with basic nutrition know-how. From a nutritional standpoint, it's easier to eat too many fats (like butter) than excess carbohydrates or proteins (like rice or chicken). Fats contain more than twice the calories of carbohydrates and proteins. Each gram of carbohydrate or protein has 4 calories, while each gram of fat has 9 calories. This means that it takes far less food to eat excessive amounts of calories from fat than from carbohydrates or proteins. As a result, people often passively overeat fat calories or eat them without even knowing they are exceeding a healthy limit.

So here's what many experts recommend. "Cut down on fatty foods, limiting total fat to 20 to 25 percent of calories," says Hanson. "Also limit saturated fat to just 8 to 10 percent of calories—possibly even less if your blood cholesterol level is too high." Depending on your daily calorie level, that means eating anywhere from 30 to 70 grams of total fat per day.

Taking our cue from the experts, we adopted the 25 percent standard for this book. Every menu gets 25 percent or less of its calories from fat. In other words, when you eat from these menus, your diet will meet or beat the official recommendations for optimal

4. Get moving. To eliminate the other 250 calories, step up your physical activity. Nothing drastic. Just taking a brisk hour-long walk will burn about 250 calories. Generally, 45 minutes of any moderately intense aerobic activity each day will burn that much. Examples are biking at 8 to 10 miles per hour, tennis, and swimming.

5. Watch the weight come off. It's that simple. Cut or burn 500 calories a day and in just two months, you will have lost nearly 10 pounds.

6. Keep going. This method of weight loss may seem slow, but it's the safest way to peel pounds without gaining them all back. By making small changes, you gradually shift to a more healthy lifestyle. Through changes you can live with and stick with, you'll keep the weight off for good.

The Science of Fats

Nature constructed fats, proteins, and carbohydrates from the same basic building blocks: carbon, hydrogen, and oxygen. What makes them different is the proportions and structure of these elements. The major difference between fat and its lower-calorie counterparts is oxygen. There's far less oxygen in fat. You might say that the air has been squeezed out of fats, making them compact little calorie packages.

So what about the different types of fats—saturated, monounsaturated, and polyunsaturated? As complicated as it sounds, saturation just describes how much hydrogen a fat contains. Saturated fats are saturated with hydrogen; they contain as many hydrogen atoms as they possibly can. They're also solid at room temperature, like butter or cooled pan drippings. Monounsaturated fats are missing one pair of hydrogen atoms, and polyunsaturated fats are missing more than a pair. Both types are liquid at room temperature.

(continued)

health. When you're not eating from these menus, be aware of how much fatty food you eat, and cut back gradually. For a good start, ditch that extra handful of deep-fried potato chips or limit yourself to just one chunk of full-fat cheese. Better yet, switch to baked chips instead of fried and eat part-skim cheese.

The bottom line for food-lovers is that if you eat more carbohydrates and proteins (like whole grains, pasta, seafood, and legumes), you can actually consume a greater volume of food and still remain within healthy calorie levels.

Fiber Up

Now here's a nutrient that you should eat more of instead of less. "Americans come up dangerously short on dietary fiber," says John Weisburger, Ph.D., senior member of the American Health Foundation in Valhalla, New York. "As a result, we're increasing our risk of cancer and heart disease." A study in the prestigious *Journal of the American Medical Association* backs up Dr. Weisburger's claim. For six years, researchers studied the eating habits of 43,000 male health-care professionals. Men who ate more than 25 grams of fiber a day were 36 percent less likely to develop heart disease than those who ate less than 15 grams a day. Indeed, most Americans get only 12 grams of the 20 to 35 grams of fiber recommended per day by the National Cancer Institute.

To get your fair share of fiber, here's what dietitians recommend.

Go for real food. Some people turn to fiber supplements— powders to stir into juice, pills to pop, or wafers to chew on. Will they do the trick? "Absolutely not," says Dr. Weisburger. "Fiber supplements generally contain just one type of fiber, but the body needs many different varieties. Bran breakfast cereals and whole-grain breads provide insoluble fibers, and fruits and vegetables are a good source of soluble fibers." It also makes good nutritional sense to get fiber from food instead of supplements. High-fiber foods are loaded with vitamins and minerals that the pills don't have. Eat real food and you'll come out ahead nutritionally. Plus, high-fiber foods make you feel full longer, which helps you eat less and control your weight.

Concentrate on fruits, vegetables, and especially, whole grains. "Whole-grain foods are virtually absent from American kitchens," says grain researcher Joanne Slavin, R.D., Ph.D., professor of food science and nutrition at the University of Minnesota in St. Paul. Surveys reveal that the average American eats less than one of the three recommended servings of whole-grain food each day. And while the U.S. Department of Agriculture recommends eating a minimum of five servings of fruits and/or vegetables daily—with some officials recommending double that—Americans average just two servings daily. Here's how to make up the difference: Have a bagel or a banana with breakfast; go for a bowl of whole-grain cereal; eat a piece of fruit with lunch; plan on a vegetable side dish with dinner; eat more beans; and opt for whole-grain breads instead of white.

Drink more water. Be sure to wash down your high-fiber foods with lots of water or other healthy liquids, such as fruit juices or herbal teas. Soaking up fluid is one of the ways fiber works to cleanse your system. Without enough water, fiber can actually be constipating. So drink at least eight cups of water, juice, or other liquids every day. But avoid filling up on sugary sodas, because most sodas are loaded with empty calories.

Build up gradually. If you're just starting to boost your fiber intake, take it slow. That will help avoid abdominal discomfort and gas. Give yourself a two-week grace period to work up to the recommended daily intake of 20 to 35 grams.

Be a label reader. Check the serving size, then check the grams of fiber per serving. You can often boost your fiber intake just by having two servings. For instance, the average serving size for whole-grain cereal is less than a cup. Pour two servings into your cereal bowl, and you'll get twice as much fiber.

The Scoop on Sodium

Like many people, you may have put away your saltshaker because you've heard that salt is bad for you. But the headlines say that salt may not be such a villain after all. How does it all shake down?

First, let's review a few salt basics. Your body needs sodium to function. Sodium works in concert with potassium and other minerals to balance body fluids. But when you eat a lot of sodium, your blood draws in extra fluid to dilute the sodium, creating a larger volume of fluid in your arteries. While some people respond easily to the extra fluid by filtering it off through the kidneys, others cannot. The result? The increased volume in the arteries puts pressure on the arteries, which is reflected in a higher blood pressure reading.

About half of all people with high blood pressure are salt-sensitive. Their bodies respond to extra sodium with increased blood pressure. But most people without high blood pressure, and even a significant portion of those with it, are not salt-sensitive. The reason is that other factors can contribute to high blood pressure readings, including a high-fat diet, too little exercise, and too much stress. Plus, studies show that when you lower the salt intake of people with normal blood pressure readings, they experience barely noticeable changes in their readings. That's why some health officials have

What about margarine? If margarine is high in poly- and monounsaturated fats, why is it solid at room temperature? The truth is, margarine was once liquid and is nothing more than artificially hardened vegetable oil. To make margarine hard, the missing hydrogen atoms in vegetable oil are artificially added. This process (hydrogenation), which also keeps fats from becoming rancid at room temperature, creates something called trans-fatty acids. As you may have read, trans-fatty acids are thought to function somewhat like saturated fats, which means that they can raise your low-density lipoprotein, or LDL, cholesterol, the "bad" kind. Some nutrition experts, in fact, think that trans-fatty acids are just as dangerous as saturated fats.

Cholesterol Myths

No dietary substance is as misunderstood as cholesterol.

Myth #1: All foods contain cholesterol. Not true. There's no cholesterol in plant foods. Cholesterol exists only in the animal kingdom—in foods such as meat, poultry, seafood, dairy products, and eggs.

Myth #2: Cholesterol is synonymous with fat. Cholesterol isn't fat at all, but a white, waxy substance closely related to fat.

Myth #3: Dietary cholesterol automatically raises blood cholesterol. Although it can raise blood cholesterol a little, dietary cholesterol is a far less important contributor to blood cholesterol levels than saturated fat. The majority of cholesterol found in your bloodstream is produced right inside your body—in the liver. In most people, dietary cholesterol has a minor impact on blood cholesterol levels. That's because your body has an amazing ability to limit cholesterol absorption, turning down its absorptive

(continued)

begun to say that we've placed too much emphasis on restricting sodium for the population as a whole. If you have high blood pressure, check with your doctor to see if you are salt-sensitive. If you don't have high blood pressure, you may not need to be as concerned about restricting sodium. Of course, that doesn't mean that you should go overboard with the salt. Experts say that it's still a good idea to be sensible about sodium. Here's why.

High blood pressure is the silent killer. "Many people who have high blood pressure don't even know they have it," says Hanson. In fact, the first sign of high blood pressure might be a stroke or a heart attack. If you're in doubt about your blood pressure, visit your doctor or a health clinic to get a reading.

Preventive health makes sense. You may not have high blood pressure today, but you could develop it in the future. If you have become increasingly sedentary and stressed out, using a little less salt may help prevent high blood pressure readings down the road.

There's no harm in cutting down. Reducing salt intake generally means eating less processed meat and fewer high-fat snacks, which often translates into eating more fruits and vegetables. And there's nothing wrong with that. Many people who reduce their salt intake say that they enjoy the true taste of the food even more.

Less salt preserves bone strength. Nutrition researchers have long known that the more sodium you eat, the more calcium you lose. Calcium loss can be especially dangerous for postmenopausal women, who have trouble hanging on to the calcium in their bones. Researchers at the University of Western Australia studied more than 100 postmenopausal women for two years, comparing sodium intake with bone density. They found that women who took in an average of 3,000 milligrams of sodium daily needed to consume about 1,700 milligrams of calcium to prevent bone loss. In comparison, women who averaged only 2,300 milligrams of sodium needed just 1,200 milligrams of calcium to hang on to the calcium in their bones.

It's true that calories and fat are the most important factors in a healthy diet, but to ensure optimal health, we also set sodium limits for the menus in this book. At the 1,500-calorie level, the maximum sodium intake is 2,400 milligrams a day; at 2,000 calories, sodium is limited to 3,300 milligrams; and at 2,500 calories, the limit is 4,000 milligrams. These are the upper limits. In most menus, sodium levels fall well below these figures.

Eat Fresh for More Vitamins

It's no coincidence that *vitality* and *vitamin* have the same root word—the Latin word *vita*, which means "life." Vitamins keep you

alive and make you thrive. Dozens of vitamins and minerals are used by your body every day for basic functioning. Your body craves these nutrients to digest, absorb, and metabolize the foods you eat. You also need them to grow, heal injuries, fight disease, and support thousands of chemical reactions that are occurring right now in your body.

While you might hear that one or another vitamin or mineral is important to help a certain system of the body function normally, nutrition science is much more complex. It's the rare nutrient that works alone to accomplish a task—most work in concert with others. For example, red blood cells need at least six nutrients to form normally and function properly: iron, copper, vitamin C, riboflavin, vitamin B_6, and vitamin B_{12}. That's why it's best to get your nutrients from fresh foods instead of supplements. Fresh foods maximize your vitamin and mineral intake. In addition, nutritionists are still discovering exactly how all the nutrient combinations in foods affect your health. If you take supplements, you might miss out.

To get a handle on why you need these substances, let's take a quick look at the three main types of nutrients: fat-soluble vitamins, water-soluble vitamins, and minerals.

Fat-soluble vitamins. The four essential nutrients in this category (vitamins A, D, E, and K) get their name because of their relationship to fat. They cannot be absorbed without some fat in the diet, and they are stored in your body's fatty tissues and organs. That means if you get too many fat-soluble vitamins, they are not readily discarded. To an extent, that's good news because you can store the excess to make up for days when you come up short. But for some fat-soluble vitamins, megadoses could spell trouble. Getting too much vitamin A, for instance, can be toxic to the liver. And too much vitamin D can cause calcium to be deposited in the heart and kidneys, which could cause them to function improperly. Such problems are rare, however, if you get your vitamins directly from food.

Water-soluble vitamins. While you may hear more about vitamin C and folate than about B-complex vitamins, not one of the nine water-soluble vitamins is optional or even just a little important. Nor can one substitute for another. Consider this analogy: If you leave out the yeast when baking bread, the bread will taste fine but will have an unacceptable texture. If you omit the salt and sugar, the bread won't taste very good. Every single ingredient, in just the right amount, is necessary for the best-tasting, best-looking bread. And while yeast is a necessary ingredient, too much can cause the bread to overrise and be full of holes. So it is with vitamins and your health—just the right amount produces the best results.

Water-soluble vitamins get their name because they dissolve in

machinery in response to a particularly large cholesterol load. In addition, your body will actually produce less internal cholesterol on days when you eat cholesterol-rich foods.

Myth #4: All cholesterol is bad. Contrary to popular belief, you couldn't live without cholesterol. Your body churns out about 1,000 milligrams a day. Without it, you couldn't make new membranes or manufacture vital hormones like estrogen, testosterone, and cortisol. It's only when there is too much cholesterol in the blood or when the undesirable version—low-density lipoprotein, or LDL, cholesterol—becomes overabundant that you get into trouble. So how do you avoid that? The best way to prevent high blood cholesterol is to eat less saturated fat.

the watery fluids of the body. That means you don't store them; the excess is excreted. There's less risk of toxicity because it's more difficult to take too much. On the other hand, because the body doesn't store any extra water-soluble vitamins, it's much easier to come up short. A diverse diet is the best way to ensure getting adequate amounts each day.

Minerals. Amazingly, our bodies need at least 24 minerals to function normally—for such varied jobs as energy production, blood pressure regulation, nerve conduction, and wound healing. The amount we need changes considerably according to the mineral. While quantity varies, the importance of each mineral does not. The 0.15 milligram of iodine we need daily is just as critical to health as the 1,000 to 1,500 milligrams of calcium required.

To make sure that you're getting all the nutrients you need, we packed the recipes in this book with super-nutritious foods. To see how healthy each day's menu is, check the "Nutrient Bonus" listing that appears beside it. They show that every menu exceeds the daily recommendations for important vitamins and for minerals like calcium, iron, potassium, and zinc.

Health-Boosting Nutrients

Nutrition scientists have uncovered a whole world of substances in food beyond the traditional vitamins and minerals. And they're realizing that these nutrients can offer disease protection. Two of the most prominent are antioxidants and phytochemicals. The best way to get them is to eat more fresh fruits, vegetables, and whole grains.

Antioxidants. Every cell in your body needs oxygen to function. After using oxygen, your body churns out by-products called free radicals. Free radicals also come from cigarette smoke, exhaust fumes, radiation, excessive sunlight, certain medications, and stress. These by-products become loose cannons—high-energy particles that ricochet wildly, scarring and punching holes in healthy cells. This process, known as oxidation, weakens your immune system and puts you at risk for more serious illnesses.

Fortunately, your body has several internal defense systems that disable free radicals and repair the damage caused by the oxidation process. What else helps? Foods high in the antioxidant vitamins A, C, E, and beta-carotene (which the body converts to vitamin A). Antioxidants can boost your immune system and protect you from disease.

Having heard this news, you may be one of the millions of Americans who take antioxidant supplements in the hope of beating cancer and heart disease. Although you are on the right track, studies show that it's best to get your antioxidants from food.

Research done with antioxidant supplements has been disappointing at best. The most famous was a study investigating whether or not vitamin E and beta-carotene supplements prevented lung cancer in Finnish smokers. Vitamin E, they found, had no impact on lung cancer risk. Worse yet, those who took the most beta-carotene actually increased their chances of developing lung cancer. Several other studies with antioxidant supplements have been equally disappointing. So stick with fruits and vegetables. Fresh foods provide immune-boosting antioxidants plus a host of other nutrients that ensure peak health.

Phytochemicals. The term *phytochemicals* might well be the buzzword in nutrition these days. Although it sounds complicated, the term simply means "plant chemicals." These chemicals have been around for millions of years, but food and nutrition experts have only recently discovered that phytochemicals may play critical roles in the prevention of disease, especially cancer and heart disease.

Here's how experts say phytochemicals evolved. Back when life was just beginning on earth, plants were anaerobic, meaning that they lived in a world without oxygen. As time progressed, plants began to turn carbon dioxide into oxygen. But they weren't equipped to deal with the by-products of oxygen production: free radicals. So plants developed defenses against free radicals, and phytochemicals became the key to these defenses. They enable plants to guard against an array of adversities, including viruses, insects, harsh weather, even rough handling. Researchers say that when you eat plant foods, you also benefit from some of the healing properties in phytochemicals.

One or more phytochemicals fight cancer at every step of the cancerous process, reversing or reducing the likelihood of progressing to the next stage. For example, indoles and isothiocyanates (also called mustard oils), which are compounds found in cruciferous vegetables like broccoli, cabbage, and brussels sprouts, are ideal anti-cancer agents.

As with vitamins and antioxidants, go for the real thing. "It's possible that phytochemicals team up with fiber, minerals, and other vitamins in foods to prevent cancer and heart disease," says cancer researcher Johanna W. Lampe, R.D., Ph.D., of the Fred Hutchinson Cancer Research Center in Seattle. She adds that while supplement manufacturers can extract some phytochemicals and squeeze them into tablets, several cannot be effectively extracted, and others probably haven't yet been discovered. What's more, phytochemicals in food may work synergistically with each other; that is, their cooperative effects are greater than their individual effects.

(continued on page 14)

Vitamins and Minerals at a Glance

The following nutrients are called essential because your body cannot make them. They must be harvested from a healthy diet.

Nutrient	Why You Need It
Vitamin A	Essential for vision; enhances immunity; builds and maintains bone
Thiamin (B_1)	Helps turn carbohydrates, proteins, and fats into energy; essential for nerve impulses
Riboflavin (B_2)	Helps turn carbohydrates, proteins, and fats into energy; regulates hormones and red blood cells
Niacin (B_3)	Acts as a co-enzyme in the release of energy from carbohydrates, proteins, and fats
Biotin	Necessary for energy metabolism; makes fatty acids; breaks down amino acids
Pantothenic acid	Helps metabolize carbohydrates, proteins, and fats; helps produce cholesterol, red blood cells, and neurotransmitters
Vitamin B_6 (pyridoxine)	Helps lower blood levels of homocysteine, an amino acid linked to heart disease
Folate	Helps form DNA in new cells; lowers levels of homocysteine, an amino acid linked to heart disease
Vitamin B_{12} (cobalamin)	Helps make new cells; protects and maintains sheath around nerve fibers
Vitamin C	An antioxidant; helps form hormones that regulate metabolic rate during illness or stress
Vitamin D	Promotes bone mineralization by raising calcium and phosphorus levels in blood
Vitamin E	An antioxidant; helps protect cells from damage
Vitamin K	Synthesizes proteins involved in blood clotting and other proteins in plasma, bones, and kidneys
Calcium	Essential in bone formation and maintenance
Iron	Helps to carry oxygen in the bloodstream
Magnesium	Helps metabolize food and transmit messages between cells
Potassium	Helps transmit nerve impulses, contract muscles, and maintain normal blood pressure
Zinc	Necessary for growth, immune function, blood clotting, wound healing, and sperm production

For each nutrient, check the chart to see why you need it and which foods are good choices.

Best Food Choices

Liver, fish-liver oil, milk, fortified reduced-fat and nonfat milk, eggs, carrots, orange fruits, dark green vegetables

Yeast, lean pork, organ meats, legumes, seeds, nuts, unrefined cereals

Milk, yogurt, cottage cheese, meats, dark green vegetables, whole-grain breads

Meats, fish, legumes, nuts, whole-grain breads

Liver, egg yolks, soybeans, yeast

Meats, whole-grain cereals, legumes

Chicken, fish, kidney, liver, pork, eggs

Yeast, liver, fruits, dark green and leafy vegetables

Liver, clams, oysters, milk, seafood, eggs

Citrus fruits, dark green vegetables, peppers, tomatoes, berries, potatoes

Fish-liver oil, fatty fish, egg yolks, milk

Vegetable oils, wheat germ, nuts, dark green vegetables

Dark green vegetables

Milk and dairy products, dark green vegetables, sardines, salmon, tofu

Meat, poultry, fish, fortified cereals, dark green vegetables

Nuts, legumes, whole grains, green vegetables, bananas

Fruits, vegetables, legumes, meats

Meat, liver, eggs, oysters, seafood

11 Easy Ways to Get Moving

Who has time for exercise? Almost every free minute gets eaten up by family or work commitments. Don't worry. You can still benefit from exercise by taking small steps. If you've been inactive for a while, try these supereasy ways to get moving again.

1. Park your car in the farthest parking space and walk the extra steps to where you're going. Or get out of the subway, taxi, or bus a few blocks before your stop.
2. When the weather is nice, walk, bike, or inline skate to work.
3. Take the stairs instead of the elevator.
4. In the office, hand deliver packages to co-workers instead of using interoffice mail.
5. Take a half-hour walk during your lunch hour.
6. When you can, run errands on foot instead of by car.
7. Before dinner or 30 minutes after, take a stroll to get your heart

(continued)

To reap the full health benefits of phytochemicals, choose fresh vegetables like broccoli, cauliflower, cabbage, brussels sprouts, and mustard greens. Also opt for vegetables and fruits that have deep, rich colors, another key to phytochemical content. Strive to get at least 5—and possibly as many as 11—servings of fruits and/or vegetables a day. Whole grains contain phytochemicals, too. A minimum of 3 servings a day of foods like whole-grain cereal and whole-wheat bread will help you get a full day's supply.

The eating plan in this book incorporates every disease-fighting, health-boosting factor mentioned so far. The menus have been designed to emphasize variety and moderation. Because we haven't focused on one food or one food group, you'll be eating a well-balanced diet that will help you feel great and also give you a leg up on preventing illnesses like cancer, heart disease, diabetes, and arthritis.

The Rewards of Physical Activity

A healthy diet goes far toward guaranteeing good health. But what gets you the rest of the way is physical activity. Believe it or not, what you do (or don't do) today has a huge impact on your future health. But there are short-term rewards too, according to Barry A. Effron, M.D., medical director at Synergy and director of the lipid disorders center at University Hospitals of Cleveland. "Adopting a healthy lifestyle not only reduces the chance that you'll suffer a heart attack or stroke but also improves your quality of life. You'll feel better. And you'll have more physical and mental energy." That's the best reason we've come across for getting on your feet again. It feels good!

Whether you're 17 or 70, it's never too late to reap the benefits of regular exercise, says exercise physiologist Michael Scholtz, interim director of fitness at the Duke University Diet and Fitness Center in Durham, North Carolina. "The most important thing is to get moving today—even if it means setting out on a five-minute stroll. That's a great start for someone who would otherwise have spent the time watching television."

The benefits of physical activity cannot be overstated. Here are just a few.

Physical activity lowers blood pressure. In fact, regular physical activity may be one of the most effective nondrug therapies there is for reducing blood pressure. When researchers studied people with normal blood pressure, they found that regular walking lowered systolic blood pressure by six to eight points and diastolic blood pressure by seven points (those are the top and bottom numbers, respectively, on a blood pressure reading).

Heavy breathing lowers heart attack risk. A Finnish study of nearly 1,500 men revealed that those who exercised regularly cut their risk of heart attack by about one-third. Researchers took into account the effect of exercise on blood pressure and cholesterol, and exercise itself stood out as a separate protector. In other words, lack of exercise in and of itself is a risk factor for increased heart attack risk.

Working up a sweat increases longevity. According to an eight-year study of 800 middle-aged and older adults, exercise helped prevent disability, disease, and even premature death. Study participants who engaged in some form of vigorous physical activity had lower blood pressure, took fewer medications, visited their doctors less frequently, and were less likely to die at an early age.

Working out reduces stress. It's no secret that physical activity can help release tension. Reducing stress helps you cope with obstacles better, work more efficiently, and look at life's cup as half-full rather than half-empty.

Being active gives you that "glow." Regular exercise has been shown to give you a positive self-image, improve your mood, and even enhance your ability to think more clearly.

So how much should you exercise? "Research indicates that everyone should exercise a minimum of 30 minutes most days of the week," says Dr. Effron. That doesn't mean you have to buy expensive exercise equipment and set up a rigid routine. It simply means that burning as few as 1,000 calories a week in physical activity is enough to improve your health and lower your risk of heart attack and stroke. "That translates into walking at a pace of $2\frac{1}{2}$ to 3 miles per hour for 30 minutes about five days a week," says Dr. Effron. If you exercise more—at greater intensity, for more days, or for longer bouts—you'll reap even more benefits.

The good news is that if you don't have time for a 30-minute brisk walk every day, you can divide up the 30 minutes into several smaller sessions. "For example, you can park your car a brisk 10-minute walk away from the office," says Dr. Effron. Making that trip twice will wipe out 20 of the 30 minutes. To get the other 10 minutes, jump on your exercise bike or hustle the dog off for a quick constitutional after dinner. It's not as hard as it seems.

"It's important, however, to consult your doctor before embarking on any new exercise program," says Carl E. Orringer, M.D., a cardiologist at University Hospitals of Cleveland. "Your physician will determine if you have any risk factors that make exercising at a certain intensity unsafe and will also gather some initial information about heart health." This information will help assess the impact of

pumping and boost metabolism.
8. Go outside and play with your kids or walk the dog.
9. Rent an exercise video and try it out.
10. Walk at a local high school track or indoor shopping mall.
11. Do some active house-cleaning or yard work.

regular exercise on your health. Here are some expert tips that make exercise just a little bit easier.

Frequency is the key. "Consistent workouts are the key to long-term success," says Michelle Innocenzi, exercise physiologist and director of Fitness Services at Synergy. It's important to set aside a time in the day that you can devote to exercise. Once a routine is established, you can focus on other goals. "But start slowly, since overdoing the intensity in the beginning will only frustrate you and possibly lead to injury." As your fitness level improves, you can gradually pick up the pace to challenge yourself.

Do what you love. It's important to pick a physical activity that you enjoy. It could be walking, running, biking, swimming, aerobics, weight lifting, racquet sports, or almost anything that gets your heart rate up and keeps it there for a while. Says Innocenzi, "Make sure that the exercise plan you choose is one that you can easily incorporate into your daily lifestyle."

Don't buy exercise equipment. . .yet. Do you actually need exercise equipment? "Absolutely not," says Scholtz. "While most equipment has some benefit, there's no reason to rush into things. It's better to start with a walking program or perhaps a swimming program. Don't spend money on equipment, hoping that it will change your lifestyle. First, change your lifestyle and then carefully consider what one piece of equipment might enhance your exercise routine."

Eat Smart in Restaurants

Picture this: It's your birthday, and your spouse has whisked you off to a great restaurant for dinner. Your all-time favorite dish is on the menu—pepper steak with béarnaise sauce. Should you order it, or choose the leaner broiled trout?

"Instead of depriving yourself, be flexible when it comes to special dinners, says Hayes. Realize that there is no need to worry about any one meal. What's important is to balance your food and your activity over several days." If you're following the menus and nutrition guidelines in this book, your overall diet should be healthy. That means you can afford to have an occasional, moderate indulgence—especially if those once-in-a-while splurges help you stick with a healthy eating plan.

If you dine out daily, be sensible and realistic. Choose from the incredible variety of delicious and healthful choices on menus everywhere. To help you steer clear of restaurant fat and calorie traps, here are a few tips from nutrition experts who eat out often.

Ask for it on the side. Loads of dressing can turn a healthy salad into a fat land mine. So order the dressing on the side. Or ask for a

reduced-fat dressing. Better yet, request balsamic vinegar and extra-virgin olive oil at the table. Then you can just drizzle on a little of each.

Be picky. Don't get fooled. Ask how your food is being prepared. If you don't want butter on bread or a sandwich bun, ask for it toasted without butter. If your dish is sautéed, ask the chef to use oil instead of butter. If the food is deep-fried, ask for it to be brushed lightly with oil and baked instead. If it's pan-fried, ask for it pan-seared with little or no added fat. After all, you're paying for the food. You should get what you want.

Sleuth out sandwich fats. A turkey sandwich might sound healthy, but mayonnaise could make it a fat nightmare. Ditch the mayo, and you'll save about 11 grams of fat per tablespoon. Try mustard instead for only 1 gram of fat per tablespoon and lots of flavor.

See if there's something fishy. Seafood is generally a healthy choice. But ask how it's prepared. Broiled fish might be drenched in seasoned butter. Ask for it grilled and add your own lemon juice or lime juice at the table.

Get a naked potato. Baked potatoes are filling, but sour cream can make them sky high in fat. Ask for a plain potato and add your own sour cream or butter at the table—but just a little. Or try lemon juice, salt, and pepper. Or ask for warmed salsa as a topping, with a bit of shredded reduced-fat cheese.

Order apps to curb your hunger. Did you enter the restaurant ready to eat a horse? Quickly order a low-fat appetizer to take the edge off. A fruit cup might do the trick. Or some shrimp cocktail. You'll then be in a better position to make smart choices for the rest of the meal.

Make your own menu. Don't see anything light and lean on the bill of fare? Ask if the chef can broil a fish fillet or a lean hamburger. Complete the meal with a baked potato, steamed vegetables, and a salad with light dressing on the side.

Pass on the dessert cart. Right when you sit down, when your resolve is highest, ask the server not to bring the dessert cart by your table after dinner. If you do decide to treat yourself, look for leaner desserts like fruit sorbet, sherbet, angel-food cake, fruit compote, a low-fat frozen dessert, or cappuccino made with skim milk.

Cut Fat in the Kitchen

There are two main myths about healthy cooking. One: It takes too long. Two: It doesn't taste too good.

Let's put them to rest. Food that's good for you doesn't take any longer to prepare than food that isn't good for you. Yes, some healthy recipes may have slightly longer ingredient lists. But these extra

Get the Right Tools

Healthy cooking is easy when you have the right equipment. What you need depends upon the type of meals that you generally make. Here's a list of basics and extras that'll get your kitchen off to a healthy start.

Basics

- Baking dishes, no-stick; 9" × 9", 13" × 9"
- Baking sheets, no-stick
- Cake pans, no-stick; two 9" round
- Can opener
- Casserole, 2-quart or 3-quart
- Colander
- Cutting board
- Electric mixer, handheld or freestanding
- Food processor, full-size
- Grater, 4-sided
- Knife sharpener
- Knives, paring, serrated for bread, and 8" chef's
- Loaf pans, no-stick
- Measuring cups, graduated for dry ingredients, glass for wet ingredients
- Measuring spoons
- Mixing bowls, graduated; stainless steel, glass, or ceramic
- Muffin pans, no-stick

(continued)

ingredients are often just herbs or spices, which can be added in seconds. Once you're familiar with cooking healthy, it's just as quick.

As for taste, believe it or not, there's research that suggests healthy food actually tastes better. It all comes down to something called palate shift, according to John La Puma, M.D., director of the CHEF (Cooking Healthy Eating Fitness) pilot study at Alexian Brothers Medical Center in Elk Grove Village, Illinois. "Palate shift is a change in a person's ability to appreciate flavor," says Dr. La Puma. "We've found that food with less fat allows people to more fully enjoy the experience of eating. It's almost as if fats have formed a layer over your palate, preventing an appreciation of the other flavors and textures in food." After 10 to 12 weeks of lower-fat food, subjects in the pilot study actually reported an increase in their range of flavor appreciation. "There is a shift from appreciating mainly the full, rich, heavy, round flavors in fat to appreciating the bright, clean, citrusy, fresh flavors of food with less fat. Eating less fat may actually broaden your palate and your enjoyment of food," says Dr. La Puma.

The only other thing that you need to know is *how* to cook healthy. Of course, perfection comes with practice, but "having the right equipment and learning a few tricks is a tremendous help in cooking healthier food," says Michelle Gavin, director of the Synergy culinary school. As one of the first cooking schools in the country dedicated to low-fat cooking, Synergy's professional culinary staff are the experts on how to pack good-for-you food with great taste. On the next few pages, they reveal their secrets for transforming your kitchen so that you can whip up healthy, high-flavor food with ease.

Tricks of the Trade

Healthy cooking involves many of the same methods used for higher-fat food preparation. You still bake, boil, steam, broil, sauté, poach, microwave, stir-fry, grill, and marinate. The difference is using less fat (and an absence of deep-frying). To make up for the flavor lost by cutting fat, it helps to know a few tricks. With baked goods, in particular, knowing what works and what doesn't is crucial. Here's how the low-fat experts at Synergy make great-tasting food.

- For cooking meat, fish, and poultry, roast, poach, braise, broil, steam, bake in parchment paper, stir-fry (with just a little oil), or stir-sizzle (like stir-frying, but use broth instead of oil).
- Choose lean cuts of meat. Marinate them, as well as vegetables, in reduced-fat and fat-free mixtures to intensify flavor. Replace oil with fruit juices, vegetable juices, or broth; season the marinade with soy sauce, herbs, and spices.

- Replace fat with sweet. Instead of slathering on the butter, use fruit salsas or chutneys to flavor pork, lamb, and fish. For poultry, use marmalade.
- Replace high-fat ingredients with lower-fat alternatives. For example, use Canadian bacon or turkey bacon instead of regular bacon. Use turkey sausage instead of pork sausage. But read labels to make sure that you're getting a real fat savings.
- Intensify the flavor of butter or margarine. Use less, but melt fresh herbs or spices in it.
- Extend butter or margarine by mixing it with fruit juice, vegetable juice, or flavored vinegars.
- To reduce fat in baked goods, replace half of the butter with a combination of oil and milk. Or replace up to one-fourth of the fat with applesauce. This method works well in muffins, quick breads, and snack cakes.
- Substitute two egg whites for each whole egg in baking.
- To reduce the fat in chocolate desserts, use cocoa powder, a small amount of oil, and just a bit of grated baking chocolate. You can also cut fat in desserts like brownies by replacing some of it with prune puree.
- Use evaporated skim milk instead of cream for soups and sauces.
- Use extracts to replace high-calorie ingredients such as coconut and rum.
- Use smaller amounts of high-fat, high-calorie ingredients. To get the most flavor, cut them smaller so that they disperse throughout the food. For example, instead of coarsely chopped nuts or olives, chop them finely. When a recipe calls for chocolate chips, use mini-morsels, but cut the quantity in half.
- Toast nuts and spices to intensify flavor. Place the spices or nuts in a dry no-stick skillet and cook, stirring often, over medium heat for 3 to 4 minutes, or until toasted and fragrant.
- Use intensely flavored foods or ingredients. For example, choose extra-virgin olive oil over other types. It may be a little more expensive, but you'll actually use less. Use kosher or sea salt instead of regular table salt. Likewise, strong-tasting cheeses such as feta and goat cheese are packed with flavor, so you don't need much.
- Grease pans and muffin tins with no-stick spray instead of oil. To vary the flavor, try olive oil spray for sautéing and butter-flavored spray for baked goods.
- Stir-fry with no-stick spray and broth instead of oil or butter. Or use very small amounts of an intensely flavored oil, such as dark sesame oil.

- Pie plate, no-stick, 9"
- Saucepans, regular or no-stick with lids; 1-, 2-, and 3-quart
- Skillet, no-stick, 10"
- Spatulas, rubber, stainless steel
- Spoons, wooden, rubber, and slotted
- Steamer basket, collapsible or insert
- Stockpot
- Thermometer, instant-read
- Timer
- Tongs
- Toothpicks, wooden
- Vegetable peeler
- Whisk
- Wire rack

Extras

- Basting brush
- Blender
- Citrus juicer, handheld
- Citrus zester
- Fat skimmer
- Food mill
- Food processor, small
- Food scale
- Garlic press
- Griddle, no-stick
- Ladle
- Microwave
- Mills, peppermill, electric spice mill
- Melon baller
- Salad spinner
- Skewers, metal
- Toaster oven
- Yogurt strainer

Make It Lean Meat

You don't have to eliminate red meat to eat healthy. The trick is choosing the leanest cuts, trimming all visible fat, and watching portion size. Generally, a good-for-you portion of meat is about 3 ounces after cooking. At that serving size, you get all the benefits of protein and iron, without a lot of fat. Here's a quick list of the leanest cuts. A 3-ounce trimmed serving of each provides less than 200 calories and less than 9 grams of fat.

Beef: Tenderloin, top loin, sirloin, top round, eye of round, tip, flank steak

Lamb: Whole leg, loin chop, blade chops, foreshank, sirloin roast

Pork: Canadian bacon, tenderloin, sirloin, lean boneless ham

Veal: All cuts except commercially ground

Stock Up

A well-stocked pantry means healthy meals at your fingertips. "At the Synergy cooking school, our biggest secret is turning up the volume on flavor when we take out the fat," says Michelle Gavin, director of the University Hospitals Synergy culinary school. Here's what to keep on hand for maximum flavor and minimum fat.

Many of these ingredients are used throughout the recipes in this book. Add these items to your kitchen, and you will broaden the range of flavors in your food. Most of these ingredients can be stored for weeks or months in your pantry or refrigerator. The list doesn't include standard items like baking powder or fresh high-flavor ingredients like lemons and oranges. As for perishable items, be sure to keep some reduced-fat dairy products in the refrigerator, such as nonfat buttermilk, low-fat yogurt, reduced-fat cream cheese, and reduced-fat sour cream. A variety of cheeses can come in handy as well. Start with feta cheese, reduced-fat mozzarella, reduced-fat Cheddar, and Parmesan or Romano.

Basics
- Canned beans: white, kidney, chickpeas, lentils, black-eyed peas
- Canned tomato products, no-salt-added: tomato paste, sauce, whole, crushed
- Capers
- Cocoa powder
- Corn syrup, light and dark
- Dried fruit: apricots, cherries, cranberries, currants, dates, peaches, prunes, raisins
- Extracts: almond, chocolate, coconut, rum, vanilla
- Flours: all-purpose, cake, whole-wheat, whole-wheat pastry
- Fruit butters: apple, pineapple
- Fruit juices: apple, apricot, papaya, peach, pear
- Fruit nectars: apricot, peach, pear
- Garlic
- Herbs: dried basil, dill, oregano, rosemary, thyme
- Hoisin sauce

- Plan bulk into your menus. Strive to include whole grains at every meal because the extra fiber will help fill you up with fewer calories. Similarly, include a fruit and two vegetables at each of your meals to help satisfy your hunger without piling on the calories.
- Use no-stick cookware, bakeware, and other utensils to make low-fat cooking easier.

- Honey
- Jams and jellies: all-fruit, assorted flavors
- Ketchup
- Kosher salt or sea salt
- Maple syrup
- Molasses
- Mustards: Dijon, whole-grain, yellow
- No-stick spray
- Nuts: almonds, pecans, walnuts
- Oils: canola, olive, toasted sesame
- Rice: Arborio, basmati, brown, white, wild
- Roasted sweet red peppers, water-packed
- Salsa
- Soy sauce, reduced-sodium
- Spices, ground or whole: black peppercorns, chili powder, cinnamon, cumin, curry powder, garlic powder, ginger, ground red pepper, paprika, red-pepper flakes
- Sun-dried tomatoes, dry-pack
- Vinegar: balsamic, fruit-flavored, rice wine, white wine
- Worcestershire sauce

Extras

- Anchovy paste
- Chili-garlic paste
- Chili peppers, assorted dried
- Chutney
- Coconut milk, reduced-fat
- Hot-pepper oil
- Miso (Asian soybean paste)
- Mushrooms, assorted dried
- Olives: black, green stuffed with pimentos
- Roasted garlic paste
- Spices, ground or whole: allspice, cardamom, Chinese five-spice powder, cloves, coriander, Italian herb seasoning, nutmeg, saffron, turmeric

- When making soups and stocks, let them chill so you can skim off the solidified fat.
- Replace high-fat dairy products (such as whole milk, sour cream, yogurt, cream cheese, and other cheeses) with reduced-fat and nonfat varieties. Experiment to find the best uses for each. For example, nonfat cream cheese works fine in many recipes—including desserts—but it just doesn't taste good on a

Quick-Shopping Tips

There's no doubt that shopping takes time. But there are ways to cut the time that you spend at the grocery store.

- Shop the same store. You'll know where things are, and that's the biggest time-saver.
- Make a list. Keep it on the refrigerator. When you run out of an item, jot it down.
- Plan for the week. Include anything that you might need for the week's meals. If you're buying meats for later in the week, you can freeze them until needed. Planning is the best way to ensure fewer trips to the store.
- Buy precut vegetables and bagged salads. The nutritional quality of these items is excellent, and they save you loads of prep time.
- Choose precut stew and stir-fry meat. Again, prep time is cut to a minimum. If your time is limited, the added expense is worth it.
- Go low-fat and low-sodium. There's no question that you'll eat

(continued)

bagel. Similarly, reduced-fat Cheddar cheese may melt on top of a casserole, but nonfat won't.
- Use low-fat or nonfat yogurt cheese to replace cream cheese, butter, and sour cream in recipes. For directions on how to make it, see page 158.
- To save time, use a food processor to chop, slice, shred, and grate vegetables.
- If you don't have fresh vegetables, use frozen ones.
- If you don't have time to chop fresh vegetables, buy them already cut in your supermarket salad bar or produce section.

Stop and Shop for Maximum Health

Do you get confused in the supermarket? It's no wonder, since the average store has about 30,000 items, according to the Food Marketing Institute. On top of that, not every store has the same 30,000 items. You might encounter thousands of additional ones just by shopping in different stores. "That makes finding healthy choices quite difficult—even intimidating," says Nelda Mercer, R.D., author of *The M-Fit Grocery Shopping Guide.*

Here's how Mercer solves the riddle of the supermarket sphinx. It's called the stoplight system. As you enter the store, mentally divide it into sections—green light, yellow light, and red light.
- Green-light foods represent the healthiest food choices. They're lowest in fat. All systems "go" on these foods.
- Yellow-light foods are acceptable food choices. They may be a little higher in total fat, saturated fat, cholesterol, sodium, or sugar. Or they may be lower in fiber than green-light foods. So use yellow-light foods with caution and careful planning.
- Red-light foods are considered occasional choices rather than often-used items. These foods are the highest in total fat or saturated fat. Stop, think, and read the label before purchasing red-light foods.

"This system doesn't mean that you can use green-light foods indiscriminately. Nor does it mean that you should swear off red-light foods completely," says Mercer. The stoplight system simply shows you what foods to eat more of and what to use with caution. It's entirely possible, Mercer explains, to fit in bacon and cheesecake on occasion and in reasonable portion sizes.

Generally, the green-light and yellow-light areas are located around the perimeter of the store. So spend most of your time there. The center aisles are where you will often find the red-light foods. In these aisles, you'll need to read labels carefully to make sure that you choose the healthiest item available. Here's a section-by-section map to help you through the supermarket maze.

Produce section = green light. The produce section has the healthiest food choices. It's best to spend the majority of your grocery-store time lingering over the produce and choosing carefully. The only questionable choices here are coconuts and avocados, which are high in fat and should be used sparingly. Otherwise, fill your cart with enough produce to get at least three vegetables and at least two fruit servings a day. Go for variety by choosing lots of different colors and textures. Brightly colored red vegetables generally have a different blend of nutrients than dark green leafy types. Similarly, assorted berries offer a different nutrient mix than apples and bananas.

Seafood counter = green light. Almost all fresh seafood is considered a healthy choice. Most fish is low in fat and calories. And fatty fish, including salmon, mackerel, and albacore tuna, are high in heart-healthy omega-3 fatty acids. Even things like shrimp are considered healthy despite the fact that they have more cholesterol than other seafood. Experts say that shrimp is a good choice because it's very low in saturated fat. One caveat here: If breaded fish sticks or fish fillets are on the menu, choose those made with a low-fat batter or no batter at all.

Bakery = yellow light. Most supermarket bakeries are stocked with a host of delicious whole-grain foods that are naturally low in fat and high in vitamins and minerals. Go for baked goods like whole-grain bagels, whole-wheat breads, or rye dinner rolls. But try to steer clear of high-fat cookies, cakes, and confections.

Dairy section = yellow light. Choose with caution here. Dairy foods offer great nutrition benefits, but they're typically high in fat. Choose low-fat or nonfat yogurt and milk, nonfat cream cheese and sour cream, and reduced-fat hard cheeses (search out those that are 50 percent reduced-fat). Experts say that you should get to know this section well. Take time to read labels, try different brands, and stick with those that work for you. Make it a goal to work your way down the fat ladder for foods in this section. For example, if you currently use whole milk, try 2 percent. Then switch to 1 percent. Eventually, you may find that skim milk tastes just fine. Do the same thing with cream cheese and sour cream. By using low-fat dairy products, you can add wonderful flavors and textures to healthy meals.

Poultry section = yellow light. Most foods in the poultry section are green light, but some may require a little caution. For instance, skinless chicken and turkey breast are good choices, but some ground turkey may be high in fat. When choosing ground turkey, look for 100 percent ground turkey breast. And watch out for prepared items like chicken nuggets. The batter may be high in fat. Check the

healthier—if you stick to reasonable serving sizes.
- Stock up on frequently used foods. Buy cereal, rice, pasta, and tomato sauce in bulk. Prepare a large batch of pesto or chop lots of onions and freeze the extra. That way you'll always have these basics on hand.

serving size to make sure that you're really getting a healthy food.

Meat case = yellow light. Surprise again: Meat is not off-limits. "There are many healthy choices in the meat case—you just have to choose lean cuts," says Gavin. Also, keep in mind that a healthy portion of cooked meat is about 3 ounces per person, the size of a deck of playing cards. Most experts recommend limiting red meat to four servings per week. Because meat shrinks when cooked, plan on buying 4 ounces of uncooked meat per person.

Center aisles = blinking red light. Regard packaged and convenience foods as red-light items. Stop to read labels when choosing them. Many of these foods are super-high in sodium or fat (especially saturated fat). On the other hand, many center-aisle foods, such as whole-grain cereal, dried pasta, low-sodium canned beans, and low-sodium canned tomato products, are green-light staples in a healthy diet. So choose wisely in the center aisles.

Freezer section = blinking red light. This section also contains some very healthy and some less healthy choices. Frozen dinners are generally red-light foods. Check the labels and serving sizes to see if these foods fit into your healthy-eating plan. Likewise, frozen desserts should be chosen with caution. Some items, like low-calorie frozen fruit-juice bars are perfectly acceptable. Others, like full-fat frozen yogurt, can be a fat and calorie nightmare. Look for reduced-fat or nonfat frozen yogurt. Choose frozen vegetables without added sauces. Frozen fruits are green-light foods, especially if they're not packed in sugar syrup. So fill up the cart.

"Getting to know and understand food labels is the most important thing that you can do to make shopping for healthy foods easier," says Mercer. She offers the following quick guidelines.

- The Daily Value (DV) tells you what percentage of the Recommended Dietary Allowance one serving of the food provides. If an item contains 5 percent or less of the DV per serving, that means it's low in that particular nutrient.
- An item containing 20 percent or more of the DV per serving is considered a significant source of that nutrient. If a food contains 20 percent of the DV for fiber, it's a good choice. On the other hand, foods containing 20 percent of the DV for saturated fat are not such a good choice.

What's the best overall advice for healthy shopping? "Go for balance, moderation, and variety," says Mercer. "Also, make it a goal to try a new vegetable each week." That way, you'll eat a variety of foods and maximize your nutrient intake. Plus, you'll enjoy a wide range of flavors and textures in your food. And that will keep your taste buds happy.

How to Use This Book

By now, it's no secret that your diet has a major impact on your health. But who wants to wade through endless nutrition guidelines, calculate complex percentages, tally up nutritional figures for dozens of foods, and develop the perfect eating plan—just to decide what's for dinner? Believe it or not, we do. And we did. We know that nutrition advice is confusing, frustrating, and time-consuming to decode. So we made things easy for you. We took the most up-to-date and reliable nutrition advice from health officials around the country and distilled it all down to one simple eating plan.

Here's the plan: Eat from the menus in this book and your diet is guaranteed to be healthy. That's all there is to it.

There are 240 recipes in this book. The recipes are organized into 80 full-day menus. Every menu provides breakfast, lunch, dinner, and a snack. (Quick-to-fix foods like tossed salads supplement the actual recipes in each menu.) And here's the best part: Every menu also comes in three different calorie levels. That means the eating plan is tailor-made to meet your individual health needs. Just pick the calorie level that works for you and follow the menus. You can put your calculator away because all the tallying has been done. The menus are low in everything Americans tend to eat too much of—like total fat, saturated fat, cholesterol, and sodium. What's more, they're high in the things Americans don't get enough of—like fiber, calcium, and vitamin C. When you eat from these menus, you'll be doing everything you possibly can, from a nutrition standpoint, to prevent disease and achieve peak health. And by including moderate exercise in your lifestyle, you can also steadily lose weight if you need to.

About the Menus

The menus were designed with every detail in mind. We chose full-day menus because that puts the focus on your diet as a whole rather than on individual foods. The full-day approach shows that it's possible to have a low-fat dish at one meal and a slightly higher-

fat one at another while still remaining within healthy limits. Here are some other things that you can expect from these menus.

Great taste. Does going healthy mean giving up flavor? Absolutely not. We found the perfect recipe for great-tasting food that's good for you, too: a chef and a dietitian. This combination has been thriving for years in Cleveland at University Hospitals Synergy—one of the country's top healthy-lifestyle clinics. All of the recipes in this book were created and tested by Synergy's trained chefs. They know that if the food doesn't taste good, you won't keep eating it. So we made sure that the menus in this book will tickle your taste buds and leave you feeling satisfied. Each recipe has been at least double-tested by Synergy's culinary staff. In fact, many went through three rigorous taste tests. And we did further testing at the Rodale Test Kitchen for extra measure.

Nutritional excellence. The menus provide all the nutrients that you need while maintaining healthy limits for calories, fat, cholesterol, and sodium. Each day includes at least 10 different foods and, in many cases, more than 15. "Variety is one of the most important ways of ensuring that you get all nutrients," says Nelda Mercer, R.D., author of *The M-Fit Grocery Shopping Guide*. Every menu meets or exceeds daily recommendations for a host of essential nutrients. Although a single day's menu may come up slightly short on one or two nutrients, that's okay, says licensed dietitian Chavanne B. Hanson, R.D., director of nutrition services at Synergy. "The goal is to balance out nutrient intake over a week's time. If you do, you'll be in great shape nutritionally."

The menus are also consistent with the U.S. Department of Agriculture's Dietary Guidelines for the Food Guide Pyramid. These national guidelines recommend eating the following foods every day for optimal health.

- 6 to 11 servings of bread, cereal, rice, or pasta
- 2 to 4 servings of fruit
- 3 to 5 servings of vegetables
- 2 to 3 servings of milk, yogurt, or cheese
- 2 to 3 servings of meat, poultry, fish, dry beans, eggs, or nuts

Minimum fat. Every menu gets less than 25 percent of its calories from fat. So all the fat budgeting has been done for you. Once you pick your calorie level, the right amount of fat is automatically figured in.

What about when you're not eating from these menus? How do high-fat foods fit into a low-fat diet? For example, how does margarine—which is 100 percent fat—fit into a 25 percent fat eating plan? "The key is using such foods in moderation and balancing

them with low-fat and nonfat foods," says Hanson. For example, using 1 teaspoon of margarine on a dinner roll is fine when the rest of the meal consists of grilled salmon, steamed broccoli, a baked potato, applesauce, and nonfat milk. The margarine gets 100 percent of its calories from fat, and the salmon gets 42 percent. But the broccoli, potato, applesauce, and milk total just 3 percent. As a whole, the meal shakes down to 22 percent fat. "That's one of the reasons variety is so important when planning meals," notes Hanson.

Limited sodium. Many health officials say that we've placed too much emphasis on restricting sodium for the population as a whole. That's because salt may not be a significant factor in raising blood pressure for many people. Nonetheless, the nutrition experts at Synergy and *Prevention* magazine recognize that too much sodium may be harmful in the long run. So we set modest sodium limits for each calorie level. At the 1,500-calorie level, the sodium limit is 2,400 milligrams; at 2,000 calories, it's 3,300 milligrams; and at 2,500 calories, the limit is 4,000 milligrams. Rest assured, most menus fall well below these figures. If you are on a severely sodium restricted diet, consult with your physician about appropriate sodium levels for you. You can easily lower the sodium in most recipes by omitting salt (except in baking, where it may be needed for the recipe to work) and using reduced-sodium varieties of other ingredients.

Another important note: Most of the recipes in this book specify exact amounts of salt to add. However, some recipes list simply "salt" or "salt and ground black pepper." In these cases, the amount of salt used for both the recipe and the nutritional analysis is one "pinch," or the equivalent of $1/16$ teaspoon.

Visual excitement. You may not realize it, but you "taste" food with your eyes first. If a plate of food doesn't look good, you won't be tempted to eat it. Mashed potatoes, steamed cauliflower, and a grilled chicken breast may be balanced nutritionally, but together they make a boring-looking meal because they're all the same color. If you don't outright pass it by, you're less likely to feel satisfied than if you had a meal that was visually exciting. That's why we've taken such care to create meals that look great on the plate. In addition to flavor and nutritional quality, these recipes and menus focus on three very important characteristics of food: color, texture, and size. No one likes skimpy portions of food, so we made sure that the serving sizes are generous.

Seasonal foods. Eating fresh foods in season makes a lot of sense. They're readily available, full of nutrients, and less expensive. You know the frustration of making a special trip to the store to buy ingredients for a new recipe—only to find that they're unavailable or

Pick Your Calorie Level

Eating the right number of calories is crucial to managing your weight, warding off disease, and tuning your body for optimal health. Essentially, the number of calories that you need depends on how much you weigh. Bigger people have more living tissue to support, so they need more calories to maintain weight than smaller folks.

Here's how to pick the calorie level that's right for you. First, convert your weight in pounds to kilograms by dividing by 2.2. Next, multiply your weight in kilograms by the "energy allowance" figure from the chart on the opposite page.

For example, if you are a 150-pound, 52-year-old woman, your daily calorie level is 2,040 calories. Here's the math: 150 pounds ÷ 2.2 = 68 kilograms × 30 = 2,040 calories. At the 2,000-calorie level, you will be getting the perfect diet for maintaining your current weight and staying healthy.

If you want to lose weight, decrease your calo-

(continued)

out of season. That's why we organized the menus in this book by season. The menus take into account what's scarce in December and what's abundant in July. In addition, we know how a bowl of hot stew warms you up after shoveling the driveway. And how a crisp, cold salad hits the spot on a sweltering summer day. Our winter menus emphasize cool-weather foods and cooking methods like roasting and baking, while summer menus often take to the grill.

Minimal time commitment. The menus in this book don't require you to be in the kitchen all day. Many items are ready-to-eat foods or easy dishes that require very little preparation time, such as grilled chicken breast. You can cut prep time even further by using precut vegetables or frozen ones. For example, if a chicken stir-fry calls for cut-up broccoli, carrots, and cauliflower, one bag of mixed frozen vegetables will do the trick. "While this is a great shortcut, realize that frozen ingredients don't have the robust taste of fresh," adds Michelle Gavin, director of the Synergy culinary school.

Menus at a Glance

We've done everything possible to make it easy for you to have a healthy diet. All you need to do is follow the menus. Just so you know exactly what we're talking about, let's take a quick look at the important elements in each menu.

1. *Calorie level.* Every menu comes with three different calorie levels: 1,500 calories, 2,000 calories, and 2,500 calories. Remember that once you pick your calorie level, fat budgeting is automatically calculated. That means you'll be eating less than 43 grams of fat per day at the 1,500-calorie level, less than 56 grams at 2,000 calories, and less than 69 grams at 2,500 calories.

2. *Recipes and other foods.* The purple color indicates recipes that you'll find in the book. There are three recipes in each menu, and they appear on the pages following the menu. The other items listed are simple foods that complete the day's meals, such as granola with banana slices and skim milk. For both the recipes and the other foods, simply measure out the serving sizes listed at your calorie level.

   Note: If you're feeding a family of four or more, be sure to check the number of servings that each recipe makes. In some cases, you may need to double a recipe.

3. *Daily Totals.* This section gives you a nutritional profile for the entire day's meals at every calorie level. You may notice that the meals don't always add up to exactly 1,500, 2,000, or 2,500 calories. Yet every menu falls within 30 calories. Other things listed are fat, percent of calories from fat, protein, carbohy-

drates, dietary fiber, cholesterol, and sodium.

4. *Nutrient Bonus.* Here's where you find out just how packed with nutrients these meals really are. We use the freshest, healthiest foods to maximize your intake of vitamins and minerals. This list shows that every menu meets or exceeds the daily recommendations for many important nutrients like calcium, iron, folate, and vitamin A. The figures shown are a percentage of the daily recommendation, or Daily Value. These percentages have been calculated at the 2,000-calorie level, the average level for moderately active adults.

5. *Healthy Tip of the Day.* These helpful hints cover such things as how to snack all day long and not gain weight, how to choose between butter and margarine, and how to eat smart at parties. From cooking to weight loss and from exercise to nutrition, you'll find 80 tips that make it easier to live a healthy lifestyle.

Mix-and-Match Menus

You can tailor the menus to suit your personal preferences, substituting foods in any given menu, creating your own special calorie level, or building original menus to satisfy your tastes. Here's how to plan your own menus and personalize them to meet your needs.

Pick a calorie level. The math for planning a full day's meals is simple. Once you pick a calorie level, just divide your total calorie intake among three meals and one snack. Plan on consuming just under one-third of your total calorie needs at breakfast. (A hearty breakfast will give you all-day energy and help you resist bingeing on high-calorie snacks later on.) Likewise, lunch and dinner (including dessert) should each account for about one-third of your day's calories. The remaining calories are for a snack; ½ cup of grapes or a handful of pretzels, for example, adds up to about 75 calories. To calculate the percentage of fat calories in your full-day menu, multiply the total fat grams by 9, then divide by the number of calories. For instance, 45 grams of fat × 9 ÷ 2,000 calories equals 20 percent of calories from fat.

Use the lists. This book contains two very useful lists. They are your keys to making the book work for you. Whether you want to use a favorite recipe from the book more often, omit recipes that don't appeal to you, or just modify the calorie level to meet your health needs, you can use these lists to do it.

The first list, on page v, includes all the recipes in this book. It's organized by food category, and the recipes are listed from highest to lowest based on calories. When building full-day menus, use the recipe list to find foods that fit your calorie needs. You can also use this

rie level by 250 calories per day and increase your exercise to burn off 250 calories per day. That will allow you to lose 1 pound a week, which is an excellent rate of weight loss, according to health officials. "Slow, gradual weight loss is the kind that lasts," says Michelle Innocenzi, exercise physiologist and director of Fitness Services at University Hospitals Synergy in Cleveland.

Age	Energy Allowance	
	Female	*Male*
19–24	38	40
25–50	36	37
51+	30	30

Watch Portion Sizes

Paying attention to serving size is a key factor in the success of any eating plan. Let's say that you're following the menus in this book at the 2,000-calorie level. And let's suppose that the menu for one particular day specifies 1 cup pasta and 3 ounces eye of round beef roast for dinner. The pasta, at that serving size, contributes about 160 calories and the beef, approximately 148.

But if, like many people, you measure with your eyes instead of with measuring tools, you may actually serve yourself 1½ cups of pasta and 5 ounces of meat. The extra pasta would add about 80 additional calories and the meat, 100. That's nearly 200 extra calories at that meal alone.

If you added 200 calories to your daily diet, you would gain ¼ pound every week. That's about 1 pound a month. No wonder it's so easy to gain weight—and so hard to lose it.

Portion control is crucial. Use measuring

(continued)

list to see at a glance how many fat grams are in your favorite recipes.

The second list, on page 32, includes common foods that you can buy at the supermarket. Use it to help plan snacks and fill out the day's meals. It's also handy if you want to know how much fat is in certain foods, such as ½ cup of corn (about 1 gram).

When using these two lists, remember that the figures for most foods are based on 1 serving. Depending on your calorie level, you may need to eat 2 or more servings. Here are a few examples to guide you through the process of meal planning.

Example 1: 1,700 calories. Let's say you'd like to eat a different amount of calories than the three choices that we've given you, such as 1,700 calories a day. Plus, you love the Glorious Morning Muffins and want to eat them more often. Because you eat breakfast early, you want one muffin for breakfast and one for a morning coffee break. And it's summer, so you'd like to include lots of fresh fruit and salad in this day's menu. Here's how to design the day's meals.

First, go to the recipe list on page v. Look under "Breakfasts" and find Glorious Morning Muffins. You'll see that each muffin has 167 calories. Let's say you decide to add to your early breakfast muffin a tall glass of skim milk and a banana. Check the common foods list for calorie figures on these items.

For lunch, you want to include cantaloupe because it was on special at the supermarket and very fresh. You find 1 cup of cubed cantaloupe in the list of common foods and add a cup of low-fat cottage cheese for a good low-fat source of protein. To round out this light lunch, you decide on a cup of sliced carrots and a whole-wheat bagel. (Note that some bagel shops make very large bagels—up to 5 ounces each. Our figures are for a typical 2-ounce bagel.) Again, use the lists to add up the total calories.

For a mid-afternoon snack, you plan to have fresh raspberries and blueberries. Choosing 1 cup of each, you add 141 calories to your daily total. Knowing that you usually get hungry again later in the day, you also plan to have some low-fat popcorn. You check the snacks list and find that 3 cups of low-fat popped popcorn total 71 calories; you opt to have just 2 cups for 47 calories.

For dinner, you choose the Grilled Shrimp and Corn Salad, which has 234 calories per serving. Because it's one of your favorite recipes, you decide to have 2 servings, which adds up to 468 calories. To add bread to the meal, you decide to have another bagel. Your calorie total for the day is now 1,620 calories, and you have 80 calories left over. So you check the snacks and frozen-foods list for dessert, finding a frozen fudge bar at 90 calories. To recap the calorie figures, here's how the day's diet adds up.

Food Item	Calories	Running Total
2 Glorious Morning Muffins	334	334
1½ cups skim milk	129	463
1 small banana	104	567
1 cup cantaloupe cubes	56	623
1 cup low-fat cottage cheese	160	783
1 cup sliced carrots	35	818
1 whole-wheat bagel	73	891
1 cup raspberries	60	951
1 cup blueberries	81	1,032
2 cups low-fat popped popcorn	47	1,079
2 servings Grilled Shrimp and Corn Salad	468	1,547
1 whole-wheat bagel	73	1,620
1 frozen fudge bar	90	1,710

cups, if necessary. For foods measured in ounces, use a food scale. Here's a quick tip: A 3-ounce piece of cooked meat (the recommended healthy serving) is about the size of a deck of playing cards.

Example 2: 1,500 calories. Suppose the 1,500-calorie level is right for you, and you like three meals a day with no snacks in between. You'd also like to have salmon fillets today because they are fresh at the market. You'd like a generous portion but still want to stick to the 1,500-calorie level. So you decide to have 6 ounces of baked salmon. Using the lists, you see that this adds up to 312 calories (52 calories per ounce). You round out the dinner menu with a baked potato (with low-fat sour cream) and steamed broccoli. Using the lists, you see that your running total comes to 489 calories.

For breakfast, you choose the Banana-Pecan Pancakes and double the portion. And you add a glass of skim milk. Adding things up, you see that you have 634 calories left. Knowing that you'd like to have another glass of milk at lunch, you check the sandwich listing for something that works. You find the Yellow Submarine Sandwiches, and that finishes lunch. Here's how this day's meals add up.

Food Item	Calories	Running Total
6 ounces baked salmon	312	312
1 small baked potato	93	405
2 tablespoons low-fat sour cream	40	445
1 cup steamed chopped broccoli	44	489
2 Banana-Pecan Pancakes	248	737
1½ cups skim milk	129	866
Yellow Submarine Sandwich	568	1,434
1 cup skim milk	86	1,520

Example 3: 3,000 calories. Suppose you are a young male athlete, and you need 3,000 calories to maintain your weight. Beginning the day with a hearty breakfast is key, especially before a game. You pick

(continued on page 36)

Common Foods at a Glance

Did you ever wonder how many grams of fat are in an egg? Or how much fat is in the egg white alone? Egg whites alone are fat-free. Each whole egg, on the other hand, has 5 grams of fat (all of it concentrated in the yolk). Here are fat and calorie figures for many of the foods that we eat day in and day out. Use this list to help plan healthy menus. Note that this list contains only foods that we recommend as part of a healthy diet. Things like butter and bacon are omitted because there are healthier choices. For example, in place of butter on toast, we recommend tub-style margarine, which has less saturated fat. In place of regular bacon, try Canadian bacon, which is very lean. Likewise, all of the poultry items listed here are skinless, and the meats are trimmed of all visible fat. Notice that we list meats by the ounce so that you can easily calculate figures for the number of ounces that you will eat.

Fruits	Amount	Calories	Fat (g.)
Apple	1 medium	67	0.4
Applesauce, unsweetened	1/2 cup	52	0
Apricots	4	75	0.6
Banana	1 small	104	0.5
Blueberries	3/4 cup	61	0.4
Cantaloupe	1 cup cubed	56	0.4
Cherries	12	61	0.8
Fruit salad, without citrus	1/2 cup	51	0.3
Grapefruit	1/2 large	37	0.1
Grapes	17 small	69	0.5
Kiwifruit	1 medium	61	0.4
Mangoes	1/2 cup sliced	54	0.2
Orange	1 small	87	0.2
Papaya	1 cup cubed	55	0.1
Peach	1 medium	56	0.1
Pear	1 small	67	0.4
Plum	2 small	78	0.8
Raisins	2 tablespoons	62	0
Raspberries	1 cup	60	0.6
Strawberries	1 1/4 cups whole	54	0.6
Watermelon	1 1/4 cups cubed	64	0.8

Vegetables			
Baked potato, with skin	1 small	93	0
Broccoli, chopped, cooked	1/2 cup	22	0.2

	Amount	Calories	Fat (g.)
Carrots	½ cup sliced	35	0.1
Celery	1 cup chopped	19	0.1
Corn kernels	½ cup	89	1
Green beans, cooked	½ cup	22	0.1
Green peas, cooked	½ cup	67	0.1
Lettuce, loose-leaf	2 leaves	4	0
Mixed-green salad	1 cup	9	0.1
Pickle spears	2	7	0.1
Spinach, cooked	½ cup	3	0
Sweet pepper	1 cup chopped	27	0.1
Sweet potato, with skin	1 small	105	0
Tomato, plum	1	13	0.2
Zucchini, cooked	½ cup chopped	14	0

Eggs, Cheese, and Dairy Products

	Amount	Calories	Fat (g.)
Cheese, low-fat, low-sodium (all types)	1 ounce	50	2
Cottage cheese, low-fat	¼ cup	40	0.7
Cream cheese, nonfat	2 tablespoons	30	0
Cream cheese, reduced-fat	2 tablespoons	69	5
Egg substitute, fat-free	¼ cup	30	0
Egg whites	2 large	33	0
Egg	1 large	75	5
Milk, 1% low-fat	1 cup	102	2.6
Milk, skim	1 cup	86	0.4
Sour cream, low-fat	2 tablespoons	40	2.5
Sour cream, nonfat	2 tablespoons	31	0
Yogurt, nonfat fruit	1 cup	227	0

Condiments and Dressings

	Amount	Calories	Fat (g.)
Balsamic vinegar	1 tablespoon	13	0
Barbecue sauce, low-sodium	2 tablespoons	23	0.5
Honey	1 tablespoon	64	0
Honey mustard	1 tablespoon	38	0.3
Jam, preserves, jelly	1 tablespoon	48	0
Ketchup, reduced-sodium	1 tablespoon	16	0
Maple syrup	1 tablespoon	52	0
Margarine, reduced-fat tub-style	1 tablespoon	65	7
Mayonnaise, nonfat	1 tablespoon	10	0

(continued)

Common Foods at a Glance—Continued

Condiments and Dressings—Continued

	Amount	Calories	Fat (g.)
Mayonnaise, reduced-fat	1 tablespoon	36	3
Mustard	1 tablespoon	12	0.7
Oil	1 teaspoon	40	4.5
Peanut butter, reduced-fat	2 tablespoons	190	12
Ranch dressing, nonfat	1 tablespoon	17	0
Refried beans, nonfat	½ cup	110	0
Salsa	¼ cup	20	0
Spaghetti sauce	½ cup	94	4.7
Syrup, reduced-calorie	2 tablespoons	57	0
Vinaigrette dressing, nonfat	1 tablespoon	6	0

Breads and Cereals

Bagel, all types	½	73	0.3
Bran flake cereal	¾ cup	114	0.5
Bread, whole-wheat	1 slice	75	1.3
Cream of rice cereal, cooked	½ cup	63	0.1
Cream of wheat cereal, cooked	½ cup	66	0.2
English muffin	½	67	0.5
Granola, low-fat	¼ cup	91	1.5
Oatmeal, cooked	½ cup	73	1.1
Pita bread	½ medium	75	0.7
Shredded wheat cereal	½ cup	77	0.4

Meats, Poultry, and Seafood

Beef round, lean roasted	1 oz.	40	1.5
Chicken breast, skinless, cooked	1 oz.	30	0.6
Halibut, baked	1 oz.	68	5
Ham, extra-lean, baked	1 oz.	37	1.4
Pork tenderloin, lean, roasted	1 oz.	53	1.7
Roast beef, lean, cooked	1 oz.	33	0.8
Salmon, baked	1 oz.	52	2.3
Salmon, smoked	1 oz.	33	1.2
Scallops, steamed	1 oz.	30	0.8
Shrimp, steamed	1 oz.	28	0.3
Snapper, steamed	1 oz.	36	0.4
Sole, flounder, steamed	1 oz.	32	0.4
Swordfish, baked	1 oz.	44	1.4

	Amount	Calories	Fat (g.)
Tuna, canned in water	1 oz.	37	0.1
Turkey breast, skinless, cooked	1 oz.	25	0.3

Snacks and Cookies

	Amount	Calories	Fat (g.)
Fig cookies	2	110	2.5
Gingersnaps	3	90	1.8
Graham crackers	1½ whole sheets	90	2.2
Granola bar, low-fat	1	110	2
Popcorn, low-fat	3 cups popped	71	1.6
Potato chips, baked	1 oz.	111	1.5
Pretzels	¾ ounce	81	0.7
Pudding, nonfat	½ cup	100	0
Soft pretzel	1	190	1.7
Tortilla chips, baked	1 oz.	110	1

Grains (cooked)

	Amount	Calories	Fat (g.)
Couscous	½ cup	100	0.1
Pasta	½ cup	98	0.4
Rice, brown or white	½ cup	133	0.3
Wild rice	½ cup	83	0.3

Soups

	Amount	Calories	Fat (g.)
Black bean, low-fat	1 cup	170	1.5
Lentil, low-fat	1 cup	130	1.5
Tomato, low-fat	1 cup	90	2
Vegetable, low-fat	1 cup	80	1.5

Frozen Foods

	Amount	Calories	Fat (g.)
Fruit-juice bar	1	63	0
Fudge bar	1	90	0.2
Waffles, whole-grain	1 (4" diameter)	116	4.6
Yogurt, nonfat	½ cup	104	0.8

Beverages

	Amount	Calories	Fat (g.)
Apple juice, apple cider	½ cup	58	0.1
Cranberry juice cocktail	½ cup	72	0.1
Grape juice, unsweetened	½ cup	47	0.1
Grapefruit juice	½ cup	47	0.1
Orange juice	½ cup	56	0.2
Tomato juice	½ cup	21	0

the Oat-Berry Pancakes with Vanilla-Ricotta Cream and double up by having four pancakes. You add a glass of low-fat milk to complete the meal. Tallying the calories, you see that breakfast adds up to 927 calories.

Midmorning, a glass of calcium-fortified orange juice boosts your energy partway through your workout, adding 112 calories. For lunch, you grab a ham sandwich on whole-wheat bread with 2 tablespoons reduced-fat mayonnaise, romaine lettuce, and tomato slices. Knowing that athletes need strong bones, you include more low-fat milk. To round out your lunch, you add one banana and three Chewy Oatmeal Cookies, bringing your running total to 1,878 calories.

For dinner, you choose Parmesan Chicken Strips and Caribbean Rice. One cup of cooked peas fills out the meal. Your calories now total 2,923. So you search for something light to satisfy that dessert craving and fill out your total calories for the day. You find that a big bowl of strawberries topped with low-fat milk is just right. Here's how your day shakes down calorie-wise.

Food Item	Calories	Running Total
4 Oat-Berry Pancakes with Vanilla-Ricotta Cream	774	774
1½ cups 1% low-fat milk	153	927
1 cup calcium-fortified orange juice	112	1,039
3 ounces extra-lean ham	111	1,150
2 slices whole-wheat bread	150	1,300
2 tablespoons reduced-fat mayonnaise	72	1,372
4 leaves romaine lettuce	8	1,380
4 plum tomato slices	13	1,393
1½ cups 1% low-fat milk	153	1,546
1 small banana	104	1,650
3 Chewy Oatmeal Cookies	228	1,878
1 serving Parmesan Chicken Strips	531	2,409
1 serving Caribbean Rice	380	2,789
1 cup green peas	134	2,923
1¼ cups whole strawberries	54	2,977
¼ cup 1% low-fat milk	26	3,003

Example 4: 2,200 calories. Let's say that you're an active adult, and 2,200 calories a day is the right amount to maintain your healthy weight. You prefer not to plan the day's meals ahead of time. You'd rather eat according to your tastes and add up the calories as you go along. Yet, you often eat the same foods every day. At breakfast, you usually have a big bowl of bran-flake cereal (1½ cups) with 1 cup of low-fat milk and ½ cup of orange juice. Later in the morning, you often eat a banana as a snack. In the afternoon, you usually snack on a bag of pretzels and a piece of fruit, such as an apple. Using the lists,

you see that these foods add up to 638 calories. So you have more than 1,500 calories left for lunch, dinner, and dessert.

You opt for last night's leftover soup at lunchtime. You have 2 cups of low-fat black bean soup and 2 slices of whole-wheat toast with 2 teaspoons reduced-fat tub-style margarine. You round out lunch by having 1 cup of mixed-green salad with 2 tablespoons of nonfat ranch dressing. You're still hungry, so you munch on 1 ounce of baked tortilla chips with ¼ cup of salsa. Using the lists, you see that your running total is now at 1,344 calories. That leaves plenty of room for a satisfying dinner with dessert. You make the Lamb Racks with Rosemary-Mustard Crust from this book. For side dishes, you add the Oregano-Roasted New Potatoes and the Herb and Mustard Beans. Now your calorie total is at 1,939. For dessert, you try a piece of Peppermint Patty Cake. That brings your daily calorie total to 2,193. To recap, here's the day's total calories at a glance.

Food Item	Calories	Running Total
1½ cups bran-flake cereal	228	228
1 cup 1% low-fat milk	102	330
½ cup orange juice	56	386
1 small banana	104	490
¾ ounce pretzels	81	571
1 medium apple	67	638
2 cups low-fat black bean soup	340	978
2 slices whole-wheat toast	150	1,128
2 teaspoons reduced-fat tub-style margarine	43	1,171
1 cup mixed-green salad	9	1,180
2 tablespoons nonfat ranch dressing	34	1,214
1 ounce baked tortilla chips	110	1,324
¼ cup salsa	20	1,344
1 serving Lamb Racks with Rosemary-Mustard Crust	304	1,648
1 serving Oregano-Roasted New Potatoes	169	1,817
1 serving Herb and Mustard Beans	122	1,939
1 serving Peppermint Patty Cake	254	2,193

These examples show how easy it is to tailor this book to your needs. Try different food combinations. Above all, eat what you like (within healthy limits, of course). If something doesn't look fresh at the supermarket or if you run out of an ingredient, use the lists on pages v and 32 to adapt the menus or recipes and still meet your calorie needs. The goal is to pick the daily calorie level that is right for you, then stick with it. Once that is done, a healthy diet is as simple as savoring the delicious foods that make it all possible.

Spring Menus

Spring Asparagus Soup
(page 54)

Spring Menu One

	1,500 CALORIES	2,000 CALORIES	2,500 CALORIES
	33-43 G. FAT	44-56 G. FAT	57-69 G. FAT

Breakfast

Banana-Pecan Pancakes	3	4	6
warmed applesauce	½ cup	1 cup	1 cup
skim milk	1 cup	1 cup	1½ cups

Lunch

Rolled Garden Sandwiches	1	1½	1½
baby carrots	6	6	12
celery sticks	6	6	12
sliced mango	½	1	1

Dinner

Stuffed Sole with Saffron Sauce	1 serving	1 serving	1 serving
mixed green salad with	1 cup	1 cup	2 cups
nonfat dressing	1 tablespoon	1 tablespoon	2 tablespoons
steamed broccoli with	½ cup	1 cup	2 cups
reduced-fat margarine	1 teaspoon	1 teaspoon	2 teaspoons
crusty French roll	1	1	2

Snack

orange	1	1	1

DAILY TOTALS

Calories	1,527	1,979	2,494
Fat (g.)	28	34	46
% of calories from fat	16	15	16
Protein (g.)	109	122	143
Carbohydrates (g.)	205	291	376
Dietary fiber (g.)	21	31	43
Cholesterol (mg.)	247	297	344
Sodium (mg.)	2,307	2,759	3,633

NUTRIENT BONUS

This menu (at 2,000 calories) exceeds the Daily Value for:

Dietary fiber	122%
Vitamin A	443%
Thiamin	141%
Riboflavin	180%
Niacin	102%
Vitamin B$_6$	118%
Vitamin B$_{12}$	102%
Folate	114%
Vitamin C	544%
Vitamin E	123%
Calcium	182%
Potassium	131%

HEALTHY TIP OF THE DAY

Darker is better. Whenever possible, choose dark leafy greens for your salads. In general, the darker the fruit or vegetable, the more nutritious it will be.

Banana-Pecan Pancakes (page 42)

Banana-Pecan Pancakes

These hotcakes are light, fluffy, and a breeze to put together. We've lowered the fat by using less oil and toasting small amounts of pecans for a nutty flavor. We also added ripe bananas to create a moist pancake that's rich in potassium.

1¼	cups all-purpose flour
1	tablespoon brown sugar
½	teaspoon baking powder
½	teaspoon baking soda
¼	teaspoon ground cinnamon
¼	teaspoon salt
1¼	cups 1% low-fat buttermilk or soured milk (see hint)
1	large egg, lightly beaten
1	tablespoon canola oil
1	cup chopped ripe bananas (about 2 bananas)
2	tablespoons chopped toasted pecans

In a large bowl, combine the flour, brown sugar, baking powder, baking soda, cinnamon, and salt. Using a whisk, blend together so the dry ingredients are uniformly distributed.

In a small bowl, combine the milk, egg, and oil. Mix well and add to the flour mixture, stirring until just combined. Fold in the bananas and pecans. The batter will appear lumpy.

Coat a large no-stick skillet or griddle with no-stick spray. Set over medium-high heat until hot. Pour out approximately ⅓ cup batter per pancake. When bubbles appear on top and the edges are barely dry, turn the pancakes and finish cooking. The pancakes are done if the center springs back when touched.

Nutrition Notes

Per pancake

Calories 124
Fat 3.5 g.
% of calories from fat 25
Protein 3.6 g.
Carbohydrates 19 g.
Dietary fiber 1.1 g.
Cholesterol 22 mg.
Sodium 180 mg.

Kitchen Hints

◆ Soured skim milk can be substituted for buttermilk in almost any recipe. To make 1¼ cups soured milk, pour a generous 1⅛ cups 1% low-fat milk into a measuring cup and add enough lemon juice to make 1¼ cups. Let stand for 5 minutes.

◆ Extra pancakes can be double-wrapped in plastic and foil. Freeze them for up to 3 months. To reheat, thaw the pancakes and warm them in a no-stick skillet over medium-low heat for 3 minutes per side.

Rolled Garden Sandwiches

MAKES 3

Looking for an easy picnic dish? Here, thin slices of turkey and Swiss are rolled up with fresh vegetables and a creamy herb spread in lavash, a flexible Middle Eastern flatbread. (Use whatever herbs you like. Italian parsley, tarragon, basil, oregano, and chives—alone or in combination— are good choices.) Slice the sandwiches on an angle for easy handling at picnics.

4	ounces nonfat cream cheese, at room temperature
1/3	cup nonfat yogurt cheese (see hint)
2	tablespoons chopped fresh herbs
1	scallion, chopped
1/4	teaspoon garlic powder
3	whole-wheat lavash (12" size)
9	ounces thinly sliced no-salt-added turkey breast
4	ounces thinly sliced low-fat, low-sodium Swiss cheese
1/3	cup shredded carrots
1/4	English cucumber, thinly sliced
1	large tomato, sliced
3	large leaves romaine lettuce, ribs removed

In a small bowl, combine the cream cheese, yogurt cheese, herbs, scallions, and garlic powder. Mix well.

Spread 2 tablespoons of the mixture on 1 lavash, covering the entire area. On the end closest to you, place a third of the turkey in a thin layer and top with a third of the Swiss.

Top with a third of the carrots, a third of the cucumbers, and a third of the tomatoes. Finish with 1 leaf of the lettuce, tearing it if needed so it extends to both ends of the lavash. Tightly roll the sandwich away from you.

At a 45° angle, slice the sandwich roll into 6 equal-size pieces.

Repeat the layering, rolling, and slicing to prepare the remaining 2 sandwiches.

Nutrition Notes

Per sandwich

Calories 372
Fat 5.4 g.
% of calories from fat 13
Protein 27.6 g.
Carbohydrates 48 g.
Dietary fiber 3.6 g.
Cholesterol 48 mg.
Sodium 750 mg.

Kitchen Hints

◆ To make 1/3 cup yogurt cheese, place 2/3 cup nonfat plain yogurt in a strainer or colander lined with cheesecloth (or use a special yogurt strainer). Place the strainer over a bowl and refrigerate for 3 to 4 hours or overnight to drain the whey (liquid). Discard the whey. The drained yogurt is yogurt cheese.

◆ Whole-wheat lavash is available in Middle Eastern grocery stores and the dairy cases of many super- markets.

◆ English cucumbers are longer and thinner than regular cukes, with fewer seeds. They're often found wrapped in plastic.

Nutrition Notes

Per serving

Calories 314
Fat 5.5 g.
% of calories from fat 16
Protein 44.9 g.
Carbohydrates 9.8 g.
Dietary fiber 1.2 g.
Cholesterol 134 mg.
Sodium 331 mg.

Kitchen Hint

◆ Saffron is the stamen of a particular crocus flower and is highly valued for the beautiful golden color and delicate flavor that it imparts to dishes. When purchasing saffron, be sure to buy the threads and not the powdered form, which is often mixed with other ingredients.

Stuffed Sole with Saffron Sauce

MAKES 4 SERVINGS

Don't be put off by the number of ingredients here. This elegant dish is quick to assemble and can easily be prepared ahead. Lean, delicate sole is stuffed with shrimp, scallops, fresh herbs, and bread crumbs. The crowning touch is a golden saffron sauce.

Stuffed Sole

1	teaspoon olive oil
1½	teaspoons minced garlic
½	cup chopped fennel bulbs
⅓	cup chopped scallions
2	tablespoons chopped fresh Italian parsley
1½	teaspoons dried Italian herb seasoning
3	tablespoons chopped shallots
4	ounces large shrimp, peeled, deveined, and sliced into thirds
4	ounces bay scallops
½	cup unseasoned dry bread crumbs
2	tablespoons fat-free egg substitute
1	tablespoon lemon juice
	Ground black pepper
4	sole fillets (6 ounces each)
1	cup dry sherry or nonalcoholic white wine

Saffron Sauce

1	teaspoon olive oil
1½	teaspoons minced garlic
⅛	teaspoon crushed saffron threads
3	tablespoons hot water
½	teaspoon Dijon mustard
½	teaspoon rinsed and drained capers
½	teaspoon arrowroot or cornstarch
1	tablespoon nonfat sour cream
	Salt and ground black pepper
1	tablespoon chopped fresh Italian parsley (optional)

To make the stuffed sole: Preheat the oven to 400°F.

Warm the oil in a large no-stick skillet over medium heat. Add the garlic, fennel, scallions, parsley, Italian herb seasoning, and 2

tablespoons of the shallots. Cook for 4 minutes, or until the fennel is just tender. Add the shrimp and scallops; cook for 2 to 3 minutes, or until the shrimp and scallops are opaque and cooked through.

Transfer the mixture to a large bowl and stir in the bread crumbs, egg substitute, and lemon juice. Season with the pepper.

Place the sole, skin side up, on a work surface. Divide the stuffing into 4 equal portions. Slightly mound the stuffing in the center of each fillet and roll up the fillets jelly-roll style.

Coat a shallow 1-quart baking dish with no-stick spray. Sprinkle the dish with the remaining 1 tablespoon shallots and place the fillets, seam side down, on top of the shallots. Pour the sherry or wine around the fillets. Cover with a piece of wax paper.

Bake for 15 minutes, or until the fish is opaque and flakes easily when tested with a fork. Remove from the baking dish and keep warm on a covered serving platter. Reserve the cooking liquid.

To make the saffron sauce: Warm the oil in a small no-stick skillet over medium heat. Add the garlic and cook for 1 minute. Mix the saffron with 2 tablespoons of the water. Add to the skillet. Stir in the mustard, capers, and the reserved cooking liquid. Cook until the liquid is reduced to about $\frac{2}{3}$ cup.

Place the arrowroot or cornstarch in a cup. Add the remaining 1 tablespoon water and stir until smooth. Stir into the skillet and cook over medium heat until slightly thick. Remove from the heat and whisk in the sour cream. Season with the salt and pepper. Spoon 2 tablespoons of the sauce over each fillet. Sprinkle with the parsley (if using).

Spring Menu Two

	1,500 CALORIES	2,000 CALORIES	2,500 CALORIES
	33-43 G. FAT	44-56 G. FAT	57-69 G. FAT
Breakfast			
Salmon-Artichoke Hash	1 serving	1½ servings	2 servings
Dill Sauce	½ cup	½ cup	½ cup
cantaloupe cubes	½ cup	1¼ cups	1½ cups
Lunch			
lean roast beef on	3 ounces	6 ounces	6 ounces
whole-wheat bread with	2 slices	2 slices	2 slices
lettuce,	1 leaf	1 leaf	2 leaves
tomato, and	2 slices	2 slices	3 slices
grainy mustard	1 tablespoon	1 tablespoon	1 tablespoon
pear	1	1	1
Dinner			
Isle of Capri Pasta	2 servings	2 servings	3 servings
mixed green salad with	1 cup	1 cup	1½ cups
nonfat dressing	1 tablespoon	1 tablespoon	1½ tablespoons
Italian bread	1 slice	2 slices	2 slices
Snack			
Strawberry-Kiwi Smoothies	½ cup	1½ cups	2 cups

DAILY TOTALS			
Calories	1,500	2,010	2,522
Fat (g.)	32	43	54
% of calories from fat	19	19	19
Protein (g.)	74	104	124
Carbohydrates (g.)	237	313	401
Dietary fiber (g.)	30	38	49
Cholesterol (mg.)	85	147	159
Sodium (mg.)	1,803	2,190	2,650

Isle of Capri Pasta (page 49)

Salmon-Artichoke Hash

Try this hearty hash as an alternative to corned beef hash. You get health-boosting omega-3 fatty acids (a beneficial type of fat that may protect against coronary artery disease) from the fish, complex carbohydrates from the potatoes, and a full plate of flavor. It's delicious served with Dill Sauce (page 60).

1	pound new potatoes, cut into ½" cubes
1	tablespoon olive oil
1	large leek, chopped (white and light green parts only)
6	ounces smoked salmon, skin removed
1	package (10 ounces) frozen quartered artichoke hearts, thawed and patted dry
½	teaspoon ground black pepper
1	medium tomato, seeded and finely chopped
4	sprigs fresh dill (optional)

Preheat the oven to 400°F. Line a baking sheet with foil. Spread the potatoes on the sheet and coat with no-stick spray. Bake for 25 minutes, or until lightly browned. Set aside.

Warm 1½ teaspoons of the oil in a large no-stick skillet over medium heat. Add the leeks and cook for 3 to 4 minutes, or until softened. Transfer to a large bowl.

Cut the salmon into 1" pieces and add to the bowl. Stir in the artichokes, potatoes, and pepper.

In the same skillet used for the leeks, warm the remaining 1½ teaspoons oil over medium-high heat. Add the salmon mixture and shape into a shallow mound with the back of a spatula. Cover and cook for 3 to 4 minutes, or until lightly browned and crisp on the bottom. Using the spatula, cut the hash into 4 sections. Flip the hash in sections and cook for 3 to 4 minutes on the other side.

Serve sprinkled with the tomatoes and dill (if using).

Nutrition Notes

Per serving

Calories 216
Fat 5.8 g.
% of calories from fat 23
Protein 12.4 g.
Carbohydrates 30.6 g.
Dietary fiber 6.4 g.
Cholesterol 10 mg.
Sodium 382 mg.

Kitchen Hints

◆ To clean leeks, trim the root end and cut off the dark green tops. Cut each leek in half lengthwise. Separate the leaves with your fingers while running under cold water to remove any grit. Pat dry.

◆ If frozen artichoke hearts are unavailable, you can replace them with 1 can (14 ounces) water-packed artichoke hearts, rinsed, drained, and quartered.

Isle of Capri Pasta

MAKES 6 SERVINGS

Roasted peppers and peas give you a day's worth of vitamin C.

1½ cups packed fresh spinach, stemmed and washed
⅔ cup packed fresh basil
¼ cup packed fresh Italian parsley
3 tablespoons grated Parmesan cheese
6 tablespoons defatted reduced-sodium chicken broth
5 teaspoons olive oil
1 clove garlic, chopped
⅛ teaspoon crushed red-pepper flakes
Salt and ground black pepper
12 ounces penne
2 roasted sweet red peppers, chopped
1 package (10 ounces) frozen baby peas, thawed

In a food processor or blender, combine the spinach, basil, parsley, Parmesan, broth, oil, garlic, red-pepper flakes, salt, and black pepper. Process for 2 to 3 minutes, or until the mixture is smooth and creamy. Stop occasionally to scrape down the sides of the bowl.

Cook the penne in a large pot of boiling water according to the package directions. Drain and place in a large serving bowl. Add the spinach-basil pesto and toss to coat well. Add the roasted red peppers and peas. Toss to mix.

Roasted Peppers

Roasted sweet red peppers are a key ingredient in low-fat cooking. They provide a slightly sweet, smoky flavor with no added fat. You can add them to pizza, pasta, risotto, salads, and sandwiches. Or you can puree the peppers to make sauces and spreads.

In most recipes, you can use either freshly roasted peppers or the jarred variety. To save time and cut fat, use the jarred variety packed in water, not oil. Look for them in the produce section or with the canned vegetables in your supermarket.

Here's how to make freshly roasted peppers.

- Place whole peppers on a hot grill or under the broiler, about 4 inches from the heat. Cook, turning occasionally, until the skin becomes bubbly and blackened all over.
- Transfer the peppers to a paper bag, seal, and set aside for 5 minutes, or until softened and cool enough to handle.
- Remove and discard the skin and the inner ribs and seeds.
- Avoid rinsing the peppers because this washes away the flavorful liquids released during the roasting process.

Nutrition Notes

Per serving (1½ cups)

Calories 294
Fat 6.7 g.
% of calories from fat 21
Protein 15 g.
Carbohydrates 46.3 g.
Dietary fiber 5.2 g.
Cholesterol 5 mg.
Sodium 204 mg.

Kitchen Hint

◆ Any short, shaped pasta works well in this recipe. Try ziti, rotini, or medium shells.

Nutrition Notes

Per serving

Calories 75
Fat 0.3 g.
% of calories from fat 3
Protein 0.6 g.
Carbohydrates 18.9 g.
Dietary fiber 1.5 g.
Cholesterol 0 mg.
Sodium 3 mg.

Kitchen Hint

◆ Here's an easy way to peel kiwifruit. Cut off the ends. Starting from one of the cut ends, put a spoon just under the skin and turn the kiwifruit until the spoon has gone around the circumference of the fruit. Repeat the process on the other end, and the kiwifruit will "pop" out of its skin.

Strawberry-Kiwi Smoothies

MAKES 5 SERVINGS

Silky-smooth and positively refreshing, this fruit drink is a snap to whip up. The bananas, kiwifruit, strawberries, and apple juice give you a burst of flavor and a healthy jolt of vitamin C and potassium.

1	banana, sliced
1	kiwifruit, sliced
5	frozen whole strawberries
1¼	cups apple juice
1½	teaspoons honey

In a blender, combine the banana, kiwifruit, strawberries, apple juice, and honey. Puree until thick and smooth. Pour into tall glasses and serve.

Spring Menu Three

	1,500 CALORIES	2,000 CALORIES	2,500 CALORIES
	33-43 G. FAT	44-56 G. FAT	57-69 G. FAT

Breakfast

bran flakes with	1½ cups	1½ cups	2 cups
skim milk	1 cup	1 cup	1½ cups
sliced strawberries	1 cup	1 cup	1½ cups

Lunch

Spring Asparagus Soup	1½ servings	2 servings	3 servings
sliced cucumbers and	12 slices	12 slices	12 slices
tomatoes with	8 slices	8 slices	8 slices
nonfat vinaigrette	2 tablespoons	2 tablespoons	2 tablespoons
toasted whole-wheat			
pita bread	2	2	2
orange	1	1	1

Dinner

London Broil	1 serving	1½ servings	1½ servings
roasted new potatoes	1 cup	1½ cups	2 cups
Herb and Mustard Beans	1 serving	1½ servings	2 servings

Snack

baked tortilla chips and	13	26	39
salsa	¼ cup	½ cup	¾ cup

DAILY TOTALS			
Calories	1,518	1,977	2,487
Fat (g.)	24	35	43
% of calories from fat	14	15	15
Protein (g.)	79	105	125
Carbohydrates (g.)	262	328	423
Dietary fiber (g.)	41	50	64
Cholesterol (mg.)	75	120	122
Sodium (mg.)	2,091	3,038	3,888

HEALTHY TIP OF THE DAY

Sail beyond sour cream. Top your next baked potato with salsa, barbecue sauce, or nonfat dressing. You'll add lots of flavor without fat.

London Broil (page 53) and Herb and Mustard Beans (page 55)

London Broil

MAKES 4 SERVINGS

You thought steak was off a healthy menu? Think again! Trimmed top round is a top pick for lean protein. Here, it's marinated in a tangy herb mixture, then broiled for a tender texture and superior flavor. Serve this dish with roasted new potatoes for a meal that can't be beat.

3	tablespoons reduced-sodium soy sauce
3	tablespoons balsamic vinegar
3	tablespoons lemon juice
3	tablespoons dry red wine or defatted reduced-sodium chicken broth
1	tablespoon olive oil
3	large shallots, chopped
3	cloves garlic, minced
$1\frac{1}{2}$	teaspoons dried thyme
$\frac{1}{2}$	teaspoon ground black pepper
$1\frac{1}{4}$	pounds top round or flank steak, trimmed of all visible fat

In a 9" × 9" baking dish, combine the soy sauce, vinegar, lemon juice, wine or broth, oil, shallots, garlic, thyme, and pepper. Mix well.

Using the tip of a sharp knife, puncture the meat all over to tenderize it. Turn the steak over and repeat on the other side. Place the meat in the marinade and turn over. Cover and refrigerate for at least 4 hours.

Coat a broiler pan with no-stick spray. Preheat the broiler. Place the steak on the broiler pan and broil 4" from the heat for 3 to 4 minutes per side per $\frac{1}{2}$" thickness of meat. Let the meat rest for 5 minutes before slicing. Cut the meat across the grain.

Nutrition Notes

Per serving

Calories 234
Fat 7.6 g.
% of calories from fat 30
Protein 28.6 g.
Carbohydrates 10.1 g.
Dietary fiber 0.4 g.
Cholesterol 70 mg.
Sodium 437 mg.

Kitchen Hints

◆ Roasted new potatoes with rosemary are delicious with this dish. To make them, quarter $1\frac{1}{2}$ pounds new potatoes and toss them with 1 teaspoon olive oil and 2 tablespoons chopped fresh rosemary. Place the potatoes on a baking sheet and roast at 375°F for 30 to 35 minutes. Season with salt and ground black pepper.

◆ This steak can also be grilled. Grill the steak 4" from the heat for 4 minutes per side per $\frac{1}{2}$" thickness of meat.

Nutrition Notes

Per serving

Calories 101
Fat 2 g.
% of calories from fat 17
Protein 5.8 g.
Carbohydrates 16.2 g.
Dietary fiber 3.1 g.
Cholesterol 0 mg.
Sodium 280 mg.

Kitchen Hint

◆ Toasting flour helps get rid of the raw flour taste when using flour to thicken creamy soups and sauces. Place ¼ cup flour in a small no-stick skillet over medium-high heat. Cook, stirring constantly, for 3 minutes, or until lightly browned; do not let the flour burn. In recipes calling for butter and flour thickening, use ¼ cup toasted flour mixed with 1 tablespoon oil.

Spring Asparagus Soup

MAKES 8 SERVINGS

Gently cooking asparagus in the microwave makes this soup a fast springtime meal. Pureed vegetables and nonfat sour cream replace the fat of a regular cream soup and add calcium. This soup packs vitamins A and C, potassium, and fiber into your day.

2	pounds asparagus, trimmed
½	cup water
1	tablespoon olive oil
1	cup chopped onions
1	cup chopped leeks (white and light green parts only)
¼	cup all-purpose flour, toasted (see hint)
8	cups defatted reduced-sodium chicken broth
⅓	cup nonfat sour cream
2	tablespoons chopped fresh tarragon
	Salt and ground black pepper

Cut the tips from the asparagus and chop them into 1" pieces; reserve the stalks. Place the tips in a microwave-safe bowl and add the water. Cover with vented plastic wrap and microwave on high power for a total of 3 minutes, or until crisp-tender; stop and stir after 1 minute. Plunge the asparagus into a bowl of cold water, drain, and lightly pat dry.

Warm the oil in a large saucepan over medium heat. Add the onions and leeks; cook for 4 minutes, or until softened. Cut the asparagus stalks into 1" pieces and add to the saucepan; cook for 2 minutes. Add the flour, stirring to coat the vegetables; cook for 2 minutes.

Add the broth and cook for 20 minutes, or until the asparagus is tender. Working in batches if necessary, transfer the soup to a food processor or blender and puree. Return the soup to the saucepan. Whisk in the sour cream. Stir in the tarragon and the reserved asparagus tips. Season with the salt and pepper. Rewarm over low heat.

Herb and Mustard Beans

MAKES 4 SERVINGS

Yellow wax beans are an easy, colorful side dish. Here, the beans are steamed, then mixed with a zesty mustard sauce. If you prefer, use green beans, broccoli, or asparagus instead of the yellow wax beans.

1	pound yellow wax beans
⅓	cup water
1	teaspoon olive oil
3	shallots, quartered
	Juice of 1 lime
1	teaspoon honey
1½	tablespoons whole-grain mustard
1	teaspoon chopped fresh basil
1	teaspoon chopped fresh Italian parsley
¼	cup chopped toasted hazelnuts
	Salt and ground black pepper

Place the beans and water in a large microwave-safe bowl. Cover with vented plastic wrap and microwave on high power for a total of 7 minutes, or until tender; stop and stir after 3 minutes. Drain and return the beans to the bowl.

Warm the oil in a small no-stick skillet over medium-low heat. Add the shallots and cook for 8 minutes, or until soft and brown all over.

In a small bowl, stir together the lime juice and honey. Add to the skillet. Stir in the mustard, basil, and parsley. Pour the shallot mixture over the beans. Add the hazelnuts and toss to coat. Season with the salt and pepper. Serve warm or at room temperature.

Nutrition Notes

Per serving

Calories 122
Fat 5.9 g.
% of calories from fat 43
Protein 3.6 g.
Carbohydrates 15.5 g.
Dietary fiber 4.2 g.
Cholesterol 0 mg.
Sodium 208 mg.

Kitchen Hint

◆ To toast the hazelnuts and remove their outer skins, preheat the oven to 400°F. Place the nuts on a foil-lined baking sheet and bake for 5 minutes, or until fragrant and lightly browned under the skin. Remove from the oven and cool. Rub the nuts to loosen and remove the skins.

	1,500 CALORIES	**2,000** CALORIES	**2,500** CALORIES
	33-43 G. FAT	44-56 G. FAT	57-69 G. FAT

Breakfast

Glorious Morning Muffins	2	3	4
calcium-fortified orange juice	1 cup	1½ cups	2 cups

Lunch

baked low-sodium ham and	4 ounces	4 ounces	5 ounces
low-fat, low-sodium			
Swiss cheese on	2 ounces	2 ounces	2 ounces
rye bread	2 slices	2 slices	2 slices
apple	1	1	2
kiwifruit	2	2	2
pretzels	1 ounce	2½ ounces	3 ounces

Dinner

Pan-Seared Red Snapper			
with Olive Crust	1 serving	1 serving	1½ servings
steamed asparagus with	10 spears	14 spears	16 spears
Dill Sauce	¼ cup	½ cup	½ cup

Snack

nonfat fruit yogurt	1 cup	1½ cups	2 cups

DAILY TOTALS			
Calories	1,504	2,001	2,482
Fat (g.)	23	28	36
% of calories from fat	14	12	13
Protein (g.)	89	107	140
Carbohydrates (g.)	238	338	409
Dietary fiber (g.)	19	25	29
Cholesterol (mg.)	164	176	234
Sodium (mg.)	2,167	2,903	3,528

NUTRIENT BONUS

This menu (at 2,000 calories) exceeds the Daily Value for:

Dietary fiber	100%
Vitamin A	190%
Thiamin	111%
Riboflavin	116%
Folate	131%
Vitamin C	660%
Calcium	173%
Potassium	115%

HEALTHY TIP OF THE DAY

Fiber up. Studies show that fiber helps prevent heart disease, colon cancer, and diabetes. Good sources include most fruits, vegetables, beans, and whole grains. Try eating whole-grain bread instead of plain white. Have brown rice instead of white; many people actually prefer the nutty taste of brown rice. Add small amounts of rolled oats, oat bran, or wheat bran to homemade pancakes, muffins, and cookies. Or substitute whole-wheat pastry flour for up to half of the all-purpose flour, as in the Glorious Morning Muffins recipe on page 58.

Pan-Seared Red Snapper with Olive Crust (page 59)

Glorious Morning Muffins

<u>MAKES 12</u>

Wake up to nutritious muffins loaded with flavor!

1 cup all-purpose flour
¾ cup whole-wheat pastry flour
1½ teaspoons baking powder
1½ teaspoons ground cinnamon
½ teaspoon baking soda
¼ teaspoon salt
1 cup nonfat vanilla yogurt
½ cup packed brown sugar
1 egg
2 tablespoons canola oil
1 teaspoon vanilla
¼ cup finely shredded carrots
½ cup drained crushed pineapple
⅓ cup currants or raisins
¼ cup chopped toasted walnuts

Preheat the oven to 400°F. Coat a 12-cup muffin pan with no-stick spray.

In a large bowl, mix the all-purpose flour, pastry flour, baking powder, cinnamon, baking soda, and salt.

In a medium bowl, mix the yogurt, brown sugar, egg, oil, and vanilla. Pour over the flour mixture and stir until just moistened. Add the carrots, pineapple, currants or raisins, and walnuts; stir just until evenly distributed.

Divide the batter evenly among the muffin cups, filling them about two-thirds full. Bake for 20 to 25 minutes, or until a toothpick inserted into the center of a muffin comes out clean.

Cool on a wire rack for 5 minutes, then remove the muffins from the pan.

Nutrition Notes

Per muffin

Calories 167
Fat 4.6 g.
% of calories from fat 24
Protein 4.5 g.
Carbohydrates 28.3 g.
Dietary fiber 2.1 g.
Cholesterol 18 mg.
Sodium 183 mg.

Kitchen Hints

◆ To give the muffins beautifully rounded tops, use an ice-cream scoop to transfer the batter. A ¼-cup scoop is just the right size.

◆ For a more hearty muffin, replace ¼ cup of the whole-wheat pastry flour with ¼ cup oat bran or wheat bran. Also try adding ¼ cup chopped dried apricots and ¼ cup semisweet chocolate chips.

Pan-Seared Red Snapper with Olive Crust

MAKES 4 SERVINGS

Pan-searing is a great low-fat way to prepare fish. In this savory dish, searing keeps the crumb crust crisp, while sealing in the juices of the moist and tender snapper.

1⅓	cups fresh bread crumbs
¼	cup chopped fresh oregano
16	pitted and finely chopped kalamata olives
2	tablespoons grated Parmesan cheese
½	teaspoon ground black pepper
4	red snapper fillets (4 ounces each)

In a shallow bowl, combine the bread crumbs, oregano, olives, Parmesan, and pepper. Firmly press the fillets into the mixture to create a uniform coating on both sides. Coat the top of the fillets with no-stick spray.

Coat a large cast-iron skillet with no-stick spray. Set over medium-high heat until hot. Add the fillets and cook for 3 to 4 minutes on each side, or until the fish is opaque and flakes easily with tested with a fork.

Nutrition Notes

Per serving

Calories 202
Fat 4.1 g.
% of calories from fat 19
Protein 30.9 g.
Carbohydrates 8.6 g.
Dietary fiber 0.4 g.
Cholesterol 56 mg.
Sodium 252 mg.

Kitchen Hint

◆ Here's a quick sauce to serve with the fish. In a food processor, combine 1 can (14½ ounces) no-salt-added stewed tomatoes, 1 tablespoon chopped fresh oregano, and 1 tablespoon balsamic vinegar. Process until the mixture is chunky. Warm the sauce on the stove top or in the microwave.

Nutrition Notes

Per ¼ cup

Calories 45
Fat 0.3 g.
% of calories from fat 7
Protein 2.8 g.
Carbohydrates 7.1 g.
Dietary fiber 0 g.
Cholesterol 1 mg.
Sodium 38 mg.

Kitchen Hints

◆ This sauce keeps in the refrigerator for up to 1 week.

◆ Crème fraîche is the classic tangy, thickened cream used so much in France. It is usually made by adding a small amount of buttermilk to heavy cream. This low-fat version, minus the dill, makes a deliciously rich addition to soups, salad dressings, and dessert sauces.

Dill Sauce

MAKES 1 CUP

Lighten your favorite creamy sauces with nonfat sour cream. This quick, calcium-rich sauce gets flavor from fresh dill and cracked pepper.

½ cup nonfat sour cream
½ cup 1% low-fat milk
1 tablespoon chopped fresh dill
¼ teaspoon sugar
  Salt and cracked black pepper

In a small bowl, mix the sour cream and milk. Cover with plastic wrap and set aside at room temperature for 8 hours or overnight.

Stir in the dill and sugar. Season with the salt and pepper. Refrigerate until cold.

Bone Up for Baby

If you're expecting, expect your diet and lifestyle to change a little. Your body's needs are changing to accommodate the growing baby. To cope with the physical changes, experts recommend getting plenty of rest and exercise. And remember that you're eating for two. So increase your daily calorie intake by about 300 calories. Drink lots of water—about 10 cups a day—and limit or avoid caffeine, alcohol, nicotine, artificial sweeteners, raw meat (such as steak tartare), and raw fish (such as sushi). Eat a well-balanced diet that's high in fiber (about 25 to 35 grams a day). Check this chart for easy ways to meet your other nutritional needs during pregnancy.

Nutrient	Daily Intake	Good Sources
Calcium	1,200 mg.	Low-fat milk, low-fat cheese, low-fat yogurt, figs, tofu
Folate	400 mcg.	Wheat germ, melons, oranges, fortified cereals, dark green vegetables
Iron	25 mg.	Beef, pork, prunes, beans, fortified cereals
Phosphorus	1,200 mg.	Wheat germ, low-fat milk, low-fat cheese, low-fat yogurt, whole-grain bread, eggs, beans
Protein	60 g.	Beef, pork, poultry, beans, legumes, cheese, yogurt
Magnesium	280 mg.	Wheat germ, melons, oranges, fortified cereals, fresh fruits, dark leafy greens
Vitamin D	400 IU	1% low-fat milk

Spring Menu Five

	1,500 CALORIES	2,000 CALORIES	2,500 CALORIES
	33-43 G. FAT	44-56 G. FAT	57-69 G. FAT

Breakfast

cream of rice cereal	1 cup	1¼ cups	1¼ cups
toasted mixed-grain bread with	1½ slices	2 slices	2 slices
Strawberry-Orange Marmalade	1½ tablespoons	2 tablespoons	2 tablespoons
skim milk	1 cup	1 cup	1 cup

Lunch

Hungry Man's Hoagies	1	1½	2
baked potato chips	12	12	24
nectarines	2	2	2

Dinner

Fiery Fusilli	1 serving	1½ servings	2 servings
spinach salad with	1 cup	2 cups	2 cups
nonfat dressing	1 tablespoon	2 tablespoons	2 tablespoons

Snack

low-fat frozen sorbet bar	1	1	1

Daily Totals

Calories	1,524	2,029	2,517
Fat (g.)	16	23	30
% of calories from fat	10	10	11
Protein (g.)	66	92	115
Carbohydrates (g.)	283	371	454
Dietary fiber (g.)	23	32	40
Cholesterol (mg.)	50	73	96
Sodium (mg.)	1,307	1,828	2,301

NUTRIENT BONUS

This menu (at 2,000 calories) exceeds the Daily Value for:

Dietary fiber	126%
Vitamin A	273%
Thiamin	109%
Riboflavin	103%
Folate	168%
Vitamin C	467%
Iron	110%

HEALTHY TIP OF THE DAY

Snack before you go. The next time you head off to a party, have a quick snack beforehand. It will take the edge off your appetite and help control your portions at the buffet table. Try "bready" foods such as a bagel, muffin, or some whole-grain cereal.

Fiery Fusilli

Fiery Fusilli

Fiber and spice make this pasta dish healthy and hot. Colorful banana peppers, roasted sweet red peppers, and chickpeas provide vitamin C and fiber, while olive oil, garlic, and sage pump up the flavor.

8	ounces fusilli
1	tablespoon olive oil
1	clove garlic, minced
2	banana chili peppers, minced (wear plastic gloves when handling)
4	plum tomatoes, diced
1	tablespoon chopped fresh sage
2	tablespoons chopped fresh Italian parsley
2	teaspoons chopped fresh oregano
1	can (19 ounces) chickpeas, rinsed and drained
½	cup defatted reduced-sodium chicken broth
¼	teaspoon crushed red-pepper flakes
1	large roasted sweet red pepper, diced
⅛	teaspoon salt

Cook the fusilli in a large pot of boiling water according to the package directions. Drain and place in a large serving bowl.

Meanwhile, warm the oil in a large no-stick skillet over medium-high heat. Add the garlic and banana peppers; cook for 2 minutes, or until the peppers are tender. Add the tomatoes, sage, parsley, and oregano; cook for 4 to 5 minutes, or until the tomatoes begin to release their juice. Add the chickpeas, broth, and red-pepper flakes; cook for 2 minutes. Pour the sauce over the cooked pasta. Top with the red peppers and sprinkle with the salt. Toss to combine.

Nutrition Notes

Per serving

Calories 420
Fat 7.4 g.
% of calories from fat 15
Protein 17.2 g.
Carbohydrates 73.1 g.
Dietary fiber 8.3 g.
Cholesterol 0 mg.
Sodium 115 mg.

Kitchen Hint

◆ Banana chili peppers are also known as Hungarian wax chilies. They are 3 to 5 inches long, up to 1½ inches in diameter, and yellow in color. The flavor ranges from mild to medium hot. Most supermarkets carry fresh banana chili peppers.

Nutrition Notes

Per hoagie

Calories 334
Fat 4 g.
% of calories from fat 11
Protein 24.9 g.
Carbohydrates 48.5 g.
Dietary fiber 3.5 g.
Cholesterol 46 mg.
Sodium 530 mg.

Kitchen Hint

◆ To create a vegetarian hoagie, omit the meat and replace it with any combination of the following: grilled or oven-roasted vegetables, artichoke hearts, olives, rehydrated sun-dried tomatoes, grilled firm tofu, shredded cabbage, or bean sprouts.

Hungry Man's Hoagies

MAKES 4

These well-balanced sandwiches have all the important food groups in them: crusty bread, an assortment of marinated vegetables, nonfat cheeses, and lean meats. Topped with a zesty vinaigrette, they'll satisfy the heartiest of appetites.

4	crusty mini-baguettes, sliced lengthwise
4	leaves romaine lettuce, ribs removed
1	large portobello mushroom, thinly sliced
¼	cup balsamic vinegar
½	teaspoon dried basil
¼	teaspoon dry mustard
¼	teaspoon ground black pepper
1	large clove garlic, minced
1	medium tomato, chopped
½	cup peeled, seeded, and chopped cucumbers
5	ounces thinly sliced no-salt-added turkey breast
5	ounces thinly sliced lean, low-sodium ham
2½	ounces thinly sliced nonfat low-sodium Swiss cheese
2½	ounces thinly sliced nonfat low-sodium Cheddar cheese
1	small red onion, thinly sliced crosswise
1	banana chili pepper, seeded and sliced crosswise (wear plastic gloves when handling)

Create hollowed-out "boats" with the bottom halves of the baguettes by pulling out the soft bread, leaving a crusty rim ¼" thick. Save the removed bread for another use. Line each boat with a lettuce leaf.

Coat a small no-stick skillet with no-stick spray and warm over medium heat. Add the mushrooms and cook for 3 to 5 minutes, or until softened and golden brown.

In a medium bowl, combine the vinegar, basil, mustard, black pepper, and garlic. Add the mushrooms, tomatoes, and cucumbers. Set aside for 5 minutes.

Divide the vegetable mixture among the boats. Top with the turkey, ham, Swiss, Cheddar, onions, and banana peppers. Drizzle with any remaining vinaigrette. Top with the remaining baguette halves.

Strawberry-Orange Marmalade

MAKES 4 CUPS

Why waste fat grams on butter, cream cheese, and other fattening spreads? This fat-free topping is full of sweet flavor and is easy to make. It perks up bagels, toast, English muffins, pancakes, and more.

- 3 cups Seville orange marmalade
- 1/3 cup orange juice or Chambord liqueur
- 1/3 cup sugar
- 3 tablespoons water
- 2 tablespoons grated orange rind
- 1/4 teaspoon ground cloves
- 1 pint strawberries, sliced

In a large saucepan, combine the marmalade, orange juice or liqueur, sugar, water, orange rind, and cloves. Stir over medium-high heat until the marmalade melts. Stir in the strawberries. Bring to a boil, stirring occasionally to prevent burning. Cook for 20 minutes, or until the mixture has thickened. Cool completely.

Spoon into hot, scalded half-pint or pint jars, leaving 1/8" headspace. Wipe the rims clean, attach the lids, and tightly screw on the caps. Invert the jars for 10 seconds.

Cool on a rack. Store in the refrigerator.

Nutrition Notes

Per tablespoon

Calories 43
Fat 0 g.
% of calories from fat 0
Protein 0.1 g.
Carbohydrates 12 g.
Dietary fiber 0.1 g.
Cholesterol 0 mg.
Sodium 9 mg.

Kitchen Hints

◆ This marmalade will keep in the refrigerator for up to 4 weeks. For longer storage, freeze the jars.

◆ Seville oranges are very sour Mediterranean oranges that are unsurpassed for making marmalade. If you want to make your own marmalade, look for Seville oranges in the market in the months of January and February.

Spring Menu Six

	1,500 CALORIES	2,000 CALORIES	2,500 CALORIES
	33-43 G. FAT	44-56 G. FAT	57-69 G. FAT

Breakfast

Italian Frittata	1 serving	1½ servings	2 servings
calcium-fortified orange juice	1 cup	1¼ cups	2 cups
whole-wheat toast with	2 slices	2 slices	2 slices
jam	2 tablespoons	2 tablespoons	2 tablespoons

Lunch

White Bean and Tomato Soup	1 serving	2 servings	2 servings
pumpernickel roll	1	2	2

Dinner

Chicken Potpie	1 serving	1½ servings	2 servings
romaine lettuce with	1 cup	2 cups	3 cups
nonfat Italian dressing	1 tablespoon	2 tablespoons	3 tablespoons

Snack

banana	1	1	2
bagel with	1	1	1½
nonfat flavored cream cheese	2 tablespoons	2 tablespoons	3 tablespoons

DAILY TOTALS			
Calories	1,498	1,977	2,495
Fat (g.)	21	31	37
% of calories from fat	12	13	13
Protein (g.)	77	107	134
Carbohydrates (g.)	261	330	421
Dietary fiber (g.)	28	40	49
Cholesterol (mg.)	164	255	325
Sodium (mg.)	2,387	3,296	3,955

Italian Frittata (page 68)

Italian Frittata

MAKES 2 SERVINGS

A frittata is a simple one-pan egg dish from Italy. This savory version is high in folate, vitamins A and C, and fiber. It packs a double-shot of flavor and nutrition into the morning meal.

1	teaspoon olive oil
1	shallot, chopped
1	medium new potato, cooked and cut into ½" cubes
½	cup sliced artichoke hearts
1	roasted sweet red pepper, chopped
1	teaspoon chopped fresh thyme
1	egg
5	egg whites
1	tablespoon water
	Salt and ground black pepper
2	tablespoons grated Parmesan cheese
1	tablespoon chopped fresh Italian parsley

Warm the oil in a medium ovenproof no-stick skillet over medium heat. Add the shallots; cook for 2 minutes, or until tender. Add the potatoes, artichokes, red peppers, and thyme; cook for 2 minutes.

In a medium bowl, whisk together the egg, egg whites, and water. Season with the salt and black pepper. Pour over the vegetables and cook while gently moving a spatula across the bottom of the skillet for 3 minutes, or until the base of the frittata is almost set.

Coat a broiler pan with no-stick spray. Preheat the broiler.

Place the frittata on the prepared pan. Sprinkle the frittata with the Parmesan and parsley. Broil 3" from the heat for 1 to 2 minutes, or until the frittata is cooked through and golden.

Nutrition Notes

Per serving

Calories 204
Fat 7.1 g.
% of calories from fat 30
Protein 17.5 g.
Carbohydrates 18.7 g.
Dietary fiber 4.3 g.
Cholesterol 111 mg.
Sodium 381 mg.

Kitchen Hints

◆ The vegetables for this breakfast dish can be cooked the night before. For variety, use your favorite leftover side dishes. The combination of fillings for frittatas is endless.

◆ To make 4 servings, double the recipe and use 2 separate skillets. Or keep one frittata warm while preparing the second one.

White Bean and Tomato Soup

MAKES 8 SERVINGS

Pair this light soup with a sunny spring day for a memorable meal. White beans provide a hearty texture, while tomatoes add a delicate sweetness and a healthy helping of vitamin C.

4	cups defatted reduced-sodium chicken broth
3	sprigs fresh Italian parsley
2	bay leaves
¼	teaspoon whole black peppercorns
1	teaspoon dried thyme
2	teaspoons olive oil
2	cups chopped onions
1	tablespoon chopped garlic
2	cans (19 ounces each) low-sodium cannellini beans, rinsed and drained
2	cans (14½ ounces each) no-salt-added diced tomatoes (with juice)
3	tablespoons chopped fresh basil
2	tablespoons chopped fresh Italian parsley
1	tablespoon grated Parmesan cheese
2	teaspoons balsamic vinegar
1¼	teaspoons paprika

Place the broth in a medium saucepan over medium-high heat. Place the parsley sprigs, bay leaves, peppercorns, and thyme in a square of cheesecloth. Tie with kitchen string and add to the saucepan. Bring to a boil. Reduce the heat to medium-low and simmer for 20 minutes. Remove from the heat. Remove and discard the seasoning bundle.

Meanwhile, warm the oil in a large saucepan over medium heat. Add the onions. Cook for 3 minutes. Add the garlic and cook for 1 minute. Add the beans, tomatoes (with juice), basil, chopped parsley, Parmesan, vinegar, paprika, and the broth. Reduce the heat to low and simmer for 20 minutes.

Working in batches if necessary, puree 4 cups of the soup in a blender or food processor. Add the pureed soup back to the saucepan. Simmer, stirring occasionally, for 20 minutes.

Nutrition Notes

Per serving

Calories 107
Fat 1.8 g.
% of calories from fat 15
Protein 6.5 g.
Carbohydrates 19.9 g.
Dietary fiber 5.5 g.
Cholesterol 1 mg.
Sodium 213 mg.

Kitchen Hint

◆ This soup can be made ahead and frozen for a later date.

Nutrition Notes

Per serving

Calories 372
Fat 5.9 g.
% of calories from fat 14
Protein 27.4 g.
Carbohydrates 48.1 g.
Dietary fiber 5.5 g.
Cholesterol 49 mg.
Sodium 687 mg.

Kitchen Hints

◆ If you prefer a solid crust on your potpie, arrange the dough pieces on a lightly floured baking sheet so they form a square. Pinch together the edges. Using a rolling pin, roll the dough into a 9" × 9" square. Lift the baking sheet and carefully slide the dough on top of the potpie. Bake as directed.

◆ If using frozen peas, you needn't defrost them; they'll thaw while the sauce cooks.

Chicken Potpie

MAKES 4 SERVINGS

Here's a potpie that's heartwarming and low in fat.

 1 cup sliced carrots
 1 cup sliced celery
 1½ cups defatted reduced-sodium chicken broth
 12 ounces boneless, skinless chicken breasts, cut into 1" cubes
 1 teaspoon olive oil
 1 cup chopped onions
 8 ounces button mushrooms, sliced
 1 teaspoon dried thyme
 1 teaspoon dried tarragon
 ½ cup white wine or nonalcoholic wine
 ⅓ cup all-purpose flour
 1 cup 1% low-fat milk
 ½ cup peas
 ⅛ teaspoon grated nutmeg
 Salt and ground black pepper
 1 tube (7½ ounces) low-fat biscuit dough

Preheat the oven to 425°F. Coat a 9" × 9" baking dish with no-stick spray.

Place the carrots in a steamer basket. Steam over boiling water in a large covered saucepan for 1 minute. Add the celery and steam for 2 minutes, or until the vegetables are tender. Transfer to a large bowl and set aside.

Place the broth in a large saucepan. Bring to a boil over medium heat. Add the chicken and stir. Cook for 5 minutes, or until the chicken is no longer pink. Add to the bowl with the vegetables.

Add the oil to the saucepan. Warm over medium heat. Add the onions, mushrooms, thyme, and tarragon. Cook, stirring often, for 8 minutes, or until the vegetables are tender. Add the wine; cook for 2 to 4 minutes, or until almost all of the liquid has evaporated.

Place the flour in a small bowl. Whisk in the milk until smooth. Add to the saucepan. Stir in the chicken mixture and the peas. Cook, stirring constantly, over medium heat for 5 to 8 minutes, or until the mixture thickens and begins to bubble. Add the nutmeg and season with the salt and pepper.

Pour the filling into the prepared baking dish. Cover the top with pieces of the biscuit dough in a single layer. Bake for 10 minutes, or until the biscuits are golden brown and cooked through.

Spring Menu Seven

	1,500 CALORIES	2,000 CALORIES	2,500 CALORIES
	33-43 G. FAT	44-56 G. FAT	57-69 G. FAT

Breakfast

Strawberry Scones	1 serving	2 servings	2 servings
skim milk	1½ cups	1½ cups	1¾ cups

Lunch

Parmesan Chicken Strips	1 serving	1 serving	1 serving
mashed Yukon gold potatoes	1 cup	1¼ cups	1½ cups
tomatoes	6 slices	6 slices	8 slices

Dinner

Black-Bean Burritos with Verde Sauce	1 serving	2 servings	3 servings
baked tortilla chips	13	13	26

Snack

Granny Smith apple	1	1	1½
strawberries	6	10	10

DAILY TOTALS

Calories	1,484	1,984	2,478
Fat (g.)	24	37	47
% of calories from fat	14	16	17
Protein (g.)	88	111	134
Carbohydrates (g.)	241	318	403
Dietary fiber (g.)	21	30	40
Cholesterol (mg.)	135	178	200
Sodium (mg.)	2,285	3,013	3,708

NUTRIENT BONUS

This menu (at 2,000 calories) exceeds the Daily Value for:

Dietary fiber	119%
Vitamin A	118%
Thiamin	107%
Riboflavin	112%
Niacin	147%
Vitamin B$_6$	119%
Vitamin C	538%
Calcium	155%
Potassium	108%

HEALTHY TIP OF THE DAY

Steer clear of the center aisles. Supermarkets generally stock the most highly processed foods and high-fat snacks in the center aisles. Next time you shop, stick to the periphery, where you'll find fresh fruits and vegetables, low-fat dairy products, fresh fish, and lean meats and poultry. Make these your primary choices, and you'll reduce the fat, calories, and sodium in your diet.

Parmesan Chicken Strips

Parmesan Chicken Strips

MAKES 4 SERVINGS

These lean chicken strips are coated in an herb-and-cheese crust, then baked instead of fried. Serve them hot or cold with the honey-mustard dipping sauce.

Chicken Strips

- ½ cup all-purpose flour
- ½ cup fat-free egg substitute
- 1½ cups fresh bread crumbs
- 2 tablespoons grated Parmesan cheese
- 1 tablespoon grated lemon rind
- 1½ teaspoons crab-boil seasoning, such as Old Bay
- 1 teaspoon dried Italian herb seasoning
- ¼ teaspoon garlic powder
- ¼ teaspoon ground red pepper
- 1¼ pounds boneless, skinless chicken breast halves, cut into short strips

Honey-Mustard Dipping Sauce

- ½ cup honey
- ¼ cup whole-grain mustard
- ¼ cup Dijon mustard

To make the chicken strips: Preheat the oven to 375°F. Line a baking sheet with foil.

Place the flour in a shallow bowl. Place the egg substitute in a second shallow bowl. In a third shallow bowl, combine the bread crumbs, Parmesan, lemon rind, crab-boil seasoning, Italian herb seasoning, garlic powder, and pepper. Mix well with a fork.

Dredge the chicken strips first in the flour, then in the egg substitute, and finally in the bread-crumb mixture. Place on a plate or a large sheet of wax paper. Coat the tops of the chicken with no-stick spray.

Coat a large no-stick skillet with no-stick spray. Set over medium-high heat until hot. Place the chicken in the skillet in a single layer (work in batches, if necessary). Cook for 1 minute on each side, or until the bread crumbs are toasted. Transfer the strips to the baking sheet. Bake for 12 to 15 minutes, or until cooked through and no longer pink in the center when tested with a sharp knife.

To make the honey-mustard dipping sauce: In a small bowl, combine the honey, whole-grain mustard, and Dijon mustard. Mix well. Serve with the chicken.

Nutrition Notes

Per serving

Calories 531
Fat 8.4 g.
% of calories from fat 14
Protein 46 g.
Carbohydrates 70.3 g.
Dietary fiber 2.7 g.
Cholesterol 84.7 mg.
Sodium 1,211 mg.

Kitchen Hint

◆ To make fresh bread crumbs, tear bread slices into large pieces and place in a food processor or blender. Process until crumbs form. Depending on the size of your slices, 2 slices should make about 1½ cups crumbs.

Black-Bean Burritos with Verde Sauce

MAKES 8 SERVINGS

These mildly spiced burritos are loaded with sautéed vegetables and beans, boosting the fiber to meet over half of your daily need. The sauce is a delicious nonfat mixture made with tomatillos (Mexican tomatoes).

Verde Sauce

1	pound tomatillos
8	ounces poblano chili peppers (wear plastic gloves when handling)
2	tablespoons chopped onions
2	tablespoons chopped fresh cilantro
1½	teaspoons chopped garlic
	Pinch of salt

Burritos

½	teaspoon olive oil
1	cup sliced scallions
1	cup chopped zucchini
1	cup chopped yellow squash
½	cup chopped sweet red peppers
1	teaspoon ground cumin
½	teaspoon chili powder
1	can (19 ounces) low-sodium black beans, rinsed and drained
1	cup nonfat chunky tomato salsa
¾	cup cooked white rice
	Ground black pepper
8	flour tortillas (6" diameter)
1	cup shredded reduced-fat Monterey Jack cheese
½	cup nonfat sour cream

To make the verde sauce: Preheat the oven to 400°F.

Remove and discard the husks from the tomatillos. Line a baking sheet with foil and place the tomatillos and chili peppers on it. Bake for 10 minutes; turn the pieces and bake for 15 minutes.

Place the peppers in a brown paper bag and let stand for 5 minutes. Remove and discard the skins and seeds. Puree the peppers in a food processor. Add the tomatillos and pulse until the mixture is

chunky. Transfer to a bowl and add the onions, cilantro, garlic, and salt.

To make the burritos: Reduce the oven temperature to 350°F. Coat a 13" × 9" baking dish with no-stick spray.

Warm the oil in a large no-stick skillet over medium heat. Add the scallions, zucchini, squash, and red peppers; cook for 2 minutes. Add the cumin and chili powder; cook for 2 to 3 minutes, or until crisp-tender. Add the beans, salsa, and rice; stir until well-combined. Season with the black pepper.

Lay a tortilla on a flat surface and place ½ cup of the filling in the center. Top with 2 tablespoons of the Monterey Jack. Roll into a tight cylinder. Place, seam side down, in the prepared baking dish. Repeat with the remaining tortillas, filling, and Monterey Jack. Mist the burritos with no-stick spray. Cover with foil and bake for 20 minutes, or until the filling is hot.

To serve, top the burritos with the sauce and sour cream.

Nutrition Notes

Per scone with 2 tablespoons sauce

Calories 171
Fat 4.3 g.
% of calories from fat 22
Protein 5.4 g.
Carbohydrates 28.4 g.
Dietary fiber 2 g.
Cholesterol 23 mg.
Sodium 207 mg.

Kitchen Hint

◆ The yogurt sauce can be made 2 days ahead and refrigerated in an airtight container. The scones can be made ahead and reheated briefly in a toaster oven. For fresh-baked scones in the morning, get a head start by mixing the dry ingredients the night before and refrigerating them in a covered bowl. While the oven is preheating in the morning, measure out the wet ingredients and chop the strawberries. Mix, shape, and bake.

Strawberry Scones

<u>MAKES 12 SCONES; 1½ CUPS SAUCE</u>

Nonfat yogurt replaces most of the butter in these tender, flaky treats.

Scones

1¼	cups quick-cooking rolled oats
1	cup all-purpose flour
½	cup whole-wheat pastry flour
2	teaspoons baking powder
½	teaspoon baking soda
¼	teaspoon salt
¼	cup + 2 teaspoons sugar
2	tablespoons cold unsalted butter or margarine, cut into small pieces
1	egg
½	cup nonfat vanilla yogurt
1	tablespoon canola oil
½	teaspoon vanilla
⅔	cup chopped strawberries
1	egg white, lightly beaten

Strawberry-Yogurt Sauce

⅔	cup nonfat plain yogurt
1	tablespoon strawberry jam
1	tablespoon sugar
⅔	cup chopped strawberries

To make the scones: Preheat the oven to 400°F. Coat a baking sheet with no-stick spray.

In a large bowl, combine the oats, all-purpose flour, pastry flour, baking powder, baking soda, salt, and ¼ cup of the sugar. Add the butter or margarine and cut into the flour using the back of a fork until the mixture resembles coarse meal.

In a small bowl, lightly beat together the egg, yogurt, oil, and vanilla. Add to the flour mixture, stirring with a fork just until the dough comes together. Add the strawberries and mix gently.

Transfer the dough to a floured surface. Pat into an 8" circle; cut into 12 wedges. Place the wedges on the baking sheet. Brush with the egg white and sprinkle with the remaining 2 teaspoons sugar. Bake for 20 minutes, or until golden. Cool on a wire rack.

To make the strawberry-yogurt sauce: In a small bowl, stir together the yogurt, jam, and sugar until smooth. Stir in the strawberries. Serve with the scones.

Spring Menu Eight

	1,500 CALORIES	2,000 CALORIES	2,500 CALORIES
	33-43 G. FAT	44-56 G. FAT	57-69 G. FAT

Breakfast

Fluted Egg Cups	3	4	5
mango slices	½ cup	1 cup	1½ cups
skim milk	1 cup	1½ cups	2 cups

Lunch

Onion Soup with Croutons	1½ servings	2 servings	2 servings
spinach salad with	1 cup	1½ cups	2½ cups
nonfat dressing	1 tablespoon	1½ tablespoons	2½ tablespoons
whole-wheat roll	1	2	2

Dinner

Seafood Gratin	2 servings	2½ servings	3 servings
steamed broccoli with	½ cup	½ cup	1½ cups
lemon juice	2 teaspoons	2 teaspoons	2 tablespoons

Snack

cinnamon-raisin toast with	2 slices	2 slices	3 slices
apple butter	2 tablespoons	2 tablespoons	3 tablespoons

DAILY TOTALS

Calories	1,510	2,010	2,476
Fat (g.)	24	31	38
% of calories from fat	14	14	14
Protein (g.)	106	139	170
Carbohydrates (g.)	220	298	372
Dietary fiber (g.)	19	27	37
Cholesterol (mg.)	241	303	365
Sodium (mg.)	2,321	3,069	3,762

NUTRIENT BONUS

This menu (at 2,000 calories) exceeds the Daily Value for:

Dietary fiber	110%
Vitamin A	339%
Thiamin	110%
Riboflavin	142%
Vitamin B_{12}	196%
Folate	127%
Vitamin C	293%
Calcium	151%
Potassium	113%

HEALTHY TIP OF THE DAY

Fewer drinks, less fat. Beer, wine, and liquor may be fat-free, but they're still loaded with calories. Unless you work them off, those extra calories will be stored as body fat. If you're trying to lose weight, monitor the amount of alcohol you consume each week. Cutting back to 1 or 2 drinks per week will help you lose weight faster.

Onion Soup with Croutons

Onion Soup with Croutons

MAKES 8 SERVINGS

Caramelized onions add rich flavor to this savory spring soup. Plus, onions are a good source of health-boosting phytochemicals. Try this soup with an assortment of onions, such as Vidalia, Spanish, and red onions.

2	quarts water
2	cans (14½ ounces each) reduced-sodium beef broth, defatted
3	carrots
3	stalks celery
4	ounces parsley root
1	leek, halved lengthwise (white and light green parts only)
1	green pepper, halved
1	medium tomato
2	bay leaves, crumbled
1	teaspoon dried thyme
1	teaspoon black peppercorns
¼	teaspoon salt
1	tablespoon olive oil
2½	pounds onions, thinly sliced
4	shallots, quartered
1	teaspoon sugar
½	cup port or apple juice
3	tablespoons all-purpose flour
2	cups reduced-fat croutons

In a large pot, combine the water, broth, carrots, celery, parsley root, leek, green pepper, tomato, bay leaves, thyme, peppercorns, and salt. Bring to a boil over high heat. Reduce the heat to medium and simmer for 45 minutes. Strain, discarding the solids. Measure the liquid; if necessary, boil until reduced to 2 quarts.

Meanwhile, warm the oil in a large saucepan over medium heat. Add the onions, shallots, and sugar. Cook, stirring occasionally, for 25 minutes, or until the onions are soft and brown. Stir in the port or apple juice; cook until the liquid has evaporated. Stir in the flour and cook for 3 minutes.

Add 3 cups of the reduced liquid and stir until slightly thickened. Add the remaining liquid and simmer for 10 minutes.

Serve sprinkled with the croutons.

Nutrition Notes

Per serving

Calories 133
Fat 2 g.
% of calories from fat 13
Protein 5.5 g.
Carbohydrates 24.5 g.
Dietary fiber 2.7 g.
Cholesterol 0 mg.
Sodium 204 mg.

Kitchen Hints

◆ This soup freezes well for up to 6 months.

◆ Be sure to thoroughly clean leeks because soil collects between the leaves as they grow. Trim off the root end and dark green tops. Make a slit the length of the leek, then thoroughly rinse between the layers.

◆ To make your own croutons, slice a French baguette into thin diagonal slices. Place in a single layer on a baking sheet and mist the slices with no-stick spray. Crumble 1 teaspoon dried basil evenly over the slices. Sprinkle with 2 tablespoons grated Parmesan cheese. Bake for 10 minutes at 350°F, or until lightly browned and crisp. Store at room temperature in an airtight container for up to 3 days.

Nutrition Notes

Per egg cup

Calories 54
Fat 1.1 g.
% of calories from fat 17
Protein 4.9 g.
Carbohydrates 7.1 g.
Dietary fiber 1.4 g.
Cholesterol 1 mg.
Sodium 126 mg.

Kitchen Hints

◆ To save time, make the bread cups the night before and store them at room temperature in an airtight container. Return the cups to the muffin pan when ready to bake.

◆ These egg cups make an impressive brunch entrée. Prepare the egg cups up to the point of topping them with the Parmesan and paprika. Cover them with plastic wrap and refrigerate overnight. Before serving, top with the Parmesan and paprika. Bake at 350° for 5 to 7 minutes, or until heated through.

Fluted Egg Cups

MAKES 12

Thin slices of whole-wheat bread create a healthy new way to enjoy scrambled eggs—in a bread cup. Scrambled cholesterol-free egg whites are placed in the cups, then run under the broiler. Delicious!

  6 slices whole-wheat bread
  1 teaspoon olive oil
⅓ cup chopped scallions
  1 tablespoon chopped fresh basil
  1 tablespoon chopped fresh Italian parsley
  8 egg whites, lightly beaten
      Salt and ground black pepper
⅓ cup reduced-fat shredded Cheddar cheese
  1 tablespoon grated Parmesan cheese
½ teaspoon paprika

Preheat the oven to 350°F.

With a rolling pin, slightly flatten the bread slices. Using a 3" round cookie cutter, cut 12 bread circles. Coat a 12-cup mini-muffin pan with no-stick spray and line each cup with a bread round. Bake for 15 to 20 minutes, or until the edges are golden.

Warm the oil in a large no-stick skillet over medium heat. Add the scallions, basil, and parsley; cook for 1 to 2 minutes, or until the scallions are softened. Add the egg whites. Season with the salt and pepper. Cook, stirring with a wooden spoon, for 1 to 2 minutes, or until almost set. Add the Cheddar and cook until the cheese has melted and the eggs are set.

Preheat the broiler.

Spoon 1 tablespoon of the egg mixture into each bread cup and top evenly with the Parmesan and paprika. Broil 4" from the heat for 1 to 2 minutes, or until hot and lightly browned.

Seafood Gratin

MAKES 6 SERVINGS

This gratin is loaded with flavor instead of fat.

- 2 tablespoons nonfat mayonnaise
- 2 tablespoons nonfat sour cream
- 2 tablespoons lemon juice
- 1 tablespoon Dijon mustard
- 1 tablespoon dry sherry (optional)
- ¼ teaspoon ground black pepper
- ¼ teaspoon ground red pepper
- 1 cup orzo
- 2 teaspoons olive oil
- 1 cup chopped scallions
- 2 teaspoons chopped garlic
- 8 ounces peeled and deveined shrimp
- 8 ounces crabmeat
- 8 ounces scallops
- 3 tablespoons all-purpose flour
- 1 can (15 ounces) evaporated skim milk
- 1 cup skim milk
- 4 tablespoons grated Parmesan cheese
- 2 tablespoons unseasoned dry bread crumbs
- ½ teaspoon paprika

Preheat oven to 350°F. Coat a 9" × 9" baking dish with no-stick spray.

In a large bowl, combine the mayonnaise, sour cream, lemon juice, mustard, sherry (if using), black pepper, and red pepper.

Cook the orzo in a medium saucepan of boiling water for 10 minutes, or until tender. Drain and add to the bowl. Stir to combine.

Meanwhile, warm the oil in a large no-stick skillet over medium-high heat. Add the scallions and garlic; cook for 1 minute. Add the shrimp, crab, and scallops; cook for 5 minutes, or until the seafood is opaque. Transfer the mixture to the bowl and stir to combine.

Place the flour in a small saucepan. Gradually whisk in the evaporated milk until smooth. Whisk in the skim milk. Cook over medium heat, stirring constantly, for 5 minutes, or until thickened. Whisk in 2 tablespoons of the Parmesan. Pour into the bowl and stir to combine. Spoon into the prepared baking dish.

In a small bowl, combine the bread crumbs, paprika, and the remaining 2 tablespoons Parmesan. Sprinkle over the gratin. Bake for 25 to 30 minutes, or until golden brown and bubbling.

Nutrition Notes

Per serving

Calories 317
Fat 5.2 g.
% of calories from fat 16
Protein 32.5 g.
Carbohydrates 30.7 g.
Dietary fiber 1.4 g.
Cholesterol 117 mg.
Sodium 515 mg.

Kitchen Hint

◆ To peel and devein shrimp, hold the shrimp under a slow stream of cold water and run the tip of a sharp knife or shrimp deveiner down the back of the shrimp. This will remove both the shell and the vein while leaving the shrimp whole.

	1,500 CALORIES	2,000 CALORIES	2,500 CALORIES
	33-43 G. FAT	44-56 G. FAT	57-69 G. FAT

Breakfast

Lemon Poppy Seed Bread with Lemon Glaze	1 slice	1 slice	1½ slices
nonfat fruit yogurt	½ cup	1 cup	1¼ cups

Lunch

Salmon Burgers with	1 serving	1 serving	1½ servings
salsa	¼ cup	¼ cup	½ cup
steamed corn on the cob	1 ear	2 ears	2 ears
Stuffed Vidalia Onions	1 serving	1 serving	1 serving

Dinner

grilled pork loin with	3 ounces	6 ounces	6 ounces
applesauce	½ cup	½ cup	¾ cup
cooked wild rice	½ cup	½ cup	¾ cup

Snack

kiwifruit	½	1	1
banana	½	1	1

NUTRIENT BONUS

This menu (at 2,000 calories) exceeds the Daily Value for:

Dietary fiber	112%
Thiamin	219%
Riboflavin	132%
Niacin	149%
Vitamin B6	166%
Vitamin B12	101%
Vitamin C	326%
Potassium	123%

HEALTHY TIP OF THE DAY

Eat smart. When dining out, take a healthy approach to your menu selections. High-fat dishes can often be spotted with the following descriptions: alfredo, au gratin, batter-dipped, breaded, buttery, creamy, crispy, flaky, deep-fried, in cheese sauce, prime, parmigiana, and tempura. Look for lower-fat items that are baked, braised, broiled, grilled, pan-seared, poached, roasted, or steamed.

DAILY TOTALS

Calories	1,526	1,991	2,485
Fat (g.)	37	47	57
% of calories from fat	21	20	20
Protein (g.)	83	117	140
Carbohydrates (g.)	227	294	373
Dietary fiber (g.)	21	28	34
Cholesterol (mg.)	162	231	277
Sodium (mg.)	1,508	1,658	2,402

Stuffed Vidalia Onions (page 87)

Per slice

Calories 396
Fat 6.5 g.
% of calories from fat 14
Protein 9.8 g.
Carbohydrates 77.1 g.
Dietary fiber 3.6 g.
Cholesterol 27 mg.
Sodium 377 mg.

Kitchen Hints

◆ To save time, the all-purpose flour, whole-wheat flour, wheat germ, baking powder, baking soda, and salt can be mixed ahead of time and stored in an airtight container.

◆ When baking with less fat, be sure not to use too much flour. Extra flour toughens low-fat baked goods.

Lemon Poppy Seed Bread with Lemon Glaze

MAKES 8 SLICES

We lightened this popular quick bread by replacing the butter with nonfat lemon yogurt. Whole-wheat pastry flour and toasted wheat germ add a slightly nutty flavor. Crowned with a sweet and zesty lemon glaze, this makes a great pick-me-up for breakfast or an afternoon snack.

Lemon Poppy Seed Bread

3	tablespoons poppy seeds
1	cup skim milk
2	cups all-purpose flour
¾	cup whole-wheat pastry flour
¼	cup toasted wheat germ
1	tablespoon baking powder
½	teaspoon baking soda
¼	teaspoon salt
1	large egg
2	egg whites
1	cup sugar
½	cup nonfat lemon yogurt
2	tablespoons canola oil
2	tablespoons grated lemon rind
⅓	cup lemon juice

Lemon Glaze

½	cup sugar
¼	cup lemon juice

To make the lemon poppy seed bread: Grind the poppy seeds in a spice grinder or crush with a mortar and pestle. Transfer to a small saucepan and add the milk. Bring to a boil. Stir once, remove from the heat, and allow to cool.

Preheat the oven to 350°F. Coat a 9" × 5" loaf pan with no-stick spray.

In a medium bowl, whisk together the all-purpose flour, whole-wheat flour, wheat germ, baking powder, baking soda, and salt.

In a large bowl, combine the egg, egg whites, and sugar. Using an electric mixer, beat on high speed for 4 to 6 minutes, or until the

mixture doubles in volume and is a pale creamy-yellow. Beat in the yogurt, oil, and lemon rind.

Add the lemon juice to the cooled milk mixture.

To the egg mixture, alternately beat in the flour mixture and the milk mixture on low speed until incorporated. Pour the batter into the prepared pan.

Bake for 50 to 60 minutes, or until a toothpick inserted into the center comes out clean. Using a metal or bamboo skewer, poke holes all over the bread. Set aside on a wire rack.

To make the lemon glaze: In a small saucepan over high heat, bring the sugar and lemon juice to a boil, stirring constantly. Pour over the warm bread. Let the bread cool in the pan.

Go the Whole Way

Eating more whole grains can lower diabetes risk, according to Harvard University researchers. That's partly because whole grains have the outer layers of the grain intact—where most of the vitamins, minerals, and fiber are located. Try using whole grains like whole-wheat bread or whole-grain breads, whole-wheat tortillas, and whole-grain cereals. For baking, replace up to half of the all-purpose flour with whole-wheat pastry flour. Whole-wheat pastry flour is more finely milled than regular whole-wheat flour, so it produces lighter results. Look for whole-wheat pastry flour in the baking aisle of your local supermarket or health food store.

Nutrition Notes

Per serving

Calories 345
Fat 12.2 g.
% of calories from fat 32
Protein 28.3 g.
Carbohydrates 30.3 g.
Dietary fiber 2.7 g.
Cholesterol 62 mg.
Sodium 566 mg.

Kitchen Hints

◆ To remove the skin from salmon, place the fillet, skin side down, on a work surface. Hold a sharp knife at a 45° angle at the thin end of the fillet. Use a sawing motion to draw the knife along the bottom of the fillet, between the flesh and the skin.

◆ Top the burgers with papaya salsa. Bake 8 ounces halved unpeeled sweet onions, cut side down, at 400° for 1 hour. Cool, peel, and chop. Add 1 chopped papaya, ½ cup pineapple chunks, 2 chopped plum tomatoes, 1 chopped jalapeño pepper (wear plastic gloves when handling), 3 tablespoons chopped scallions, 1 chopped roasted red pepper, 3 tablespoons lime juice, 2 tablespoons chopped fresh cilantro, and a pinch of salt and pepper.

Salmon Burgers

MAKES 4 SERVINGS

Salmon is a deliciously lean alternative to high-fat ground beef in burgers like these. In addition, salmon is one of the fish highest in heart-smart omega-3 fatty acids. Spread some salsa on the bottom of buns for added kick and vitamin C.

Mayonnaise Spread

- 3 tablespoons nonfat mayonnaise
- 1 tablespoon lemon juice
- 2 teaspoons whole-grain mustard

Salmon Burgers

- 1 salmon fillet (1 pound), skin removed
- 1 tablespoon Dijon mustard
- 1 teaspoon Worcestershire sauce
- 1 teaspoon reduced-sodium soy sauce
- 1 teaspoon lemon juice
- 1 teaspoon grated fresh ginger
- 1 clove garlic, minced
- ¼ teaspoon ground black pepper
- 2 teaspoons olive oil
- 4 whole-wheat hamburger buns
- 4 tomato slices
- 4 red onion slices
- 4 leaves lettuce

To make the mayonnaise spread: In a small bowl, combine the mayonnaise, lemon juice, and mustard. Mix well.

To make the salmon burgers: Remove and discard any bones from the salmon. Using a sharp knife, finely chop the salmon. Place in a large bowl. Add the mustard, Worcestershire sauce, soy sauce, lemon juice, ginger, garlic, and pepper. Mix well. Shape into 4 patties.

Warm the oil in a large no-stick skillet over medium-high heat. Add the patties and cook for 2 to 3 minutes per side, or until the salmon is opaque and no longer bright pink.

Serve on the buns, topped with the mayonnaise spread and the tomatoes, onions, and lettuce.

Stuffed Vidalia Onions

*Vidalia onions create a wonderful spring side dish that's low in fat.
Choose large onions that weigh about 8 ounces each.*

4	Vidalia onions
½	teaspoon olive oil
3	cups shredded zucchini
3	cloves garlic, minced
1	teaspoon dried thyme
1	teaspoon dried basil
3	tablespoons unseasoned dry bread crumbs
1½	tablespoons chopped toasted pine nuts
3	tablespoons grated Parmesan cheese
	Salt and ground black pepper

Preheat the oven to 400°F.

Cut about ½" off the top of each onion; slightly trim the bottoms so
the onions stand upright. Line a baking sheet with foil. Add the
onions, cut side up, and coat with no-stick spray. Bake for 1 hour,
or until soft when tested with a sharp knife. Set aside for 15 minutes, or until cool enough to handle.

Reduce the oven temperature to 350°F.

Remove and discard the onion peels. Using a spoon, scoop out the
onion centers, leaving a ½" shell. Chop the centers and reserve 1
cup for the stuffing; save the remainder for another use.

Warm the oil in a large no-stick skillet over medium heat. Add the
zucchini, garlic, thyme, basil, and chopped onions. Cook for 6 to
8 minutes, or until the zucchini is softened and most of the
liquid has evaporated. Remove from the heat and stir in the
bread crumbs, pine nuts, and 2½ tablespoons of the Parmesan.
Season with the salt and pepper. Mix well.

Divide the filling among the onion shells. Coat a 9" × 9" baking dish
with no-stick spray. Add the onions. Sprinkle the tops with the
remaining ½ tablespoon Parmesan.

Bake for 20 minutes, or until golden.

Nutrition Notes

Per serving

Calories 200
Fat 7.3 g.
% of calories from fat 31
Protein 7.8 g.
Carbohydrates 28.3 g.
Dietary fiber 6.0 g.
Cholesterol 4 mg.
Sodium 175 mg.

Kitchen Hint

◆ The onions can be
roasted a day in advance.
Serve cold, at room temperature, or reheated in a
microwave.

Spring Menu Ten

	1,500 CALORIES 33-43 G. FAT	2,000 CALORIES 44-56 G. FAT	2,500 CALORIES 57-69 G. FAT
Breakfast			
low-fat granola with	1 cup	1¼ cups	1½ cups
sliced banana	1	1	1
skim milk	1 cup	1¼ cups	1½ cups
Lunch			
Turkey Barbecue Sandwiches	1 serving	1 serving	1½ servings
baked potato	1	1	2
Dinner			
Springtime Risotto	1 serving	1½ servings	2 servings
mixed green salad with	2 cups	3 cups	3 cups
Country Cider Vinaigrette	2 tablespoons	3 tablespoons	3 tablespoons
Snack			
baby carrots and	5	10	10
cut celery with	2 stalks	4 stalks	4 stalks
nonfat creamy dressing	¼ cup	½ cup	½ cup

DAILY TOTALS			
Calories	1,517	1,985	2,522
Fat (g.)	30	45	50
% of calories from fat	17	20	17
Protein (g.)	62	76	101
Carbohydrates (g.)	264	333	433
Dietary fiber (g.)	24	32	40
Cholesterol (mg.)	85	109	140
Sodium (mg.)	2,274	3,259	3,915

NUTRIENT BONUS

This menu (at 2,000 calories) exceeds the Daily Value for:

Dietary fiber	126%
Vitamin A	261%
Thiamin	181%
Riboflavin	185%
Niacin	180%
Vitamin B$_6$	230%
Vitamin B$_{12}$	135%
Folate	226%
Vitamin C	265%
Iron	115%
Potassium	145%

HEALTHY TIP OF THE DAY

Snacks are good for you. For all-day energy, eat three balanced meals—plus one or two healthy snacks. They can keep you from bingeing on high-fat foods or eating too much at main meals. Healthy snacks include cut vegetables, baked potatoes, baked tortilla chips or potato chips, hard or soft pretzels, air-popped popcorn, fig bar cookies, gingersnap cookies, low-fat granola bars, graham crackers, whole-grain cereal, nonfat pudding, yogurt, and fresh fruit.

Turkey Barbecue Sandwiches (page 90) and coleslaw

Nutrition Notes

Per serving

Calories 233
Fat 1.8 g.
% of calories from fat 7
Protein 22.7 g.
Carbohydrates 33.9 g.
Dietary fiber 2 g.
Cholesterol 55 mg.
Sodium 652 mg.

Kitchen Hint

◆ This recipe calls for a relatively small amount of cabbage. To avoid waste, use packaged shredded cabbage from the produce section of your supermarket. Or buy shredded cabbage from the salad bar.

Turkey Barbecue Sandwiches

MAKES 6 SERVINGS

Barbecue gets a healthy makeover when the beef is replaced by tender strips of shredded turkey. Topped with creamy coleslaw, this sandwich will satisfy any cowboy's hunger. (The less adventuresome may want their coleslaw on the side.)

Creamy Coleslaw

1¼	cups shredded green or red cabbage
¼	cup chopped sweet red peppers
1	tablespoon finely chopped onions
2	tablespoons nonfat mayonnaise
2	tablespoons nonfat sour cream
2	teaspoons lemon juice
1½	teaspoons sugar
1	teaspoon cider vinegar
¼	teaspoon celery seeds
¼	teaspoon dried basil
	Pinch of ground black pepper

Turkey Barbecue

1¼	teaspoons paprika
½	teaspoon dried basil
½	teaspoon garlic powder
¼	teaspoon ground red pepper
1	pound turkey breast tenders
1	cup chopped scallions
½	cup reduced-sodium ketchup
¼	cup packed brown sugar
¼	cup Dijon mustard
¼	cup honey
¼	cup cider vinegar
3	tablespoons reduced-sodium soy sauce
2	tablespoons Worcestershire sauce
1	tablespoon water
1	tablespoon chopped fresh rosemary
2	teaspoons minced garlic
1	teaspoon hot-pepper sauce
6	sesame seed sandwich buns

To make the creamy coleslaw: In a large bowl, toss together the cabbage, red peppers, and onions.

In a small bowl, whisk together the mayonnaise, sour cream, lemon juice, sugar, vinegar, celery seeds, basil, and black pepper. Pour over the cabbage and toss to coat. Set aside.

To make the turkey barbecue: Coat a grill rack or broiler pan with no-stick spray. Preheat the grill or broiler.

In a small bowl, combine the paprika, basil, garlic powder, and red pepper. Rub the spice mixture all over the turkey tenders.

Place the turkey on the prepared rack or pan. Cook 4" from the heat for 4 to 5 minutes per side, or until no longer pink in the center when tested with a sharp knife.

Using a fork, shred the turkey following the grain of the meat. Discard the tendon that runs the length of each tender.

In a large no-stick skillet, combine the scallions, ketchup, brown sugar, mustard, honey, vinegar, soy sauce, Worcestershire sauce, water, rosemary, garlic, and hot-pepper sauce. Mix well. Add the shredded turkey and cook over medium heat for 3 to 4 minutes, or until heated through.

Divide the turkey mixture along the bottom halves of the sandwich buns. Top with the coleslaw and the bun tops.

Nutrition Notes

Per serving

Calories 318
Fat 4.9 g.
% of calories from fat 14
Protein 11.9 g.
Carbohydrates 53.9 g.
Dietary fiber 5.6 g.
Cholesterol 4 mg.
Sodium 476 mg.

Kitchen Hints

◆ To prepare the fennel, start with a large bulb. Trim off the stalks and feathery tops; trim the bottom. Cut the bulb into quarters lengthwise. Remove any thick core. Cut the flesh into thin slices.

◆ To shred basil easily, stack the leaves on top of one another. Roll up lengthwise. Using a sharp knife, cut the roll crosswise into $1/8$" widths.

◆ To make 1"-long Parmesan curls, run a vegetable peeler along a large piece of Parmesan. (Use this same technique to make chocolate curls.)

Springtime Risotto

MAKES 4 SERVINGS

Risotto is a great source of complex carbohydrates and B vitamins. In this version, the creamy golden rice complements an array of spring vegetables.

8	cups reduced-sodium vegetable broth
1	tablespoon olive oil
8	ounces asparagus, trimmed and cut into 2" pieces
$1\frac{1}{2}$	cups peas
2	cups thinly sliced fennel bulb
$\frac{1}{2}$	cup chopped shallots or onions
1	clove garlic, chopped
$1\frac{1}{2}$	cups Arborio rice
$\frac{1}{2}$	cup white wine or nonalcoholic white wine
$\frac{1}{8}$–$\frac{1}{4}$	teaspoon crushed saffron threads
1	cup finely chopped tomatoes
$\frac{1}{2}$	cup shredded fresh basil
4	tablespoons Parmesan curls (see hint)

Bring the broth to a simmer in a large saucepan over medium heat. Reduce the heat to low and simmer until needed.

Warm $1\frac{1}{2}$ teaspoons of the oil in a large, deep no-stick skillet over medium-high heat. Add the asparagus, peas, and fennel; cook for 4 to 6 minutes, or until the vegetables are crisp-tender. Transfer the vegetables to a bowl. Return the skillet to the heat.

Reduce the heat to medium and warm the remaining $1\frac{1}{2}$ teaspoons oil. Add the shallots or onions and garlic; cook for 2 to 3 minutes. Add the rice; cook for 2 minutes. Increase the heat to medium-high and add the wine. Stir until all the liquid has been absorbed.

Add 1 cup of the broth; stir constantly until most of the broth has been absorbed. Add 1 cup of broth at a time until a total of 4 cups broth have been stirred in and absorbed (about 15 minutes).

Add $\frac{1}{2}$ cup of broth at a time until another 2 cups have been stirred in and absorbed (about 10 minutes). Stir the saffron into the remaining 2 cups broth.

Stir the tomatoes and the reserved vegetables into the rice. Add $\frac{1}{4}$ cup of broth at a time until the rice is tender yet firm to the bite (you might not need all the broth; reserve for another use).

Stir in the basil. Serve sprinkled with the Parmesan curls.

Country Cider Vinaigrette

MAKES ½ CUP

This tangy vinaigrette beats store-bought versions by a mile. The basic ingredient is frozen apple juice concentrate instead of oil.

- 3 tablespoons frozen apple juice concentrate, thawed
- 1 tablespoon whole-grain mustard
- 1 tablespoon lemon juice
- 1 tablespoon dry sherry or nonalcoholic white wine
- 1 tablespoon minced shallots
- 1 tablespoon walnut or canola oil
- 2 teaspoons Dijon mustard
- Ground black pepper

In a medium bowl, whisk together the apple juice concentrate, whole-grain mustard, lemon juice, sherry or wine, shallots, oil, and Dijon mustard. Season with the pepper.

Nutrition Notes

Per tablespoon

Calories 32
Fat 2 g.
% of calories from fat 55
Protein 0.2 g.
Carbohydrates 3.3 g.
Dietary fiber 0.1 g.
Cholesterol 0 mg.
Sodium 73 mg.

Kitchen Hint

◆ To reduce the fat in your favorite vinaigrettes, replace up to three-fourths of the oil with fruit juice, broth, or water.

Spring Menu Eleven

	1,500 CALORIES	2,000 CALORIES	2,500 CALORIES
	33-43 G. FAT	44-56 G. FAT	57-69 G. FAT

Breakfast

Stuffed French Toast	2 slices	2 slices	3 slices
calcium-fortified orange juice	1 cup	1 cup	1¼ cups

Lunch

Chili Baked Potatoes	1 serving	1½ servings	2 servings
mixed green salad with	1 cup	1 cup	2 cups
nonfat dressing	1 tablespoon	1 tablespoon	2 tablespoons

Dinner

Thai Chicken Stir-Sizzle	1 serving	2 servings	2 servings
dinner roll	1	1	2
papaya slices with	1 cup	1 cup	1 cup
lime juice	1 teaspoon	1 teaspoon	1 teaspoon

Snack

frozen fruit-juice bar	1	1	1

DAILY TOTALS			
Calories	1,478	1,976	2,516
Fat (g.)	31	42	55
% of calories from fat	18	19	19
Protein (g.)	72	108	131
Carbohydrates (g.)	235	302	387
Dietary fiber (g.)	19	26	33
Cholesterol (mg.)	97	151	178
Sodium (mg.)	1,521	1,871	2,589

NUTRIENT BONUS

This menu (at 2,000 calories) exceeds the Daily Value for:

Dietary fiber	103%
Vitamin A	202%
Thiamin	117%
Niacin	160%
Vitamin B₆	105%
Vitamin C	678%
Calcium	123%

HEALTHY TIP OF THE DAY

Get moving! According to the American Heart Association, a sedentary lifestyle may increase the risk of heart disease. To help build a healthy heart, step up your physical-activity level. Regular physical activity has been shown to increase blood circulation, strengthen the heart muscle, improve oxygen use, and provide the energy needed for other activities. Physical activity also decreases stress, stimulates your mind, and helps fight fatigue. If you're not sure where to begin, start with simple changes, like taking the stairs instead of the elevator.

Thai Chicken Stir-Sizzle (page 98)

Nutrition Notes

Per slice

Calories 231
Fat 6.4 g.
% of calories from fat 25
Protein 11 g.
Carbohydrates 31.1 g.
Dietary fiber 1.6 g.
Cholesterol 17 mg.
Sodium 446 mg.

Kitchen Hints

◆ In a pinch, you can replace the confectioners' sugar with granulated sugar that has been powdered in a spice grinder or mini food processor.

◆ After soaking, the stuffed French toast can be stored in resealable freezer bags and frozen for up to 1 month. Place the frozen French toast on a baking sheet coated with no-stick spray and bake at 375°F for 15 to 20 minutes per side, or until golden.

Stuffed French Toast

MAKES 10 SLICES

You needn't fuss with this dish at breakfast time. Since the bread slices need to soak in the egg mixture, you can get everything ready the night before and bake the French toast in the morning. You'll need a loaf of French or Italian bread that's at least 16" long to get slices thick enough to hold the strawberry and cream cheese filling.

Filling

    1   package (8 ounces) reduced-fat cream cheese, at room
        temperature
  ⅓   cup confectioners' sugar
    1   teaspoon almond extract or vanilla
1½   cups sliced strawberries

French Toast

    1   loaf day-old French or Italian bread
1¼   cups fat-free egg substitute
    1   cup skim milk
    1   tablespoon vanilla

To make the filling: In a medium bowl, stir the cream cheese until smooth. Stir in the confectioners' sugar and almond extract or vanilla. Fold in the strawberries.

To make the French toast: Cut a small diagonal slice off each end of the bread and discard. Cut the bread diagonally into 10 thick slices. Cut a slit through the top crust of each slice to form a pocket. Divide the filling among the bread slices, stuffing each pocket with the cream-cheese mixture. Lay the slices in a 13" × 9" baking dish.

In a medium bowl, whisk together the egg substitute, milk, and vanilla. Slowly pour over the bread, then turn the slices to coat completely. Cover with plastic wrap and refrigerate for at least 4 hours or up to 12 hours. Turn the slices at least once while soaking.

Preheat the oven to 450°F. Coat a baking sheet with no-stick spray. Place the bread slices about 1" apart on the sheet. Bake for 6 to 10 minutes per side, or until golden. Serve warm.

Chili Baked Potatoes

MAKES 4 SERVINGS

Tucked into each potassium-rich baked potato half is a scoop of quick and easy chili. This is a great make-ahead, fiber-filled lunch item.

- 2 large baking potatoes
- 1 teaspoon olive oil
- 1½ cups sliced mushrooms
- 1 cup chopped onions
- ½ cup chopped green peppers
- 1 large clove garlic, minced
- 1 can (14½ ounces) low-sodium kidney beans, rinsed and drained
- 1 can (14½ ounces) no-salt-added stewed tomatoes (with juice)
- 1 cup frozen corn kernels
- 3 tablespoons canned chopped green chili peppers
- 2 teaspoons dried oregano
- 1 teaspoon ground cumin
- 1 teaspoon chili powder
- ½ cup shredded reduced-fat hot-pepper Monterey Jack cheese
- 4 tablespoons nonfat sour cream
- 4 tablespoons sliced scallions

Preheat the oven to 400°F.

Line a baking sheet with foil and place the potatoes on it. Bake for 1 hour, or until tender when pierced with a sharp knife.

Meanwhile, warm the oil in a large saucepan over medium heat. Add the mushrooms, onions, green peppers, and garlic. Cook for 4 to 6 minutes, or until tender.

Stir in the beans, tomatoes (with juice), corn, chili peppers, oregano, cumin, and chili powder. Cook for 15 minutes.

Cut the potatoes in half lengthwise and gently crumble the insides of each half with a fork. Place the potatoes, cut side up, on the baking sheet. Spoon 1 cup of the chili mixture over each potato half and sprinkle with 2 tablespoons of the Monterey Jack. Return the potatoes to the oven and bake for 3 to 5 minutes, or until the cheese is melted.

Top each potato half with 1 tablespoon of the sour cream and 1 tablespoon of the scallions.

Nutrition Notes

Per serving

Calories 340
Fat 8 g.
% of calories from fat 20
Protein 17.8 g.
Carbohydrates 55.6 g.
Dietary fiber 8.4 g.
Cholesterol 20 mg.
Sodium 90 mg.

Kitchen Hints

◆ Chili powder offers little in the way of heat but adds a depth of flavor that varies from brand to brand. To increase the chili's voltage, try adding chopped fresh jalapeño peppers (wear plastic gloves when handling), ground red pepper, red-pepper flakes, or hot-pepper sauce to the dish.

◆ To save time, make the chili in advance and freeze it in individual servings in freezer bags.

Nutrition Notes

Per serving

Calories 328
Fat 7.4 g.
% of calories from fat 20
Protein 26.5 g.
Carbohydrates 38.6 g.
Dietary fiber 2.8 g.
Cholesterol 44 mg.
Sodium 304 mg.

Kitchen Hints

◆ You can make your own spicy ketchup by stirring ground red pepper or red-pepper flakes into regular ketchup.

◆ The sauce can be made up to 2 days in advance.

◆ For a more intense flavor, grill the uncut chicken breasts for 4 to 5 minutes per side, or until no longer pink in the center when tested with a sharp knife. Slice the chicken crosswise into 1/2" strips. Add to the skillet along with the peanut sauce.

◆ This dish reheats well in a microwave, making it a great packable lunch.

The spices of southeast Asia and an aromatic peanut sauce enrich this low-fat "stir-sizzle"—our version of a stir-fry with just a small amount of oil.

Peanut Sauce

1/3 cup defatted reduced-sodium chicken broth
1/3 cup reduced-fat chunky peanut butter
2 tablespoons reduced-sodium soy sauce
2 tablespoons packed light brown sugar
2 tablespoons minced red onions
1 tablespoon reduced-sodium spicy ketchup
1 tablespoon lime juice
1 tablespoon rice-wine vinegar
1/2 teaspoon ground coriander

Stir-Sizzle

6 ounces soba noodles or linguine
1 teaspoon toasted sesame oil
1 pound boneless, skinless chicken breast halves, sliced crosswise into 1/2" pieces
1 bunch scallions, sliced diagonally into 1" pieces
1 tablespoon minced garlic
2 teaspoons grated fresh ginger
1 cup snow peas
1 sweet red pepper, cut into thin strips
1/2 cup grated carrots
2 tablespoons chopped fresh cilantro

To make the peanut sauce: In a food processor or blender, combine the broth, peanut butter, soy sauce, brown sugar, onions, ketchup, lime juice, vinegar, and coriander. Process for 30 seconds, or until well-combined but still chunky.

To make the stir-sizzle: Cook the noodles in a large pot of boiling water according to the package directions. Drain and return to the pot.

Meanwhile, warm the oil in a large no-stick skillet over medium-high heat. Add the chicken and cook for 3 to 4 minutes, or until no longer pink in the center. Add the scallions, garlic, and ginger; cook for 2 minutes, stirring often and being careful not to let the garlic burn. Add the snow peas, peppers, and carrots; cook for 2 minutes. Mix in the peanut sauce. Pour over the noodles. Sprinkle with the cilantro. Toss to coat. Place over heat for 2 minutes, or until heated through.

Spring Menu Twelve

	1,500 CALORIES	2,000 CALORIES	2,500 CALORIES
	33-43 G. FAT	44-56 G. FAT	57-69 G. FAT

Breakfast

Herbed Asparagus Omelets	1	1	1
pumpernickel toast	1 slice	1 slice	3 slices
skim milk	1 cup	1 cup	1¼ cups

Lunch

Hoppin' John Salad	1 serving	1½ servings	1½ servings
no-salt-added turkey breast on	4 ounces	6 ounces	6 ounces
sourdough roll	1	1	1
pineapple chunks	¾ cup	1 cup	1½ cups

Dinner

Lasagna Bundles	2	3	4
mixed greens with	1 cup	1 cup	2 cups
nonfat Italian dressing	1 tablespoon	1 tablespoon	2 tablespoons

Snack

low-fat popcorn	2 cups popped	3 cups popped	4 cups popped

NUTRIENT BONUS

This menu (at 2,000 calories) exceeds the Daily Value for:

Dietary fiber	129%
Vitamin A	257%
Thiamin	117%
Riboflavin	133%
Folate	135%
Vitamin C	211%
Calcium	145%
Iron	102%

HEALTHY TIP OF THE DAY

Build a network. Friends and family can help you achieve your ultimate health goals. If you fall off track, their friendly encouragement can help motivate you again. Encourage your friends or family to join you in exercise. Or invite them over for a low-fat meal to celebrate when you reach one of your health goals.

DAILY TOTALS

Calories	1,498	1,998	2,494
Fat (g.)	24	30	37
% of calories from fat	14	14	13
Protein (g.)	113	152	179
Carbohydrates (g.)	211	283	369
Dietary fiber (g.)	24	32	44
Cholesterol (mg.)	347	409	434
Sodium (mg.)	2,088	2,631	3,482

Lasagna Bundles

Lasagna Bundles

MAKES 8

Nonfat ricotta cheese reduces the fat in this innovative spin-off of tra-ditional lasagna. Topped with a chunky tomato sauce, this dish provides a hearty serving of antioxidant vitamins. Forming the lasagna into bundles makes it easy to control portion size.

8	lasagna noodles
1	teaspoon olive oil
1	cup chopped onions
2	teaspoons minced garlic
1	container (15 ounces) nonfat ricotta cheese
1	package (10 ounces) frozen chopped spinach, thawed and squeezed dry
2	egg whites, lightly beaten
¼	cup chopped fresh basil
2	tablespoons grated Parmesan cheese
¼	teaspoon ground black pepper
⅛	teaspoon grated nutmeg
¾	cup shredded reduced-fat mozzarella cheese
1	jar (25½ ounces) reduced-sodium marinara sauce

Preheat the oven to 350°F.

Cook the noodles in a large pot of boiling water according to the package directions. Drain. Lay the noodles flat on a work surface to prevent them from sticking together.

Warm the oil in a medium no-stick skillet over medium heat. Add the onions and garlic. Cook for 3 to 5 minutes, or until softened. Transfer to a medium bowl.

To the bowl, add the ricotta, spinach, egg whites, basil, Parmesan, pepper, nutmeg, and ¼ cup of the mozzarella. Mix well.

Spread ⅓ cup of the ricotta filling over the length of each noodle and roll up from one end.

Spread one-half of the marinara sauce on the bottom of a 13" × 9" baking dish. Add the rolls, seam side down. Top with the remaining sauce and the remaining ½ cup mozzarella.

Cover with foil and bake for 25 minutes. Remove the foil and bake for another 5 minutes.

Nutrition Notes

Per bundle

Calories 230
Fat 3.5 g.
% of calories from fat 14
Protein 17.2 g.
Carbohydrates 32 g.
Dietary fiber 3.7 g.
Cholesterol 24 mg.
Sodium 311 mg.

Kitchen Hint

◆ Substitute eggplant for the lasagna noodles for a tasty variation. Cut 1 large eggplant lengthwise into ¼"-thick slices. Grill the slices for 2 to 3 minutes per side, or until soft and pliable. Prepare the bundles as directed.

Nutrition Notes

Per serving

Calories 281
Fat 2.2 g.
% of calories from fat 7
Protein 12 g.
Carbohydrates 54.8 g.
Dietary fiber 6.5 g.
Cholesterol 5 mg.
Sodium 373 mg.

Kitchen Hint

◆ You can replace the frozen black-eyed peas with 1 cup rinsed and drained canned black-eyed peas.

Hoppin' John Salad

MAKES 4 SERVINGS

Hoppin' John is a savory southern rice and bean dish that dates back to the 1700s, when dietary fat and sodium were not a concern. Early versions of the recipe call for more than a pound of bacon or smoked ham hocks. Turkey bacon provides the flavor in this lighter version. For a unique twist, we serve the mixture in hollowed-out beefsteak tomatoes.

2	slices turkey bacon
1	cup chopped onions
1	teaspoon minced garlic
3	cups defatted reduced-sodium chicken broth
1/2	cup wild rice, rinsed
1	bay leaf
1	teaspoon dried thyme
1/2	cup long-grain white rice
1	cup frozen black-eyed peas, thawed
1	stalk celery, chopped
1/2	green pepper, chopped
1/2	cup chopped tomatoes
1/4	cup chopped fresh Italian parsley
2	tablespoons lemon juice
1/2	teaspoon hot-pepper sauce
1/4	teaspoon ground black pepper
1/8	teaspoon salt
4	large beefsteak tomatoes

In a medium saucepan over medium-high heat, cook the bacon for 2 to 3 minutes, or until crisp. Remove from the saucepan and set aside until cool; crumble.

Add the onions and garlic to the same saucepan. Cook for 3 to 5 minutes, or until softened. Add the broth, wild rice, bay leaf, and thyme; bring to a boil. Cover, reduce the heat to low, and cook for 20 minutes.

Add the white rice. Cover and cook for 20 minutes, or until the rice is tender. Fluff the rice with a fork, loosely cover, and let cool completely.

Stir in the black-eyed peas, celery, green peppers, chopped tomatoes, parsley, lemon juice, hot-pepper sauce, black pepper, salt, and crumbled bacon. Remove and discard the bay leaf.

Slice the tops from the beefsteak tomatoes; carefully scoop out the insides and discard. Divide the rice mixture among the tomatoes.

Herbed Asparagus Omelets

MAKES 4

Omelets aren't off-limits! We cut the fat and cholesterol in these delicious omelets by replacing some of the whole eggs with egg whites. Goat cheese and asparagus pack this breakfast with flavor. Use whatever fresh herbs you have on hand—basil and dill are especially good.

8	egg whites
4	eggs
¼	cup skim milk
2	tablespoons chopped scallions
¼	cup chopped fresh herbs
½	teaspoon ground black pepper
⅛	teaspoon salt
8	ounces asparagus, trimmed and cut into 1" pieces
¼	cup water
4	tablespoons crumbled goat cheese

In a medium bowl, whisk together the egg whites, eggs, and milk. Stir in the scallions, herbs, pepper, and salt.

Place the asparagus and water in a large microwave-safe bowl. Cover with vented plastic wrap and microwave on high power for a total of 4 to 6 minutes, or until crisp-tender; stop and stir after 2 minutes. Drain, pat dry, and add to the egg mixture.

Coat a medium no-stick skillet with no-stick spray. Set over medium heat until hot. Pour one-fourth of the egg mixture into the skillet and cook, occasionally scraping the bottom of the skillet, for 2 to 3 minutes. Sprinkle with 1 tablespoon of the goat cheese. Add one-fourth of the asparagus pieces. Continue to cook for 4 to 5 minutes, or until the eggs are almost set.

Using a large spatula, fold the omelet in half. Cook for 3 minutes, or until the omelet is golden and the cheese is melted. Turn onto a plate to keep warm.

Coat the skillet with no-stick spray and repeat the process with the remaining ingredients to make 3 more omelets.

Nutrition Notes

Per omelet

Calories 177
Fat 8.8 g.
% of calories from fat 45
Protein 18.6 g.
Carbohydrates 5.9 g.
Dietary fiber 1.7 g.
Cholesterol 220 mg.
Sodium 321 mg.

Kitchen Hint

◆ For perfect omelets every time, beat your eggs just before you are ready to cook them and use a no-stick pan with sloping sides. As for doneness, an omelet should be tender yet firm—golden brown on the outside and creamy on the inside. Since omelets are best made individually, try using 2 skillets so you can make 2 at a time. If you prefer to make a larger omelet, increase the cooking time until the eggs are set.

Spring Menu Thirteen

	1,500 CALORIES	2,000 CALORIES	2,500 CALORIES
	33-43 G. FAT	44-56 G. FAT	57-69 G. FAT

Breakfast

shredded wheat cereal with	1¼ cups	1¼ cups	2 cups
sliced strawberries and	½ cup	1¼ cups	1½ cups
skim milk	1 cup	1¼ cups	1½ cups

Lunch

Oh-So-Sloppy Joes	1 serving	1 serving	1 serving
shredded cabbage salad with	1 cup	1 cup	2 cups
nonfat dressing	1 tablespoon	1 tablespoon	2 tablespoons

Dinner

Veal Marsala	1 serving	1 serving	2 servings
rotini with fresh herbs	½ cup	2 cups	2½ cups
Tiramisu	1 serving	1 serving	1 serving

Snack

graham crackers	2 whole sheets	4 whole sheets	4 whole sheets

DAILY TOTALS

Calories	1,513	1,989	2,518
Fat (g.)	34	39	50
% of calories from fat	20	17	17
Protein (g.)	84	99	133
Carbohydrates (g.)	217	311	381
Dietary fiber (g.)	15	20	27
Cholesterol (mg.)	298	299	391
Sodium (mg.)	1,476	1,731	2,215

NUTRIENT BONUS

This menu (at 2,000 calories) exceeds the Daily Value for:

Vitamin A	110%
Riboflavin	108%
Niacin	117%
Vitamin B$_{12}$	102%
Vitamin C	283%

HEALTHY TIP OF THE DAY

Travel savvy: When you're on the run, plan ahead for snacks and meals. Don't be tempted by the high-fat, highly processed foods found at convenience stores and fast-food restaurants. Healthy foods like fresh fruit, bagels, and dry cereal are filling and nutritious to snack on. For a quick mini-meal, carry along roasted vegetable sandwiches or pita bread filled with grain salad.

Tiramisu (page 108)

Nutrition Notes

Per serving

Calories 353
Fat 7.9 g.
% of calories from fat 20
Protein 31.2 g.
Carbohydrates 41.1 g.
Dietary fiber 4.5 g.
Cholesterol 61 mg.
Sodium 500 mg.

Kitchen Hints

♦ The beef can be replaced with 1 pound ground turkey breast or chicken breast for even less fat. For a vegetarian version, use 1 cup frozen, thawed, and crumbled tofu in place of the meat.

♦ To take this dish along for lunch, pack the beef mixture in an airtight container. Pack the buns in a separate plastic bag. Microwave the beef mixture for 2 to 4 minutes, or until heated through; stop and stir after every 1 minute. Assemble the sandwiches.

Where can you get a satisfying sandwich that's low in fat too? Right here! These hearty Joes are filled with lean ground beef and an array of nourishing vegetables. With vitamin B_{12} and vitamin A, they also pack quite a nutritional punch.

½ teaspoon olive oil
¾ cup chopped red onions
½ cup chopped green peppers
½ cup finely chopped carrots
½ cup chopped celery
1 clove garlic, minced
2 teaspoons dried oregano
1 pound lean ground beef round
½ cup reduced-sodium tomato sauce
¼ cup water
1 tablespoon balsamic vinegar
1 tablespoon Worcestershire sauce
2 tablespoons packed light brown sugar
¼ teaspoon ground black pepper
¼ teaspoon hot-pepper sauce
4 sesame seed buns

Warm the oil in a large no-stick skillet over medium-high heat. Add the onions, green peppers, carrots, celery, garlic, and oregano; cook for 4 to 5 minutes, or until the vegetables are softened. Add the ground beef. Cook, breaking up the meat with a wooden spoon, for 3 minutes, or until no longer pink. Stir in the tomato sauce, water, vinegar, Worcestershire sauce, brown sugar, black pepper, and hot-pepper sauce. Cook for 3 minutes, or until heated through.

Lightly toast the buns. Place ½ cup of the mixture on the bottom half of each bun. Top with the other half.

Veal Marsala

MAKES 4 SERVINGS

Lean, delicately flavored veal marries well with the richer flavors of mushrooms and Marsala. This elegant yet quick-to-prepare dish can be on the table in 30 minutes.

1/3	cup dried wild mushrooms
1	cup boiling water
1/3	cup all-purpose flour
1/2	teaspoon ground black pepper
1/4	teaspoon salt
1	pound veal scallops, pounded to 1/8" thickness
1	teaspoon olive oil
2	cups sliced mushrooms
1	shallot, finely chopped
1	clove garlic, minced
1/2	cup dry Marsala or apple juice
3/4	cup defatted reduced-sodium chicken broth
2	teaspoons unsalted butter or margarine
4	teaspoons chopped fresh Italian parsley

Place the dried mushrooms in a small bowl and cover with the water. Let stand for 10 minutes.

Combine the flour, pepper, and salt on a large plate. Dredge the veal in the flour mixture to coat both sides and shake off any excess.

Warm the oil in a large no-stick skillet over medium-high heat. Working in batches if necessary, quickly cook the veal until browned, about 1 minute per side. Transfer to a platter.

Reduce the heat to medium and coat the skillet with no-stick spray. Add the sliced mushrooms, shallots, and garlic. Cover and cook, stirring occasionally, for 3 to 4 minutes, or until browned. Add the Marsala or apple juice, increase the heat to medium-high, and cook for 2 to 3 minutes, or until the liquid is reduced by half.

Using a fine mesh strainer, strain the liquid from the dried mushrooms into the skillet. Reserve the mushrooms for another use. Add the broth and cook until the liquid in the skillet is reduced by one-third.

Return the veal to the skillet and cook for 1 to 2 minutes, or until warmed through. Stir in the butter or margarine. Serve sprinkled with the parsley.

Nutrition Notes

Per serving

Calories 250
Fat 9 g.
% of calories from fat 33
Protein 24.1 g.
Carbohydrates 12.8 g.
Dietary fiber 1.3 g.
Cholesterol 91 mg.
Sodium 316 mg.

Kitchen Hints

◆ When buying veal scallops, look for ivory-colored pieces with a hint of pink. Ask your butcher to make scallops from the top round, cutting across the muscle's grain rather than parallel to it. Then have him pound the scallops to an even thickness.

◆ Here are some good uses for the leftover reconstituted wild mushrooms: Chop and add to jarred tomato sauce for a quick spaghetti supper, sprinkle over pizza or lean grilled beef or chicken, or mix into a pasta salad.

Nutrition Notes

Per serving

Calories 357
Fat 11.4 g.
% of calories from fat 28
Protein 7.5 g.
Carbohydrates 54.5 g.
Dietary fiber 0.4 g.
Cholesterol 142 mg.
Sodium 175 mg.

Kitchen Hints

◆ If you don't have instant espresso powder, substitute 3 tablespoons instant coffee powder.

◆ Ladyfingers are delicate sponge cakes shaped like a wide finger and are available in most super-markets. Mascarpone is a dense Italian triple-cream cheese made from cow's milk and is available in Italian markets and in some supermarkets.

◆ The egg-white mixture in this recipe is a type of partially cooked meringue. According to the U.S. Department of Agriculture, this type of meringue is safe to eat because the egg whites reach a temperature of more than 160°F, which is enough to eliminate any harmful bacteria.

Tiramisu

MAKES 8 SERVINGS

Finally! A healthy triumph over the traditional Italian "pick-me-up."

64	ladyfingers, split
3	tablespoons brandy (optional)
1½	tablespoons instant espresso powder (see hint)
½	cup + 1½ tablespoons hot water
3	tablespoons seedless raspberry jam
3	egg whites, at room temperature
1	cup + 2 tablespoons sugar
3	tablespoons cold water
¼	teaspoon cream of tartar
4	ounces mascarpone cheese
4	ounces reduced-fat cream cheese, at room temperature
1	tablespoon semisweet chocolate shavings

Preheat the oven to 350°F.

Arrange the ladyfingers on a baking sheet and bake for 3 minutes, or until golden brown. Let cool.

In a small bowl, stir together the brandy (if using), espresso powder, and ½ cup of the hot water. Using a pastry brush, lightly brush the flat side of each ladyfinger with the mixture.

In another small bowl, combine the jam with the remaining 1½ tablespoons hot water to make a spreadable mixture. Brush the top side of each ladyfinger with a light coating of the mixture.

Bring about 2" water to a simmer in a large saucepan. In a medium heatproof bowl that will fit over the saucepan, combine the egg whites, sugar, cold water, and cream of tartar. Place the bowl over the saucepan. Using an electric mixer, beat on low speed for 4 to 5 minutes. Increase the speed to high and beat for 4 minutes, or until very thick. Remove the bowl from the saucepan. Beat for another 4 minutes, or until the mixture is very light and fluffy.

In a large bowl, combine the mascarpone and cream cheese. Using the same mixer, beat until creamy. Add 1 cup of the egg-white mixture and beat until smooth, scraping the sides of the bowl as necessary. Gradually fold in the remaining egg-white mixture.

Line the bottom of a 9" × 9" baking dish with 16 of the ladyfingers, jam side up; top with one-fourth of the filling. Repeat 3 times to use all the ladyfingers and filling. Sprinkle with the chocolate.

Cover and refrigerate for at least 4 hours or up to 3 days before serving.

Spring Menu Fourteen

	1,500 CALORIES	2,000 CALORIES	2,500 CALORIES
	33-43 G. FAT	44-56 G. FAT	57-69 G. FAT

Breakfast

frozen whole-grain waffles with	1	2	2
maple syrup	1 tablespoon	2 tablespoons	3 tablespoons
calcium-fortified orange juice	1 cup	1 cup	1½ cups

Lunch

Herbed Chicken Pinwheels	½ serving	1 serving	1½ servings
cooked brown rice	1 cup	1 cup	1½ cups
sliced pears with	¾ cup	1 cup	1 cup
orange sections	¾ cup	1 cup	1 cup

Dinner

New Iberia Seafood Gumbo	1 serving	1 serving	1 serving
soda crackers	8	8	8
Italian Parfaits	1	1	1

Snack

whole-grain crackers with	4	8	8
reduced-fat, reduced-sodium cheese	1 ounce	2 ounces	2 ounces

DAILY TOTALS			
Calories	1,484	1,998	2,503
Fat (g.)	29	46	56
% of calories from fat	17	20	20
Protein (g.)	74	112	143
Carbohydrates (g.)	236	290	362
Dietary fiber (g.)	16	21	25
Cholesterol (mg.)	220	335	431
Sodium (mg.)	1,190	1,625	2,046

NUTRIENT BONUS

This menu (at 2,000 calories) exceeds the Daily Value for:

Vitamin A	106%
Niacin	154%
Vitamin B$_6$	105%
Vitamin C	569%
Calcium	166%

HEALTHY TIP OF THE DAY

Take five for yourself. To help meet your health goals, make a 5-minute appointment with yourself. Take this opportunity to assess your dietary patterns, plan your next exercise workout, or just relax. If you find that you've strayed from your goals, don't despair. Use those 5 minutes to come up with a plan to get yourself back on track.

Herbed Chicken Pinwheels

Herbed Chicken Pinwheels

MAKES 4 SERVINGS

These chicken pinwheels are rolled with a goat-cheese filling, then baked. Each roll is sliced to display a beautiful spiral of color.

Chicken

- 2 roasted sweet red peppers, chopped
- 4 ounces goat cheese
- 1/2 cup chopped fresh basil
- 1/2 cup chopped fresh Italian parsley
- 2 tablespoons nonfat sour cream
- 1 tablespoon lemon juice
- 1 tablespoon chopped fresh thyme
- 1 teaspoon ground black pepper
- 4 boneless, skinless chicken breast halves (about 6 ounces each)

Sauce

- 1 teaspoon olive oil
- 3 large shallots, finely chopped
- 1 cup defatted reduced-sodium chicken broth
- 2 1/2 cups reduced-sodium canned crushed tomatoes

To make the chicken: In a medium bowl, combine the red peppers, goat cheese, basil, parsley, sour cream, lemon juice, thyme, and black pepper. Mix well.

With a sharp knife, split each chicken breast half open so the thick sides butterfly out like a thin open book. Place between pieces of plastic wrap and pound lightly with a meat mallet to 1/2" thickness.

Remove the plastic wrap from each breast. Divide the cheese mixture among the breasts and spread it evenly. Roll the breasts into cylinders to enclose the filling. Tightly wrap each breast in foil and twist the ends to close.

Bring about 2" of water to a boil in a large wide saucepan over high heat. Add the rolls to the saucepan. Reduce the heat to medium-low, cover and simmer for 20 minutes, turning the rolls every 5 minutes.

To make the sauce: Warm the oil in a medium saucepan over medium heat. Add the shallots and cook for 4 minutes, or until soft. Add the broth and cook for 5 minutes, or until the liquid is slightly reduced. Add the tomatoes and simmer for 5 minutes.

Use tongs to remove the chicken rolls from the water; drain on paper towels. Let cool for 1 minute. Unwrap and cut each roll on the diagonal into 1/2"-thick slices. Serve with the sauce.

Nutrition Notes

Per serving

Calories 366
Fat 9.5 g.
% of calories from fat 24
Protein 49.2 g.
Carbohydrates 19.3 g.
Dietary fiber 4 g.
Cholesterol 112 mg.
Sodium 528 mg.

Kitchen Hints

◆ If buying chicken breasts that include the tenders, remove them, lifting the end of each tender and pulling it toward you. Within each chicken tender is a tough, chewy tendon. To remove it, grab the end of the tendon and cut away some of the surrounding meat to expose it. Then hold the tendon against the surface of a cutting board. Using a knife held at a 45° angle, push the tendon away from you along the length of the tender.

◆ For a decorative presentation, spoon some tomato sauce on each serving plate. Arrange the sliced chicken rolls on top of the sauce. Serve the additional sauce on the side.

Per serving

Calories 193
Fat 3.3 g.
% of calories from fat 15
Protein 18.2 g.
Carbohydrates 22.4 g.
Dietary fiber 2.1 g.
Cholesterol 103 mg.
Sodium 390 mg.

Kitchen Hints

◆ Filé powder is an essential ingredient in many gumbos. Used as a thickener, it's made from dried sassafras leaves and has a flavor reminiscent of root beer. It is available in most supermarkets.

◆ The stock can be prepared up to 3 months in advance and frozen.

New Iberia Seafood Gumbo

MAKES 8 SERVINGS

Louisiana lightens up with this lean version of the classic gumbo. Low-fat kielbasa stands in for ham, while filé powder and Cajun seasoning intensify the flavors. Buy shrimp in the shell because you'll need the shells for the stock.

Seafood Stock

- 1 pound small unpeeled shrimp
- 2 quarts water
- 1 onion, quartered
- 1 large clove garlic, halved
- 1 stalk celery
- 1 bay leaf
- ½ teaspoon black peppercorns
- ½ teaspoon dried thyme

Gumbo

- 1 tablespoon olive oil
- 1 cup chopped onions
- 1 cup chopped celery
- ½ cup chopped green peppers
- ½ cup chopped sweet red peppers
- 2 large cloves garlic, minced
- 1 tablespoon filé powder (see hint)
- 2 teaspoons Cajun seasoning
- 1 can (14½ ounces) no-salt-added chopped tomatoes (with juice)
- 1 cup frozen okra
- 4 ounces low-fat kielbasa, diced
- ⅔ cup long-grain white rice
- 6 ounces crabmeat
- ¼ teaspoon salt

To make the stock: Peel the shrimp and place the shells in a large saucepan. Devein the shrimp and refrigerate until needed.

To the saucepan, add the water, onions, garlic, celery, bay leaf, peppercorns, and thyme. Bring to a boil over high heat. Reduce the heat to medium-low and gently simmer for 1 hour, skimming off any accumulated foam. If necessary, add more water to keep

about 5 cups liquid in the saucepan at all times. Strain the stock and measure out 5 cups (reserve any excess for another use).

To make the gumbo: Warm the oil in a Dutch oven over medium-high heat. Add the onions, celery, green peppers, and red peppers. Cook, stirring often, for 5 minutes. Reduce the heat to medium and add the garlic, filé powder, and Cajun seasoning; cook, stirring constantly, for 5 minutes. Stir in the tomatoes (with juice), okra, and kielbasa; cook for 5 minutes.

Add the stock and bring to a boil over high heat. Reduce the heat to medium-low and simmer for 45 to 50 minutes.

Meanwhile, cook the rice according to the package directions.

Stir the shrimp, crabmeat, and salt into the gumbo. Cover and remove from the heat. Let stand for 5 minutes, or until the shrimp are opaque and cooked through. Remove and discard the bay leaf. Serve over the rice.

Healthy Shellfish

If you're monitoring your cholesterol intake, you might shy away from shellfish—especially shrimp, which have a reputation for being high in cholesterol. However, many shellfish are comparable in cholesterol content to finfish and skinless poultry. Even shrimp are lower in cholesterol than previously thought. And all shellfish are very low in saturated fat, which has a greater effect on raising blood cholesterol. In general, mollusks are lower in cholesterol than crustaceans. Mollusks include clams, mussels, oysters, and scallops as well as squid and octopus. In the crustacean category, there are crabs, lobsters, crayfish, and shrimp. Here are the most popular types of shellfish and their cholesterol counts.

Seafood (3 oz.)	Cholesterol (mg.)
Clams	29
Crab	60
Crayfish	113
Lobster	81
Mussels	24
Octopus	82
Oysters	52
Scallops	14
Shrimp	121
Squid	239

Nutrition Notes

Per parfait

Calories 186
Fat 1.3 g.
% of calories from fat 6
Protein 7.6 g.
Carbohydrates 36.8 g.
Dietary fiber 0.2 g.
Cholesterol 2 mg.
Sodium 100 mg.

Kitchen Hints

◆ Biscotti are crunchy Italian cookies often made with no added fat. They can be purchased in most supermarkets and in Italian food stores. To crush the biscotti, place them in a heavy-duty resealable plastic bag and coarsely crush with a rolling pin.

◆ Create your own version of this recipe by using different flavors of nonfat frozen yogurt and biscotti.

Italian Parfaits

This tempting dessert is deceptively low in fat—and supereasy to prepare. Just layer crushed biscotti in goblets with frozen yogurt, shaved chocolate, and espresso.

2	teaspoons instant espresso powder
1/2	cup boiling water
8	nonfat chocolate chip biscotti, crushed
2 2/3	cups nonfat vanilla frozen yogurt
4	teaspoons grated semisweet chocolate

In a small bowl, dissolve the espresso powder in the water. Set aside to cool.

Divide one-third of the biscotti crumbs among 4 parfait glasses. In each glass, layer 1/3 cup of the frozen yogurt, 1 tablespoon of the espresso, and 1/2 teaspoon of the chocolate. Repeat. Top with the remaining biscotti crumbs and the remaining chocolate. Serve immediately or freeze for up to 1 hour.

Spring Menu Fifteen

	1,500 CALORIES	2,000 CALORIES	2,500 CALORIES
	33-43 G. FAT	44-56 G. FAT	57-69 G. FAT

Breakfast

oatmeal	1 cup	1 cup	1¼ cups
skim milk	1 cup	1¼ cups	1¼ cups
orange	1	2	2

Lunch

Casablanca Couscous	1 serving	1½ servings	2 servings
tomato	1	2	2

Dinner

Turkey Piccata	1 serving	1½ servings	2 servings
steamed carrots and broccoli	1 cup	1½ cups	1½ cups
roasted new potatoes	½ cup	1 cup	1¼ cups
Lemon Cheesecake	1 slice	1 slice	1 slice

Snack

soft pretzel with	1	1	2
hot mustard	2 tablespoons	2 tablespoons	4 tablespoons

DAILY TOTALS

Calories	1,527	1,991	2,506
Fat (g.)	25	31	38
% of calories from fat	14	14	13
Protein (g.)	85	114	145
Carbohydrates (g.)	249	327	412
Dietary fiber (g.)	28	41	51
Cholesterol (mg.)	141	184	226
Sodium (mg.)	1,625	1,949	2,714

NUTRIENT BONUS

This menu (at 2,000 calories) exceeds the Daily Value for:

Dietary fiber	164%
Vitamin A	738%
Thiamin	113%
Riboflavin	137%
Niacin	123%
Vitamin B$_6$	118%
Vitamin C	798%
Vitamin E	128%
Calcium	120%
Iron	204%
Potassium	154%

HEALTHY TIP OF THE DAY

Shop like a pro. To make healthy shopping easier, take 10 minutes out of your day to plan dinners for the upcoming week. Make a shopping list so you take only one trip to the store. And avoid shopping while you're hungry. Grab a piece of fruit, a couple of pretzels, or half a bagel before you head out. That way, you'll buy only what you need and avoid the temptation of high-fat snacks.

Lemon Cheesecake

Lemon Cheesecake

MAKES 12 SLICES

This one is sure to impress you and your guests. The graham cracker crust perfectly complements the smooth lemony filling.

Crust

1¼	cups graham cracker crumbs
¼	cup pecans, toasted and ground
¼	cup sugar
3	tablespoons butter or margarine, melted
1	egg white

Filling and Topping

2	packages (8 ounces each) nonfat cream cheese
1	package (8 ounces) reduced-fat cream cheese
¼	cup all-purpose flour
2	cups sugar
½	cup fresh lemon juice
2	eggs
2	egg whites
2	cups nonfat sour cream

To make the crust: Preheat the oven to 350°F. Coat a 9" springform pan with no-stick spray.

In a large bowl, combine the cracker crumbs, pecans, sugar, and butter or margarine. Lightly beat the egg white in a cup. Add half of the egg white to the bowl; reserve the remainder for another use or discard. Mix well. Press the mixture into the bottom and 1" up the sides of the prepared pan. Bake for 10 minutes, or until lightly browned. Cool on a wire rack.

To make the filling and topping: Place the nonfat cream cheese and reduced-fat cream cheese in a food processor. Process for 1 to 2 minutes, or until smooth. Add the flour and 1½ cups of the sugar. Process for 3 minutes, or until light and fluffy; stop and scrape the sides of the bowl as necessary. Add the lemon juice and process briefly. Add the eggs and egg whites, one at a time, and process until just incorporated.

Pour the mixture into the prepared pan. Bake for 1 hour. Remove from the oven.

In a small bowl, mix the sour cream and the remaining ½ cup sugar. Spread over the hot cheesecake. Bake for 10 minutes. Place on a wire rack and let cool to room temperature. Cover and refrigerate for at least 8 hours.

Nutrition Notes

Per slice

Calories 388
Fat 10.4 g.
% of calories from fat 24
Protein 13.2 g.
Carbohydrates 60.6 g.
Dietary fiber 0.6 g.
Cholesterol 52 mg.
Sodium 416 mg.

Kitchen Hint

◆ This cheesecake is equally delicious served with a fresh fruit topping. Omit the sour-cream topping. Toss 3 cups berries, sliced peaches, or orange segments with 2 tablespoons melted jam or jelly. Decoratively arrange the fruit on top of the cooled cheesecake.

Nutrition Notes

Per serving

Calories 237
Fat 4.3 g.
% of calories from fat 16
Protein 32.5 g.
Carbohydrates 14.6 g.
Dietary fiber 1.8 g.
Cholesterol 84 mg.
Sodium 340 mg.

Kitchen Hint

◆ Capers are the unopened floral buds of a shrub that grows in the mild, dry climate of the Mediterranean region. The buds are picked while still closed, then pickled and packed in brine. Capers add zing to many sauces, salads, and fish dishes. Packed capers are high in sodium, so remember to rinse them before using.

Veal is traditionally used in piccata dishes, but turkey breast makes a wonderful substitute with a lot less saturated fat and cholesterol. The mellow flavor of the turkey marries well with the piquant lemon-caper sauce.

2	lemons
$1/3$	cup all-purpose flour
$1/2$	teaspoon ground black pepper
$1/4$	teaspoon salt
1	pound turkey breast, cut into $1/4$"-thick slices
2	teaspoons olive oil
2	cups sliced mushrooms
1	shallot, minced
1	large clove garlic, minced
$1/4$	cup dry vermouth or nonalcoholic white wine
$3/4$	cup defatted reduced-sodium chicken broth
2	tablespoons rinsed and drained capers
$1/4$	teaspoon sugar
2	tablespoons chopped fresh Italian parsley
1	teaspoon unsalted butter or margarine

With a sharp knife, carefully remove the rind and white membrane from one of the lemons. Cut the lemon segments away from their surrounding membranes and place in a small bowl. Squeeze any juice from the membranes into the bowl. Discard the rind, membranes, and seeds. Thinly slice the remaining whole lemon.

Combine the flour, pepper, and salt on a large plate. Dredge the turkey in the flour mixture to coat both sides and shake off any excess.

Warm the oil in a large no-stick skillet over medium-high heat. Working in batches if necessary, add the turkey to the skillet and cook for 2 minutes per side, or until no longer pink in the center when tested with a sharp knife. Transfer to a platter.

Coat the skillet with no-stick spray and add the mushrooms, shallots, and garlic. Reduce the heat to medium, cover, and cook for 2 minutes, stirring occasionally. Add the vermouth or wine to the skillet and raise the heat to medium-high. Bring to a boil and stir constantly for 30 seconds. Add the broth, capers, sugar, and the lemon segments (with juice). Return to a boil and cook for 1 to 2 minutes.

Return the turkey to the skillet and add the parsley, butter or margarine, and the lemon slices. Cook and stir for 1 minute, or until heated through.

Casablanca Couscous

MAKES 4 SERVINGS

This is a quick-cooking meatless meal. A seasoned couscous mixture is stuffed into juicy beefsteak tomatoes. Serve at room temperature or chilled.

¼	cup red lentils
1	cup orange juice
¼	cup water
⅔	cup couscous
1	sweet red pepper, chopped
½	cup chopped dates
⅓	cup sliced scallions
⅓	cup currants
3	tablespoons toasted slivered almonds
2	tablespoons chopped fresh mint
	Grated rind of 1 lemon
½	teaspoon ground cinnamon
⅛	teaspoon salt
4	beefsteak tomatoes

Place the lentils in a small saucepan and add enough water to cover by ½". Bring to a simmer over medium heat. Cook for 5 minutes, or until the lentils are just tender. Drain and rinse under cold water, pressing firmly to remove any excess water. Place in a large bowl.

Add the orange juice and water to the saucepan. Bring to a boil over high heat. Stir in the couscous. Cover, remove from the heat, and let stand for 5 minutes. Fluff with a fork. Add to the bowl with the lentils.

Stir in the peppers, dates, scallions, currants, almonds, mint, lemon rind, cinnamon, and salt.

Slice the tops from the tomatoes and discard; carefully scoop out the insides and discard. Divide the couscous mixture among the tomatoes.

Nutrition Notes

Per serving

Calories 250
Fat 4 g.
% of calories from fat 13
Protein 8.7 g.
Carbohydrates 49.4 g.
Dietary fiber 8.1 g.
Cholesterol 0 mg.
Sodium 99.5 mg.

Kitchen Hint

◆ Couscous is a tiny round pasta made from semolina flour. The mild flavor of this North African staple is the perfect backdrop for more flavorful ingredients and seasonings. Couscous can be served hot or cold as a base for salads, entrées, or side dishes.

Spring Menu Sixteen

Breakfast

toasted bagel with	1	1	1½
jam	2 tablespoons	2 tablespoons	3 tablespoons
grapefruit	½	1	1½

Lunch

Mediterranean Pizza with Shrimp and Feta	2 slices	3 slices	4 slices
mixed green salad with	1 cup	1 cup	2 cups
balsamic vinegar	1 tablespoon	2 tablespoons	2 tablespoons

Dinner

Cornish Hens with Orange-Rosemary Sauce	1 serving	1 serving	1 serving
Snow Peas with Red Peppers	1 serving	2 servings	2 servings

Snack

nonfat fruit yogurt	1 cup	1½ cups	1½ cups

DAILY TOTALS			
Calories	1,493	1,992	2,498
Fat (g.)	30	42	53
% of calories from fat	17	18	19
Protein (g.)	99	124	145
Carbohydrates (g.)	212	287	372
Dietary fiber (g.)	29	39	49
Cholesterol (mg.)	234	276	316
Sodium (mg.)	1,826	2,496	3,150

NUTRIENT BONUS

This menu (at 2,000 calories) exceeds the Daily Value for:

Dietary fiber	154%
Vitamin A	177%
Niacin	125%
Folate	106%
Vitamin C	659%
Iron	169%
Calcium	199%

HEALTHY TIP OF THE DAY

Easy does it. Take it slow and safe when beginning a weight-loss or exercise plan. Unrealistic expectations can lead to anxiety and stress, which may discourage you to the point of quitting your routine. Choose an activity—and an activity level—that is personally satisfying, rather than one that promises instant bene-fits. You'll be more likely to stick with activities that you enjoy and an activity level that you are comfortable with.

Cornish Hens with Orange-Rosemary Sauce (page 122)

Cornish Hens with Orange-Rosemary Sauce

MAKES 4 SERVINGS

Sliced oranges and rosemary infuse these lean birds with heady aromas and flavors—instead of extra fat and calories.

Hens

1	large onion, thickly sliced
2	oranges
2	Cornish hens (1½ pounds each), trimmed of excess fat and giblets discarded
1½	teaspoons dried rosemary
½	teaspoon ground black pepper
⅛	teaspoon salt
6	sprigs fresh rosemary
2	cloves garlic, thinly sliced
1	cup orange juice

Orange-Rosemary Sauce

1	tablespoon cornstarch
¾	cup water
½	cup orange marmalade
2	teaspoons finely chopped fresh rosemary
½	teaspoon ground black pepper
2	tablespoons brandy (optional)

To make the hens: Preheat the oven to 375°F.

Coat a 13" × 9" baking dish with no-stick spray. Scatter the onions in the dish.

Grate the rind from the oranges. Reserve 1 tablespoon rind for the sauce. Slice the oranges crosswise.

Season the cavities of the hens with the dried rosemary, pepper, and salt. Stuff with the orange slices. Work your fingers underneath the skin of each hen (being careful not to break through the skin). Slide 3 rosemary sprigs, half of the garlic, and 1 tablespoon of the orange rind under the skin of each hen. Place the hens, breast side up, on top of the onions in the baking dish.

Pour the orange juice over the hens. Cover with foil and bake for 40 to 50 minutes. Remove the foil, spoon the juices over the hens, and increase the heat to 400°F. Bake, uncovered, for 20 to 25 minutes,

or until the skin is crispy and the juices run clear when the thigh is pierced with a sharp knife. Remove and discard the skin. Cut each bird in half lengthwise. Discard the orange slices and onions.

To make the orange-rosemary sauce: Place the cornstarch in a cup. Add ¼ cup of the water and stir until smooth.

In a small saucepan, combine the marmalade and the remaining ½ cup water. Stir over low heat for 4 minutes to form a smooth sauce. Add the rosemary, pepper, and the reserved orange rind. Stir in the cornstarch mixture. Cook over medium heat, stirring constantly, for 2 to 3 minutes, or until thickened. Add the brandy (if using) and cook for 2 minutes. Spoon the sauce over the hens.

Maximize Your Microwave

Why limit your microwave to reheating leftovers? Microwaves can cut cooking time for fresh foods, too. Steamed vegetables are done quickly, and they retain more of their water-soluble vitamins than when boiled or braised. Potatoes can be "baked" in no time at all; serve them in their skins for added fiber. For other foods, use the microwave as you would use any other moist-heat cooking method. Even chicken breasts can be steam-sautéed in your microwave.

The following tips will assure you consistently good results.

- Cut foods into same-size pieces so they cook at the same rate.
- To promote thorough cooking, place the food in a deep dish and wrap tightly with plastic wrap. Poke steam vents in the wrap or fold back an edge to allow steam to escape. (You can also use vented plastic wrap, available in most supermarkets.) Make sure the plastic wrap doesn't touch the food during cooking.
- For steamed vegetables, add about ¼ cup water to every 8 ounces vegetables. For added flavor, use broth and dried herbs.
- Microwaves cook foods quickly on the perimeter and more slowly in the center. For even cooking, arrange stalk vegetables like broccoli and cauliflower with the thick stems around the edge and the tender heads toward the center. For chicken and other meats, place the thickest part toward the edge and the thinner parts toward the center.
- Rotate the cooking vessel at least once during cooking to promote even cooking. Also stir the food.
- Observe the "standing time" if specified in a recipe. The food will finish cooking during this time.
- Lift plastic wrap or microwave lids away from you to avoid steam burns.

Nutrition Notes

Per slice

Calories 205
Fat 6.5 g.
% of calories from fat 29
Protein 13.6 g.
Carbohydrates 23.2 g.
Dietary fiber 3.7 g.
Cholesterol 40 mg.
Sodium 340 mg.

Kitchen Hint

◆ Restaurant pizzas are often baked in a wood-fired brick oven to create a crisp, delicate crust. Get the same effect at home by using a pizza stone or unglazed quarry tiles. Place them on an oven rack and preheat them for 30 minutes before placing the pizza directly on the stone or tiles. A pizza peel (a flat wooden paddle with a long handle) is useful for moving the pizza in and out of the oven. Or try using a flat baking sheet. Dust the peel or baking sheet with cornmeal so the pizza will slide off the surface easily.

Mediterranean Pizza with Shrimp and Feta

MAKES 8 SLICES

Add zest to your pizza with a low-fat, iron-rich pesto. Your favorite ingredients can stand in for the shrimp and feta cheese called for here. Just remember to choose fresh vegetables and reduced-fat cheeses when creating your own topping.

2	tablespoons cornmeal
1	tube (10 ounces) refrigerated pizza dough
1	cup water
5	ounces large shrimp, peeled and deveined
1	tablespoon toasted pine nuts
1	large clove garlic
1½	cups loosely packed fresh basil
2	tablespoons grated Parmesan cheese
2–3	tablespoons defatted reduced-sodium chicken broth
2	teaspoons lemon juice
2	ounces feta cheese, crumbled
2	tablespoons minced red onions
½	cup shredded reduced-fat low-sodium mozzarella cheese

Preheat the oven to 450°F. Coat a baking sheet with no-stick spray. Sprinkle with the cornmeal.

Unroll the pizza dough and spread on the prepared sheet.

Bring the water to a simmer in a small saucepan. Add the shrimp and cook for 1 to 2 minutes, or until opaque and cooked through. Drain and cut each shrimp into thirds.

Place the pine nuts and garlic in a food processor or blender. Process until minced. Add the basil, Parmesan, broth, and lemon juice; process for 2 to 3 minutes, or until a paste forms. Add more broth, if necessary, to achieve the desired consistency.

Spread the pesto on the crust, leaving a ½" border. Sprinkle with the shrimp, feta, and onions. Top with the mozzarella. Bake for 14 to 16 minutes, or until the bottom is browned and the cheese is melted.

Snow Peas with Red Peppers

MAKES 4 SERVINGS

A sweet and tangy glaze replaces butter in this spring side dish. It's a great way to boost your vitamin C and folate intake, too.

3	cups snow peas
2	tablespoons water
1/3	cup balsamic vinegar
1	tablespoon packed light brown sugar
1/2	teaspoon olive oil
1/2	large sweet red pepper, cut into short strips
1	clove garlic, minced
1/8	teaspoon salt
1/8	teaspoon ground black pepper

Place the snow peas and water in a large microwave-safe bowl. Cover with vented plastic wrap and microwave on high power for a total of 5 minutes, or until crisp-tender; stop and stir after 3 minutes. Drain.

In a small saucepan over medium-high heat, bring the vinegar and brown sugar to a boil. Cook, stirring constantly, for 3 minutes, or until the mixture is reduced to 2 tablespoons. Remove from the heat.

Warm the oil in a large no-stick skillet over medium heat. Add the red peppers and garlic; cook for 2 minutes, or until crisp-tender. Add the snow peas, salt, black pepper and the glaze. Toss to mix.

Nutrition Notes

Per serving

Calories 69
Fat 0.8 g.
% of calories from fat 10
Protein 2.4 g.
Carbohydrates 13.8 g.
Dietary fiber 2.2 g.
Cholesterol 0 mg.
Sodium 76 mg.

Kitchen Hint

◆ Sweet red peppers are usually sold by the pound. To save money when buying them, compare size against weight in your hands. Look for large, long, narrow peppers. They often weigh less (and cost less) than small, short, round peppers. Remember, you'll use only the fleshy part of the pepper, not the stem and ribs (where most of the weight is concentrated).

HEALTHY TIP OF THE DAY

For long-lasting energy, eat complex carbohydrates like bread, grains, pasta, rice, and cereal. These foods supply time-released energy with less than half the calories per gram than fat. Choose from a variety of foods at the base of the Food Guide Pyramid.

	1,500 CALORIES	2,000 CALORIES	2,500 CALORIES
	33-43 G. FAT	44-56 G. FAT	57-69 G. FAT
Breakfast			
toasted English muffin with	1	1½	1½
jam	2 tablespoons	3 tablespoons	3 tablespoons
mixed fresh fruit salad	1 cup	1½ cups	1½ cups
Lunch			
Tuna-Pasta Salad	1 serving	1½ servings	2 servings
nonfat fruit yogurt	1 cup	1¼ cups	1½ cups
dinner roll	1	2	2
Dinner			
grilled chicken breast with	4 ounces	5 ounces	6 ounces
low-sodium barbecue sauce	2 tablespoons	2½ tablespoons	3 tablespoons
baked sweet potato	1	1	1½
steamed peas	½ cup	1 cup	1½ cups
Strawberry-Rhubarb Cobbler	1 serving	1 serving	1 serving
Snack			
Kiwifruit Shakes	1 serving	1 serving	2 servings

DAILY TOTALS			
Calories	1,517	2,002	2,509
Fat (g.)	17	23	28
% of calories from fat	10	10	10
Protein (g.)	76	100	131
Carbohydrates (g.)	271	355	444
Dietary fiber (g.)	23	33	41
Cholesterol (mg.)	88	113	142
Sodium (mg.)	1,387	1,854	2,168

Tuna-Pasta Salad (page 128)

Nutrition Notes

Per serving

Calories 200
Fat 5.2 g.
% of calories from fat 23
Protein 13.5 g.
Carbohydrates 25.3 g.
Dietary fiber 3.1 g.
Cholesterol 18 mg.
Sodium 127 mg.

Kitchen Hints

◆ To create your own spin-offs of this recipe, try substituting cooked chicken, turkey breast, crabmeat, or shrimp for the tuna. Add steamed green beans or wax beans, diced tomatoes, chopped cooked egg whites, rinsed capers, or your favorite fresh herbs.

◆ This salad keeps in the refrigerator for 2 to 3 days in an airtight container.

Tuna-Pasta Salad

This salad makes a low-calorie yet filling lunch. A lemony vinaigrette lends zip to the salad.

4	ounces rigatoni
¼	cup defatted reduced-sodium chicken broth
2	tablespoons lemon juice
1	tablespoon chopped fresh oregano
2	teaspoons extra-virgin olive oil
1	teaspoon minced garlic
½	teaspoon sugar
¼	teaspoon ground black pepper
1	can (4 ounces) no-salt-added water-packed solid white tuna, drained and flaked
4	ounces frozen artichoke hearts, thawed and patted dry
1	roasted sweet red pepper, chopped
½	cup thinly sliced scallions
1	ounce feta cheese, crumbled

Cook the rigatoni in a large pot of boiling water according to the package directions. Drain and place in a large bowl. Let cool for 10 minutes.

In a small bowl, whisk together the broth, lemon juice, oregano, oil, garlic, sugar, and black pepper. Pour over the pasta.

Add the tuna, artichokes, red peppers, scallions, and feta. Toss to combine.

Kiwifruit Shakes

Frozen yogurt and kiwifruit make a high-calcium drink.

  2 kiwifruit, sliced
  4 cups nonfat vanilla frozen yogurt

In a food processor or blender, combine the kiwifruit and yogurt. Process until smooth. Serve in tall glasses.

Give Me 5

The National Cancer Institute recommends eating at least five servings of fruits and/or vegetables per day. These foods boost your intake of cancer-preventing fiber and immunity-boosting antioxidants. It's easy to get five servings. Let's say you have fruit juice with breakfast, a vegetable side dish with lunch, a piece of fruit as a snack, a vegetable with dinner, and a fruit-based dessert. That's five servings for the whole day. Here's what counts as a serving.

One Serving of Fruit Equals...(each item contains about 60 calories)

- $\frac{1}{2}$ cup cut-up fruit
- $\frac{1}{2}$ cup applesauce
- $\frac{1}{2}$ banana
- 1 medium piece of fruit (such as an apple or orange)
- 15 grapes
- $1\frac{1}{4}$ cups berries (such as strawberries or blueberries)
- $\frac{1}{4}$ cup dried fruit
- $\frac{3}{4}$ cup fruit juice

High-Fiber Fruits Include...

- Apples
- Blackberries
- Blueberries
- Figs
- Nectarines
- Prunes
- Strawberries

One Serving of Vegetables Equals...(each item contains about 25 calories)

- $\frac{1}{2}$ cup cooked vegetables
- $\frac{1}{2}$ cup vegetable juice
- 1 cup raw vegetables

High-Fiber Vegetables Include...

- Asparagus
- Cabbage
- Cauliflower
- Broccoli
- Brussels sprouts
- Green beans
- Sweet potatoes (with skin)

Nutrition Notes

Per serving

Calories 214
Fat 0.5 g.
% of calories from fat 2
Protein 10 g.
Carbohydrates 43.6 g.
Dietary fiber 0.7 g.
Cholesterol 3 mg.
Sodium 131 mg.

Kitchen Hint

◆ This recipe is infinitely variable. A few suggestions: chocolate frozen yogurt with strawberries, vanilla yogurt with peaches, and banana yogurt with mango and papaya.

Nutrition Notes

Per serving

Calories 235
Fat 4.6 g.
% of calories from fat 17
Protein 3.7 g.
Carbohydrates 46.9 g.
Dietary fiber 3.7 g.
Cholesterol 0 mg.
Sodium 239 mg.

Kitchen Hint

◆ Another delicious cobbler combination is sweet peaches and Bing cherries. Use 4 cups peeled and sliced peaches and 2 cups pitted and halved Bing cherries. Replace the raspberry liqueur or orange juice with lemon juice.

Strawberry-Rhubarb Cobbler

MAKES 6 SERVINGS

The secret to this cobbler's low-fat top crust is a combination of nonfat yogurt and a reduced amount of margarine or butter.

Filling

1	quart strawberries, halved or quartered if large
3	cups sliced rhubarb
½	cup sugar
¼	cup water
1	tablespoon cornstarch
2	tablespoons raspberry liqueur or orange juice

Top Crust

¾	cup all-purpose flour
¼	cup whole-wheat flour
1	teaspoon baking powder
½	teaspoon baking soda
⅛	teaspoon salt
4	teaspoons sugar
2	tablespoons unsalted margarine or butter, cut into pieces
1	tablespoon nonfat plain yogurt
1–2	tablespoons skim milk
¼	teaspoon ground cinnamon

Preheat oven to 400°F. Coat a 9" × 9" baking dish with no-stick spray.

To make the filling: Place half of the berries in a large saucepan. Add the rhubarb, sugar, and water. Cover and cook over medium heat, stirring occasionally, for 10 minutes.

Place the cornstarch in a cup. Add the liqueur or orange juice and stir until smooth. Add to the saucepan and cook, stirring constantly, for 1 minute, or until thickened. Stir in the remaining strawberries. Pour the mixture into the prepared baking dish.

To make the top crust: In a medium bowl, combine the all-purpose flour, whole-wheat flour, baking powder, baking soda, salt, and 2 teaspoons of the sugar. Cut in the margarine or butter and yogurt until the mixture resembles coarse meal. Add the milk, 1 tablespoon at a time, and stir until the dough just holds together. Turn out onto a lightly floured surface and roll into a 9" × 9" square. Carefully lay the dough over the strawberry mixture.

In a cup, stir together the cinnamon and the remaining 2 teaspoons sugar. Sprinkle over the dough. Bake for 20 to 25 minutes, or until bubbling and the crust is golden brown.

Spring Menu Eighteen

	1,500 CALORIES	2,000 CALORIES	2,500 CALORIES
	33-43 G. FAT	44-56 G. FAT	57-69 G. FAT

Breakfast

egg-white omelet with	2 egg whites	3 egg whites	4 egg whites
sautéed spinach	¼ cup	¼ cup	½ cup
banana	1	1	1
rye toast with	1 slice	3 slices	3 slices
jam	1 tablespoon	3 tablespoons	3 tablespoons

Lunch

Goat Cheese Quesadillas	1	2	3
nonfat refried beans	½ cup	½ cup	1 cup
plum tomato slices with	5	5	6
chopped fresh basil	1 tablespoon	1 tablespoon	1 tablespoon

Dinner

Singapore Shrimp Noodles	2 servings	2 servings	2 servings
sautéed greens	½ cup	½ cup	1 cup
(escarole, Swiss chard)			

Snack

Triple Chocolate Drops	3	3	4

DAILY TOTALS			
Calories	1,505	1,994	2,470
Fat (g.)	32	48	66
% of calories from fat	19	22	24
Protein (g.)	77	95	118
Carbohydrates (g.)	226	295	353
Dietary fiber (g.)	23	29	39
Cholesterol (mg.)	302	318	339
Sodium (mg.)	1,763	2,541	3,556

NUTRIENT BONUS

This menu (at 2,000 calories) exceeds the Daily Value for:

Dietary fiber	115%
Vitamin A	248%
Thiamin	106%
Riboflavin	113%
Vitamin C	436%
Iron	125%

HEALTHY TIP OF THE DAY

Add flavor, not fat. Get creative with low-fat toppings and dips. Top pita chips with reduced-fat cream cheese and chopped fresh herbs. Dip baked tortilla chips into zesty salsa. Spread French bread with marinara sauce and reduced-fat cheese, then bake it for a quick pizza. Cook rice in defatted broth for extra flavor. Toss pasta with grilled vegetables, chicken broth, and grated Parmesan cheese. Top bagels with jam, marmalade, or fruit butter.

Triple Chocolate Drops

Triple Chocolate Drops

MAKES 36

Three types of chocolate make a fudgy cookie with little fat.

1¾ cups all-purpose flour
½ cup unsweetened cocoa powder
1 teaspoon baking powder
½ teaspoon baking soda
¼ teaspoon salt
1 ounce unsweetened chocolate
3 tablespoons canola oil
4 egg whites
1 egg
1 cup sugar
½ cup packed light brown sugar
¼ cup prune puree
2 tablespoons light corn syrup
1 teaspoon vanilla
¼ cup miniature semisweet chocolate chips
Confectioners' sugar (optional)

In a medium bowl, mix together the flour, cocoa, baking powder, baking soda, and salt.

Place the chocolate and oil in a small microwave-safe bowl. Microwave on high power for 1 minute, or until softened. Stir until the chocolate is melted and smooth.

In a large bowl, combine the egg whites, egg, sugar, and brown sugar. Using an electric mixer, beat on high speed for 3 to 5 minutes, or until smooth and pale yellow. Reduce the speed to low and add the melted chocolate mixture, prune puree, corn syrup, and vanilla. Beat for 1 minute, or until incorporated.

Gradually add the flour mixture and stir until blended. Fold in the chocolate chips. Cover and refrigerate for 1 hour or up to 24 hours.

Preheat the oven to 350°F. Coat 2 baking sheets with no-stick spray.

Let the dough soften at room temperature for 5 to 10 minutes. Drop tablespoons of the dough onto the baking sheets, spacing them about 2" apart. Bake the sheets on separate racks for 11 to 13 minutes, or until the centers just begin to set; switch the sheets halfway through baking to ensure even cooking. Remove from the oven and let stand for 1 minute. Transfer the cookies to a wire rack and let cool completely.

Lightly dust the cookies with the confectioners' sugar (if using).

Nutrition Notes

Per cookie

Calories 85
Fat 2.3 g.
% of calories from fat 23
Protein 1.6 g.
Carbohydrates 15.7 g.
Dietary fiber 0.8 g.
Cholesterol 6 mg.
Sodium 57 mg.

Kitchen Hints

◆ Prune puree is a great fat replacer in chocolate baked goods—as long as you don't use too much. Substitute the puree for up to two-thirds of the fat. To make your own, combine 12 ounces pitted prunes and 3 tablespoons corn syrup in a food processor. Process for 10 seconds. Add ½ cup water and process until smooth. Refrigerate in an airtight container for up to 2 months.

◆ Alternatives to homemade prune puree include pureed baby food prunes, lekvar, and commercial fat substitutes made with prunes and sweeteners like corn syrup. These products are not quite as thick and flavorful as homemade prune puree, but they are adequate substitutes.

Kitchen Hint

◆ Pesto is a concentrated sauce made by creating a paste from various herbs, nuts, Parmesan cheese, garlic, and often a large amount of olive oil. This reduced-fat version is a great addition to soups, baked potatoes, pasta, roasts, and sandwiches. Make a double recipe of the pesto and freeze the remainder in small amounts in resealable freezer bags so you always have some ready.

Goat Cheese Quesadillas

MAKES 6

How do you say "satisfying lunch"? Flour tortillas stuffed with tangy goat cheese, roasted red-pepper sauce, and pesto.

Roasted Red-Pepper Sauce

1	small onion, chopped
2	cloves garlic, minced
1	tablespoon olive oil
2	roasted sweet red peppers, coarsely chopped
2	tablespoons chopped fresh basil
1/4	teaspoon ground black pepper

Pesto

2 1/2	cups packed fresh basil
1/2	cup packed fresh Italian parsley
1/3	cup defatted reduced-sodium chicken broth
3	tablespoons grated Parmesan cheese
5	teaspoons olive oil
1	clove garlic, chopped
1/8	teaspoon crushed red-pepper flakes
	Salt and ground black pepper
12	flour tortillas (6" diameter)
4 1/2	ounces goat cheese

To make the roasted red-pepper sauce: In a medium skillet, combine the onions, garlic, and oil. Cook over medium heat for 4 minutes, or until the onions are soft. Transfer to a food processor or blender. Add the red peppers, basil, and black pepper. Process until smooth.

To make the pesto: In a food processor or blender, combine the basil, parsley, broth, Parmesan, oil, garlic, and red-pepper flakes. Process until smooth. Season with the salt and black pepper.

Lay 6 of the tortillas on a work surface. Divide the goat cheese among them and spread evenly to cover the tortillas. Divide the red-pepper sauce among them and spread evenly. Sprinkle with the pesto. Top with the remaining 6 tortillas.

Coat a large cast-iron or no-stick skillet with no-stick spray. Place over medium heat for 1 to 2 minutes. Transfer 1 quesadilla to the skillet and cook for 3 to 4 minutes per side, or until lightly browned. Remove to a plate and cover with foil to keep warm.

Coat the skillet with no-stick spray and cook another quesadilla. Repeat to cook all the quesadillas.

Singapore Shrimp Noodles

The intense flavors and colors of shrimp and curry powder star in this Indian noodle dish, which is rich in beta-carotene, vitamin C, and fiber. Reduced-fat coconut milk significantly decreases the fat with no loss of flavor. Look for light coconut milk in the international section of your supermarket.

  6 ounces angel hair
  1 teaspoon olive oil
  1 bunch scallions, cut on the diagonal into 1" pieces
  1 sweet red pepper, cut into short strips
  1 cup snow peas
  2 teaspoons minced garlic
$1\frac{1}{2}$ teaspoons grated fresh ginger
  1 pound medium shrimp, peeled and deveined
  1 tablespoon curry powder
$\frac{2}{3}$ cup defatted reduced-sodium chicken broth
$\frac{1}{2}$ cup light coconut milk
$\frac{1}{4}$ teaspoon harissa or chili paste (see hint)
  1 teaspoon coconut extract (optional)
$\frac{1}{4}$ teaspoon salt (optional)

Cook the angel hair in a large pot of boiling water according to the package directions. Drain and return to the pot.

Warm the oil in a large no-stick skillet over medium heat. Add the scallions, peppers, snow peas, garlic, and ginger; cook, stirring frequently, for 1 minute. Add the shrimp and curry powder; cook for 2 to 3 minutes, or until the shrimp are opaque. Add the broth, coconut milk, harissa or chili paste, coconut extract (if using), and salt (if using). Bring to a simmer.

Pour over the pasta and toss well. Cook, stirring constantly, over low heat for 1 to 2 minutes, or until the pasta has absorbed most of the sauce.

Nutrition Notes

Per serving

Calories 303
Fat 4 g.
% of calories from fat 13
Protein 21.5 g.
Carbohydrates 40.5 g.
Dietary fiber 3.3 g.
Cholesterol 135 mg.
Sodium 202 mg.

Kitchen Hints

◆ Save the shells when you peel shrimp. Freeze them in resealable plastic bags to make shrimp stock. To make the stock, combine the shells from 1 pound shrimp with 1 quart water in a large saucepan. Chop 1 small onion, 2 stalks celery, 1 leek, and 1 carrot; add to the pan. Add 1 cup white wine, 1 bay leaf, $\frac{1}{2}$ teaspoon peppercorns, $\frac{1}{2}$ teaspoon salt, and $\frac{1}{2}$ teaspoon dried thyme. Simmer, partially covered, for 1 hour. Strain and refrigerate for up to 4 days or freeze for up to 6 months.

◆ Harissa is a fiery chili paste used in North African cooking. Look for it in the international section of large supermarkets and in specialty food markets. Adjust the amount you use to suit your taste.

Easter Menu

	1,500 CALORIES	2,000 CALORIES	2,500 CALORIES
	33-43 G. FAT	44-56 G. FAT	57-69 G. FAT

Breakfast

bagel with	1	1	1
smoked salmon,	1 ounce	1 ounce	1 ounce
red onions, and	3 slices	3 slices	3 slices
nonfat cream cheese	2 tablespoons	2 tablespoons	4 tablespoons
cantaloupe and strawberry slices	1 cup	1½ cups	2 cups

Lunch

lentil soup	1¼ cups	2 cups	2½ cups
whole-wheat pita bread	1½	2	2½

Dinner

Herb-Crusted Leg of Lamb	1½ servings	2 servings	2 servings
Oregano-Roasted New Potatoes	1½ servings	2 servings	2½ servings
Sautéed Greens	1½ servings	2 servings	2½ servings

Snack

nonfat vanilla frozen yogurt blended with	¾ cup	1 cup	1¼ cup
frozen raspberries	¼ cup	½ cup	¾ cup

DAILY TOTALS			
Calories	1,488	1,970	2,507
Fat (g.)	31	41	47
% of calories from fat	18	18	17
Protein (g.)	99	131	160
Carbohydrates (g.)	210	279	374
Dietary fiber (g.)	46	66	87
Cholesterol (mg.)	124	162	169
Sodium (mg.)	2,126	2,692	3,599

Herb-Crusted Leg of Lamb (page 138), Oregano-Roasted New Potatoes (page 140), and Sautéed Greens (page 141)

Nutrition Notes

Per serving

Calories 191
Fat 7.7 g.
% of calories from fat 37
Protein 23.6 g.
Carbohydrates 4 g.
Dietary fiber 0.9 g.
Cholesterol 73 mg.
Sodium 72 mg.

Kitchen Hints

◆ Ask your butcher to bone and butterfly the lamb to save you time in the kitchen.

◆ If you're making the complete Easter dinner, put the potatoes in the oven about 20 minutes before the lamb is due to be removed. The potatoes can continue to roast while the lamb is resting, and the greens can be sautéed.

Herb-Crusted Leg of Lamb

MAKES 12 SERVINGS

For this traditional Mediterranean Easter dish, lean leg of lamb is first marinated, then coated with a garlic-herb paste for an intensely aromatic roast. It's also a great way to boost your intake of vitamin B_{12}, niacin, zinc, and iron.

Marinade and Lamb

- ²/₃ cup defatted reduced-sodium beef broth
- ½ cup dry vermouth or nonalcoholic white wine
- ¼ cup balsamic vinegar
- 3 tablespoons lemon juice
- 1 tablespoon chopped fresh rosemary
- 2 cloves garlic, minced
- 1 teaspoon dried thyme
- 1 bay leaf
- ¼ teaspoon ground black pepper
- 1 leg of lamb (5–6 pounds), boned, butterflied, and trimmed of all visible fat (see hint)

Garlic-Herb Paste

- 1 whole bulb garlic
- 2 tablespoons water
- 2 tablespoons chopped fresh rosemary
- 2 tablespoons chopped fresh oregano
- 2 tablespoons chopped fresh Italian parsley
- 1 tablespoon olive oil
- ½ teaspoon ground black pepper
- ¼ cup brandy (optional)
- 1 teaspoon cornstarch

To make the marinade and lamb: In a 13" × 9" baking dish, combine the broth, vermouth or wine, vinegar, lemon juice, rosemary, garlic, thyme, bay leaf, and pepper. Place the lamb in the marinade and turn to coat. Cover, refrigerate, and marinate for at least 4 hours or up to 12 hours, turning the lamb occasionally.

To make the garlic-herb paste: Preheat the oven to 400°F.

Slice ¼" off the top of the garlic bulb and discard. Set the bulb on a large piece of foil, sprinkle with 1 tablespoon of the water, and wrap loosely. Bake for 25 to 30 minutes, or until very soft. Remove from the oven, unwrap, and let cool. Squeeze the garlic into a small bowl and discard the papery skins. Using a fork,

mash the garlic to a paste. Add the rosemary, oregano, parsley, oil, and pepper. Mix well.

Increase the oven temperature to 450°F.

Remove the lamb from the marinade; roll it up and tie together with kitchen string. Pour the marinade into a small bowl; refrigerate until needed.

Place the lamb on a rack in a small roasting pan and roast for 15 minutes. Reduce the heat to 350°F and roast for 30 minutes.

Remove the lamb from the oven and slather with the garlic-herb paste, spreading it on with a small metal spatula. Rotate the pan and return to the oven. Roast for 40 to 50 minutes, or until an instant-read thermometer inserted in the thickest part of the roast registers 130°F for medium-rare. (For medium-well, continue to roast, checking every 5 minutes, until the temperature registers 140°F.)

Transfer the lamb to a cutting board, cover lightly with foil, and let stand for 15 to 20 minutes before carving.

Pour off and discard any fat from the roasting pan; remove and discard the bay leaf. Add the brandy (if using) and the reserved marinade to the pan. Place over medium-high heat and bring to a boil, scraping the browned bits from the bottom of the pan. Boil gently until the liquid is reduced by one-third.

Place the cornstarch in a cup. Add the remaining 1 tablespoon water and stir to dissolve. Add to the pan, stirring constantly. Cook, stirring, for 2 to 3 minutes, or until thickened. Serve with the lamb.

Nutrition Notes

Per serving

Calories 169
Fat 2.6 g.
% of calories from fat 14
Protein 5.3 g.
Carbohydrates 29.8 g.
Dietary fiber 3.9 g.
Cholesterol 0 mg.
Sodium 96 mg.

Kitchen Hint

◆ New potatoes are less starchy than russets and hold their shape better when boiled, roasted, or diced for salads. Choose the smallest potatoes that you can find with smooth red or light brown skin. Scrub them under cool water to remove any dirt, being careful not to break through the skin. Leave the skin on whenever possible for the most vitamins and fiber.

Oregano-Roasted New Potatoes

MAKES 6 SERVINGS

These crispy potatoes make the perfect "plate mate" for your favorite lean meat. Oven-roasting requires little oil and brings out the natural sweetness of the potatoes, which are a good source of vitamins A and C plus potassium and fiber.

2	pounds small new potatoes, cubed
2	tablespoons lemon juice
1	tablespoon olive oil
¼	cup chopped fresh oregano
¼	teaspoon salt
¼	teaspoon ground black pepper

Preheat the oven to 425°F.

Place the potatoes in a large bowl, sprinkle with the lemon juice, and toss to combine.

Pour the oil into a shallow baking dish just large enough to hold all the potatoes in a single layer. Place the dish in the oven for 2 minutes to heat the oil. Add the potatoes and stir to coat. Bake for 15 minutes.

Turn the potatoes and mist with no-stick spray. Bake for 20 minutes. Spray again and toss with the oregano. Bake for 5 to 10 minutes, or until the potatoes are browned on the outside and tender when tested with a sharp knife. Sprinkle with the salt and pepper.

Sautéed Greens

MAKES 4 SERVINGS

Sautéed greens are a great way to add vitamins A and C, iron, folate, and magnesium to your diet. This quick-to-prepare dish leaves you time to enjoy the holiday. Choose greens like escarole, spinach, and Swiss chard.

2	pounds assorted greens, stems and ribs removed
2	cups 1% low-fat milk
1	small shallot, chopped
2	cloves garlic, chopped
1	bay leaf
6	black peppercorns
½	teaspoon dried thyme
1	teaspoon canola oil
1	teaspoon unsalted butter or margarine
1½	tablespoons all-purpose flour
¼	teaspoon salt
1	tablespoon chopped fresh tarragon

Bring a large pot of water to a boil over high heat. Add the greens and cook for 1 to 2 minutes, or until bright green and tender. Pour into a colander. Run cold water over the greens to cool them. Squeeze out the excess liquid and coarsely chop.

In a small saucepan, combine the milk, shallots, garlic, bay leaf, peppercorns, and thyme. Bring just to the boiling point over medium heat. Reduce the heat to low and simmer for 20 minutes.

In a medium saucepan, combine the oil and butter or margarine. Place over medium heat for 1 minute, or until the butter or margarine is melted. Add the flour and cook, stirring constantly, for 1 minute. Strain the milk into the flour mixture, stirring constantly. (Discard the solids from the milk mixture.) Cook, stirring, for 5 to 10 minutes, or until thickened. Add the salt, tarragon, and chopped greens. Stir for 2 to 3 minutes, or until the greens are heated through.

Nutrition Notes

Per serving

Calories 112
Fat 3.8 g.
% of calories from fat 29
Protein 7.1 g.
Carbohydrates 13.9 g.
Dietary fiber 3 g.
Cholesterol 7 mg.
Sodium 324 mg.

Kitchen Hint

◆ Here's a timesaving tip for preparing greens. Wash them when you first bring them home from the market. Then dry them, loosely wrap in paper towels, and store in resealable plastic bags. Stored this way, greens have a longer shelf life and are ready for instant salads or side dishes.

Graham Kerr

Television's former Galloping Gourmet, Graham Kerr is widely recognized as America's most inspirational healthy chef. His books and cooking shows have won countless culinary awards. He selected this menu for its lively, mouth-tingling tastes and healthy profile. "The Crêpes Julia," notes Kerr, "are named after my culinary pal Julia Child, from when we went head-to-head on *Good Morning America* with our versions of crêpes suzette."

Graham Kerr's Menu

	1,500 CALORIES 33-43 G. FAT	2,000 CALORIES 44-56 G. FAT	2,500 CALORIES 57-69 G. FAT
Breakfast			
scrambled egg whites with	2	3	3
chopped fresh herbs	1 tablespoon	1½ tablespoons	1½ tablespoons
multigrain toast	1 slice	2 slices	3 slices
skim milk	1 cup	1¼ cups	1½ cups
Lunch			
Canadian Bacon and			
Roasted-Pepper Sandwiches	1	1½	2
Dinner			
pineapple and mango chunks	¾ cup	1½ cups	2 cups
Sea Bass Fillets in			
Saffron-Lemon Sauce	1 serving	1½ servings	2 servings
steamed broccoli	½ cup	1 cup	1½ cups
baked potato	1	1½	2
multigrain roll	1	2	2
Crêpes Julia	1 serving	1 serving	1 serving
Snack			
bagel with	1	1	1
lime marmalade	2 tablespoons	2 tablespoons	2 tablespoons

DAILY TOTALS			
Calories	1,468	1,981	2,478
Fat (g.)	26	37	46
% of calories from fat	15	16	16
Protein (g.)	92	130	164
Carbohydrates (g.)	227	291	363
Dietary fiber (g.)	17	26	34
Cholesterol (mg.)	263	337	411
Sodium (mg.)	1,779	2,540	3,126

Sea Bass Fillets in Saffron-Lemon Sauce (page 144)

Nutrition Notes

Per serving

Calories 202
Fat 6.3 g.
% of calories from fat 29
Protein 32.4 g.
Carbohydrates 2.2 g.
Dietary fiber 0.1 g.
Cholesterol 116 mg.
Sodium 215 mg.

Kitchen Hints

◆ Black sea bass is a delicate yet firm fish commonly used in Chinese cuisine. Sea bass is delicious grilled, poached, or broiled. If sea bass is unavailable, substitute grouper, black cod, or striped bass.

◆ Arrowroot is a starchy powder used for thickening. It is made from the root of a tropical plant and can be substituted for cornstarch in equal amounts. For this recipe, arrowroot is preferred because it turns clear when cooked (cornstarch has a tendency to remain a bit cloudy). The arrowroot lends the sauce the look of clarified butter, enhancing its overall appeal.

◆ This recipe is adapted from *Graham Kerr's Swiftly Seasoned* (G.P. Putnam's Sons, 1997).

Sea Bass Fillets in Saffron-Lemon Sauce

MAKES 4 SERVINGS

This succulent fish is microwave-poached in just 4 minutes. A low-fat lemon-saffron sauce adds the elegant finishing touches.

¼	cup lemon juice
½	teaspoon dried dill
⅛	teaspoon salt
¼	cup + 2 teaspoons nonalcoholic Chardonnay or water
4	sea bass fillets (6 ounces each)
1	teaspoon rinsed and drained capers
	Pinch of crushed saffron threads
1	teaspoon arrowroot or cornstarch
	Pinch of paprika
	Pinch of ground black pepper

In a 9" × 9" microwave-safe baking dish, combine the lemon juice, dill, salt, and ¼ cup of the wine or water. Add the sea bass and turn to coat. Cover loosely with wax paper and microwave on high power for 4 minutes, or until opaque and cooked through. Divide among individual plates and cover with wax paper to keep warm.

Pour the cooking liquid into a small saucepan. Add the capers and cook over medium-high heat for 1 to 2 minutes, or until hot. Place the arrowroot or cornstarch in a cup. Stir in the remaining 2 teaspoons wine or water until dissolved. Add the saffron to the cup. Stir into the saucepan. Cook, stirring constantly, for 1 to 2 minutes, or until thickened and clear.

Pour the sauce over the sea bass. Sprinkle with the paprika and pepper.

Canadian Bacon and Roasted-Pepper Sandwiches

MAKES 4

These robust sandwiches make a scrumptious alternative to high-fat grilled cheese sandwiches. The creaminess of roasted sweet red peppers lends a wonderful mouthfeel without a speck of fat. If you have a sandwich maker, you'll get a delicious grilled flavor. Otherwise, a no-stick skillet works just fine.

4	English muffins, halved
4	very thin slices Canadian bacon
1	teaspoon Dijon mustard
1/2	cup sliced roasted sweet red peppers
	Pinch of ground black pepper
4	large basil leaves
4	slices reduced-fat Swiss cheese

Warm a large no-stick skillet over medium-high heat until hot. Add the English muffins in a single layer, cut sides down, and toast for 1 minute, or until crisp and brown (work in batches, if necessary).

Divide the Canadian bacon among 4 of the muffin halves. Spread with the mustard, top with the red peppers, and sprinkle with the black pepper. Top with the basil, Swiss, and the remaining muffin halves.

Place the sandwiches in the skillet and cook over medium heat for 3 minutes per side, or until the cheese is melted.

Nutrition Notes

Per sandwich

Calories 262
Fat 8.6 g.
% of calories from fat 30
Protein 16.9 g.
Carbohydrates 28.6 g.
Dietary fiber 1.9 g.
Cholesterol 31 mg.
Sodium 596 mg.

Kitchen Hints

◆ Canadian bacon is a leaner alternative to regular bacon. It imparts a similar smoky flavor and can be used in much the same way as bacon. Per ounce, Canadian bacon has 2 grams of total fat and only 1 gram of saturated fat; the same amount of regular bacon has 14 grams of total fat and 5 grams of saturated fat.

◆ This recipe is adapted from *Graham Kerr's Swiftly Seasoned* (G.P. Putnam's Sons, 1997).

Kitchen Hints

◆ To make 2 tablespoons yogurt cheese, place ¼ cup nonfat plain yogurt in a strainer or colander lined with cheesecloth (or use a special yogurt strainer). Place the strainer over a bowl and refrigerate for 3 to 4 hours or overnight to drain the whey (liquid). Discard the whey. The drained yogurt is yogurt cheese.

◆ Crêpes are very versatile and easy to prepare. If you have ever made pancakes, you can fearlessly attempt crêpes. They are delicious at breakfast with a filling of sweetened low fat-ricotta cheese and melted jam. For a light lunch or supper, make savory crêpes; omit the vanilla and lemon rind called for in the batter and add 1 tablespoon chopped fresh herbs. Fill with

(continued)

Crêpes Julia

MAKES 4 SERVINGS

This is a lower-fat takeoff of classic crêpes suzette, a dish in which delicate crêpes are filled with a citrus-flavored butter, then set ablaze with cognac and Grand Marnier. This version is considerably lighter yet just as irresistible. Low-fat milk lightens up the batter, then the crêpes are topped with a wonderfully aromatic citrus-yogurt sauce.

Crêpes

    1 egg
    1 egg yolk
    1 cup 2% milk
    ½ cup all-purpose flour
    1 teaspoon finely grated lemon rind
    ½ teaspoon vanilla
    1 teaspoon light olive oil

Orange Syrup

    ½ teaspoon light olive oil
    1 tablespoon finely grated orange rind
    ½ cup + 2 tablespoons nonalcoholic white Zinfandel or orange juice
    1 cup orange juice
    2 tablespoons light brown sugar
    1 tablespoon lemon juice
    1 tablespoon arrowroot or cornstarch
    2 tablespoons yogurt cheese (see hint)
    4 navel oranges, sectioned
    1 teaspoon chopped fresh mint

To make the crêpes: In a small bowl, whisk together the egg, egg yolk, and milk.

Sift the flour into a large bowl and make a well in the center. Pour the egg mixture into the well and whisk until well-blended. Stir in the lemon rind and vanilla. Let stand for 30 minutes.

Warm the oil in a medium no-stick skillet over medium-high heat. Pour the oil into the crêpe batter and mix well. Pour ¼ cup of the batter into the skillet and quickly swirl the skillet to make a thin, round crêpe. Cook for about 1 minute per side, or until lightly browned. Remove to a plate and cover with a towel to keep warm. Repeat with the remaining batter. Make 8 crêpes.

To make the orange syrup: Warm the oil in a large no-stick skillet over medium-high heat. Add the orange rind and cook for 2 minutes. Add ½ cup of the white Zinfandel or orange juice and cook for 3 minutes, or until slightly reduced and thickened. Gradually stir in the 1 cup orange juice, ¼ cup at a time, allowing the sauce to reduce slightly after each addition. Add the brown sugar and lemon juice. Stir until the brown sugar is dissolved.

Strain the syrup through a fine sieve and return to the skillet.

Place the arrowroot or cornstarch in a cup. Add the remaining 2 tablespoons white Zinfandel or orange juice and stir to dissolve. Add to the skillet. Cook, stirring, for 1 to 2 minutes, or until thickened and clear.

Place the yogurt cheese in a small bowl. Stir in a little of the syrup until smooth. Add the remaining syrup in a slow, steady stream and stir until smooth. Return to the skillet and reduce the heat to low.

Transfer a crêpe to the skillet and turn to coat with the sauce. Fold the crêpe in half and in half again to form a small triangle. Repeat with the rest of the crêpes, piling them on top of one another to make room in the skillet. Stir the orange sections and mint into the syrup alongside the crêpes. Warm briefly.

sautéed vegetables or lean fish or chicken and top with a low-fat sauce, such as tomato sauce (page 211).

◆ The light olive oil used in this recipe is light in flavor, not calories or fat.

◆ This recipe is adapted from *Graham Kerr's Best* (G.P. Putnam's Sons, 1996).

Strawberry-Watercress Salad
(page 177)

Summer Menus

Summer Menu One

	1,500 CALORIES 33-43 G. FAT	2,000 CALORIES 44-56 G. FAT	2,500 CALORIES 57-69 G. FAT
$\mathcal{B}$reakfast			
Buttermilk Pancakes with Fruit Compote	2	3	4
skim milk	1 cup	1 cup	1½ cups
$\mathcal{L}$unch			
Julius Caesar Salad	1 serving	1½ servings	2 servings
soft breadsticks	2	2½	3
$\mathcal{D}$inner			
Spicy Pecan-Crusted Grouper	1 serving	1 serving	1½ servings
nonfat tartar sauce	2 tablespoons	2 tablespoons	3 tablespoons
grilled corn on the cob	2 ears	2 ears	2 ears
steamed broccoli	½ cup	1 cup	1½ cups
$\mathcal{S}$nack			
watermelon slices	2	2	2

DAILY TOTALS			
Calories	1,507	1,978	2,507
Fat (g.)	34	45	58
% of calories from fat	20	20	20
Protein (g.)	98	125	169
Carbohydrates (g.)	211	280	338
Dietary fiber (g.)	15	20	25
Cholesterol (mg.)	168	223	307
Sodium (mg.)	1,765	2,262	3,124

NUTRIENT BONUS

This menu (at 2,000 calories) exceeds the Daily Value for:

Vitamin A	235%
Thiamin	152%
Riboflavin	111%
Niacin	137%
Vitamin B$_6$	162%
Folate	108%
Vitamin C	463%
Calcium	102%
Potassium	120%

HEALTHY TIP OF THE DAY

Try grouper. A member of the sea bass family, grouper is a firm, mild-flavored fish and a lean source of protein. Three ounces of uncooked grouper has less than 1 gram of fat. Grouper is also a good source of omega-3 fatty acids, a beneficial type of fat that may protect against coronary artery disease. The fish with the highest concentrations of omega-3's include mackerel, herring, trout, sardines, tuna, salmon, and halibut.

Spicy Pecan-Crusted Grouper (page 154)

Nutrition Notes

Per serving

Calories 139
Fat 1.9 g.
% of calories from fat 12
Protein 4.7 g.
Carbohydrates 25.9 g.
Dietary fiber 2 g.
Cholesterol 19 mg.
Sodium 269 mg.

Kitchen Hints

◆ The fruit compote can be made a day in advance and reheated in the microwave for 2 minutes on high power.

◆ The secret to light and fluffy pancakes is not over-mixing the batter. Stir together the wet and dry ingredients just until the flour is moistened. Small lumps are acceptable.

◆ For a more hearty winter variation, replace the peaches and blackberries with 1 cup dried fruits, such as apricots, peaches, prunes, and currants. Increase the nectar to 1 cup. Cook over medium heat for 8 to 10 minutes, or until the fruit is soft.

Buttermilk Pancakes with Fruit Compote

<u>MAKES 12 SERVINGS</u>

Buttermilk and one egg make these hotcakes healthier than most.

Compote

2	peaches or nectarines, sliced
1/4	cup apricot nectar or orange juice
3	tablespoons apricot preserves
1	teaspoon minced crystallized ginger
1/4	teaspoon ground cinnamon
1	cup blackberries

Buttermilk Pancakes

1 1/2	cups all-purpose flour
1/2	cup whole-wheat flour
1	tablespoon sugar
1	teaspoon baking soda
1/2	teaspoon baking powder
1/2	teaspoon salt
1	egg
1	egg white
2	cups 1% low-fat buttermilk
1	tablespoon vanilla
2	teaspoons canola oil

To make the compote: In a small saucepan, combine the peaches or nectarines, apricot nectar or orange juice, preserves, ginger, and cinnamon. Cook over medium heat for 5 minutes, or until the fruit is soft. Add the blackberries and cook for another 2 minutes. Keep warm over very low heat.

To make the buttermilk pancakes: In a large bowl, whisk together the all-purpose flour, whole-wheat flour, sugar, baking soda, baking powder, and salt until well-combined.

In a medium bowl, whisk together the egg and egg white until very foamy. Whisk in the buttermilk, vanilla, and oil. Stir into the flour mixture just until the batter is combined and pourable.

Place a large no-stick skillet over medium heat. Coat with no-stick spray. Pour 1/3 cup batter into the skillet to form a 4" pancake. Cook for 2 to 3 minutes, or until the underside is browned. Turn and cook for 1 to 2 minutes, or until golden brown. Transfer to a warm oven. Repeat to make a total of 12 pancakes. Serve the pancakes with the warm compote.

Julius Caesar Salad

MAKES 4 SERVINGS

This salad is fit for an emperor. Strips of grilled chicken are tossed with calcium-rich dark leafy greens and carotene-packed peppers. Nonfat cottage cheese and skim milk significantly reduce the fat in the dressing.

Dressing

    1   tablespoon balsamic vinegar
    1   tablespoon lemon juice
    1   teaspoon anchovy paste (see hint)
    1   teaspoon Dijon mustard
    1   teaspoon Worcestershire sauce
    1   clove garlic, minced
  ½   cup nonfat cottage cheese
  ½   cup skim milk
    3   tablespoons grated Parmesan cheese

Salad

    1   pound boneless, skinless chicken breasts
    6   cups lightly packed torn romaine lettuce
    2   roasted sweet red peppers, cut into strips
  ¼   cup chopped fresh basil
    3   tablespoons toasted pine nuts

To make the dressing: In a blender or food processor, combine the vinegar, lemon juice, anchovy paste, mustard, Worcestershire sauce, and garlic. Process until well-blended. Add the cottage cheese, milk, and Parmesan. Process until very smooth and creamy.

To make the salad: Coat a grill rack or broiler pan with no-stick spray. Preheat the grill or broiler. Cook the chicken 4" from the heat for 5 to 7 minutes per side, or until no longer pink in the center when tested with a sharp knife. Slice into ½" strips.

In a large salad bowl, toss together the lettuce, peppers, basil, and pine nuts. Top with the chicken and drizzle with the dressing. Toss well to combine.

Nutrition Notes

Per serving

Calories 278
Fat 11.5 g.
% of calories from fat 38
Protein 33.4 g.
Carbohydrates 9.3 g.
Dietary fiber 2.3 g.
Cholesterol 71 mg.
Sodium 404 mg.

Kitchen Hints

◆ Anchovy paste is a mixture of ground anchovies, vinegar, and olive oil. It makes a flavorful addition to sauces and dressings for vegetables or pasta. The flavor is very concentrated, so you need only a small amount. It is available in the international section of most supermarkets.

◆ The dressing will keep for up to 5 days in an airtight container in the refrigerator.

Nutrition Notes

Per serving

Calories 251
Fat 7.4 g.
% of calories from fat 26
Protein 31.3 g.
Carbohydrates 15 g.
Dietary fiber 1.6 g.
Cholesterol 54 mg.
Sodium 383 mg.

Kitchen Hints

◆ To make fresh bread crumbs, grind soft bread cubes or slices in a food processor or blender until crumbs form.

◆ You can use any firm white fish, such as red snapper or halibut, in place of the grouper in this recipe. When purchasing fish fillets or steaks, look for flesh that is moist and firm without dark bruised spots or dried-out edges. The fish should smell sweet, not "fishy." To store the fillets, wrap them in plastic and place in an ice-filled colander. Set the colander in a bowl and refrigerate; try to use within a day.

Spicy Pecan-Crusted Grouper

MAKES 4 SERVINGS

Whole-grain cereal flakes contribute fiber to the coating of these marinated fillets. By pan-searing this very lean fish and using just a small amount of toasted pecans, we keep the fat content low.

½	cup chopped scallions
3	tablespoons reduced-sodium teriyaki sauce
1	large clove garlic, minced
1	teaspoon minced fresh ginger
4	grouper fillets (4 ounces each)
1	cup fresh bread crumbs
½	cup whole-grain cereal flakes, coarsely crushed
¼	cup chopped toasted pecans
1	teaspoon ground black pepper
2	tablespoons shredded fresh basil

In a 9" × 9" glass baking dish, combine the scallions, teriyaki sauce, garlic, and ginger. Place the grouper in the marinade and turn to coat both sides. Cover and refrigerate for 1 to 2 hours.

In a pie plate, combine the bread crumbs, cereal flakes, pecans, and pepper. Remove the grouper from the marinade; discard the marinade. Press each fillet into the crumb mixture to coat all sides.

Coat a large no-stick skillet with no-stick spray and place over medium-high heat until hot. Add the grouper and cook for 3 to 4 minutes, or until golden brown on the bottom. Mist the top of the fillets with no-stick spray, then flip and cook for 3 to 4 minutes more, or until the grouper flakes easily when tested with a fork. Sprinkle with the basil.

Summer Menu Two

	1,500 CALORIES	2,000 CALORIES	2,500 CALORIES
	33-43 G. FAT	44-56 G. FAT	57-69 G. FAT

Breakfast
shredded wheat cereal with	1½ cups	1½ cups	1½ cups
skim milk and	1 cup	1 cup	1 cup
raspberries	½ cup	½ cup	½ cup

Lunch
Barbecued Fish Tacos	1	2	2
baked tortilla chips with	13	26	26
tomato salsa	¼ cup	½ cup	½ cup

Dinner
Lamb Kabobs	1 serving	1 serving	2 servings
Cucumber Chutney	¼ cup	¼ cup	½ cup
couscous	1 cup	1 cup	1½ cups

Snack
Bing cherries	1 cup	1¼ cups	1½ cups

DAILY TOTALS
Calories	1,502	2,002	2,506
Fat (g.)	22	32	41
% of calories from fat	13	14	14
Protein (g.)	94	131	168
Carbohydrates (g.)	240	309	378
Dietary fiber (g.)	24	30	36
Cholesterol (mg.)	133	187	261
Sodium (mg.)	1,511	2,381	2,886

NUTRIENT BONUS

This menu (at 2,000 calories) exceeds the Daily Value for:

Dietary fiber	122%
Vitamin A	137%
Riboflavin	200%
Niacin	101%
Vitamin B6	100%
Vitamin B12	131%
Vitamin C	317%
Vitamin E	109%
Calcium	114%
Potassium	106%

HEALTHY TIP OF THE DAY

Add back flavor when reducing or replacing the fat in your family's favorite recipes. Look to the following ingredients for extra pizzazz: defatted chicken broth or vegetable broth, sun-dried tomatoes (dry-pack), roasted red peppers, balsamic vinegar, herb vinegar, mustard, salsa, hot-pepper sauce, chili peppers, fresh herbs, spices, fresh fruits, fruit juices, and grated orange or lemon rind.

Lamb Kabobs (page 157) and Cucumber Chutney (page 158)

Lamb Kabobs

MAKES 4 SERVINGS

Fire up your grill for these skewers of fresh summer vegetables and marinated leg of lamb. This lean cut of lamb provides iron, niacin, vitamin B_{12} and zinc.

- 2 tablespoons lemon juice
- 2 tablespoons chopped fresh oregano
- 1 teaspoon olive oil
- 1 teaspoon ground cumin
- ½ teaspoon ground coriander
- 1 bay leaf
- 1 pound leg of lamb, trimmed of all visible fat and cut into 1" cubes
- 2 sweet yellow peppers, each cut into 8 pieces
- 2 zucchini, each cut into 8 pieces
- 16 cherry tomatoes
- 1 large red onion, cut into 16 chunks
- Salt and ground black pepper
- 4 pita breads (8" diameter)

In a medium bowl, combine the lemon juice, oregano, oil, cumin, coriander, and bay leaf. Add the lamb and toss to evenly coat. Cover and refrigerate the lamb. Let marinate for at least 2 hours or up to 8 hours.

Coat a grill rack or broiler pan with no-stick spray. Preheat the grill or broiler.

Divide the lamb into 4 equal portions; thread onto 4 metal skewers, leaving ¼" space between the pieces of meat. Discard the marinade.

Divide the yellow peppers, zucchini, tomatoes, and onions into 8 portions; thread onto 8 metal skewers, alternating the vegetables. Sprinkle the meat and vegetables with the salt and black pepper.

Cook the skewers 4" from the heat for 4 to 5 minutes per side, or until the lamb is light pink inside when tested with a sharp knife and the vegetables are tender. (Cook for 3 to 4 minutes longer if you prefer the lamb well-done.)

Warm the pitas on the grill or under the broiler for 1 to 2 minutes per side. Serve with the meat and vegetables.

Nutrition Notes

Per serving

Calories 375
Fat 8.8 g.
% of calories from fat 21
Protein 30.3 g.
Carbohydrates 43.4 g.
Dietary fiber 3.4 g.
Cholesterol 73 mg.
Sodium 420 mg.

Kitchen Hints

◆ It's well worth the effort to cut your own lamb cubes. The resulting lean, tender pieces of meat are far superior to the tough precut cubes found in most supermarkets.

◆ If you don't have metal skewers, use bamboo ones. Soak them in cold water for 30 minutes before grilling so they don't burn.

Nutrition Notes

Per ¼ cup

Calories 53
Fat 0.3 g.
% of calories from fat 4
Protein 4.4 g.
Carbohydrates 8.8 g.
Dietary fiber 0.9 g.
Cholesterol 1 mg.
Sodium 83 mg.

Kitchen Hint

◆ English cucumbers have a more reliable flavor than regular cucumbers, which are sometimes bitter. English cucumbers are longer, more slender, and contain fewer seeds. Most supermarkets carry them wrapped in plastic in the produce section.

Cucumber Chutney

MAKES 1 CUP

This quick and cool companion to grilled lamb is made of calcium-rich yogurt cheese, shredded cucumber, fresh mint, and lemon juice. Pair it with grilled chicken, too.

> 1 English cucumber, peeled, seeded, and finely shredded
> Salt
> ½ cup nonfat yogurt cheese
> ¼ cup minced onions
> 1 tablespoon lemon juice
> 1 tablespoon chopped fresh mint
> 1 clove garlic, minced
> Ground black pepper

Place the cucumber in a colander and set over a bowl or in the sink. Sprinkle lightly with the salt and allow to drain for at least 30 minutes. Rinse the cucumber with cold water, squeeze dry, and transfer to a medium bowl.

Stir in the yogurt cheese, onions, lemon juice, mint, and garlic. Season with the pepper and additional salt.

Yogurt Cheese

Looking for a low-fat alternative to full-fat cream cheese and sour cream? Try yogurt cheese. It's easy to make and has a thick, creamy consistency. Use it for low-fat cheesecakes, dips, spreads, and sauces.

To make 1 cup yogurt cheese, place 2 cups nonfat or low-fat plain yogurt in a strainer or colander lined with cheesecloth (or use a special yogurt strainer available in kitchen stores). Place the strainer over a bowl and refrigerate for 3 to 4 hours or overnight to drain the whey (the liquid). Discard the whey.

When making yogurt cheese with flavored yogurt, such as vanilla, avoid yogurt sweetened with aspartame. It won't separate properly. Gelatin used as a thickening agent in some yogurts will also prevent the whey from draining.

Barbecued Fish Tacos

MAKES 4

Grilled lean swordfish stands in for the traditional ground beef filling in these tacos and reduces the fat considerably. Serve these tacos with a side dish of fresh fruit to get every tier of the Food Guide Pyramid in just one meal.

- 1 pound swordfish fillet
- ¼ cup + 1 tablespoon taco sauce
- 4 corn or flour tortillas (8" diameter)
- 2 cups shredded leaf lettuce
- ½ cup chopped scallions
- ½ cup shredded reduced-fat Monterey Jack cheese
- ½ cup nonfat salsa
- ½ cup nonfat sour cream
- 1 lime

Coat a grill rack with no-stick spray. Preheat the grill.

Brush the swordfish with ¼ cup of the taco sauce and place on the hot grill. Grill 4" from the heat for 5 minutes per side per 1" thickness of fish, or until the fish is opaque and flakes easily when tested with a fork. Transfer to a medium bowl and flake with a fork. Add the remaining 1 tablespoon taco sauce and toss to coat.

Wrap the tortillas in plastic wrap and microwave on high power for 1 minute to soften. Place the tortillas on a flat surface. Divide the lettuce among them, arranging it in a row in the center of each. Top with the fish. Sprinkle with the scallions and Monterey Jack. Top with the salsa and sour cream.

Cut the lime into quarters and squeeze the juice over the filling. Fold the tortillas around the filling to enclose it.

Nutrition Notes

Per taco

Calories 302
Fat 8.1 g.
% of calories from fat 24
Protein 31.5 g.
Carbohydrates 25.9 g.
Dietary fiber 3 g.
Cholesterol 54 mg.
Sodium 493 mg.

Kitchen Hint

◆ Instead of using a grill, you can broil the swordfish 4" from the heat on a baking sheet coated with no-stick spray.

HEALTHY TIP OF THE DAY

Take steps to help prevent osteoporosis. Studies show that weight-bearing exercise and increased calcium intake can prevent and even reverse the loss of bone density (which often leads to osteoporosis) among women. Weight-bearing exercise includes walking, dancing, running, jogging, skiing, and aerobics. To boost calcium, eat more dairy products, dark green leafy vegetables, calcium-enriched foods such as orange juice, and even canned salmon with the bones.

Summer Menu Three

	1,500 CALORIES	2,000 CALORIES	2,500 CALORIES
	33-43 G. FAT	44-56 G. FAT	57-69 G. FAT

Breakfast

Garden Bounty Omelets	1	1	1
oatmeal toast with	2 slices	2 slices	3 slices
jam	2 tablespoons	2 tablespoons	3 tablespoons
grapefruit juice	½ cup	1 cup	1½ cups

Lunch

Creamy Parmesan Pasta Salad	1 serving	2 servings	2 servings
whole-grain roll	1	2	2

Dinner

Roast Beef Sandwiches	1	1	1½
oven-fried potatoes	1 potato	1 potato	2 potatoes
spinach salad with	1 cup	2 cups	2 cups
mandarin orange segments and	¼ cup	½ cup	½ cup
nonfat dressing	1 tablespoon	2 tablespoons	2 tablespoons

Snack

banana	1	1	1½

DAILY TOTALS			
Calories	1,530	2,014	2,519
Fat (g.)	29	37	42
% of calories from fat	17	17	15
Protein (g.)	87	109	131
Carbohydrates (g.)	233	315	412
Dietary fiber (g.)	20	25	31
Cholesterol (mg.)	323	335	372
Sodium (mg.)	1,914	2,402	2,767

Roast Beef Sandwiches (page 164)

Nutrition Notes

Per omelet

Calories 271
Fat 13.7 g.
% of calories from fat 47
Protein 23.7 g.
Carbohydrates 10.8 g.
Dietary fiber 3.4 g.
Cholesterol 238 mg.
Sodium 445 mg.

Kitchen Hint

◆ When storing eggs, leave them in their carton to prevent them from absorbing odors from other foods. For safe storage, place the carton on the middle refrigerator shelf toward the back—the coldest part of the refrigerator. If your refrigerator has an egg tray in the door—one of the warmest areas—remove it and use the space for other items.

Garden Bounty Omelets

MAKES 2

Fresh dill accents these garden-fresh omelets. By using 2 egg whites and 1 whole egg per omelet, we've reduced the fat and cholesterol.

> 1 cup chopped plum tomatoes
> ¾ cup chopped sweet red peppers
> ⅓ cup chopped scallions
> ¼ cup chopped fresh dill
> 4 egg whites
> 2 eggs
> 2 teaspoons skim milk
> Salt and ground black pepper
> 4 tablespoons shredded reduced-fat smoked Jarlsberg cheese

Coat a medium no-stick skillet with no-stick spray and place over medium heat. Add the tomatoes, red peppers, scallions, and dill; sauté for 7 to 10 minutes, or until soft. Transfer the vegetables to a small bowl. Wipe out the skillet and coat with no-stick spray. Return to the heat.

In a medium bowl, whisk together the egg whites, eggs, and milk. Season with the salt and black pepper. Pour half of the egg mixture into the skillet and cook, occasionally scraping the bottom of the pan, for 2 to 3 minutes. Sprinkle half of the vegetable mixture over the eggs and top with 2 tablespoons of the Jarlsberg. Continue to cook for 3 to 4 minutes, or until the Jarlsberg is melted, the bottom is golden brown, and the eggs are set.

Using a large spatula, flip the omelet in half and transfer to a plate. Place the plate in a warm oven.

Coat the skillet with no-stick spray. Use the remaining egg mixture, vegetables, and Jarlsberg to make another omelet.

Creamy Parmesan Pasta Salad

MAKES 4 SERVINGS

Rich, creamy, delicious, and—yes—lean! In this cool summer salad, penne, vegetables, and herbs are tossed with a creamy dressing made with low-fat dairy products. And the whole salad is a great source of complex carbohydrates for all-day energy.

8	ounces penne
1	cup 1% low-fat buttermilk
½	cup nonfat sour cream
2	tablespoons nonfat mayonnaise
1	teaspoon roasted garlic paste (see hint)
½	cup grated Parmesan cheese
¼	cup chopped fresh basil
1½	tablespoons chopped fresh chives
¼	teaspoon garlic powder
¼	teaspoon ground black pepper
4	cups broccoli florets
1½	cups chopped plum tomatoes

Cook the penne in a large pot of boiling water according to the package directions. Drain, rinse with cold water, and place in a large bowl.

In a medium bowl, whisk together the buttermilk, sour cream, mayonnaise, and garlic paste until smooth. Add the Parmesan, basil, chives, garlic powder, and pepper; whisk until smooth.

Place the broccoli in a medium microwave-safe bowl. Cover with vented plastic wrap and microwave on high power for a total of 6 minutes, or until bright green and tender; stop and stir after 3 minutes. Plunge the broccoli into a bowl of cold water, drain, and lightly pat dry. Add to the bowl with the pasta. Add the tomatoes; toss to combine. Add the dressing and toss well.

Nutrition Notes

Per serving

Calories 326
Fat 5.6 g.
% of calories from fat 15
Protein 18 g.
Carbohydrates 51.4 g.
Dietary fiber 5.2 g.
Cholesterol 12 mg.
Sodium 411 mg.

Kitchen Hint

◆ Roasted garlic paste can be found in the produce section or gourmet aisle of most supermarkets. You can also make your own by wrapping a few cloves of unpeeled garlic in foil (sprinkle the cloves with water before closing the foil). Bake at 400°F for 25 minutes, or until soft. Squeeze the pulp out of its skin before using. If desired, you can replace the roasted garlic paste with 1 teaspoon minced fresh garlic.

Nutrition Notes

Per sandwich

Calories 309
Fat 5.3 g.
% of calories from fat 16
Protein 31.6 g.
Carbohydrates 31.8 g.
Dietary fiber 0.8 g.
Cholesterol 74 mg.
Sodium 399 mg.

Kitchen Hints

◆ Mango chutney is an Indian relish made with mangoes, sugar, vinegar, and spices. It is available in the international aisle of most supermarkets.

◆ If you are trying to limit the sodium in your diet, replace the pickles with cucumber spears.

◆ Lunchmeats should be stored in the refrigerator for no more than 3 days in their original wrappers.

Roast Beef Sandwiches

MAKES 4

A zesty nonfat horseradish spread adds zip to these hearty sandwiches.

Horseradish Spread

$\frac{1}{3}$ cup nonfat cream cheese, at room temperature
2 tablespoons nonfat mayonnaise
2 tablespoons mango chutney
2 teaspoons prepared horseradish
Ground black pepper

Roast Beef Sandwiches

4 crusty rolls, halved
1 pound thinly sliced lean roast beef
4 leaves lettuce
4 slices tomato
4 very thin slices red onion
4 spears kosher dill pickles (optional)

To make the horseradish spread: In a small bowl, stir together the cream cheese, mayonnaise, chutney, and horseradish until well-combined. Season with the pepper.

To make the roast beef sandwiches: Spread the horseradish mixture on the top and bottom half of each roll. Divide the roast beef among the bottom halves of the rolls. Top with the lettuce, tomatoes, and onions. Top with the remaining roll halves. Serve with the pickles (if using).

Summer Menu Four

	1,500 CALORIES	2,000 CALORIES	2,500 CALORIES
	33-43 G. FAT	44-56 G. FAT	57-69 G. FAT

Breakfast

Breakfast Parfaits	1	1	1
bagel with	1	1	2
jam	2 tablespoons	2 tablespoons	4 tablespoons

Lunch

Breast of Duck Salad	1 serving	2 servings	2 servings
multigrain roll	1	2	2
honeydew melon cubes	1 cup	1½ cups	2 cups

Dinner

Crab Cakes	1 serving	1 serving	1½ servings
steamed sugar snap peas	½ cup	¾ cup	1 cup
orzo	½ cup	1 cup	1½ cups

Snack

graham crackers	4 whole sheets	4 whole sheets	4 whole sheets

DAILY TOTALS

Calories	1,481	1,975	2,486
Fat (g.)	23	34	38
% of calories from fat	14	15	13
Protein (g.)	82	113	137
Carbohydrates (g.)	245	309	408
Dietary fiber (g.)	22	30	39
Cholesterol (mg.)	205	295	352
Sodium (mg.)	1,986	2,354	3,146

NUTRIENT BONUS

This menu (at 2,000 calories) exceeds the Daily Value for:

Dietary fiber	118%
Vitamin A	146%
Thiamin	181%
Riboflavin	139%
Niacin	155%
Vitamin B$_6$	173%
Vitamin B$_{12}$	214%
Folate	168%
Vitamin C	438%
Vitamin E	250%
Iron	130%
Potassium	107%

HEALTHY TIP OF THE DAY

Sweet red peppers are an excellent source of the antioxidant vitamins A and C, which have been shown to reduce the risk of heart disease and certain types of cancer. Experts say to get 15 to 20 milligrams a day of beta-carotene (which the body converts to vitamin A) and 60 milligrams of vitamin C. One cup of sweet red peppers provides 90 percent of the daily recommendation for beta-carotene and more than 300 percent of vitamin C.

Crab Cakes with roasted pepper sauce

Crab Cakes

MAKES 4 SERVINGS

The secret to healthy crab cakes is good-quality lump crabmeat.

Roasted Pepper Sauce

2	roasted sweet red peppers
1/2	cup nonfat mayonnaise
	Ground black pepper

Crab Cakes

1	teaspoon olive oil
1/3	cup finely chopped onions
1/3	cup finely chopped celery
1	egg white
2	tablespoons crushed reduced-sodium crackers
2	tablespoons chopped fresh Italian parsley
2	tablespoons nonfat mayonnaise
1	tablespoon lemon juice
1 1/2	teaspoons crab boil seasoning, such as Old Bay
2	teaspoons Worcestershire sauce
1/2	teaspoon dry mustard
1/4	teaspoon celery seeds, crushed
1/4	teaspoon paprika
1	pound lump crabmeat
1/4	teaspoon hot-pepper sauce
1	cup fresh bread crumbs

To make the sauce: Puree the red peppers in a food processor or blender. Add the mayonnaise and black pepper. Process briefly to combine. Transfer to a small bowl.

To make the crab cakes: Warm the oil in a medium no-stick skillet over medium-high heat. Add the onions and celery. Cook for 5 minutes, or until soft. Transfer to a large bowl.

Stir in the egg white, crackers, parsley, mayonnaise, lemon juice, crab boil seasoning, Worcestershire sauce, mustard, celery seeds, and paprika. Blend with a fork. Stir in the crabmeat and hot-pepper sauce. Mix thoroughly. Form into 8 patties. Roll in the bread crumbs to coat completely.

Place a large no-stick skillet over medium-high heat. Coat with no-stick spray. Add the crab cakes and cook for 2 minutes; cover and cook for 1 minute, or until browned on the bottom. Coat the tops with no-stick spray and turn over. Cook for 2 to 3 minutes, uncovered, or until golden brown. Serve with the sauce.

Nutrition Notes

Per serving

Calories 244
Fat 4.7 g.
% of calories from fat 18
Protein 26.2 g.
Carbohydrates 21.2 g.
Dietary fiber 1.8 g.
Cholesterol 114 mg.
Sodium 983 mg.

Kitchen Hints

◆ The sauce can be made 1 day in advance and stored, covered, in the refrigerator.

◆ To clean the food processor blade after making the sauce, remove as much of the sauce as you can with a rubber spatula, return the bowl to the base, and pulse once or twice. The remaining food will come away from the blade. To soak a food processor bowl, invert a jigger or shot glass over the stem of the opening. Add liquid soap and fill the bowl with water.

Nutrition Notes

Per parfait

Calories 333
Fat 3.6 g.
% of calories from fat 9
Protein 10.2 g.
Carbohydrates 70.5 g.
Dietary fiber 5.4 g.
Cholesterol 2 mg.
Sodium 160 mg.

Kitchen Hint

◆ These parfaits are perfect to serve for brunch or snacks. Assemble smaller versions in champagne glasses or custard cups.

Breakfast Parfaits

MAKES 4

This nourishing breakfast is a lot of fun and refreshing on a hot morning. Vary the fruits according to your taste and seasonal availability.

> 2 cups nonfat vanilla yogurt
> 2 cups low-fat granola
> 1 cup blueberries
> 1 cup sliced strawberries
> 2 kiwifruit, chopped

Layer half of the yogurt, granola, blueberries, strawberries, and kiwifruit in 4 parfait glasses or bowls. Repeat.

Breast of Duck Salad

MAKES 4 SERVINGS

In this protein-rich salad, lean slices of grilled duck breast are fanned on a bed of mixed baby lettuces and dressed with a low-fat raspberry vinaigrette. The pungent flavors of blue cheese and toasted walnuts mean that small quantities can be used to top the salad, keeping fat at bay without sacrificing depth of flavor.

Raspberry Vinaigrette

1–2	tablespoons raspberry jam
½	cup raspberry vinegar (see hint)
3	tablespoons defatted reduced-sodium chicken broth
1	teaspoon walnut or canola oil
½	teaspoon Dijon mustard

Salad

1¼	pounds duck breast, trimmed of all visible fat
	Salt and ground black pepper
¼	cup dry red wine or cranberry juice
1	pear, chopped
4	cups mixed baby lettuce
2	tablespoons chopped toasted walnuts
2	tablespoons crumbled blue cheese

To make the raspberry vinaigrette: Place the jam in a small microwave-safe bowl and microwave on high power for 1 minute, or until melted. Whisk in the vinegar, broth, oil, and mustard.

To make the salad: Coat a grill rack or broiler pan with no-stick spray. Preheat the grill or broiler.

Season the duck with the salt and pepper. Cook 4" from the heat for 4 to 5 minutes per side. Transfer to a cutting board and let stand for 5 minutes. Cut the duck across the grain into 12 thin slices.

In a small saucepan, combine the wine or cranberry juice and pears. Place over medium-high heat and cook, stirring often, for 4 to 5 minutes, or until the liquid has evaporated.

Divide the lettuce among dinner plates. Sprinkle with the walnuts and blue cheese. Divide the pears and duck among the plates. Drizzle with the vinaigrette.

Nutrition Notes

Per serving

Calories 254
Fat 9.6 g.
% of calories from fat 34
Protein 25.5 g.
Carbohydrates 14.2 g.
Dietary fiber 2.2 g.
Cholesterol 90 mg.
Sodium 187 mg.

Kitchen Hints

◆ Adjust the amount of jam to counterbalance the tartness and acidity of the vinegar. The quality and flavor of vinegar vary significantly from brand to brand. Look for a raspberry vinegar that lists raspberries as the first ingredient, has a good-quality vinegar—such as champagne—as its base, and ideally, has a bit of added sugar.

◆ You can replace the duck with 1 pound boneless, skinless chicken breasts.

Summer Menu Five

	1,500 CALORIES 33-43 G. FAT	2,000 CALORIES 44-56 G. FAT	2,500 CALORIES 57-69 G. FAT
Breakfast			
bran flakes with	1½ cups	1½ cups	2¼ cups
skim milk and	1 cup	1 cup	1½ cups
peach slices	½ cup	1 cup	1¼ cups
Lunch			
Berry-Yogurt Soup	1 serving	1 serving	1½ servings
mixed green salad with	2 cups	2 cups	3 cups
nonfat dressing	2 tablespoons	2 tablespoons	3 tablespoons
pumpernickel roll	1	2	3
Dinner			
Apricot Grilled Shrimp	2 servings	2 servings	2 servings
Confetti Rice Salad	1 serving	2 servings	2 servings
sautéed zucchini and			
sweet red peppers	1 cup	1½ cups	2 cups
Snack			
cantaloupe cubes	½ cup	1 cup	1½ cups

DAILY TOTALS			
Calories	1,510	1,978	2,473
Fat (g.)	8	11	15
% of calories from fat	5	5	5
Protein (g.)	69	80	98
Carbohydrates (g.)	316	423	530
Dietary fiber (g.)	37	48	64
Cholesterol (mg.)	275	275	278
Sodium (mg.)	1,738	1,956	2,635

NUTRIENT BONUS

This menu (at 2,000 calories) exceeds the Daily Value for:

Dietary fiber	190%
Vitamin A	383%
Thiamin	151%
Riboflavin	152%
Niacin	155%
Vitamin B6	152%
Vitamin B12	121%
Folate	177%
Vitamin C	803%
Iron	148%
Potassium	139%

HEALTHY TIP OF THE DAY

Pad your pasta for more fiber. It may be versatile, delicious, and a complex carbohydrate, but pasta is actually very low in fiber. The goal for fiber is 20 to 35 grams per day, and a ¾-cup serving of cooked pasta provides only 2 grams. To boost the amount in your favorite pasta dishes, toss in some chick-peas, kidney beans, or a variety of vegetables. Most vegetables are good sources of fiber, and beans provide 8 grams per ½ cup.

Apricot Grilled Shrimp (page 173)

Nutrition Notes

Per serving

Calories 321
Fat 1.9 g.
% of calories from fat 5
Protein 8.7 g.
Carbohydrates 73.1 g.
Dietary fiber 8.9 g.
Cholesterol 2 mg.
Sodium 77 mg.

Kitchen Hint

◆ For a decorative look, pour the yogurt into a small resealable plastic bag. Cut the tip off one of the corners and squeeze the yogurt on top of the soup in a swirl or zigzag pattern. Pull a knife through the center of the zigzag to create a pretty design.

Berry-Yogurt Soup

MAKES 4 SERVINGS

Sun-ripened fruit blends with orange juice and yogurt to create this sweet cold soup. It makes a refreshing lunch on a hot summer day. And it's high in fiber and water-soluble vitamins.

1	cup blackberries
$\frac{1}{3}$	cup sugar
$\frac{1}{2}$	teaspoon ground cinnamon
$2\frac{1}{2}$	cups quartered strawberries
2	cups blueberries
3	nectarines, sliced
$1\frac{1}{2}$	cups raspberries
$1\frac{1}{2}$	cups orange juice
$1\frac{1}{2}$	cups nonfat plain yogurt

In a medium saucepan, combine the blackberries, sugar, and cinnamon. Add $1\frac{1}{2}$ cups of the strawberries, 1 cup of the blueberries, two-thirds of the nectarines, and $\frac{3}{4}$ cup of the raspberries. Cook over medium heat, stirring occasionally, for 10 minutes, or until the fruit is very soft.

Remove from the heat and let cool for 5 minutes. Transfer the mixture to a food processor or blender. Puree. Strain through a sieve into a large bowl; discard the seeds.

Whisk in the orange juice and 1 cup of the yogurt. Gently stir in the remaining 1 cup strawberries, 1 cup blueberries, one-third nectarines, and $\frac{3}{4}$ cup raspberries. Refrigerate for 1 hour.

In a small bowl, whisk the remaining $\frac{1}{2}$ cup yogurt until very smooth. Ladle the soup into bowls and top with the yogurt.

Apricot Grilled Shrimp

MAKES 8 SERVINGS

Shrimp are low in fat and calories—ideal for weight watchers.

- 1 cup apricot preserves
- 1 lemon
- 4 teaspoons reduced-sodium soy sauce
- 2 cloves garlic, minced
- 2 teaspoons grated fresh ginger
- 1 teaspoon ground black pepper
- 2 pounds large shrimp, peeled and deveined

Place the preserves in a large microwave-safe bowl. Microwave on high power for 30 seconds, or until melted.

Grate 2 teaspoons rind from the lemon and add to the bowl. Cut the lemon in half and squeeze 2 tablespoons juice into the bowl. Stir in the soy sauce, garlic, ginger, and pepper. Add the shrimp and toss to coat. Cover and refrigerate for 30 minutes.

Coat a grill rack or broiler pan with no-stick spray. Preheat the grill or broiler. Remove the shrimp from the marinade and divide into 8 portions; reserve the marinade. Thread the shrimp onto 8 metal skewers, leaving ¼" between the pieces. Cook 4" from the heat, basting often with the marinade, for 2 to 3 minutes per side, or until the shrimp are opaque.

Transfer the remaining marinade to a saucepan. Bring to a boil over medium-high heat. Cook for 2 minutes. Serve with the shrimp.

Nutrition Notes

Per serving

Calories 171
Fat 0.9 g.
% of calories from fat 4
Protein 15.1 g.
Carbohydrates 27 g.
Dietary fiber 0.6 g.
Cholesterol 135 mg.
Sodium 255 mg.

Kitchen Hint

◆ Jams, jellies, and preserves make delicious glazes for seafood, poultry, and meats. Add various herbs and seasonings, such as fresh or candied ginger, soy sauce, Worcestershire sauce, and grated citrus rind. To make a tasty glaze for cooked pork tenderloin, add cinnamon, cloves and allspice to peach preserves.

Handy Thermometer

Summer's here, and it's time to fire up the grill. But how hot should the grill be? And how do you test the heat? Here's how. Hold your hand, palm down, approximately 2 inches above where the food will be grilled. The number of seconds you count before needing to pull your hand away tells you the temperature. If you can hold your hand over the heat for only 4 seconds, the grill is medium to medium-high, the perfect temperature for most foods. For thicker foods, use medium to medium-low heat so the food cooks through before getting burned.

Seconds	Temperature
2	High
3	Medium-high
4	Medium
5	Medium-low
6	Low

Nutrition Notes

Per serving

Calories 300
Fat 0.8 g.
% of calories from fat 2
Protein 6.4 g.
Carbohydrates 70.5 g.
Dietary fiber 5.2 g.
Cholesterol 0 mg.
Sodium 43 mg.

Kitchen Hints

◆ Wild rice should be rinsed before cooking to wash off grit and debris. If you forget, simply skim off the foam that collects on the water's surface during boiling.

◆ To remove orange segments from their membranes, cut away the outer peel and white pith, keeping the orange intact. Slice along a membrane with a paring knife, then slice along the next membrane. The orange segment should slide out.

◆ This salad will keep, covered, in the refrigerator for up to 5 days.

MAKES 4 SERVINGS

Serve this colorful, fiber-rich side dish with any grilled fish, poultry, or meat.

½	cup wild rice, rinsed
½	cup long-grain white rice
2	oranges, segmented (see hint)
⅔	cup chopped dates
½	cup sliced scallions
¼	cup water
2	tablespoons apple juice concentrate
1	tablespoon lemon juice
1	tablespoon red-wine vinegar
½	teaspoon dried basil
¼	teaspoon dry mustard
	Salt and ground black pepper

Using separate saucepans, cook the wild rice and the white rice according to the package directions. Drain, if necessary. Cool and transfer to a large bowl. Stir in the oranges, dates, and scallions.

In a small bowl, whisk together the water, apple juice concentrate, lemon juice, vinegar, basil, and mustard. Pour the dressing over the salad and toss to coat. Season with the salt and pepper.

Summer Menu Six

	1,500 CALORIES	2,000 CALORIES	2,500 CALORIES
	33-43 G. FAT	44-56 G. FAT	57-69 G. FAT

Breakfast

Country-Style Blueberry Muffins	1	2	3
skim milk	1¼ cups	1¼ cups	2 cups

Lunch

low-sodium sliced turkey breast on	4 ounces	5 ounces	6 ounces
whole-wheat bread with	2 slices	2 slices	2 slices
lettuce,	1 leaf	1 leaf	1 leaf
tomato, and	2 slices	2 slices	2 slices
low-fat, low-sodium Muenster cheese	1½ ounces	2 ounces	2 ounces
plum slices and	¼ cup	½ cup	1 cup
blackberries	½ cup	½ cup	¾ cup
baked potato chips	12	24	24

Dinner

Fennel and Swiss Quiche	1 serving	1 serving	1½ servings
Strawberry-Watercress Salad	1 serving	2 servings	2 servings

Snack

nonfat fruit yogurt	1 cup	1 cup	1½ cups

DAILY TOTALS

Calories	1,475	1,975	2,484
Fat (g.)	41	55	66
% of calories from fat	25	25	23
Protein (g.)	93	111	140
Carbohydrates (g.)	192	273	348
Dietary fiber (g.)	19	26	32
Cholesterol (mg.)	229	280	367
Sodium (mg.)	1,647	2,232	2,733

NUTRIENT BONUS

This menu (at 2,000 calories) exceeds the Daily Value for:

Dietary fiber	104%
Vitamin A	138%
Riboflavin	133%
Vitamin C	273%
Calcium	199%

HEALTHY TIP OF THE DAY

Avoid hydrogenated oils. Many convenience foods, particularly crackers and cookies, are made with hydrogenated oils. These are liquid fats (such as soybean oil or vegetable oil) that have been turned into solid fats by adding extra hydrogen molecules. Hydrogenated and partially hydrogenated oils contain trans-fatty acids, which experts say may contribute to certain types of cancer. To reduce your risk, choose snacks made with little or no hydrogenated oils. Better yet, choose snacks made with heart-healthy monounsaturated oils like canola oil, peanut oil, or olive oil.

Strawberry-Watercress Salad

Strawberry-Watercress Salad

MAKES 4 SERVINGS

The calcium-rich watercress in this peppery-tasting salad supplies an outstanding array of nutrients, including fiber and the antioxidant vitamins A and C.

Poppy Seed Dressing

- ¼ cup sugar
- 6 tablespoons orange juice
- 3 tablespoons raspberry vinegar
- 1 tablespoon minced shallots
- 1 tablespoon olive oil
- 1½ teaspoons poppy seeds
- 1 teaspoon honey
- ½ teaspoon dry mustard
- ¼ teaspoon salt

Salad

- 2 cups trimmed watercress, coarsely chopped
- 2 heads Belgian endive, torn into small pieces
- 1 cup sliced strawberries
- 1 can (14 ounces) hearts of palm, rinsed, drained, and cut into 2" pieces (see hint)

To make the poppy seed dressing: In a small bowl, whisk together the sugar, orange juice, vinegar, shallots, oil, poppy seeds, honey, mustard, and salt until the sugar dissolves.

To make the salad: In a large bowl, combine the watercress, endive, and strawberries. Slice the hearts of palm into 2" pieces and add to the salad. Pour the dressing on top and toss well. Refrigerate for 5 to 10 minutes before serving.

Nutrition Notes

Per serving

Calories 154
Fat 4.9 g.
% of calories from fat 27%
Protein 3.5 g.
Carbohydrates 26.5 g.
Dietary fiber 3.5 g.
Cholesterol 0 mg.
Sodium 254 mg.

Kitchen Hints

◆ Hearts of palm are the edible terminal buds of certain palm trees. They have a mild flavor similar to artichoke hearts. The tender parts can be eaten raw and thinly sliced for salads. Hearts of palm can be found canned in most supermarkets.

◆ Good-tasting bottled nonfat or low-fat salad dressings are hard to find. Most are very tart and acidic and filled with gums, stabilizers, and artificial flavors. It's easy to prepare your own by using combinations of the following ingredients: fruit juices, high-quality vinegars, fresh herbs, chicken and vegetable stocks, nonfat mayonnaise, nonfat sour cream, low-fat buttermilk, nonfat yogurts, soy sauce, miso, ginger, garlic, and shallots.

Nutrition Notes

Per serving

Calories 293
Fat 12.7 g.
% of calories from fat 39
Protein 14.8 g.
Carbohydrates 29.3 g.
Dietary fiber 2 g.
Cholesterol 89 mg.
Sodium 280 mg.

Kitchen Hints

◆ You can replace the whole-wheat flour with 1¼ cups all-purpose flour, if desired.

◆ The dough for the crust can be prepared ahead and stored, wrapped in plastic, in the refrigerator for up to 2 days, or in the freezer for up to 1 month. Let the dough come to room temperature before rolling it out and fitting it into the pie plate.

◆ To save time, you can use a prepared low-fat pie crust from the freezer section of your supermarket.

Fennel and Swiss Quiche

MAKES 6 SERVINGS

Quiche is traditionally fat-laden, but we've lightened this version by using egg whites, skim milk, and reduced-fat Swiss cheese. Fennel and Dijon mustard enhance flavor.

Crust

1¼	cups whole-wheat pastry flour
¼	teaspoon salt
¼	teaspoon sugar
3	tablespoons canola oil
1	tablespoon cold unsalted butter or margarine, cut into small pieces
2–3	tablespoons ice water

Filling

1	cup thinly sliced fennel bulb
1	cup chopped scallions
4	egg whites
2	eggs
1	cup evaporated skim milk
½	cup skim milk
1½	teaspoons Dijon mustard
¼	teaspoon ground nutmeg
¼	teaspoon ground black pepper
½	cup shredded reduced-fat Swiss cheese
1	tablespoon grated Parmesan cheese
	Pinch of paprika

To make the crust: Preheat the oven to 425°F. Coat a 9" pie plate with no-stick spray.

In a large bowl or food processor, combine the flour, salt, and sugar. Blend with a pastry blender or process briefly to mix. Add the oil and butter or margarine and stir or process until the mixture resembles fine meal. While stirring constantly or with the motor of the food processor running, add the water, 1 tablespoon at a time, and stir or process for about 30 seconds, or until the dough barely comes together. Transfer to a counter and pat the dough into a flattened disk.

Place the dough between 2 sheets of wax paper and roll out to an 11" circle. Remove the top sheet and invert the dough into the prepared pie plate. Remove the remaining sheet of wax paper

and fit the dough into the plate. Use a fork to poke holes in the bottom and sides of the dough. Line the dough with a piece of foil and top it with a layer of pie weights or dried rice or beans.

Bake for 10 minutes, remove the weights and foil, and bake for 3 to 5 minutes, or until the dough is dry but has not begun to brown.

To make the filling: Coat a medium no-stick skillet with no-stick spray and place over medium heat. Add the fennel and cook for 5 minutes, or until soft. Add the scallions and cook for 2 minutes.

In a medium bowl, whisk together the egg whites, eggs, evaporated milk, skim milk, mustard, nutmeg, and pepper.

Sprinkle the fennel mixture over the bottom of the baked pie shell and top with the Swiss. Pour in the egg mixture and sprinkle the top with the Parmesan and paprika. Bake for 30 to 35 minutes, or until a knife inserted in the center comes out clean. Transfer to a wire rack and let cool for 5 to 10 minutes before serving.

Nutrition Notes

Per muffin

Calories 147
Fat 2.9 g.
% of calories from fat 17
Protein 3.1 g.
Carbohydrates 27.4 g.
Dietary fiber 1.2 g.
Cholesterol 21 mg.
Sodium 186 mg.

Kitchen Hint

◆ When there isn't enough batter for all the muffin cups, fill the empty cups three-quarters full of water. This prevents the unused cups from burning and also creates steam in the oven, which makes for moister muffins.

Country-Style Blueberry Muffins

MAKES 12

These streusel-topped muffins have a tender crumb with minimal fat.

Topping

2	tablespoons all-purpose flour
2	tablespoons quick-cooking rolled oats
2	tablespoons packed light brown sugar
½	teaspoon ground cinnamon
1	tablespoon cold unsalted butter or margarine, cut into small pieces

Muffins

1½	cups all-purpose flour
2	teaspoons baking powder
½	teaspoon salt
1	egg
½	cup sugar
3	tablespoons nonfat vanilla yogurt
1	tablespoon canola oil
1	teaspoon vanilla
½	cup skim milk
½	teaspoon grated lemon rind (optional)
1½	cups blueberries

To make the topping: In a small bowl, stir together the flour, oats, brown sugar, and cinnamon. Cut in the butter or margarine until the mixture resembles coarse meal.

To make the muffins: Preheat the oven to 400°F. Coat a 12-cup muffin pan with no-stick spray.

In a medium bowl, whisk together the flour, baking powder, and salt.

In a large bowl, combine the egg, sugar, yogurt, oil, and vanilla. Using an electric mixer, beat on medium-high for 2 minutes. Reduce the speed to low and alternately beat in the flour mixture and the milk in 4 additions, ending with the milk. Beat just until combined. Stir in the lemon rind (if using). Fold in the blueberries.

Divide the batter evenly among the muffin cups, filling them about two-thirds full. Top each muffin with 1 teaspoon of the topping. Bake for 17 to 20 minutes, or until a toothpick inserted into the center of a muffin comes out clean. Cool on a rack for 5 minutes, then remove the muffins from the pan.

Summer Menu Seven

	1,500 CALORIES	2,000 CALORIES	2,500 CALORIES
	33-43 G. FAT	44-56 G. FAT	57-69 G. FAT

Breakfast

toasted multigrain bagel with	1	1	2
Triple-Berry Cream Cheese	2 tablespoons	2 tablespoons	4 tablespoons
skim milk	1 cup	1½ cups	2 cups

Lunch

Southwest Bean Burgers with			
Lime Cream	1 serving	2 servings	2 servings
Spicy Rainbow Fries	1 serving	2 servings	2 servings
fresh peaches	2	2	2

Dinner

grilled chicken breast	6 ounces	6 ounces	8 ounces
marinated in			
nonfat vinaigrette	2 tablespoons	2 tablespoons	¼ cup
baked sweet potato	1	1	2
steamed broccoli	½ cup	¾ cup	1 cup
cooked brown rice	½ cup	¾ cup	1 cup

Snack

nonfat cheese with	2 ounces	2 ounces	2 ounces
whole-grain crackers	8	8	8
mixed berries	½ cup	½ cup	1 cup

DAILY TOTALS

Calories	1,470	1,980	2,496
Fat (g.)	31	38	43
% of calories from fat	18	17	15
Protein (g.)	88	107	135
Carbohydrates (g.)	222	320	412
Dietary fiber (g.)	29	42	54
Cholesterol (mg.)	145	148	188
Sodium (mg.)	889	1,104	1,683

NUTRIENT BONUS

This menu (at 2,000 calories) exceeds the Daily Value for:

Dietary fiber	167%
Vitamin A	1,477%
Riboflavin	118%
Niacin	158%
Vitamin B$_6$	155%
Vitamin C	345%
Calcium	126%
Potassium	122%

HEALTHY TIP OF THE DAY

If you crave a satisfying snack, try a baked sweet potato, which you can microwave in minutes. Simply scrub the sweet potato, pierce it in several places with a fork, and place it in a microwave-safe bowl. Cover with vented plastic wrap and microwave on high power for 7 to 10 minutes. For added sweetness, top the sweet potato with a little maple syrup or cinnamon. This tasty snack is nutritious, too—providing more than 200 percent of the recommended daily intake of beta-carotene.

Southwest Bean Burgers with Lime Cream (page 183) and Spicy Rainbow Fries (page 184)

Southwest Bean Burgers with Lime Cream

MAKES 4 SERVINGS

You'll never miss the meat! Vibrant flavors enliven this low-fat burger.

Burgers

2	dried chipotle peppers (wear plastic gloves when handling)
1	cup chopped red onions
½	cup chopped carrots
1	cup chopped mushrooms
1	cup frozen corn kernels, thawed
¼	cup chopped fresh Italian parsley
1	teaspoon ground cumin
¼	teaspoon cider vinegar
1	can (19 ounces) black beans, rinsed and drained
¼	cup blue or yellow cornmeal
⅓	cup unseasoned dry bread crumbs

Lime Cream

⅓	cup nonfat sour cream
1	tablespoon lime juice
¼	teaspoon chili powder
	Dash of hot-pepper sauce

To make the burgers: Place the peppers in a small bowl and cover with boiling water. Let soak for 10 minutes, or until softened. Drain, pat dry, and remove and discard the stems and seeds. Chop the flesh.

Coat a large no-stick skillet with no-stick spray. Add the onions and carrots. Cook over medium heat for 2 to 3 minutes, or until softened. Stir in the peppers, mushrooms, corn, parsley, cumin, and vinegar. Cook for 5 minutes, or until the vegetables are tender. Remove from the heat.

Place the beans in a large bowl. Use the back of a wooden spoon to mash about half of the beans. Stir in the cornmeal and the vegetable mixture until well-combined. Form into four 1"-thick patties. Roll in the bread crumbs to coat.

Wipe out the skillet and coat with no-stick spray. Place over medium heat until hot. Add the burgers and cook for 5 minutes per side, or until browned and hot throughout.

To make the lime cream: In a cup, combine the sour cream, lime juice, chili powder, and hot-pepper sauce. Serve with the burgers.

Nutrition Notes

Per serving

Calories 190
Fat 1.2 g.
% of calories from fat 5
Protein 9.2 g.
Carbohydrates 40 g.
Dietary fiber 6.9 g.
Cholesterol 0 mg.
Sodium 87 mg.

Kitchen Hints

◆ Chipotle peppers are mesquite-smoked jalapeño peppers. You can buy them dry or canned in a savory sauce. Most supermarkets carry the dried variety in the produce section.

◆ Beans are a rich source of protein, fiber, and other vital nutrients. They're also very filling—an added bonus for those watching their calorie intake. Serve beans with pasta, grains, rice, and vegetables for side or main dishes. Or try using them in soups, spreads, dips, and salads.

◆ If you're in a hurry, replace the lime cream with prepared salsa.

◆ Serve the burgers in buns for quick sandwiches.

Nutrition Notes

Per serving

Calories 221
Fat 5.6 g.
% of calories from fat 22
Protein 3.9 g.
Carbohydrates 40.6 g.
Dietary fiber 4.7 g.
Cholesterol 0 mg.
Sodium 62 mg.

Kitchen Hints

◆ If you are doubling the recipe, use 2 baking sheets. Switch the position of the sheets in the oven halfway through the baking process for even cooking.

◆ For extra-crispy fries, place under the broiler for 1 to 2 minutes before serving.

Spicy Rainbow Fries

<u>MAKES 4 SERVINGS</u>

These aren't your average fries. Beets and sweet potatoes add color and extra flavor to regular russet potatoes.

1½	tablespoons canola oil
1	teaspoon chili powder
1	teaspoon garlic powder
1	medium russet potato, cut into strips
1	medium sweet potato, cut into strips
2	medium beets, cut into strips

Preheat the oven to 350°F. Line a baking sheet with foil and coat with no-stick spray.

In a medium bowl, combine the oil, chili powder, and garlic powder. Add the russet potatoes, sweet potatoes, and beets. Toss to coat.

Arrange the vegetables on the prepared baking sheet in a single layer, being careful not to let the pieces touch. Bake for 15 minutes. Turn the pieces and bake for 15 to 20 minutes, or until crispy on the outside and tender inside.

Triple-Berry Cream Cheese

MAKES 1½ CUPS

Make the most of summer's berries with this reduced-fat spread, perfect for topping toast, bagels, and whole-grain muffins.

> 4 ounces reduced-fat cream cheese, at room temperature
> 4 ounces nonfat cream cheese, at room temperature
> ⅓ cup blueberries
> ⅓ cup raspberries
> ⅓ cup sliced strawberries
> 1–2 tablespoons confectioners' sugar or honey

In a medium bowl, mix together the reduced-fat cream cheese and nonfat cream cheese until smooth. Stir in the blueberries, raspberries, strawberries, and confectioners' sugar or honey until well-combined.

Careful with Caffeine

Some people thrive on it. Others can do without it. Either way, health experts recommend moderating your caffeine consumption, especially if you are pregnant, breastfeeding, or under stress. Too much caffeine can cause increased stomach acids, elevated heartbeat, irritability, anxiety, and headaches.

The American Dietetic Association recommends limiting daily caffeine intake to 230 milligrams. That's about 2½ cups (6 ounces each) of full-strength coffee. Switching to decaf will save you about 96 milligrams per 6-ounce cup. To replace calcium that may be lost through caffeine consumption, eat plenty of calcium-rich foods like low-fat dairy products. Check the chart below for sources of caffeine.

Item	Caffeine (mg.)
12 ounces coffee	197
2 Excedrin tablets	130
12 ounces tea	68
2 Anacin tablets	64
12 ounces diet soda	50
12 ounces regular soda	37
1 ounce dark or semisweet chocolate	20
1 ounce milk chocolate	7
8 ounces cocoa or hot chocolate	5
12 ounces decaffeinated coffee	3
12 ounces decaffeinated tea	0

Nutrition Notes

Per tablespoon

Calories 20
Fat 1 g.
% of calories from fat 47
Protein 1.3 g.
Carbohydrates 1.4 g.
Dietary fiber 0.2 g.
Cholesterol 4 mg.
Sodium 43 mg.

Kitchen Hints

◆ Adjust the amount of confectioners' sugar or honey according to the sweetness of the berries.

◆ When berries are out of season, try jazzing up reduced-fat or nonfat cream cheese with assorted chopped dried fruits, jams, marmalades, toasted nuts, and spices for a delicious breakfast or snack spread. Store the spread, covered, in the refrigerator for up to 4 days.

Summer Menu Eight

	1,500 CALORIES	2,000 CALORIES	2,500 CALORIES
	33-43 G. FAT	44-56 G. FAT	57-69 G. FAT

Breakfast

honeydew melon cubes	1 cup	1½ cups	2 cups
English muffin with	1	1	1½
jam	2 tablespoons	2 tablespoons	3 tablespoons
calcium-fortified orange juice	1¼ cups	1½ cups	2 cups

Lunch

Grilled Mediterranean Sandwiches	1	2	2
strawberries	1 cup	1 cup	1½ cups
baked potato chips	12	24	24

Dinner

Beef Fajitas	2	2	3
nonfat refried beans	¼ cup	¾ cup	¾ cup
Guiltless Guacamole	¼ cup	½ cup	½ cup

Snack

frozen sorbet bar	1	1	1

DAILY TOTALS

Calories	1,490	1,994	2,485
Fat (g.)	27	35	44
% of calories from fat	16	15	16
Protein (g.)	61	81	102
Carbohydrates (g.)	262	353	437
Dietary fiber (g.)	25	42	48
Cholesterol (mg.)	83	95	130
Sodium (mg.)	1,979	2,921	3,557

NUTRIENT BONUS

This menu (at 2,000 calories) exceeds the Daily Value for:

Dietary fiber	167%
Vitamin A	160%
Thiamin	125%
Folate	119%
Vitamin C	958%
Calcium	126%
Potassium	101%

HEALTHY TIP OF THE DAY

For healthier bones and to help prevent osteoporosis, try to get 1,000 to 1,500 milligrams of calcium a day. Here are some good sources: 1 cup of yogurt provides up to 415 milligrams of calcium, 8 ounces of calcium-fortified orange juice provides about 320 milligrams, and 5 dried figs provide 135 milligrams. To determine the milligrams of calcium in a packaged food, find the percent Daily Value of calcium listed on the label, drop the percent sign, and add a zero.

Beef Fajitas (page 189) and Guiltless Guacamole (page 190)

Nutrition Notes

Per sandwich

Calories 185
Fat 5.6 g.
% of calories from far 25
Protein 9.8 g.
Carbohydrates 27.4 g.
Dietary fiber 6.2 g.
Cholesterol 12 mg.
Sodium 233 mg.

Kitchen Hints

◆ Instead of discarding the soft bread centers, use them to make fresh bread crumbs, which can be frozen for up to 6 months.

◆ You can make the spread and grill the vegetables up to a day in advance and store them in the refrigerator. Reheat the vegetables and assemble the sandwiches just before serving.

◆ As long as you have the grill hot, prepare some extra vegetables such as zucchini, carrots, mushrooms, tomatoes, and fennel to have on hand for a side dish or to top pizza, pasta, couscous, or rice. Store, covered, in the refrigerator for up to 4 days.

Grilled Mediterranean Sandwiches

MAKES 4

A creamy sun-dried tomato spread gives a burst of flavor to the vegetables in these easy sandwiches.

1 large eggplant (1 pound), cut lengthwise into ¼" slices
1 pound yellow squash, cut lengthwise into ¼" slices
1 red onion, sliced crosswise
2 sweet red peppers
2 tablespoons chopped sun-dried tomatoes
2 ounces nonfat cream cheese, at room temperature
2 ounces goat cheese
2 tablespoons nonfat sour cream
2 teaspoons chopped fresh thyme
1 tablespoon chopped pistachios (optional)
1 loaf crusty multigrain French bread, halved lengthwise through the side

Coat a grill rack with no-stick spray. Preheat a grill. Position the rack 4" from the heat and let it get hot. Add the eggplant, squash, onions, and peppers in a single layer.

Cook the eggplant, squash, and onions for 2 to 3 minutes per side, or until lightly browned and softened; remove from the grill and set aside. Continue cooking the peppers until charred all over. Transfer the peppers to a paper bag and let stand for 5 minutes. Remove the tops, charred skin, ribs, and seeds from the peppers; discard. Slice the peppers into thin strips.

Place the tomatoes in a small bowl and cover with boiling water. Let soak for 10 minutes, or until softened. Drain.

In another small bowl, stir together the cream cheese, goat cheese, sour cream, thyme, pistachios (if using), and tomatoes until well-mixed.

Remove the soft insides from the crust of each half of the bread. Discard or reserve for another use (see hint). Spread the tomato mixture over both halves of the bread. Layer the grilled vegetables on the bottom half, then cover with the top half of the bread. Cut into a total of 4 sandwiches.

Beef Fajitas

MAKES 8

Say adios to high-fat fajitas when you use lean beef tenderloin and reduced-fat accompaniments.

1 pound beef tenderloin
½ teaspoon ground black pepper
1 teaspoon olive oil
1 large Spanish onion, cut into thin wedges
1 large green pepper, cut into thin strips
1 large sweet red pepper, cut into thin strips
⅓ cup defatted reduced-sodium chicken broth
¼ cup lime juice
2 tablespoons reduced-sodium soy sauce
2 teaspoons honey
2 teaspoons cornstarch
1 teaspoon minced garlic
½ teaspoon ground cumin
8 flour tortillas (8" diameter)
2 cups shredded leaf lettuce
1 cup Guiltless Guacamole (page 190)
1 cup nonfat salsa

Coat a grill rack with no-stick spray. Preheat the grill.

Slice the beef in half lengthwise and grill 4" from the heat, covered, for 7 to 10 minutes per side. Remove from the grill and let stand for 5 minutes. Sprinkle the black pepper evenly over the beef. Slice crosswise into thin strips.

Warm the oil in a large no-stick skillet over medium heat. Add the onions, green peppers, and red peppers. Cook, stirring occasionally, for 7 to 10 minutes, or until tender.

In a small bowl, combine the broth, lime juice, soy sauce, honey, cornstarch, garlic, and cumin; mix well to dissolve the cornstarch. Add to the skillet and stir constantly for 1 to 2 minutes, or until slightly thickened. Add the beef and stir to combine.

Wrap the tortillas in plastic wrap and microwave on high power for 1 minute, or until warm.

Divide the beef mixture and lettuce among the tortillas. Top with the guacamole and salsa. Roll up the tortillas to enclose the filling.

Nutrition Notes

Per fajita

Calories 265
Fat 8.1 g.
% of calories from fat 27
Protein 17.2 g.
Carbohydrates 31 g.
Dietary fiber 3 g.
Cholesterol 35 mg.
Sodium 486 mg.

Kitchen Hints

◆ The beef tenderloin can be replaced with marinated flank or round steak. Chicken or turkey breast can also be used. For a vegetarian option, try sautéed seitan, a meat substitute made from cooked wheat gluten. Seitan has a chewy texture and absorbs the flavors of whatever it's cooked in. Look for it in the freezer or refrigerator case at health food stores.

◆ To roast the beef instead of grilling it, place it on a baking sheet and bake at 475°F for 30 minutes, or until the internal temperature registers 130°F on an instant-read thermometer.

Nutrition Notes

Per ¼ cup

Calories 42
Fat 1.4 g.
% of calories from fat 29
Protein 1.7 g.
Carbohydrates 6.2 g.
Dietary fiber 2.2 g.
Cholesterol 0 mg.
Sodium 69 mg.

Kitchen Hints

◆ To pit an avocado, cut it in half lengthwise around the seed. Twist the halves apart. Carefully whack a large sharp knife into the seed, then twist and separate the avocado from the seed.

◆ To peel an avocado, place the halves cut side down. Cut 2 equally spaced lengthwise slits just through the skin. With the edge of a knife blade, lift the top corner of each strip and peel back the skin. Or, scoop the avocado out of the peel with a spoon.

Guiltless Guacamole

MAKES 3 CUPS

Green peas stand in for most of the avocado in this creamy delight. Perfect as a dip, topping, or sandwich spread, this lower-fat Mexican favorite is now a good source of vitamin A and folate.

> 1 box (10 ounces) frozen baby peas, thawed
> ½ ripe avocado, chopped
> 1 can (4 ounces) chopped green chili peppers
> 3 tablespoons lime juice
> 2 tablespoons nonfat sour cream
> 1 teaspoon minced garlic
> 1 teaspoon ground cumin
> 1 cup chopped plum tomatoes
> ⅓ cup chopped red onions
> 2 tablespoons chopped fresh cilantro
> Salt and ground black pepper

In a food processor or blender, combine the peas, avocado, chili peppers, lime juice, sour cream, garlic, and cumin. Process until smooth. Transfer to a medium bowl.

Stir in the tomatoes, onions, and cilantro. Season to taste with the salt and black pepper. Store, covered, in the refrigerator for up to 3 days.

Summer Menu Nine

	1,500 CALORIES	2,000 CALORIES	2,500 CALORIES
	33-43 G. FAT	44-56 G. FAT	57-69 G. FAT

Breakfast

Blueberry-Cornmeal Flapjacks	2	3	3
peach slices	½ cup	½ cup	½ cup
maple syrup	2 tablespoons	3 tablespoons	3 tablespoons
skim milk	1 cup	1 cup	1¼ cups

Lunch

Tarragon Chicken Salad	1 serving	1 serving	1½ servings
French bread	1 slice	2 slices	3 slices

Dinner

Tropical Gazpacho	1 serving	2 servings	2 servings
grilled halibut with	4 ounces	5 ounces	6 ounces
lemon wedge	1	1	1
orzo with	½ cup	½ cup	1 cup
chopped Italian parsley	½ tablespoon	½ tablespoon	1 tablespoon

Snack

apple slices with	½ cup	½ cup	¾ cup
reduced-fat peanut butter	2 tablespoons	2 tablespoons	3 tablespoons

DAILY TOTALS			
Calories	1,490	1,971	2,505
Fat (g.)	27	32	42
% of calories from fat	16	15	15
Protein (g.)	79	92	123
Carbohydrates (g.)	236	332	411
Dietary fiber (g.)	13	18	22
Cholesterol (mg.)	137	164	205
Sodium (mg.)	2,014	2,559	3,322

NUTRIENT BONUS

This menu (at 2,000 calories) exceeds the Daily Value for:

Vitamin A	111%
Thiamin	106%
Niacin	149%
Vitamin B6	102%
Vitamin C	251%

HEALTHY TIP OF THE DAY

Drink a lot of water. Since 40 to 60 percent of your body weight is water, proper hydration can be the key to peak performance. Fluid in your body transports glucose to muscles, helps eliminate waste products, and cools off your body during exercise. Drink 6 to 10 cups of water per day to ensure adequate fluid intake. If you're exercising, drink 1 to 2 cups of water both before and after your workout.

Tropical Gazpacho

Tropical Gazpacho

MAKES 4 SERVINGS

Here's a nifty twist on traditional gazpacho. Mango, pineapple, and a banana give the soup a lush tropical flavor—and a vitamin blast to boot. This makes a great summer lunch or starter course.

1	banana
1	tablespoon water
1½	cups papaya nectar or apricot nectar
1¼	cups pineapple juice
1	cup chopped pineapple
1	cup chopped mango
½	cup peeled, seeded, and chopped cucumbers
½	cup chopped plum tomatoes
1	jalapeño pepper, minced (wear plastic gloves when handling)
2	tablespoons chopped fresh cilantro
2	tablespoons shredded coconut, toasted (see hint)

In a large bowl, mash the banana and water until smooth. Whisk in the papaya nectar or apricot nectar and pineapple juice. Stir in the pineapple, mango, cucumbers, tomatoes, peppers, and cilantro. Serve sprinkled with the coconut.

Nutrition Notes

Per serving

Calories 195
Fat 1.7 g.
% of calories from fat 8
Protein 1.4 g.
Carbohydrates 45.7 g.
Dietary fiber 3.3 g.
Cholesterol 0 mg.
Sodium 18 mg.

Kitchen Hints

◆ To toast coconut, cook it in a dry skillet over medium heat for 2 to 3 minutes, or until fragrant and golden. Shake the pan often.

◆ Look for fruit nectars in the international or juice aisle of your supermarket.

◆ To intensify the flavors of this soup, let it stand for 15 minutes before serving.

◆ For extra flavor, add a chopped roasted onion to this soup. To roast, bake the onion on a baking sheet at 400°F for 1 hour, or until tender and golden. When cool enough to handle, peel and discard the skin. Chop the onion, refrigerate until cold, and add to the soup.

Beat the Heat

To avoid the burn of hot chili peppers, wear plastic gloves when handling them. Or try this method: Use two utensils to avoid touching the peppers. Two paring knives or a paring knife and a serrated grapefruit spoon work well. Steady the chili pepper with one utensil and cut with the other. Use the grapefruit spoon or paring knife to scrape out the seeds. Then steady the seeded pepper with one utensil as you chop the pepper with the paring knife. This method works especially well for small hot chili peppers that are difficult to handle with gloves.

Nutrition Notes

Per flapjack

Calories 109
Fat 2.2 g.
% of calories from fat 18
Protein 3.4 g.
Carbohydrates 19.1 g.
Dietary fiber 1.3 g.
Cholesterol 19 mg.
Sodium 298 mg.

Kitchen Hints

◆ If you don't have cake flour, you can make an approximation by measuring out 1 cup all-purpose flour and removing 2 tablespoons. Replace the flour with 2 tablespoons cornstarch. Mix well.

◆ Yellow, white, and blue varieties of cornmeal are available at many super-markets. Yellow cornmeal contains more beta-carotene than white. Corn-meal is most often sold degermed in order to extend its shelf life, but you can find "unbolted" cornmeal, which contains both the bran and the germ, in most health food stores.

Blueberry-Cornmeal Flapjacks

Makes 12

You can mix, pour, and flip these colorful pancakes in about 10 minutes to start your day off right. The complex carbohydrates will give you long-lasting energy. If you don't have buttermilk, use soured milk instead. To make 1½ cups soured milk, pour a generous 1⅓ cups 1% low-fat milk into a measuring cup. Add enough lemon juice to make 1½ cups. Let stand for 5 minutes.

1	cup cake flour (see hint)
¾	cup yellow cornmeal
1	tablespoon sugar
1½	teaspoons baking powder
1	teaspoon baking soda
½	teaspoon salt
1	egg
1	egg white
1½	cups 1% low-fat buttermilk
1	tablespoon canola oil
1½	cups blueberries

In a large bowl, combine the flour, cornmeal, sugar, baking powder, baking soda, and salt. Mix well.

In a medium bowl, whisk together the egg, egg white, buttermilk, and oil. Stir into the flour mixture just until smooth; do not over-mix. Fold in the blueberries.

Place a large no-stick skillet over medium heat until hot. Coat with no-stick spray. For each flapjack, pour ⅓ cup batter into the skillet and spread to form a 4" pancake. Cook for 2 to 3 minutes, or until the underside is browned and bubbles appear on the top. Turn the flapjack over and cook for another 1 to 2 minutes, or until golden brown. Repeat to make a total of 12 flapjacks.

Tarragon Chicken Salad

MAKES 4 SERVINGS

This sweet and savory salad pairs lean chicken with grapes, potatoes, and a creamy nonfat herb-mustard dressing. This is a great pack-ahead salad for a picnic or brown-bag lunch.

- 12 ounces new potatoes, cut into 1" cubes
- 1 pound boneless, skinless chicken breasts
- 1 cup defatted reduced-sodium chicken broth
- 1 cup sliced scallions
- 1 cup seedless red grapes, halved
- 1 cup nonfat mayonnaise
- 3 tablespoons Dijon mustard
- 2 tablespoons lemon juice
- 2 teaspoons dried tarragon
  Salt and ground black pepper
- 4 leaves lettuce or radicchio

Place the potatoes in a large saucepan. Add cold water to cover and bring to a boil over high heat. Reduce the heat to medium, cover, and cook for 12 to 15 minutes, or until tender when tested with a sharp knife. Drain, transfer to a large bowl, and refrigerate for 1 hour, or until cool.

Place the chicken in a single layer in a glass pie plate. Add the broth. Cover with vented plastic wrap and microwave on high power for a total of 10 minutes, or until the chicken is no longer pink in the center when tested with a sharp knife; turn the chicken after 5 minutes. Set aside until cool enough to handle.

Cut the chicken into 1" cubes and add to the bowl with the potatoes. Add the scallions and grapes. Toss to mix.

In a small bowl, whisk together the mayonnaise, mustard, lemon juice, and tarragon. Season with the salt and pepper. Pour over the chicken mixture and toss to coat. Serve on the lettuce or radicchio.

Nutrition Notes

Per serving

Calories 291
Fat 4.1 g.
% of calories from fat 13
Protein 26.7 g.
Carbohydrates 34.3 g.
Dietary fiber 2.8 g.
Cholesterol 63 mg.
Sodium 860 mg.

Kitchen Hint

◆ To prevent food-borne illnesses, avoid leaving any food that should be cold out of the refrigerator for more than 2 hours. If the food contains animal-based products, get it back to the refrigerator or cooler after 1 hour.

Summer Menu Ten

	1,500 CALORIES 33-43 G. FAT	2,000 CALORIES 44-56 G. FAT	2,500 CALORIES 57-69 G. FAT
Breakfast			
Synergy Eggs Benedict	1 serving	1 serving	1 serving
strawberries and raspberries	¼ cup	1 cup	1 cup
calcium-fortified orange juice	½ cup	1½ cups	1½ cups
Lunch			
Asian Sesame Noodles	1 serving	1 serving	2 servings
mixed baby lettuce with	1 cup	2 cups	2 cups
nonfat dressing	1 tablespoon	2 tablespoons	2 tablespoons
Dinner			
grilled beef tenderloin	4 ounces	6 ounces	7 ounces
grilled zucchini, mushrooms, and onions	½ cup	1 cup	1 cup
baked potato with	1	1	2
nonfat sour cream	2 tablespoons	2 tablespoons	4 tablespoons
Summer Dessert Pizza	1 slice	1 slice	1 slice
Snack			
gingersnaps	6	12	12

Daily Totals			
Calories	1,513	2,005	2,488
Fat (g.)	31	40	47
% of calories from fat	19	18	17
Protein (g.)	76	94	115
Carbohydrates (g.)	224	310	394
Dietary fiber (g.)	17	26	33
Cholesterol (mg.)	237	272	289
Sodium (mg.)	1,785	2,164	2,624

NUTRIENT BONUS

This menu (at 2,000 calories) exceeds the Daily Value for:

Dietary fiber	105%
Vitamin A	212%
Thiamin	118%
Folate	104%
Vitamin C	523%
Iron	124%
Calcium	108%

HEALTHY TIP OF THE DAY

Energize with a morning meal. Breakfast adds energy to your morning and keeps you going strong until lunchtime. A healthy breakfast also helps you resist bingeing on high-fat, low-fiber snacks.

Synergy Eggs Benedict (page 198)

Nutrition Notes

Per serving

Calories 317
Fat 5.1 g.
% of calories from fat 15
Protein 24.1 g.
Carbohydrates 36.4 g.
Dietary fiber 1.8 g.
Cholesterol 117 mg.
Sodium 820 mg.

Kitchen Hints

◆ Butter-flavored sprinkles or granules are flavored fat substitutes, such as Molly McButter and Butter Buds. They are available in most supermarkets.

◆ Leftover sauce can be refrigerated for 1 day and reheated in a double boiler over medium heat, whisking constantly, for 2 to 3 minutes.

Synergy Eggs Benedict

MAKES 4 SERVINGS

Yes! You can enjoy eggs Benedict and stay healthy. By using scrambled egg substitute and lean Canadian bacon, fat and cholesterol are significantly reduced. This new classic is topped with a lemony hollandaise sauce that's so creamy, you won't believe it's butter-free.

Hollandaise Sauce

½ cup white wine or nonalcoholic white wine
1 small shallot, minced
¼ teaspoon black peppercorns
¼ teaspoon dried thyme
1 tablespoon butter-flavored sprinkles
⅓ cup hot water
½ cup nonfat sour cream
2 egg yolks
1 tablespoon lemon juice
Salt and ground black pepper

Eggs

4 English muffins, split
4 ounces Canadian bacon, cut into 8 thin slices
2 cups fat-free egg substitute

To make the hollandaise sauce: In the bottom of a double boiler, combine the wine, shallots, peppercorns, and thyme. Bring to a boil over high heat, then reduce the heat to medium and simmer for 3 minutes, or until reduced to about 2 tablespoons. Remove from the heat and strain the liquid into the top of the double boiler. Set aside to cool for 5 minutes.

In a small bowl, dissolve the butter-flavored sprinkles in the water. Whisk in the sour cream until smooth.

Place about 1" of water in the bottom of the double boiler and bring to a simmer over medium heat.

Whisk the egg yolks into the wine mixture and set over the simmering water. Whisk constantly for 1 to 3 minutes, or until thickened but not hardened. (If the yolks begin to harden, remove the top of the double boiler and whisk vigorously off the heat for a few seconds.) Remove the top of the double boiler from the heat.

Add the sour-cream mixture in a steady stream, whisking constantly. Whisk in the lemon juice and season with the salt and pepper.

To make the eggs: Preheat the broiler. Place the English muffins, split side up, and bacon on a baking sheet and broil for 2 to 3 minutes, or until the muffins are toasted and the bacon is heated through.

Coat a large no-stick skillet with no-stick spray and place over medium heat. Add the egg substitute and cook, occasionally scraping the bottom of the pan, for 3 to 4 minutes, or until the eggs are scrambled.

Just before serving, place the top of the double boiler over the simmering water and whisk the sauce constantly for 1 minute, or until smooth and warm.

Top each muffin half with a slice of bacon. Divide the eggs and sauce among the muffins.

Nutrition Notes

Per slice

Calories 266
Fat 8.6 g.
% of calories from fat 29
Protein 7.2 g.
Carbohydrates 41 g.
Dietary fiber 2.1 g.
Cholesterol 49 mg.
Sodium 90 mg.

Kitchen Hints

◆ To make 1 cup vanilla yogurt cheese, place 2 cups low-fat vanilla yogurt in a strainer or colander lined with cheesecloth (or use a special yogurt strainer). Place the strainer over a bowl and refrigerate for 3 to 4 hours or overnight to drain the whey (liquid). Discard the whey. The drained yogurt is yogurt cheese.

◆ Try this arrangement when setting the fruit over the filling: Fan the sliced strawberries around the outer edge in 2 circular rows. Next, create 2 or 3 circular rows of blueberries. Arrange the kiwifruit in the inner circle to resemble a flower.

Summer Dessert Pizza

MAKES 8 SLICES

Pizza for dessert? You got it. And you'll love it! It's like a big cookie topped with a sweet, creamy spread and sliced vitamin-rich kiwifruit, strawberries, and blueberries. Dig in!

Crust

1½	cups all-purpose flour
⅓	cup sugar
3	tablespoons cold unsalted butter or margarine, cut into small pieces
1	egg yolk
3	tablespoons skim milk

Topping

4	ounces reduced-fat cream cheese, at room temperature
3	tablespoons confectioners' sugar
1	cup low-fat vanilla yogurt cheese (see hint)
½	teaspoon vanilla
2	cups sliced strawberries
1	cup blueberries
1	kiwifruit, halved lengthwise and thinly sliced
1	tablespoon currant jelly

To make the crust: Line a baking sheet with foil and coat with no-stick spray.

In a large bowl or food processor, combine the flour and sugar. Add the butter or margarine and blend with a pastry blender or process just until the mixture resembles fine meal.

In a small bowl, whisk together the egg yolk and milk. While stirring constantly or with the motor of the food processor running, pour in the milk mixture in a steady stream and stir or process for 45 seconds, or until the dough barely comes together.

Transfer the dough to a flat surface and pat into a flattened disk. Place between 2 sheets of wax paper and roll out to a 10" circle. Remove the top sheet and invert the dough onto the prepared baking sheet. Remove the remaining sheet of wax paper and cover with plastic wrap. Refrigerate for 30 minutes.

Preheat the oven to 350°F.

Bake the dough for 15 minutes, or until just golden. Transfer the crust, on the foil, to a wire rack to cool completely. Remove the foil.

To make the topping: In a small bowl, combine the cream cheese and confectioners' sugar. Mix well. Stir in the yogurt cheese and vanilla until smooth.

Spread the topping over the cooled crust, leaving a ¼" border. Decoratively arrange the strawberries, blueberries, and kiwifruit over the filling.

Place the jelly in a microwave-safe custard cup. Microwave on high power for 30 seconds, or until melted. Brush over the fruit.

Nutrition Notes

Per serving

Calories 293
Fat 4.6 g.
% of calories from fat 14
Protein 11.4 g.
Carbohydrates 52.1 g.
Dietary fiber 4.4 g.
Cholesterol 0 mg.
Sodium 419 mg.

Kitchen Hints

◆ Hot chili sauce with garlic is available in the international section of most supermarkets.

◆ The noodles will keep, covered, in the refrigerator, for up to 3 days.

◆ For added protein, toss 4 ounces sautéed shrimp, chicken breast, or tofu with the noodles.

Asian Sesame Noodles

MAKES 4 SERVINGS

Crunchy bean sprouts, shredded scallions, and angel hair pasta are tossed in a ginger-spiked soy sauce to create this cold noodle dish. The small amount of toasted sesame oil adds rich flavor without a lot of fat.

8 ounces angel hair pasta
2 teaspoons toasted sesame oil
1 tablespoon minced fresh ginger
2 teaspoons sesame seeds
1 tablespoon ground coriander
½ cup defatted reduced-sodium chicken broth
3 tablespoons reduced-sodium soy sauce
1 tablespoon hot chili sauce with garlic (see hint)
8 scallions
2 cups bean sprouts

Cook the angel hair in a large pot of boiling water according to the package directions. Drain and transfer to a large serving bowl. Set aside to cool.

Warm the oil in a medium no-stick skillet over medium-high heat. Add the ginger and sesame seeds. Cook, stirring, for 1 to 2 minutes, or until the seeds are fragrant. Add the coriander and cook for 30 seconds more. Stir in the broth, soy sauce, and chili sauce. Bring to a boil. Pour over the cooled noodles. Toss to coat.

Slice the scallions into 2" lengths, then cut each piece into shreds by slicing lengthwise. Add the scallions and bean sprouts to the noodles and toss to combine. Serve cold.

Summer Menu Eleven

	1,500 CALORIES	2,000 CALORIES	2,500 CALORIES
	33-43 G. FAT	44-56 G. FAT	57-69 G. FAT

Breakfast

toasted bagel	½	1	1
poached egg	1	1	1
calcium-fortified orange juice	1 cup	1 cup	1 cup

Lunch

multigrain toast with	1 slice	3 slices	4 slices
melted reduced-fat Swiss cheese and	1 ounce	3 ounces	4 ounces
tomato slices	1	3	4

Dinner

Breezy Chocolate Chip Milk Shakes	1 serving	1 serving	1 serving
Pan-Seared Scallop Salad	1 serving	1 serving	2 servings
crusty French rolls	2	2	2
Berry Soufflés	1	1	1

Snack

baby carrots with	1 cup	1 cup	1½ cups
nonfat dip	¼ cup	¼ cup	¼ cup

DAILY TOTALS

Calories	1,507	2,023	2,483
Fat (g.)	28	46	59
% of calories from fat	17	20	21
Protein (g.)	66	93	128
Carbohydrates (g.)	250	317	371
Dietary fiber (g.)	24	32	41
Cholesterol (mg.)	275	315	372
Sodium (mg.)	1,884	2,343	2,790

NUTRIENT BONUS

This menu (at 2,000 calories) exceeds the Daily Value for:

Dietary fiber	126%
Folate	126%
Vitamin C	392%
Calcium	168%

HEALTHY TIP OF THE DAY

When choosing low-fat desserts at restaurants, look for fruit-based items such as pies, cobblers, crisps, sorbets, or sherbets. In pies and cobblers, the fillings are generally low-fat, but crusts and toppings may be high in fat. For the least fat, enjoy the fruit and leave the crust on the plate.

Pan-Seared Scallop Salad

Pan-Seared Scallop Salad

MAKES 4 SERVINGS

This light dinner is elegant and delicious. Peppery pan-seared scallops rest on a bed of vegetables and mixed lettuce. A low-fat lime vinaigrette gives the dish refreshing flavor.

Vinaigrette

¾	cup lime juice
¼	cup balsamic vinegar
1	tablespoon honey
1	tablespoon olive oil
	Salt and ground black pepper

Salad

1½	cups thawed and chopped frozen artichoke hearts
1½	cups chopped cucumbers
2	plum tomatoes, chopped
1	tablespoon minced shallots
4	cups mixed lettuce (see hint)
6	large leaves radicchio, torn
5	large leaves basil, coarsely chopped
1	pound jumbo sea scallops
1	teaspoon ground black pepper

To make the vinaigrette: In a small bowl, whisk together the lime juice, vinegar, honey, and oil. Season with the salt and pepper.

To make the salad: In a medium bowl, combine the artichoke hearts, cucumbers, tomatoes, and shallots. Add half of the vinaigrette and toss to coat.

In a large bowl, combine the lettuce, radicchio, and basil. Add the remaining vinaigrette and toss to coat.

Coat a large no-stick skillet with no-stick spray. Place over medium-high heat until hot. Sprinkle the scallops with the pepper. Add to the skillet and cook for 2 to 3 minutes per side, or until opaque.

Divide the lettuce mixture among dinner plates. Top with the artichoke mixture and the scallops.

Nutrition Notes

Per serving

Calories 238
Fat 5.1 g.
% of calories from fat 18
Protein 23.6 g.
Carbohydrates 28.3 g.
Dietary fiber 6.7 g.
Cholesterol 37 mg.
Sodium 285 mg.

Kitchen Hints

◆ You can buy mixed baby lettuce in many supermarkets. An alternative is 3 cups frisée, 1 cup torn watercress, and 2 Belgian endives (torn).

◆ The vinaigrette can also double as a marinade for chicken or firm-fleshed fish, such as swordfish, halibut, and tuna.

Nutrition Notes

Per serving

Calories 338
Fat 5.4 g.
% of calories from fat 15
Protein 8.7 g.
Carbohydrates 61.3 g.
Dietary fiber 2.1 g.
Cholesterol 7 mg.
Sodium 137 mg.

Kitchen Hints

◆ Dutch-process cocoa powder is richer and darker than regular cocoa. It has been treated with an alkali that helps neutralize cocoa's natural acidity. It's widely available in supermarkets.

◆ You can make the chocolate sauce up to a month in advance, so this calcium-packed treat is a breeze to whip up at a moment's notice. Refrigerate the sauce in an airtight container. It's also good as a topping for angel food cake or nonfat plain yogurt. Or turn it into fondue for dipping fruit like bananas, strawberries, and dried apricots; warm the sauce briefly in the microwave or a saucepan.

Breezy Chocolate Chip Milk Shakes

MAKES 4 SERVINGS

The classic lunch-counter shake gets a new look! Low-fat ice cream and a simple cocoa sauce lighten it considerably.

Chocolate Sauce

- ½ cup water
- ¼ cup sugar
- ¼ cup unsweetened Dutch-process cocoa powder (see hint)
- ½ teaspoon vanilla

Shake

- 5 cups low-fat mint chocolate chip ice cream
- ⅓ cup skim milk

To make the chocolate sauce: In a medium saucepan, combine the water, sugar, and cocoa. Bring to a boil over medium heat, stirring constantly until the sugar and cocoa are dissolved. Remove from the heat and stir in the vanilla. Refrigerate for 30 minutes, or until cold.

To make the shake: In a blender or food processor, combine the ice cream, milk, and ⅓ cup of the chocolate sauce. Blend until smooth. Reserve the remaining chocolate sauce for another use (see hint).

Gadgets Worth Getting

Healthy cooking can be a challenge. But nifty gadgets and appliances do help. They cut time and make it easier to cook with less fat. Here are some items that make healthy cooking quicker and easier.

- Cheese grater
- Citrus zester
- Food processor or blender
- Garlic press
- Grill and grill utensils
- Microwave
- No-stick skillets
- Vegetable steamer
- Wok
- Yogurt strainer

Berry Soufflés

Makes 6

Egg whites and pureed berries give these soufflés a striking light purple color. Underneath you'll find a delicious layer of whole berries.

6	tablespoons sugar
1¾	cups blackberries
1¾	cups raspberries
1	lemon
2	tablespoons cornstarch
1	tablespoon raspberry liqueur (optional)
4	egg whites
¼	teaspoon cream of tartar
	Pinch of salt
	Confectioners' sugar

Preheat the oven to 350°F. Coat six 8-ounce soufflé cups with no-stick spray. Add 1 teaspoon of the sugar to each cup and swirl to coat the bottom and sides. Distribute ¾ cup of the blackberries and ¾ cup of the raspberries among the cups.

Grate ½ teaspoon rind from the lemon into a medium saucepan. Add the remaining 1 cup blackberries, 1 cup raspberries, and 4 tablespoons sugar. Bring to a boil over medium heat. Cook and mash the berries for 3 to 5 minutes, or until the berries are very soft. Transfer the mixture to a fine sieve set over a small saucepan. With the back of a spoon, press the berries through the sieve to extract the pulp; discard the seeds.

Cut the lemon in half and squeeze 2 tablespoons juice into a small bowl. Add the cornstarch and stir until dissolved. Stir into the berry puree and bring to a boil over medium-high heat, stirring constantly. Cook, stirring, for 30 seconds, or until thickened. Remove from the heat and stir in the liqueur (if using). Transfer to a large bowl and let cool to room temperature.

In a medium bowl, combine the egg whites, cream of tartar, and salt. Using an electric mixer, beat on medium speed until foamy. Beat on high until the whites are firm and glossy.

Fold the egg-white mixture into the berry puree. Spoon the mixture into the soufflé cups and smooth the tops.

Place the cups in a roasting pan and add about 1" of water to the pan. Bake for 25 to 30 minutes, or until the soufflés are firm when jiggled and the tops are golden brown and puffed. Dust with the confectioners' sugar.

Nutrition Notes

Per soufflé

Calories 111
Fat 0.4 g.
% of calories from fat 3
Protein 3 g.
Carbohydrates 25.2 g.
Dietary fiber 3.3 g.
Cholesterol 0 mg.
Sodium 59 mg.

Kitchen Hints

◆ You get the most volume from egg whites that are at room temperature.

◆ If you prefer, you can make one large soufflé. Use a 1½-quart soufflé dish and increase the baking time to 30 to 35 minutes.

Summer Menu Twelve

	1,500 CALORIES 33-43 G. FAT	2,000 CALORIES 44-56 G. FAT	2,500 CALORIES 57-69 G. FAT
Breakfast			
nonfat fruit yogurt with	½ cup	1 cup	1 cup
low-fat granola	1 cup	1 cup	1¼ cups
Lunch			
Pesto Chicken Picnic	1 serving	2 servings	2 servings
mixed fresh fruit salad	½ cup	1 cup	1 cup
Dinner			
Baked Ziti	1 serving	1 serving	1½ servings
mixed salad greens with	1 cup	1 cup	2 cups
balsamic vinegar	1 tablespoon	1 tablespoon	2 tablespoons
Snack			
baked tortilla chips with	13	13	26
Turkish White-Bean Dip	¼ cup	¼ cup	½ cup

DAILY TOTALS			
Calories	1,516	2,001	2,504
Fat (g.)	32	45	53
% of calories from fat	18	19	19
Protein (g.)	80	115	139
Carbohydrates (g.)	238	297	383
Dietary fiber (g.)	27	36	46
Cholesterol (mg.)	97	151	172
Sodium (mg.)	1,450	2,071	2,592

NUTRIENT BONUS

This menu (at 2,000 calories) exceeds the Daily Value for:

Dietary fiber	142%
Vitamin A	189%
Thiamin	186%
Riboflavin	178%
Niacin	242%
Vitamin B$_6$	180%
Vitamin B$_{12}$	117%
Folate	183%
Vitamin C	587%
Vitamin E	119%
Iron	168%
Calcium	122%

HEALTHY TIP OF THE DAY

Sometimes even healthy-sounding foods are loaded with fat—like stuffed vegetables, twice-baked potatoes, and frozen breaded fish. Fats are also found in bagel chips, pita chips, tortilla chips, popcorn, hot chocolate, and flavored instant coffees. Even granola bars, cereals, frozen waffles, muffins, and nondairy creamers can be suspect. Check food labels to make smart choices. Remember that labels list ingredients from the largest to the smallest quantities.

Pesto Chicken Picnic (page 210)

Nutrition Notes

Per serving

Calories 374
Fat 12.5 g.
% of calories from fat 30
Protein 28.9 g.
Carbohydrates 37 g.
Dietary fiber 6.4 g.
Cholesterol 53 mg.
Sodium 551 mg.

Kitchen Hints

◆ To butterfly a chicken breast, make a horizontal cut into the thickest part of the breast, being careful not to cut all the way through. Open as you would a book so the piece lies flat. Cover the chicken with plastic wrap and gently flatten with a smooth-bottomed meat mallet to an even thickness.

◆ Loaves of bread make wonderful serving bowls for salads, dips, and condiments, such as pickles, olives, roasted peppers, marinated mushrooms, and grilled vegetables. Try using assorted shapes and sizes of bread. Remove a slice from the top. Scoop out the soft insides. Before filling, bake at 200°F for 2 hours, or until completely dry.

Pesto Chicken Picnic

MAKES 6 SERVINGS

Layers of pesto, chicken, and vegetables fill this crusty loaf, which makes a perfect on-the-go lunch.

Pesto

2 cups packed fresh spinach leaves, trimmed and washed
1 cup packed fresh basil
1/3 cup defatted reduced-sodium chicken broth
2 tablespoons grated Parmesan cheese
2 tablespoons toasted pine nuts
1 tablespoon olive oil
1 tablespoon nonfat sour cream

Sandwiches

1 pound boneless, skinless chicken breasts, butterflied (see hint)
1 large round loaf crusty bread
2 tablespoons sliced kalamata olives
2 ounces thinly sliced prosciutto
2 roasted sweet yellow or red peppers
1 cup thawed frozen artichoke hearts, patted dry
2 tomatoes, sliced
3 ounces sliced reduced-fat mozzarella cheese

To make the pesto: In a food processor or blender, combine the spinach, basil, broth, Parmesan, pine nuts, oil, and sour cream. Process until smooth.

To make the sandwiches: Coat a grill rack or broiler pan with no-stick spray. Preheat the grill or broiler. Cook the chicken 4" from the heat for 3 to 4 minutes per side, or until no longer pink in the center when tested with a sharp knife. Transfer to a plate and coat both sides of the pieces with the pesto.

Slice the bread in half horizontally. Scoop out about 1" of the soft bread center from each half; reserve for another use. On the bottom half of the bread, layer the olives, prosciutto, chicken, peppers, artichokes, tomatoes, and mozzarella. Cover with the top half of the bread and cut into wedges.

Baked Ziti

Reduced-fat mozzarella and broiled chicken breast lighten this pasta classic.

Tomato Sauce

- 1 teaspoon olive oil
- 1 large onion, chopped
- ¼ cup chopped sun-dried tomatoes
- 2 cloves garlic, cut into matchsticks
- 1 can (15 ounces) no-salt-added chopped tomatoes (with juice)
- 1 can (15 ounces) no-salt-added crushed tomatoes
- ¼ cup vermouth or nonalcoholic white wine
- 1 tablespoon chopped fresh basil
- 2 teaspoons chopped fresh rosemary
- 2 teaspoons chopped fresh sage
- ¼ teaspoon ground black pepper

Pasta and Chicken

- 8 ounces ziti
- 8 ounces boneless, skinless chicken breasts
- 1 cup shredded reduced-fat mozzarella cheese
- 1 tablespoon chopped fresh basil
- 1 tablespoon grated Parmesan cheese

To make the tomato sauce: Warm the oil in a large saucepan over medium heat. Add the onions and sun-dried tomatoes. Cook for 5 minutes, or until softened. Add the garlic; cook for 2 minutes. Stir in the chopped tomatoes (with juice), crushed tomatoes, vermouth or wine, basil, rosemary, sage, and pepper. Simmer for 25 minutes.

To make the pasta and chicken: Cook the ziti in a pot of boiling water according to the package directions. Drain; transfer to a large bowl.

Preheat the broiler. Coat a baking sheet with no-stick spray and place the chicken on the sheet. Broil 4" from the heat for 4 to 5 minutes per side, or until no longer pink in the center when tested with a sharp knife. Slice the chicken into 2" strips. Add to the ziti. Add the tomato sauce and mix well.

Change the oven temperature to 350°F. Coat a 9" × 9" baking dish with no-stick spray. Add half of the ziti mixture. Sprinkle with ½ cup of the mozzarella. Top with the remaining ziti mixture and the remaining ½ cup mozzarella. Sprinkle with the basil and Parmesan. Cover with foil and bake for 15 minutes. Remove the foil and bake for 10 minutes, or until lightly browned.

Nutrition Notes

Per serving

Calories 428
Fat 7.6 g.
% of calories from fat 16
Protein 30 g.
Carbohydrates 56.6 g.
Dietary fiber 6.7 g.
Cholesterol 43 mg.
Sodium 453 mg.

Kitchen Hints

◆ Both the pasta and the sauce can be cooked the day before assembling. Mix the drained pasta with 2 tablespoons defatted chicken broth to prevent it from sticking together. Refrigerate the pasta and sauce in separate airtight containers.

◆ To cut the garlic into matchsticks, make a series of lengthwise cuts through the side, keeping the pieces attached at the root end. Carefully turn the garlic so it lies flat, then make another series of lengthwise cuts through the top. Cut off the root end to free the pieces.

Nutrition Notes

Per ¼ cup

Calories 55
Fat 2.1 g.
% of calories from fat 34
Protein 3.1 g.
Carbohydrates 8.6 g.
Dietary fiber 2.4 g.
Cholesterol 0 mg.
Sodium 55 mg.

Kitchen Hint

◆ Arugula, also known as rocket or roquette, is a pungent, peppery green. It's available in most markets in the summer months, and it's also very easy to grow in your home garden. The smaller the leaf, the more mellow the flavor.

Turkish White-Bean Dip

MAKES 1¼ CUPS

Serve this creamy dip with low-fat tortilla chips, pita chips, raw vegetables, crackers, or bread.

1 can (16 ounces) white beans, such as cannellini or great Northern, rinsed and drained
2 teaspoons extra-virgin olive oil
2 teaspoons lime juice
1 teaspoon ground cumin
1 teaspoon minced garlic
¼ cup chopped arugula or watercress
Salt and ground black pepper

In a food processor or blender, combine the beans, oil, lime juice, cumin, and garlic. Process until smooth.

Transfer to a small bowl. Stir in the arugula or watercress and season with the salt and pepper.

What Is Low-Fat?

Thanks to government labeling laws, terms like *low-fat* must mean the same thing to all food manufacturers. The next time you see nutrient content claims on food labels, here's what they really mean.

Food Label Claim	Legal Definition
Low-fat	3 grams (or less) of fat per serving
Fat-free	Less than 0.5 gram of fat per serving and does not contain added fats
Light or lite	One-third fewer calories or 50 percent less fat than the higher-calorie, higher-fat version
Reduced	At least 25 percent less of a nutrient (such as calories, fat, or sodium) than the original food
Lean	Less than 10 grams of fat, 4 grams or less of saturated fat, and less than 95 milligrams of cholesterol per serving
Extra-lean	Less than 5 grams of fat, less than 2 grams of saturated fat, and less than 95 milligrams of cholesterol per serving
Low-cholesterol	20 milligrams (or less) of cholesterol and 2 grams (or less) of saturated fat per serving
Cholesterol-free	Less than 2 milligrams of cholesterol and 2 grams (or less) of saturated fat per serving
Low-sodium	140 milligrams (or less) of sodium per serving

Summer Menu Thirteen

	1,500 CALORIES 33-43 G. FAT	2,000 CALORIES 44-56 G. FAT	2,500 CALORIES 57-69 G. FAT
Breakfast			
nonfat cottage cheese	½ cup	¾ cup	1 cup
mango slices	¾ cup	1 cup	1 cup
whole-grain toast with	1 slice	2 slices	3 slices
jam	1 tablespoon	2 tablespoons	3 tablespoons
Lunch			
Garden Salad Pizza	2 slices	3 slices	3 slices
nonfat reduced-sodium bean soup	1 cup	1½ cups	1½ cups
Dinner			
Home-Run Hamburgers	1	1	2
baked sweet potato	1	1	1
Peach-Blueberry Crisp with	1 serving	1 serving	1 serving
frozen nonfat vani8lla yogurt	½ cup	½ cup	½ cup
Snack			
frozen green grapes	½ cup	1 cup	1 cup

Daily Totals			
Calories	1,514	1,994	2,484
Fat (g.)	23	29	37
% of calories from fat	13	13	13
Protein (g.)	88	116	155
Carbohydrates (g.)	250	332	401
Dietary fiber (g.)	35	48	55
Cholesterol (mg.)	87	99	154
Sodium (mg.)	1,892	2,712	3,462

Nutrient Bonus

This menu (at 2,000 calories) exceeds the Daily Value for:

Dietary fiber	193%
Vitamin A	941%
Riboflavin	111%
Vitamin C	265%
Calcium	118%

Healthy Tip of the Day

Kick it up with condiments. Add zip and zest to your favorite dishes with low-fat, low-calorie condiments like ketchup, salsa, chili sauce, barbecue sauce, taco sauce, teriyaki sauce, Dijon mustard, yellow mustard, chutney, roasted red peppers, nonfat mayonnaise, nonfat sour cream, and nonfat salad dressings. These condiments save you the 11 grams of fat per tablespoon found in regular mayonnaise. Other high-fat add-ons to avoid include tartar sauce, Thousand Island dressing, cheese sauce, hollandaise sauce, and béarnaise sauce.

Peach-Blueberry Crisp

Peach-Blueberry Crisp

MAKES 8 SERVINGS

Lots of fruit plus oats in the topping make this easy dessert a good source of soluble fiber. It's great served with frozen nonfat vanilla yogurt.

Filling

2	pounds ripe peaches, peeled, pitted, and cut into $1/2$" slices
2	cups blueberries
$1/4$	cup sugar
$1/3$	cup apricot nectar or peach nectar
2	tablespoons all-purpose flour
1	tablespoon lemon juice

Topping

$1/2$	cup all-purpose flour
$1/4$	cup rolled oats
2	tablespoons sugar
2	tablespoons packed light brown sugar
$1/2$	teaspoon ground cinnamon
3	tablespoons cold unsalted butter or margarine, cut into small pieces

To make the filling: Preheat the oven to 375°F. Coat a 9" × 9" baking dish with no-stick spray.

In a large bowl, stir together the peaches, blueberries, sugar, apricot nectar or peach nectar, flour, and lemon juice. Pour into the prepared baking dish.

To make the topping: In a medium bowl, mix the flour, oats, sugar, brown sugar, and cinnamon. Cut in the butter or margarine until the mixture resembles coarse meal. Sprinkle over the fruit.

Bake for 45 to 50 minutes, or until the top is lightly browned. Let cool for 10 minutes before serving.

Nutrition Notes

Per serving

Calories 200
Fat 4.8 g.
% of calories from fat 21
Protein 2.4 g.
Carbohydrates 39.1 g.
Dietary fiber 3.2 g.
Cholesterol 12 mg.
Sodium 4 mg.

Kitchen Hint

◆ To peel peaches, drop them into boiling water for about 20 seconds. Remove with a slotted spoon and run under cold water. Use a paring knife to score the peel and remove it.

Nutrition Notes

Per slice

Calories 161
Fat 4.4 g.
% of calories from fat 24
Protein 9 g.
Carbohydrates 21.6 g.
Dietary fiber 1.4 g.
Cholesterol 7 mg.
Sodium 327 mg.

Kitchen Hints

◆ Anchovy paste is a mixture of ground anchovies, vinegar, and olive oil. It makes a flavorful addition to sauces and dressings for vegetables or pasta. The flavor is very concentrated, so you need only a small amount. It is available in the international section of most supermarkets.

◆ If desired, you can seed the tomato before slicing it. Cut it in half crosswise. Place one of the halves in the palm of your hand, invert your palm, and gently apply pressure to squeeze out the seeds (use your fingers to help draw the seeds out). Lay the tomato, flat side down, on a cutting board and slice with a serrated knife.

Garden Salad Pizza

MAKES 8 SLICES

Here are two meals in one. A crunchy romaine salad sits atop a tomato-and-onion pizza. This vegetable-rich dish is a great source of the antioxidant vitamins A and C.

2	tablespoons cornmeal
1	teaspoon olive oil
1	large red onion, halved and thinly sliced
1	tube (10 ounces) pizza dough
2	large tomatoes, thinly sliced
1	cup shredded reduced-fat mozzarella cheese
¼	cup nonfat plain yogurt
2	tablespoons grated Parmesan cheese
1	small clove garlic, minced
½	teaspoon balsamic vinegar
½	teaspoon Dijon mustard
¼	teaspoon anchovy paste (see hint)
¼	teaspoon Worcestershire sauce
2	cups packed torn romaine lettuce
¼	cup coarsely chopped fresh basil

Preheat the oven to 400°F. Coat a baking sheet with no-stick spray. Sprinkle with the cornmeal.

Warm the oil in a large no-stick skillet over medium heat. Add the onions and cook for 12 minutes, or until golden brown. Let cool for 5 minutes.

Roll the pizza dough into a 12" circle. Transfer to the baking sheet. Sprinkle the onions over the dough, arrange the tomatoes on top, and sprinkle with the mozzarella. Bake for 10 to 12 minutes, or until the bottom crust is browned and the cheese is melted.

In a medium bowl, combine the yogurt, Parmesan, garlic, vinegar, mustard, anchovy paste, and Worcestershire sauce. Mix well. Add the lettuce and basil; toss to coat.

Spread the salad over the hot pizza.

Home - Run Hamburgers

MAKES 6

These burgers are a grand slam! Lean ground round keeps fat grams in check. To give the burger a winning source a calcium, add a slice of reduced-fat cheese.

    3 tablespoons bulgur
   1/3 cup boiling water
    1 teaspoon olive oil
    1 medium Vidalia onion, thinly sliced
  1 1/2 cups sliced shiitake mushrooms
  1 1/4 pounds extra-lean ground beef round
   1/3 cup fresh bread crumbs
   1/4 cup chopped fresh Italian parsley
    2 tablespoons Worcestershire sauce
    2 tablespoons tomato paste
    2 cloves garlic, minced
    1 teaspoon ground black pepper
   1/2 teaspoon dry mustard
    3 dashes hot-pepper sauce
    2 drops liquid smoke (optional)
    6 whole-wheat hamburger buns, split
    6 leaves red leaf lettuce
    6 tomato slices

Place the bulgur in a large bowl. Add the water. Cover and let stand for 15 minutes, or until soft.

Warm the oil in a large no-stick skillet over medium heat. Add the onions and cook for 10 minutes, or until very soft. Add the mushrooms and sauté for 5 minutes, or until soft.

Drain the bulgur and return it to the bowl. Stir in the beef, bread crumbs, parsley, Worcestershire sauce, tomato paste, garlic, black pepper, mustard, hot-pepper sauce, and liquid smoke (if using). Shape the mixture into six 1"-thick patties.

Coat a grill rack or broiler pan with no-stick spray. Preheat the grill or broiler. Cook the burgers 4" from the heat for 3 to 4 minutes per side for medium doneness. Set a burger on the bottom half of each bun. Divide the sautéed onions and mushrooms among the burgers and top each with lettuce, tomato, and the top halves of the buns.

Nutrition Notes

Per hamburger

Calories 312
Fat 7.1 g.
% of calories from fat 20
Protein 27.3 g.
Carbohydrates 37.8 g.
Dietary fiber 4.4 g.
Cholesterol 51 mg.
Sodium 425 mg.

Kitchen Hint

◆ To get the leanest ground beef available, ask your butcher to trim all of the fat from a 1 1/4-pound beef round steak and then grind it. Your lean beef will derive only 26 percent of its calories from fat—a lot less than the 80 percent in typical ground beef.

Summer Menu Fourteen

	1,500 CALORIES	2,000 CALORIES	2,500 CALORIES
	33-43 G. FAT	44-56 G. FAT	57-69 G. FAT

Breakfast

Sour Cream Waffles with	2	2	3
maple syrup and	2 tablespoons	2 tablespoons	3 tablespoons
blackberries	½ cup	½ cup	¾ cup
skim milk	1 cup	1 cup	2 cups

Lunch

Portobello Burgers with Shoestring Fries	1 serving	2 servings	2 servings
spinach salad with	1 cup	2 cups	3 cups
nonfat dressing	1 tablespoon	2 tablespoons	3 tablespoons

Dinner

grilled salmon steak	4 ounces	5 ounces	6 ounces
Grilled Shrimp and Corn Salad	1 serving	1 serving	1 serving
steamed green beans	½ cup	¾ cup	1 cup
fruit sorbet	½ cup	¾ cup	1¼ cups

Snack

papaya slices	¾ cup	1 cup	1½ cups

DAILY TOTALS			
Calories	1,495	1,983	2,498
Fat (g.)	24	30	35
% of calories from fat	14	13	12
Protein (g.)	88	113	139
Carbohydrates (g.)	241	330	422
Dietary fiber (g.)	20	29	35
Cholesterol (mg.)	291	308	372
Sodium (mg.)	1,611	2,196	2,766

NUTRIENT BONUS

This menu (at 2,000 calories) exceeds the Daily Value for:

Dietary fiber	118%
Vitamin A	253%
Thiamin	111%
Riboflavin	175%
Niacin	171%
Vitamin B$_6$	147%
Vitamin B$_{12}$	150%
Folate	148%
Vitamin C	394%
Calcium	103%
Potassium	171%

HEALTHY TIP OF THE DAY

Pantothenate is a B vitamin that's essential for synthesizing and metabolizing fats in your body. The recommended intake is 4 to 7 milligrams per day. Today's menu provides more than 100 percent of the recommended intake, most of it coming from the portobello mushrooms. Other foods high in pantothenate include blue cheese, brewer's yeast, corn, eggs, lentils, liver, fish, shellfish, sunflower seeds, and green peas.

Sour Cream Waffles (page 220) with confectioners' sugar and berries

Sour Cream Waffles

Nonfat sour cream and nonfat vanilla yogurt moisten these waffles, reducing the need for added butter—and making the waffles a good source of calcium. Top them with fresh fruit and maple syrup.

¾	cup skim milk
½	cup nonfat vanilla yogurt
¼	cup nonfat sour cream
2	egg yolks
1	tablespoon canola oil
1	teaspoon vanilla
1¾	cups cake flour (see hint)
2	teaspoons baking powder
½	teaspoon baking soda
¼	teaspoon salt
½	cup sugar
4	egg whites

Preheat a waffle iron according to the manufacturer's directions.

In a small bowl, combine the milk, yogurt, sour cream, egg yolks, oil, and vanilla. Mix well.

In a large bowl, combine the flour, baking powder, baking soda, salt, and ¼ cup of the sugar. Mix well. Add the egg-yolk mixture and stir until the batter is smooth.

Place the egg whites in a medium bowl. Using an electric mixer, beat on medium speed until foamy. Gradually beat in the remaining ¼ cup sugar. Increase the speed to high and continue to beat until soft peaks form. Fold the egg-white mixture into the batter.

Spoon a scant ¾ cup batter into the center of the waffle iron. Cook until the waffle is golden brown and crispy. (Do not press on the iron during cooking or the waffle will collapse.) Repeat to make a total of 10 waffles.

Nutrition Notes

Per waffle

Calories 162
Fat 2.6 g.
% of calories from fat 14
Protein 5.1 g.
Carbohydrates 29.3 g.
Dietary fiber 0.3 g.
Cholesterol 43 mg.
Sodium 259 mg.

Kitchen Hints

◆ You can replace the cake flour with 1½ cups all-purpose flour mixed with 3 tablespoons cornstarch.

◆ To save time in the morning, partially prepare the batter the night before. In a small bowl, combine the liquid ingredients except for the eggs. Cover the bowl and refrigerate. In a large bowl, combine the dry ingredients and cover with plastic wrap. In the morning, mix the egg yolks into the liquid ingredients, beat the egg whites and sugar, and follow the rest of the directions.

◆ For a nice presentation, dust the waffles with confectioners' sugar.

◆ Store leftover waffles in the freezer. Wrap them in a double layer of plastic and foil.

Portobello Burgers with Shoestring Fries

MAKES 4 SERVINGS

Portobello mushrooms are a unique alternative to beef burgers. They grill up thick, meaty, and juicy. Crispy fries complete the meal.

Shoestring Fries

2	egg whites
½	teaspoon paprika
¼	teaspoon garlic powder
2	pounds baking potatoes, cut lengthwise into thin strips

Mushroom Burgers

1	hard-cooked egg white, finely chopped
2	tablespoons nonfat mayonnaise
1	tablespoon minced shallots
1	tablespoon chili sauce
1	teaspoon sweet pickle relish
4	large portobello mushroom caps
	Salt and ground black pepper
4	whole-wheat hamburger buns
4	leaves lettuce
4	tomato slices

To make the shoestring fries: Preheat the oven to 425°F. Line 2 baking sheets with foil and coat with no-stick spray.

In a large bowl, whisk together the egg whites, paprika, and garlic powder. Add the potatoes and toss to coat. Transfer to the prepared baking sheets, allowing the excess egg whites to drain off. Bake for 15 minutes. Switch the position of the baking sheets. Bake for 10 to 15 minutes, or until golden brown and crispy.

To make the mushroom burgers: Coat a grill rack or broiler pan with no-stick spray. Preheat the grill or broiler.

In a small bowl, combine the egg whites, mayonnaise, shallots, chili sauce, and relish.

Coat the mushroom caps with no-stick spray and season with the salt and pepper. Cook 4" from the heat for 3 to 4 minutes per side, or until soft and tender.

If desired, lightly toast the buns on the grill or under the broiler. Place a lettuce leaf and tomato slice on the bottom half of each bun. Top with a mushroom cap, the seasoned mayonnaise, and the other half of the bun. Serve with the shoestring fries.

Nutrition Notes

Per serving

Calories 348
Fat 2.9 g.
% of calories from fat 7
Protein 13.8 g.
Carbohydrates 70.1 g.
Dietary fiber 6.5 g.
Cholesterol 0 mg.
Sodium 436 mg.

Kitchen Hint

◆ Look for firm, solid-colored mushrooms that are dry to the touch. Clean mushrooms by wiping them with a damp paper towel or soft mushroom brush.

Nutrition Notes

Per serving

Calories 234
Fat 6.2 g.
% of calories from fat 22
Protein 20.7 g.
Carbohydrates 27.8 g.
Dietary fiber 4.6 g.
Cholesterol 137 mg.
Sodium 283 mg.

Kitchen Hint

◆ To get more juice out of citrus fruits, roll them on a countertop before juicing. Apply gentle pressure with the palm of your hand and roll the fruit forward and backward. Another trick is to pierce the fruit with a fork and warm in a microwave on high power for 30 seconds.

Grilled Shrimp and Corn Salad

MAKES 4 SERVINGS

This vibrant low-fat summer salad is a good source of fiber, vitamin A, folate, and potassium.

Dressing

½	ripe avocado, pitted and peeled
3	tablespoons lime juice
1	cup 1% low-fat buttermilk
1	tablespoon chopped fresh basil
1	teaspoon honey
	Ground black pepper

Salad

1	pound medium shrimp, peeled and deveined
	Salt and ground black pepper
3	ears corn, husks and silks removed
2	plum tomatoes, chopped
½	cup seeded and chopped English cucumbers
⅓	cup chopped red onions
4	cups mixed torn greens

To make the dressing: In a food processor or blender, puree the avocado and lime juice. Add the buttermilk, basil, honey, and pepper. Process until smooth.

To make the salad: Coat a grill rack or broiler pan with no-stick spray. Preheat the grill or broiler.

Season the shrimp with the salt and pepper and thread onto metal skewers, leaving about ¼" between the pieces. Cook 4" from the heat for 2 to 3 minutes per side, or until opaque and cooked through. Remove from the skewers and transfer to a large bowl.

Cook the corn in a large pot of boiling water for 3 minutes. Remove from the water and place on the grill or under the broiler for 5 minutes, turning every minute, until the corn is speckled with golden brown spots. Set aside for 5 minutes to cool. Slice the kernels off the cobs and add to the bowl with the shrimp. Stir in the tomatoes, cucumbers, and onions. Toss with the dressing.

Serve on a bed of the greens.

Summer Menu Fifteen

	1,500 CALORIES 33-43 G. FAT	2,000 CALORIES 44-56 G. FAT	2,500 CALORIES 57-69 G. FAT
Breakfast			
Caribbean Fruit Frappé	1 serving	1 serving	2 servings
scrambled fat-free egg substitute	½ cup	½ cup	¾ cup
toasted wheat pita	1	1	2
Lunch			
low-sodium ham and	4 ounces	4 ounces	5 ounces
low-fat, low-sodium Swiss cheese on	2 ounces	2 ounces	3 ounces
rye bread with	2 slices	2 slices	2 slices
country Dijon mustard,	1 tablespoon	1 tablespoon	1 tablespoon
lettuce, and	1 leaf	1 leaf	1 leaf
tomato	2 slices	2 slices	2 slices
baked potato chips	12	12	24
cherries	½ cup	¾ cup	¾ cup
Dinner			
grilled veal loin	4 ounces	6 ounces	6 ounces
sautéed tomatoes and yellow squash	1 cup	1½ cups	2 cups
Sweet-Potato Soufflé	1 serving	2 servings	2 servings
Snack			
Raspberry Swirl Brownies	1	2	2

Daily Totals			
Calories	1,500	1,995	2,507
Fat (g.)	40	53	64
% of calories from fat	23	23	22
Protein (g.)	98	119	147
Carbohydrates (g.)	194	270	351
Dietary fiber (g.)	21	27	37
Cholesterol (mg.)	222	287	323
Sodium (mg.)	2,421	2,603	3,291

Nutrient Bonus

This menu (at 2,000 calories) exceeds the Daily Value for:

Dietary fiber	107%
Vitamin A	894%
Niacin	128%
Vitamin C	223%

Healthy Tip of the Day

Go tropical. Fruits like papayas, pineapples, and mangoes are excellent sources of immunity-boosting antioxidants. The recommended daily intakes for these vitamins: 15 to 20 milligrams of beta-carotene, 60 milligrams of vitamin C, and 30 international units of vitamin E. One mango provides 5 milligrams of beta-carotene, 57 milligrams of vitamin C, and 2 milligrams of vitamin E. One cup of cubed papaya supplies 87 milligrams of vitamin C, and 1 cup of diced pineapple contains 24 milligrams vitamin C.

Raspberry Swirl Brownies

Raspberry Swirl Brownies

MAKES 12

Experience decadence without denial in these rich brownies marbled with juicy raspberries. The secret? Naturally fat-free cocoa delivers intense chocolate flavor, while a small amount of unsweetened chocolate adds rich texture.

1⅔ cups confectioners' sugar
⅔ cup cake flour (see hint)
¼ cup unsweetened cocoa powder
¾ teaspoon baking powder
⅛ teaspoon salt
1½ ounces unsweetened chocolate
2½ tablespoons canola oil
2 tablespoons dark corn syrup
2 teaspoons raspberry liqueur or vanilla
2 egg whites
2 tablespoons raspberry jam
1 cup raspberries

Preheat the oven to 350°F. Line a 9" × 9" baking dish with foil, wrapping the excess foil over the handles. Coat with no-stick spray.

In a medium bowl, combine the confectioners' sugar, flour, cocoa, baking powder, and salt. Mix well.

In a large microwave-safe bowl, combine the chocolate and oil. Microwave on high power for 1 minute. Stir until the chocolate is completely melted and smooth. Stir in the corn syrup, raspberry liqueur or vanilla, and egg whites. Mix well. Gently stir in the flour mixture just until blended.

Place the jam in a small microwave-safe bowl. Microwave on high power for 1 minute, or until melted. Stir in the raspberries. Carefully fold into the batter, keeping most of the berries whole.

Spoon the batter into the prepared baking dish and spread evenly. Bake for 22 to 26 minutes, or until the center of the surface is almost firm when tapped. Cool in the pan on a wire rack for 15 minutes. Using the overhanging foil as handles, lift the brownies from the pan and return to the wire rack. Let cool completely.

Cut into bars, wiping the knife blade between cuts.

Nutrition Notes

Per brownie

Calories 149
Fat 5.2 g.
% of calories from fat 29
Protein 1.9 g.
Carbohydrates 26.1 g.
Dietary fiber 1.7 g.
Cholesterol 0 mg.
Sodium 70 mg.

Kitchen Hints

◆ You can replace the cake flour with ½ cup all-purpose flour mixed with 2 tablespoons cornstarch.

◆ To make cutting sticky desserts easier, remove from the pan and slice with unwaxed dental floss. Cut a piece of floss several inches longer than the dessert that you're cutting. Hold the floss taut over the dessert, then lower your hands so the floss cuts through it. Let go of one end and pull the floss out through the other side.

Nutrition Notes

Per serving

Calories 115
Fat 1.4 g.
% of calories from fat 10
Protein 2 g.
Carbohydrates 25.8 g.
Dietary fiber 2.7 g.
Cholesterol 3 mg.
Sodium 27 mg.

Kitchen Hints

◆ Coconut extract is available in the spice section of most supermarkets. You can replace it with $\frac{1}{2}$ teaspoon rum extract or vanilla.

◆ Blender drinks are perfect for any time of day. Try interesting combinations such as carrot juice, lime juice, strawberries, and fresh basil; peaches, cold herb tea, and fresh mint; or watermelon, cantaloupe, and plain yogurt.

Caribbean Fruit Frappé

<u>MAKES 4 SERVINGS</u>

Nothing could be more refreshing—or easier—than this vitamin-rich combination of tropical fruits and ice cream. Just plug in your blender, and you'll be sipping your way to the islands.

$1\frac{1}{2}$ cups chopped pineapple
1 cup low-fat vanilla ice cream
1 mango, chopped
2 tablespoons lime juice
$\frac{1}{2}$ teaspoon coconut extract

In a blender or food processor, puree the pineapple, ice cream, mango, lime juice, and coconut extract until smooth. Serve in tall glasses.

Sweet-Potato Soufflé

MAKES 6 SERVINGS

If you have baked sweet potatoes on hand, it takes no time at all to whip up this light soufflé. It's a perfect complement to grilled meats. Like other soufflés, this is best served immediately.

Topping

- ¼ cup packed light brown sugar
- 2 tablespoons all-purpose flour
- 2 tablespoons chopped toasted walnuts
- 1 tablespoon cold unsalted butter or margarine, cut into small pieces

Soufflé

- 2 pounds sweet potatoes, baked
- 1 orange
- ¼ cup maple syrup
- 1 tablespoon minced crystallized ginger
- 2 egg whites
  Pinch of cream of tartar

To make the topping: In a small bowl, combine the brown sugar, flour, and walnuts. Cut in the butter or margarine until well-distributed.

To make the soufflé: Preheat the oven to 350°F. Coat a 1½-quart baking dish with no-stick spray.

Peel the sweet potatoes and place in a large bowl; mash well.

Grate 1 teaspoon rind from the orange and add to the bowl. Cut the orange in half and squeeze 3 tablespoons juice into the bowl. Discard the remaining orange or reserve for another use. Stir in the maple syrup and ginger.

Place the egg whites and cream of tartar in a medium bowl. Using an electric mixer, beat on medium speed until foamy. Increase the speed to high and continue to beat until the whites are firm and glossy. Fold the whites into the sweet-potato mixture.

Spoon the mixture into the prepared baking dish and sprinkle with the topping. Bake for 40 minutes, or until lightly browned.

Nutrition Notes

Per serving

Calories 206
Fat 3.6 g.
% of calories from fat 15
Protein 3.8 g.
Carbohydrates 41.1 g.
Dietary fiber 3 g.
Cholesterol 5 mg.
Sodium 54 mg.

Kitchen Hint

◆ Egg whites achieve more volume if they're at room temperature when you beat them. To quickly take the chill off cold raw eggs in the shell, place them in a bowl of warm water for a few minutes.

Summer Menu Sixteen

	1,500 CALORIES	2,000 CALORIES	2,500 CALORIES
	33-43 G. FAT	44-56 G. FAT	57-69 G. FAT

Breakfast

Dried Apricot and Currant Scones	2	2	3
skim milk	1 cup	1 cup	1½ cups

Lunch

Chop-Chop Salad	1 serving	2 servings	2 servings
multigrain roll	1	2	2
nonfat reduced-sodium lentil soup	1 cup	1½ cups	1½ cups

Dinner

grilled mahimahi	4 ounces	5 ounces	6 ounces
Vegetable Pancakes	2	2	4
papaya and banana slices	1 cup	2 cups	2 cups

Snack

nonfat pudding	1 cup	1¼ cups	1¼ cups

DAILY TOTALS

Calories	1,478	2,015	2,500
Fat (g.)	20	27	35
% of calories from fat	12	12	13
Protein (g.)	79	111	132
Carbohydrates (g.)	237	324	406
Dietary fiber (g.)	33	49	57
Cholesterol (mg.)	67	92	110
Sodium (mg.)	1,737	2,471	3,043

NUTRIENT BONUS

This menu (at 2,000 calories) exceeds the Daily Value for:

Dietary fiber	193%
Vitamin A	511%
Thiamin	118%
Riboflavin	118%
Niacin	122%
Vitamin B₆	104%
Vitamin C	306%
Calcium	173%
Iron	114%
Potassium	127%

HEALTHY TIP OF THE DAY

Eat a variety of foods for more minerals. Minerals are used by our bodies to regulate metabolic processes. For instance, iron in red blood cells transports oxygen from the lungs to the muscles. Meats, fish, and poultry are rich in iron, zinc, copper, and other trace minerals. Whole-grain foods are packed with iron, zinc, copper, and magnesium. Fruits and vegetables provide potassium and magnesium. Dairy products are often high in calcium and potassium.

Chop-Chop Salad (page 231)

Nutrition Notes

Per scone

Calories 162
Fat 3.4 g.
% of calories from fat 18
Protein 3.3 g.
Carbohydrates 30.5 g.
Dietary fiber 1.5 g.
Cholesterol 5 mg.
Sodium 222 mg.

Kitchen Hints

◆ Create your own signature scone with any of these dried fruit combinations: cherries and dates, cranberries and apples, or pineapple and papaya.

◆ These scones can be made the day before serving and stored in plastic bags. If desired, reheat briefly in a toaster oven.

Dried Apricot and Currant Scones

MAKES 12

Butter-packed scones have long been on the list of forbidden favorites. But you can put scones back on the healthy menu with this delicious low-fat rendition. These scones are flaky and flavorful thanks to nonfat yogurt, skim milk, and just 3 tablespoons of added fat. The currants and dried apricots provide extra fiber and vitamin A.

> 2 cups all-purpose flour
> 1/3 cup sugar
> 1 tablespoon baking powder
> 1/2 teaspoon salt
> 2 tablespoons cold unsalted butter or margarine, cut into small pieces
> 1 tablespoon canola oil
> 1/2 cup dried apricots, slivered
> 1/2 cup currants
> 1/2 cup nonfat plain yogurt
> 3 tablespoons skim milk

Preheat the oven to 425°F. Coat a baking sheet with no-stick spray.

In a large bowl, combine the flour, sugar, baking powder, and salt. Cut in the butter or margarine and oil until the mixture resembles fine meal. Add the apricots and currants and toss to combine. Stir in the yogurt and milk until just incorporated.

Transfer to a lightly floured surface and pat out to an 8" circle. Cut into 12 wedges and place on the prepared baking sheet, being careful not to let the pieces touch. Bake for 12 to 15 minutes, or until lightly browned on top. Cool slightly on a wire rack and serve warm.

Chop-Chop Salad

MAKES 4 SERVINGS

Chop, chop—and it's ready to eat! Chopped vegetables, smoked turkey breast, reduced-fat Swiss cheese, and chickpeas are tossed with a creamy low-fat herb dressing in this vitamin-packed salad. Use whatever combination of herbs you like. Basil, tarragon, dill, Italian parsley, and cilantro are good choices.

Dressing

⅔	cup 1% low-fat buttermilk
¼	cup nonfat mayonnaise
¼	cup nonfat sour cream
¼	cup chopped fresh herbs
1	tablespoon lime juice
¼	teaspoon garlic powder
¼	teaspoon ground black pepper
⅛	teaspoon ground cumin

Salad

2	cups chopped romaine lettuce
1	cup chopped Belgian endive
½	cup chopped radicchio
½	cup cooked chickpeas
½	cup sliced radishes
½	cup chopped celery
¼	cup chopped carrots
¼	cup chopped sweet red peppers
¼	cup frozen corn kernels, thawed
2	ounces smoked turkey breast, diced
2	ounces reduced-fat Swiss cheese, diced

To make the dressing: In a medium bowl, combine the buttermilk, mayonnaise, sour cream, herbs, lime juice, garlic powder, pepper, and cumin. Stir until thoroughly blended.

To make the salad: In a large bowl, combine the lettuce, endive, radicchio, chickpeas, radishes, celery, carrots, peppers, corn, turkey, and Swiss. Pour the dressing over the salad and toss to combine.

Nutrition Notes

Per serving

Calories 169
Fat 4.3 g.
% of calories from fat 23
Protein 12.7 g.
Carbohydrates 20 g.
Dietary fiber 2.7 g.
Cholesterol 17 mg.
Sodium 403 mg.

Kitchen Hints

◆ This salad is a great way to use leftover raw or cooked vegetables. You can also substitute other lean protein and reduced-fat cheese for the turkey and Swiss. Try lean ham, chicken breast, or grilled tempeh or tofu and Cheddar, Jarlsberg, or blue cheese.

◆ For a take-along salad, make the dressing up to 2 days in advance and refrigerate in a resealable plastic bag or an airtight container. Combine the vegetables the night before serving and refrigerate in a plastic bag. Add the turkey and cheese just before tossing with the dressing.

Vegetable Pancakes

MAKES 8

These tasty vegetable pancakes will make you an "ace" with the antioxidant vitamins A, C, and E.

1 cup coarsely chopped red potatoes
1 cup chopped onions
1 cup coarsely chopped mushrooms
1 teaspoon minced garlic
½ cup shredded zucchini
½ cup shredded carrots
¼ cup all-purpose flour
2 tablespoons chopped fresh Italian parsley
1 tablespoon chopped fresh thyme
¼ teaspoon salt
½ teaspoon ground black pepper
½ cup fat-free egg substitute
½ cup fresh whole-wheat bread crumbs
½ cup nonfat sour cream
½ cup mango chutney (see hint)

Place the potatoes in a medium saucepan. Cover with cold water and bring to a boil over high heat. Reduce the heat to medium and cook for 15 to 20 minutes, or until the potatoes are tender when tested with a sharp knife. Drain.

Coat a large no-stick skillet with no-stick spray and place over medium heat. Add the onions, mushrooms, and garlic. Cook, stirring often, for 5 minutes, or until the onions and mushrooms are golden. Add the potatoes, zucchini, and carrots. Cook, stirring often, for 3 minutes, or until the zucchini is wilted.

Add the flour, parsley, thyme, salt, and pepper. Cook, stirring constantly, for 3 minutes. Transfer the mixture to a large bowl and let cool for 2 minutes. Stir in the egg substitute and bread crumbs.

For each pancake, scoop out ¼ cup of the vegetable mixture and shape into a ¼"-thick patty.

Wipe out the skillet and coat with no-stick spray. Place over medium heat until hot. Add the pancakes and cook for 4 to 5 minutes, or until the bottoms are a deep golden brown. Coat the top of the pancakes with no-stick spray and turn over. Cook for 2 to 3 minutes, or until browned.

Serve with the sour cream and chutney.

Nutrition Notes

Per 2 pancakes

Calories 229
Fat 1.1 g.
% of calories from fat 4
Protein 10 g.
Carbohydrates 45.7 g.
Dietary fiber 4.6
Cholesterol 0 mg.
Sodium 364 mg.

Kitchen Hints

◆ Chutney is an Indian condiment made from fruit, spices, and vinegar. It is available in the condiment or international section of most supermarkets. Or check your local Indian or Middle Eastern grocery store.

◆ To serve these pancakes as an appetizer, drop rounded tablespoons of the batter into the pan and shape into coins with the back of a spoon. Cook for 1 to 2 minutes per side, or until browned.

Summer Menu Seventeen

	1,500 CALORIES 33-43 G. FAT	2,000 CALORIES 44-56 G. FAT	2,500 CALORIES 57-69 G. FAT
Breakfast			
bialy or bagel with	1	1½	2
nonfat cream cheese	2 tablespoons	3 tablespoons	4 tablespoons
low-sodium tomato juice	1 cup	1¼ cups	1¼ cups
nonfat fruit yogurt	½ cup	1 cup	1 cup
Lunch			
Lentil Salad	1½ servings	1½ servings	2 servings
pita bread	1	2	2
Dinner			
Grilled Swordfish with Blueberry Salsa	1 serving	1 serving	2 servings
Greek Salad	1 serving	1 serving	2 servings
cooked brown rice	1 cup	2 cups	2 cups
steamed broccoli	½ cup	1 cup	1 cup
Snack			
apricots	2	3	4
cherries	8	10	10

DAILY TOTALS			
Calories	1,522	2,025	2,519
Fat (g.)	28	35	47
% of calories from fat	16	15	16
Protein (g.)	83	107	142
Carbohydrates (g.)	250	342	408
Dietary fiber (g.)	39	52	64
Cholesterol (mg.)	68	80	126
Sodium (mg.)	1,449	2,143	2,697

NUTRIENT BONUS

This menu (at 2,000 calories) exceeds the Daily Value for:

Dietary fiber	210%
Vitamin A	233%
Thiamin	135%
Riboflavin	136%
Niacin	144%
Vitamin B$_6$	151%
Folate	184%
Vitamin C	604%
Vitamin E	120%
Calcium	129%
Iron	236%
Potassium	137%

HEALTHY TIP OF THE DAY

Check your protein intake. Protein comes mostly from foods like beef, poultry, eggs, nuts, beans, milk, and other dairy products. To determine the grams of protein that you need on a daily basis, divide your weight in pounds by 2.2 and multiply that number by 0.8. For example, 175 pounds ÷ 2.2 = 79.5 × 0.8 = 64. So a 175-pound person should get at least 64 grams of protein per day. Even without eating meat, most people can easily meet their protein needs.

Grilled Swordfish with Blueberry Salsa

Grilled Swordfish with Blueberry Salsa

MAKES 4 SERVINGS

This summery dish is high in protein and with virtually no saturated fat.

Salsa

1	cup blueberries, coarsely chopped
1	cup chopped watermelon
½	cup chopped tomatoes
¼	cup minced red onions
¼	cup minced sweet yellow peppers
⅓	cup chopped roasted sweet red peppers
1	jalapeño pepper, seeded and minced (wear plastic gloves when handling)
2	tablespoons chopped fresh basil
2	tablespoons orange juice
	Pinch of salt

Swordfish and Marinade

2	limes
1	orange
6	scallions, chopped
1	tablespoon honey
1	clove garlic, minced
1	teaspoon olive oil
½	teaspoon ground black pepper
4	swordfish fillets (4 ounces each)

To make the salsa: In a medium bowl, combine the blueberries, watermelon, tomatoes, onions, yellow peppers, red peppers, jalapeño peppers, basil, orange juice, and salt. Mix well. Cover and refrigerate for at least 2 hours.

To make the swordfish and marinade: Grate 1 teaspoon rind from 1 of the limes and place in a 9" × 9" baking dish. Cut both limes in half and squeeze ¼ cup juice into the dish. Grate 2 teaspoons rind from the orange and add to the dish. Cut the orange in half and squeeze ⅓ cup juice into the dish. Stir in the scallions, honey, garlic, oil, and pepper. Place the swordfish in the marinade and turn to coat. Cover and refrigerate for 1 hour; turn after 30 minutes. Remove 15 minutes before cooking.

Coat a grill rack or broiler pan with no-stick spray. Preheat the grill or broiler. Cook 4" from the heat for 4 to 5 minutes per side per 1" thickness, or until the fish is opaque and flakes easily when tested with a fork. Serve with the salsa.

Nutrition Notes

Per serving

Calories 197
Fat 4.8 g.
% of calories from fat 22
Protein 17.1 g.
Carbohydrates 22 g.
Dietary fiber 2.6 g.
Cholesterol 30 mg.
Sodium 113 mg.

Kitchen Hints

◆ When removing the ribs and seeds from hot chili peppers, remember to wear plastic gloves to protect your skin. Avoid touching your face and wash your hands with soap immediately after working with any hot pepper.

◆ The salsa can be made and refrigerated up to a day in advance.

Nutrition Notes

Per serving

Calories 249
Fat 6.4 g.
% of calories from fat 22
Protein 16.9 g.
Carbohydrates 33.2 g.
Dietary fiber 8.4 g.
Cholesterol 10 mg.
Sodium 172 mg.

Kitchen Hints

◆ Lentils—a nutritional powerhouse—are high in soluble fiber and folate. Because they don't need to be soaked before cooking like other beans, lentils make a great spur-of-the-moment addition to soups, stews, and salads.

◆ This salad tastes even better after the flavors have blended for a day. It can be made up to 3 days in advance.

Lentil Salad

MAKES 4 SERVINGS

Lentils are an outstanding source of plant-based protein and fiber. Here, they are tossed in a citrus vinaigrette with vegetables and goat cheese for a refreshing blend of flavors and textures.

¾ cup green or brown lentils, rinsed and drained
1 shallot, halved lengthwise
¼ teaspoon ground cloves
1 bay leaf
1 cup chopped celery
½ cup chopped sweet yellow peppers
½ cup finely chopped red onions
½ cup chopped plum tomatoes
3 ounces goat cheese, crumbled
2 tablespoons chopped fresh Italian parsley
2 tablespoons chopped fresh mint
3 tablespoons lemon juice
1 teaspoon honey
1 teaspoon walnut oil or olive oil
½ teaspoon chopped garlic
Salt and ground black pepper

Place the lentils in a medium saucepan and cover with 3" of water. Add the shallots, cloves, and bay leaf. Bring to a boil over high heat. Reduce the heat to low, cover, and simmer for 20 minutes, or until the lentils are tender. Drain in a colander and discard the bay leaf and shallots. Set the lentils aside to cool.

In a large bowl, combine the celery, yellow peppers, onions, tomatoes, goat cheese, parsley, and mint. Stir in the lentils.

In a small bowl, whisk together the lemon juice, honey, oil, and garlic. Pour over the salad and gently toss to combine. Season with the salt and pepper.

Greek Salad

MAKES 4 SERVINGS

The healthfulness of Mediterranean cooking is reflected in this traditional salad of juicy garden vegetables and feta cheese drizzled with oregano vinaigrette.

8	ounces asparagus, trimmed and cut into 2" pieces
2	tablespoons water
2	cups sliced English cucumbers
1	large tomato, halved and thinly sliced
½	large red onion, thinly sliced
3	ounces feta cheese, crumbled
¼	cup balsamic vinegar
1	tablespoon chopped fresh oregano
2	teaspoons olive oil
1	teaspoon Dijon mustard
½	teaspoon ground black pepper

Place the asparagus and water in a microwave-safe bowl. Cover with vented plastic wrap and microwave on high power for a total of 3 minutes, or until crisp-tender; stop and stir after 1½ minutes. Immediately plunge the asparagus into a bowl of cold water, drain, and lightly pat dry. Place in a large bowl. Stir in the cucumbers, tomatoes, onions, and feta.

In a small bowl, whisk together the vinegar, oregano, oil, mustard, and pepper. Pour the vinaigrette over the vegetables and toss well.

Nutrition Notes

Per serving

Calories 135
Fat 7.4 g.
% of calories from fat 47
Protein 6.3 g.
Carbohydrates 12.4 g.
Dietary fiber 2.8 g.
Cholesterol 19 mg.
Sodium 278 mg.

Kitchen Hint

◆ To prevent a cutting board from moving or sliding while you're chopping, rest it on a damp paper towel or dishcloth.

Summer Menu Eighteen

	1,500 CALORIES	2,000 CALORIES	2,500 CALORIES
	33-43 G. FAT	44-56 G. FAT	57-69 G. FAT

Breakfast

cooked cream of rice cereal with	1 cup	1 cup	1¼ cups
raisins and	2 tablespoons	2 tablespoons	2 tablespoons
brown sugar	1 tablespoon	1 tablespoon	1½ tablespoons
skim milk	½ cup	1½ cups	1½ cups

Lunch

Aegean Sea Pasta	1 serving	2 servings	3 servings
cucumber slices and	5	5	5
tomato slices with	5	5	5
nonfat dressing	1 tablespoon	1 tablespoon	1 tablespoon

Dinner

Grilled Beef Tenderloin Salad	1 serving	1 serving	1½ servings
baked potato with	1	1	1
nonfat sour cream	2 tablespoons	2 tablespoons	2 tablespoons
Summer Fruit Turnovers	1	1	1

Snack

baked tortilla chips with	13	13	20
melted reduced-fat cheese sauce	¼ cup	¼ cup	⅓ cup

DAILY TOTALS			
Calories	1,473	2,002	2,491
Fat (g.)	26	37	48
% of calories from fat	15	16	17
Protein (g.)	81	113	149
Carbohydrates (g.)	235	312	374
Dietary fiber (g.)	15	21	26
Cholesterol (mg.)	149	208	297
Sodium (mg.)	1,556	2,435	2,918

HEALTHY TIP OF THE DAY

Have fun with exercise. It can be enjoyable as well as rewarding. Choose an activity that is fun for you. And work out at a pace that feels comfortable so you'll be more likely to stick with your routine. Begin with a simple outdoor activity such as biking, gardening, or even walking your dog. Try to avoid getting caught up in the "gym syndrome" (exercising only on the treadmill, stair-climber, or stationary bicycle). Instead, enjoy outdoor activities, too.

Aegean Sea Pasta (page 240)

Nutrition Notes

Per serving

Calories 292
Fat 5 g.
% of calories from fat 15
Protein 18.7 g.
Carbohydrates 43.2 g.
Dietary fiber 3.6 g.
Cholesterol 45 mg.
Sodium 288 mg.

Kitchen Hints

◆ Clams and mussels need to be cleaned thoroughly before cooking. Soak for about an hour in a mixture of salted water and cornmeal to rid them of any excess sand. Throw out any that are open before soaking and discard any that do not open after they have been cooked.

◆ Mussels often have dark threads, called beards, protruding from the shell. Pull them out or cut them off just before cooking.

◆ To prolong the life of fresh herbs, store them in a narrow glass filled with water as you would a bouquet of flowers. Loosely cover the tops with a plastic bag and refrigerate. If you change the water daily and shake excess moisture from the tops, the herbs should last for a week.

Aegean Sea Pasta

MAKES 4 SERVINGS

This dish showcases the delights of the sea. The mussels and clams are a good source of iron, and the pasta provides a healthy dose of complex carbohydrates.

1	tablespoon olive oil
2	cups chopped red onions
4	teaspoons chopped garlic
2	cups chopped plum tomatoes
1½	cups reduced-sodium clam juice
1	cup defatted reduced-sodium chicken broth
⅔	cup no-salt-added tomato sauce
8	ounces linguine
12	mussels, scrubbed and beards removed (see hint)
12	clams, scrubbed
12	large shrimp, peeled and deveined
½	cup packed fresh basil, chopped
¼	cup fresh oregano
⅛	teaspoon salt
½	teaspoon red-pepper flakes (optional)

Warm the oil in a large no-stick skillet over medium heat. Add the onions and garlic. Cook, stirring often, for 5 minutes, or until the onions are soft. Stir in the tomatoes. Cook over medium-high heat for 2 minutes. Stir in the clam juice, broth, and tomato sauce. Bring to a boil. Reduce the heat to medium, cover, and simmer for 5 minutes.

Cook the linguine in a large pot of boiling water according to the package directions. Drain.

Stir the mussels, clams, shrimp, basil, oregano, salt, and red-pepper flakes (if using) into the sauce mixture. Cover and simmer, stirring occasionally, for 5 minutes, or until the mussels and clams open and the shrimp is opaque. Discard any unopened mussels and clams. Add the linguine and stir well.

Grilled Beef Tenderloin Salad

MAKES 4 SERVINGS

Think salads are boring? This one will change your mind.

Salad

1¼	pounds beef tenderloin, halved lengthwise
	Salt and ground black pepper
10	ounces portobello mushroom caps
3½	ounces shiitake mushrooms, stems removed
5	ounces snow peas
2	tablespoons water

Dressing

1	orange
¼	cup defatted reduced-sodium chicken broth
2	tablespoons reduced-sodium soy sauce
2	tablespoons chopped scallions
1	teaspoon grated fresh ginger
½	teaspoon minced garlic
4	cups mixed baby lettuce

To make the salad: Coat a grill rack with no-stick spray. Preheat the grill.

Coat the beef with no-stick spray and season with the salt and pepper. Grill, covered, 4" from the heat for 7 to 10 minutes per side, or until an instant-read thermometer registers 130°F for medium-rare. (For well-done, grill to a temperature of 145°F.) Transfer to a cutting board and let stand for 5 minutes. Thinly slice on a diagonal.

Grill the portobello mushrooms for 2 to 3 minutes per side, or until soft. Grill the shiitake mushrooms for 1 minute per side, or until soft. Transfer to a cutting board and thinly slice the mushrooms.

Place the snow peas and water in a microwave-safe dish. Cover with vented plastic wrap and microwave on high power for a total of 3 to 4 minutes, or until crisp-tender; stop and stir after 2 minutes. Plunge the peas into cold water, drain, and pat dry.

To make the dressing: Grate ½ teaspoon rind from the orange into a large bowl. Cut the orange in half and squeeze 3 tablespoons juice into the bowl. Whisk in the broth, soy sauce, scallions, ginger, and garlic.

Add the lettuce and snow peas. Toss to combine. Serve topped with the beef and mushrooms.

Nutrition Notes

Per serving

Calories 296
Fat 11.4 g.
% of calories from fat 34
Protein 34.6 g.
Carbohydrates 14.3 g.
Dietary fiber 3.5 g.
Cholesterol 88 mg.
Sodium 391 mg.

Kitchen Hint

◆ The beef can also be roasted. Place the whole tenderloin (do not slice in half) on a baking sheet coated with no-stick spray. Bake at 425°F for 25 to 30 minutes for medium-rare. To cook the mushrooms, heat ¼ teaspoon oil in a no-stick skillet over medium heat. Thinly slice the portobello mushrooms and cook for 2 minutes. Slice the shiitake mushroom caps; add to the skillet and cook for 2 minutes more, or until soft and lightly browned.

Nutrition Notes

Per turnover

Calories 204
Fat 2 g.
% of calories from fat 9
Protein 2.7 g.
Carbohydrates 45.1 g.
Dietary fiber 2.2 g.
Cholesterol 0 mg.
Sodium 123 mg.

Kitchen Hints

◆ If possible, use fresh phyllo instead of frozen. Fresh phyllo is more pliable and less likely to fall apart. Look for it in Middle Eastern specialty stores. To store unused sheets of fresh phyllo, double-wrap them in plastic wrap and freeze for up to 6 months. You can also refreeze frozen phyllo, but the sheets tend to fall apart easily when refrozen.

◆ Freeze unbaked turnovers in resealable freezer bags for up to 3 months. Bake frozen on a foil-lined baking sheet coated with no-stick spray at 400°F for 35 to 40 minutes, or until golden brown and crispy.

Summer Fruit Turnovers

MAKES 6

Phyllo dough is a low-fat alternative to regular pastry dough. Here, the sheets of phyllo are coated with no-stick spray instead of melted butter to reduce the fat and calories. Inside, fresh strawberries and raspberries burst with flavor.

> 2 cups sliced strawberries
> 1 cup raspberries
> $^2/_3$ cup sugar
> 3 tablespoons all-purpose flour
> $1^1/_2$ tablespoons lemon juice
> 8 sheets phyllo dough, thawed if frozen

Preheat the oven to 400°F. Line a baking sheet with foil and coat with no-stick spray.

In a medium bowl, combine the strawberries, raspberries, sugar, flour, and lemon juice. Gently stir until the sugar is dissolved.

Place a double layer of phyllo on a counter with one of the long edges facing you. (Cover the remaining sheets with a lightly moistened dish towel to keep them from drying out.) Coat with no-stick spray. Top with 2 more sheets and coat with no-stick spray.

Cut the prepared sheets from top to bottom (not from left to right) into 3 equal strips. Place $^1/_2$ cup of the fruit mixture at the bottom of each strip. Fold the lower right corner to the opposite edge to form a triangle. Continue to fold the triangle up the length of the strip until you reach the end. Coat with no-stick spray and transfer to the prepared baking sheet.

Repeat with the remaining phyllo and filling to make a total of 6 turnovers.

Place the turnovers on the prepared baking sheet. Bake for 20 to 25 minutes, or until golden brown and crispy. Cool on the baking sheet on a wire rack for 10 to 15 minutes before serving.

Fourth of July Menu

	1,500 CALORIES	2,000 CALORIES	2,500 CALORIES
	33-43 G. FAT	44-56 G. FAT	57-69 G. FAT

Breakfast

Star-Spangled Popover Pancake	2 servings	2 servings	2 servings
skim milk	¾ cup	1 cup	2 cups

Lunch

reduced-sodium tomato soup	1 cup	2 cups	2 cups
whole-grain crackers	6	12	12
kiwifruit	1	1½	2

Dinner

Apricot-Mango Barbecued Chicken	1 serving	1 serving	2 servings
Patriotic Potato Salad	1 serving	2 servings	2 servings
corn on the cob	1 ear	2 ears	3 ears

Snack

baby carrots with	6	12	12
nonfat ranch dip	¼ cup	½ cup	½ cup

DAILY TOTALS

Calories	1,485	1,989	2,482
Fat (g.)	24	31	39
% of calories from fat	14	14	14
Protein (g.)	66	87	123
Carbohydrates (g.)	262	354	430
Dietary fiber (g.)	28	42	48
Cholesterol (mg.)	187	189	256
Sodium (mg.)	1,845	3,060	3,347

NUTRIENT BONUS

This menu (at 2,000 calories) exceeds the Daily Value for:

Dietary fiber	169%
Vitamin A	430%
Thiamin	121%
Riboflavin	131%
Niacin	148%
Vitamin C	451%
Potassium	160%

HEALTHY TIP OF THE DAY

Traditional potato salad can be deceptively high in fat. A 1-cup serving of deli-style salad can have up to 360 calories and 22 grams of fat—nearly half of your daily allotment if you're on a 2,000-calorie diet. But you can enjoy today's Patriotic Potato Salad (page 246) without worry. Every cup has only 190 calories and 3.5 grams of fat.

Apricot-Mango Barbecued Chicken (page 245) and Patriotic Potato Salad (page 246)

Apricot-Mango Barbecued Chicken

MAKES 4 SERVINGS

A Fourth-of-July favorite gets a new twist. In this bold-flavored entrée, grilled chicken breasts are topped with a tangy sauce made with fresh mango and apricot nectar.

- ½ cup reduced-sodium ketchup
- ½ cup apricot nectar
- ¼ cup packed light brown sugar
- ¼ cup mango chutney
- 2 tablespoons mango vinegar (see hint)
- 1 tablespoon Worcestershire sauce
- ¼ teaspoon Cajun seasoning
- ¼ teaspoon hot-pepper sauce (optional)
- 1 tablespoon olive oil
- ⅓ cup chopped red onions
- ⅓ cup chopped sweet red peppers
- 1 mango, finely chopped
- 4 boneless, skinless chicken breast halves (about 4 ounces each)
  Salt and ground black pepper

In a medium bowl, combine the ketchup, apricot nectar, brown sugar, chutney, vinegar, Worcestershire sauce, Cajun seasoning, and hot-pepper sauce (if using).

Warm the oil in a medium no-stick skillet over medium heat. Add the onions and red peppers. Cook, stirring often, for 5 minutes, or until the onions are translucent. Stir in the mangoes and cook for 5 minutes. Stir in the ketchup mixture and simmer for 10 minutes, or until slightly reduced.

Coat a grill rack or broiler pan with no-stick spray. Preheat the grill or broiler.

Season the chicken with the salt and black pepper. Cook 4" from the heat for 4 to 5 minutes, or until browned. Turn the chicken over and brush the cooked surface with some of the sauce. Cook for 4 to 5 minutes, or until no longer pink in the center when tested with a sharp knife. Turn over again, brush with more of the barbecue sauce, and cook for 1 minute. Serve drizzled with the remaining sauce.

Nutrition Notes

Per serving

Calories 307
Fat 6.4 g.
% of calories from fat 18
Protein 24.2 g.
Carbohydrates 40.6 g.
Dietary fiber 3 g.
Cholesterol 63 mg.
Sodium 147 mg.

Kitchen Hints

◆ Mango vinegar can be found in many supermarkets and specialty food stores. You can substitute red-wine vinegar, if necessary.

◆ To chop a mango, use a sharp knife to slice the fruit lengthwise from both sides of the pit. Score the flesh like a tick-tack-toe board, invert the peel, and cut away the mango pieces. Cut away any flesh still clinging to the pit and slice the peel off.

Nutrition Notes

Per serving

Calories 190
Fat 3.5 g.
% of calories from fat 17
Protein 9.3 g.
Carbohydrates 29.6 g.
Dietary fiber 3.5 g.
Cholesterol 0 mg.
Sodium 613 mg.

Kitchen Hint

◆ This recipe can easily be doubled and is the perfect accompaniment to any summer barbecue.

Patriotic Potato Salad

MAKES 6 SERVINGS

Here's an American classic updated to today's nutritional standards. It's low-fat, low-calorie, and a delicious source of complex carbohydrates.

1½	pounds red potatoes, cut into ½" cubes
1	cup chopped celery
½	cup chopped red onions
⅓	cup chopped fresh Italian parsley
¼	cup chopped fresh dill
5	hard-cooked egg whites, coarsely chopped
¾	cup nonfat sour cream
½	cup nonfat mayonnaise
¼	cup Dijon mustard
¼	cup red-wine vinegar
1½	tablespoons olive oil
½	teaspoon ground black pepper
¼	teaspoon salt

Place the potatoes in a large saucepan. Cover with cold water and bring to a boil over high heat. Reduce the heat to medium and cook for 15 to 20 minutes, or until tender when tested with a sharp knife. Drain and transfer to a large bowl. Allow to cool for 10 minutes.

Add the celery, onions, parsley, dill, and egg whites. Toss gently to combine.

In a medium bowl, whisk together the sour cream, mayonnaise, mustard, vinegar, oil, pepper, and salt. Pour over the potato mixture and toss gently to combine. Refrigerate for about 1 hour before serving.

Star-Spangled Popover Pancake

MAKES 4 SERVINGS

Celebrate the red, white, and blue with this colorful breakfast. By the dawn's early light, you will be able to "C" the vitamin-packed blueberries, nectarines, and strawberries.

- 4 egg whites
- 1 egg
- 1 cup 1% low-fat milk
- 1 cup all-purpose flour
- 2 teaspoons unsalted butter or margarine, melted
- ¼ teaspoon salt
- 3 tablespoons apricot or peach preserves
- 2 tablespoons lemon juice
- 1 tablespoon packed light brown sugar
- 3 nectarines, sliced
- 1 cup sliced strawberries
- 1 cup blueberries

Preheat the oven to 425°F. Coat a 12" cast-iron skillet with no-stick spray. Place the skillet in the oven for 5 minutes.

Place the egg whites and egg in a medium bowl. Whisk until well-combined. Add the milk, flour, butter or margarine, and salt. Mix well.

Remove the skillet from the oven and pour in the batter. Return to the oven and bake for 20 to 25 minutes, or until golden brown and puffed. (The pancake will collapse when removed from the oven.)

In a medium saucepan, combine the preserves, lemon juice, and brown sugar. Bring to a boil over medium heat. Add the nectarines; cover and cook, stirring occasionally, for 5 minutes, or until soft. Stir in the strawberries and cook for 2 minutes. Remove from the heat and stir in the blueberries.

Pour the fruit on top of the pancake and cut into 4 wedges. Serve warm.

Nutrition Notes

Per serving

Calories 307
Fat 5.1 g.
% of calories from fat 14
Protein 8.4 g.
Carbohydrates 59.8 g.
Dietary fiber 4.5 g.
Cholesterol 61 mg.
Sodium 210 mg.

Kitchen Hint

◆ To make individual popover pancakes, use a cast-iron 8-cup muffin pan in place of the skillet and bake for 12 to 15 minutes, or until golden brown and puffed. Arrange 2 popovers on each plate and top with the warm fruit.

Diana Shaw

Author of the best-selling *Almost Vegetarian* and the *Essential Vegetarian Cookbook*, Diana Shaw says, "I never consciously consider whether a dish will be 'healthy' because I cook only with foods and methods that are whole-some from the start." Former food columnist for the *Los Angeles Times*, Shaw teaches at cooking schools and specialty stores around the country. She developed this menu to be swift and simple.

NUTRIENT BONUS

This menu (at 2,000 calories) exceeds the Daily Value for:

Dietary fiber	145%
Vitamin A	204%
Thiamin	193%
Riboflavin	180%
Niacin	130%
Vitamin B$_6$	115%
Folate	149%
Vitamin C	687%
Vitamin E	132%
Calcium	177%
Iron	109%
Potassium	162%

Diana Shaw's Menu

	1,500 CALORIES	2,000 CALORIES	2,500 CALORIES
	33-43 G. FAT	44-56 G. FAT	57-69 G. FAT

Breakfast

Oat-Berry Pancakes with Vanilla-Ricotta Cream	1 servings	2 servings	2 servings
skim milk	½ cup	1¼ cups	2 cups

Lunch

Caesar-Style Panzanella	1 serving	1 serving	1 serving
low-sodium tomato juice	1 cup	1 cup	1½ cups

Dinner

Grilled Chicken Burgers with Caramelized Onions	1	1	2
steamed red potatoes	½ cup	¾ cup	1 cup

Snack

watermelon cubes	½ cup	1½ cups	1¾ cups

DAILY TOTALS			
Calories	1,473	1,975	2,473
Fat (g.)	25	30	40
% of calories from fat	15	13	14
Protein (g.)	96	123	163
Carbohydrates (g.)	236	335	400
Dietary fiber (g.)	28	36	43
Cholesterol (mg.)	206	225	292
Sodium (mg.)	2,181	2,815	3,489

Caesar-Style Panzanella (page 252)

Nutrition Notes

Per serving

Calories 387
Fat 3.6 g.
% of calories from fat 8
Protein 21.6 g.
Carbohydrates 76.4 g.
Dietary fiber 7 g.
Cholesterol 18 mg.
Sodium 588 mg.

Kitchen Hint

◆ If you don't have buttermilk, use soured milk instead. To make 2 cups soured milk, pour a generous 1¾ cups 1% low-fat milk into a measuring cup. Add enough lemon juice to make 2 cups. Let stand for 5 minutes.

◆ Both the orange sauce and ricotta cream can be made up to 3 days in advance and stored, covered, in the refrigerator. The pancake batter can be mixed the night before and stored, covered, in the refrigerator.

Oat-Berry Pancakes with Vanilla-Ricotta Cream

MAKES 4 SERVINGS

These easy pancakes are topped with a refreshing orange sauce. What a delicious way to greet the day.

Orange Sauce

2   teaspoons cornstarch
1   cup orange juice
1   tablespoon lime juice
1   tablespoon sugar

Ricotta Cream

⅔   cup nonfat ricotta cheese
2   tablespoons nonfat cream cheese
2   tablespoons sugar
    Grated rind of 1 lemon
1   teaspoon vanilla

Pancakes

1   cup oat bran
1   cup whole-wheat pastry flour or all-purpose flour
1   tablespoon packed light brown sugar
1½   teaspoons baking powder
½   teaspoon baking soda
3   egg whites
2   cups 1% low-fat buttermilk or soured milk (see hint)
2   cups mixed berries

To make the orange sauce: Place the cornstarch in a cup. Add 2 tablespoons of the orange juice and stir until smooth.

Place the remaining orange juice in a small saucepan. Add the lime juice and sugar. Cook over medium heat, stirring constantly, for 1 minute, or until the sugar is dissolved. Stir in the cornstarch mixture. Cook, whisking constantly, for 1 minute, or until thickened. Remove from the heat and set aside to cool. Cover and refrigerate for at least 3 hours before serving.

To make the ricotta cream: In a food processor or blender, process the ricotta until smooth. Add the cream cheese, sugar, lemon rind, and vanilla. Process until smooth. Refrigerate until ready to use.

To make the pancakes: In a large bowl, whisk together the oat bran, flour, brown sugar, baking powder, and baking soda.

In a medium bowl, whisk together the egg whites and buttermilk. Add to the flour mixture and stir just until combined.

Coat a large no-stick skillet with no-stick spray and place over medium-high heat until hot. Reduce the heat to medium. For each pancake, spoon about 3 tablespoons batter into the skillet and spread to form a 3" pancake. Cook for 2 minutes, or until the top has small holes. Turn and cook for 1 to 2 minutes, or until golden brown. Repeat to make a total of 8 pancakes.

For each serving, spread a pancake with the ricotta cream and top with a second pancake. Drizzle with the orange sauce.

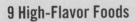

9 High-Flavor Foods

Keep these items on hand for fast, great-tasting dishes.

1. *Canned beans.* Add to salads, stews, soups, and pasta dishes.
2. *Canned reduced-sodium broths.* Use vegetable, chicken, or beef broth for cooking rice, polenta, barley, couscous, and other grains. Substitute broth for half the oil in a vinaigrette.
3. *Citrus fruit.* Both the juice and the grated rind perk up salad dressings, seafood, pasta, cakes, pies, and fruit desserts. Citrus rind also works well with pork and game birds.
4. *Flavored no-stick sprays.* Try toasted sesame oil spray for stir-fries, mesquite for grilling, Italian for a basil flavor, and olive and canola oil sprays for general cooking.
5. *Flavored vinegars.* Especially good are balsamic, raspberry, herb-infused, garlic, and rice-wine vinegars. Add them to salad dressings, sauces, and pasta dishes.
6. *Ginger.* Grate, chop, or slice for wonderful aroma and flavor in Asian dishes. For baked goods, use crystallized or ground ginger.
7. *Hot chili peppers.* Reconstitute dried chili peppers in hot water. Use fresh or dried hot peppers for rice dishes, chili, stews, salsas, enchiladas, or burritos.
8. *Roasted garlic paste.* Look for it in the international aisle. Use with sautéed lean red meats, chicken, and fish; in pestos and pasta sauces; and as a spread for toasted bread.
9. *Sun-dried tomatoes.* Reconstitute them in hot water. Use in pasta dishes, soups, casseroles, and stuffings. Save the soaking liquid for sauces and salad dressings.

Nutrition Notes

Per serving

Calories 508
Fat 11.5 g.
% of calories from fat 19
Protein 30.7 g.
Carbohydrates 78.1 g.
Dietary fiber 11.7 g.
Cholesterol 121 mg.
Sodium 885 mg.

Kitchen Hints

◆ The dressing can be made up to 4 days in advance and stored, covered, in the refrigerator.

◆ This recipe is adapted from the *Essential Vegetarian Cookbook* (Clarkson Potter, 1997).

Caesar-Style Panzanella

MAKES 4 SERVINGS

In this variation on a traditional Italian salad from Tuscany, toasted bread cubes and seasonal vegetables are tossed with a creamy low-fat buttermilk dressing.

Dressing

1	cup nonfat plain yogurt
1	cup 1% low-fat buttermilk
½	cup grated Parmesan cheese
¼	cup lemon juice
2	soft-cooked eggs
2	tablespoons balsamic vinegar
4	teaspoons reduced-sodium soy sauce
2	teaspoons Dijon mustard

Salad

4	ears corn, husks and silks removed
4	cups sugar snap peas or snow peas
2	tablespoons water
6	cups cubed day-old bread
2	heads romaine lettuce, torn into bite-size pieces
4	cups cherry tomatoes, halved or quartered

To make the dressing: In a food processor or blender, combine the yogurt, buttermilk, Parmesan, lemon juice, eggs, vinegar, soy sauce, and mustard. Process until smooth.

To make the salad: Bring a large pot of water to a boil. Add the corn, cover, and remove from the heat. Let stand for 5 minutes. Drain. When cool enough to handle, slice the kernels off the cobs. Place in a large bowl.

Combine the sugar snap peas or snow peas and water in a microwave-safe bowl. Cover with vented plastic wrap and microwave on high power for 30 seconds, or until crisp-tender. Plunge the peas into a bowl of cold water, drain, and add to the corn.

Preheat the oven to 350°F. Place the bread in 2 jelly-roll pans. Bake, stirring occasionally, for 8 to 10 minutes, or until lightly toasted. Add to the bowl with the corn.

Add the lettuce and tomatoes. Toss gently to combine. Add the dressing and toss to thoroughly coat. Let stand for 5 minutes to allow the bread to absorb the dressing. Toss again.

Grilled Chicken Burgers with Caramelized Onions

MAKES 4

Ground chicken breast is naturally lean and low in saturated fat.

Chicken Burgers

- 1 pound ground chicken breast
- 2 tablespoons minced fresh Italian parsley
- 2 tablespoons minced fresh cilantro
- 2 tablespoons nonfat plain yogurt
- 1 tablespoon lemon juice
- 1 clove garlic, minced
- 2 teaspoons reduced-sodium soy sauce
- Ground black pepper

Caramelized Onions

- 1 tablespoon olive oil
- 2 large Vidalia onions, thinly sliced
- ½ teaspoon sugar
- 2 large purple plums
- 4 hamburger buns
- 2 tablespoons Dijon mustard
- 1 large tomato, sliced
- 1 cup alfalfa sprouts

To make the chicken burgers: In a large bowl, combine the chicken, parsley, cilantro, yogurt, lemon juice, garlic, soy sauce, and pepper. Stir well. Cover and refrigerate for at least 30 minutes.

Coat a grill rack or broiler pan with no-stick spray. Preheat the grill or broiler. Shape the chicken mixture into four ½"-thick patties. Cook 4" from the heat for 5 minutes. Turn; cook for 4 minutes, or until no longer pink in the center when tested with a sharp knife.

To make the caramelized onions: Warm the oil in a large no-stick skillet over medium-high heat. Add the onions, reduce the heat to medium, and sprinkle with the sugar. Cook, stirring occasionally, for 20 minutes, or until the onions are very soft.

Bring a medium saucepan of water to a boil. Add the plums, return to a boil, and boil for 30 seconds. Remove the plums with a slotted spoon and rinse under cold water. Peel and finely chop the plums. Add to the onions and cook, stirring occasionally, for 7 minutes.

Place a burger on the bottom of each bun. Top with the mustard, onions, tomatoes, alfalfa sprouts, and the bun tops.

Nutrition Notes

Per burger

Calories 361
Fat 9.3 g.
% of calories from fat 23
Protein 31 g.
Carbohydrates 40.3 g.
Dietary fiber 4.8 g.
Cholesterol 63 mg.
Sodium 563 mg.

Kitchen Hint

◆ The onions can be made up to 14 days in advance and stored, covered, in the refrigerator.

Fall Menus

Mile-High Apple Pie
(page 356)

NUTRIENT BONUS

This menu (at 2,000 calories) exceeds the Daily Value for:

Dietary fiber	140%
Vitamin A	372%
Thiamin	177%
Niacin	140%
Vitamin B$_6$	127%
Folate	150%
Vitamin C	568%
Calcium	105%
Iron	101%
Potassium	111%

HEALTHY TIP OF THE DAY

Exercise helps you lose weight. A nutritious diet is one way to trim pounds. But add regular exercise, and you have a winning combination for permanent weight loss. Try to get in the habit of exercising four or five times a week. Pick an activity that you enjoy so you'll stick with it. If you're just starting out, take it slow at first. Park your car farther away from your destination and walk the rest of the way. Or take a 10-minute walk when you get a break from work. Small changes make a big difference.

Fall Menu One

	1,500 CALORIES	2,000 CALORIES	2,500 CALORIES
	33-43 G. FAT	44-56 G. FAT	57-69 G. FAT
Breakfast			
Very Veggie Cream Cheese	2 tablespoons	2 tablespoons	¼ cup
whole-wheat bagel	1	1	2
papaya and raspberries	½ cup	¾ cup	1 cup
calcium-fortified orange juice	1 cup	1¼ cups	1½ cups
Lunch			
mixed greens with	3 cups	4 cups	4 cups
water-packed tuna,	3 ounces	3 ounces	3 ounces
chopped carrots,	¼ cup	¼ cup	¼ cup
nonfat croutons, and	¼ cup	¼ cup	¼ cup
nonfat dressing	3 tablespoons	¼ cup	¼ cup
French bread	1 slice	2 slices	2 slices
pear slices	½ cup	1 cup	1¼ cups
Dinner			
Spaghetti Squash with Salsa	1 serving	2 servings	2 servings
grilled pork tenderloin	4 ounces	4 ounces	5 ounces
cooked long-grain white rice	½ cup	1 cup	1¼ cups
Spice Cake with Maple Glaze	1 serving	1 serving	1 serving
Snack			
baked tortilla chips with	13	13	26
fat-free salsa and	2 tablespoons	2 tablespoons	2 tablespoons
low-fat melted Cheddar	2 tablespoons	¼ cup	¼ cup
DAILY TOTALS			
Calories	1,498	1,984	2,494
Fat (g.)	27	35	44
% of calories from fat	16	16	15
Protein (g.)	79	90	111
Carbohydrates (g.)	242	341	431
Dietary fiber (g.)	23	35	45
Cholesterol (mg.)	119	119	152
Sodium (mg.)	1,742	2,168	2,966

Spice Cake with Maple Glaze (page 260)

Nutrition Notes

Per 2 tablespoons

Calories 38
Fat 3.1 g.
% of calories from fat 71
Protein 1.7 g.
Carbohydrates 1.1 g.
Dietary fiber 0.2 g.
Cholesterol 10 mg.
Sodium 64 mg.

Kitchen Hint

◆ This recipe is easily adaptable. If you like Asian flavors, try adding ginger, garlic, and a little soy sauce to the cream cheese. For a Mexican twist, stir in a little salsa, chopped cilantro, and lime juice.

Very Veggie Cream Cheese

MAKES 2 CUPS

For a quick breakfast, try this creamy spread on toast or a bagel. Vegetables and herbs perk up the flavor of the reduced-fat cream cheese. The spread is also good on crackers or as a dip for fresh-cut vegetables. You could even spread it on a baked pizza crust and top it with grilled vegetables for an easy light meal.

8 ounces reduced-fat cream cheese, at room temperature
¼ cup finely shredded carrots
¼ cup finely shredded radishes
¼ cup chopped scallions
½ roasted sweet red pepper, diced
1 tablespoon chopped fresh dill
1 teaspoon chopped fresh chives (optional)
½ teaspoon ground black pepper

In a large bowl, combine the cream cheese, carrots, radishes, scallions, red peppers, dill, chives (if using), and black pepper. Stir until well-blended.

Have a Snack

Snacking during the day helps curb your appetite so you're less likely to overeat at main meals. And if you choose wisely, snacks can provide important vitamins and minerals, too. We're not talking about downing a whole bag of cookies, though. Go for low-fat, high-fiber snacks. They'll keep your stomach from growling without slowing you down. Here are some good-tasting snacks with less than 150 calories.

- 1 cup nonfat plain or vanilla yogurt
- ¾ cup nonfat plain yogurt blended with ½ cup berries
- 1 peach
- 25 grapes
- 2 cups cubed watermelon
- ½ baked potato with 1 tablespoon nonfat sour cream
- 5 broccoli florets and ½ sweet red pepper (cut up) with 2 tablespoons nonfat dip
- 1½ full-size graham cracker sheets and 6 ounces skim milk
- 1 frozen fruit-juice pop
- ½ cup cereal with 6 ounces skim milk
- 1 ounce pretzels
- 10 baked tortilla chips with ¼ cup fat-free salsa or bean dip

Spaghetti Squash with Salsa

MAKES 4 SERVINGS

A fast, no-cook sauce makes this dish a snap. The sauce goes over cooked strands of spaghetti squash. But it's also delicious with pasta, other vegetables, lean meat or poultry, and baked tortilla chips.

1	spaghetti squash (about 3 pounds), halved lengthwise
10	plum tomatoes, chopped
¼	cup chopped fresh basil
¼	cup chopped fresh Italian parsley
3	cloves garlic, minced
1	tablespoon lemon juice
1	tablespoon olive oil
¼	teaspoon salt
¼	teaspoon ground black pepper

Preheat the oven to 400°F. Line a baking sheet with foil and coat with no-stick spray.

Place the squash, cut side down, on the prepared baking sheet. Bake for 50 minutes, or until soft and tender. Scoop out and discard the seeds. Using a fork, separate the squash into strands and transfer to a large bowl.

In a food processor, combine the tomatoes, basil, parsley, garlic, lemon juice, oil, salt, and pepper. Process until combined but slightly chunky. Pour over the squash and toss to coat.

Nutrition Notes

Per serving

Calories 159
Fat 4.8 g.
% of calories from fat 25
Protein 3.8 g.
Carbohydrates 28.8 g.
Dietary fiber 6.2 g.
Cholesterol 0 mg.
Sodium 205 mg.

Kitchen Hints

◆ Spaghetti squash gets its name from the spaghetti-like strands that appear when the flesh is cooked. Try it instead of regular pasta the next time you make your favorite pasta sauce. It has a slightly sweet, crunchy texture and a lot fewer calories than pasta.

◆ If you don't have a food processor, finely chop the salsa ingredients by hand and combine in a medium bowl.

Nutrition Notes

Per serving

Calories 241
Fat 5.7 g.
% of calories from fat 21
Protein 4 g.
Carbohydrates 44.1 g.
Dietary fiber 0.5 g.
Cholesterol 0 mg.
Sodium 196 mg.

Kitchen Hint

◆ To make your own cake flour: For each 1 cup of all-purpose flour, replace 2 tablespoons with 2 tablespoons cornstarch.

Spice Cake with Maple Glaze

<u>MAKES 10 SERVINGS</u>

Looking for a sweet low-fat snack? Apple butter and egg whites keep the fat down to a moderate level.

2	teaspoons + 1½ cups cake flour (see hint)
1	cup sugar
2	teaspoons baking powder
1	teaspoon ground cinnamon
¼	teaspoon ground cloves
¼	teaspoon ground nutmeg
¼	teaspoon salt
¼	cup canola oil
¼	cup apple butter
¼	cup apple juice
1	teaspoon vanilla
8	egg whites
4	tablespoons confectioners' sugar
¼	cup maple syrup

Preheat the oven to 350°F. Coat a 10-cup Bundt pan with no-stick spray. Sprinkle with 2 teaspoons of the flour and tap out the excess.

Place the remaining 1½ cups flour in a large bowl. Add the sugar, baking powder, cinnamon, cloves, nutmeg, and salt. Mix well.

In a small bowl, combine the oil, apple butter, apple juice, and vanilla. Mix well. Pour into the bowl with the flour. Using an electric mixer, beat on low speed just until blended. Do not overmix.

Place the egg whites in a medium bowl. Using an electric mixer with clean, dry beaters, beat on medium speed until foamy. Add 2 tablespoons of the confectioners' sugar. Increase the speed to high and beat until firm and glossy. Fold into the batter.

Pour the batter into the prepared pan and bake for 20 to 25 minutes, or until a toothpick inserted in the center comes out clean. Cool in the pan on a wire rack for 5 minutes. Unmold onto the rack and use a wooden skewer to poke holes in the top of the cake.

Place the maple syrup in a small microwave-safe bowl. Microwave on high power for 30 seconds, or until warm. Drizzle evenly over the cake and let cool completely. Dust with the remaining 2 tablespoons confectioners' sugar.

Fall Menu Two

	1,500 CALORIES	2,000 CALORIES	2,500 CALORIES
	33-43 G. FAT	44-56 G. FAT	57-69 G. FAT

Breakfast

cooked oatmeal with	½ cup	¾ cup	1¼ cups
skim milk	½ cup	¾ cup	1½ cups
cranberry juice	1 cup	1 cup	1½ cups

Lunch

Southwest Chowder	1 serving	2 servings	2 servings
cornbread muffin	1	2	2

Dinner

Beef and Spinach Lasagna	1 serving	1 serving	1½ servings
sautéed mushrooms and	¼ cup	¼ cup	¼ cup
green beans	½ cup	½ cup	½ cup
Pear Sorbet	1 serving	2 servings	2 servings

Snack

bagel with	1	1	1
nonfat cream cheese and	2 tablespoons	2 tablespoons	2 tablespoons
smoked salmon	1 ounce	1 ounce	1 ounce

DAILY TOTALS

Calories	1,491	1,992	2,495
Fat (g.)	26	37	45
% of calories from fat	16	16	16
Protein (g.)	92	108	145
Carbohydrates (g.)	228	319	389
Dietary fiber (g.)	26	37	44
Cholesterol (mg.)	135	162	214
Sodium (mg.)	1,962	2,548	2,990

NUTRIENT BONUS

This menu (at 2,000 calories) exceeds the Daily Value for:

Dietary fiber	149%
Vitamin A	258%
Thiamin	120%
Riboflavin	136%
Niacin	111%
Vitamin B6	102%
Vitamin C	990%
Calcium	142%
Iron	107%
Potassium	112%

HEALTHY TIP OF THE DAY

Satisfying desserts don't have to blow your fat budget. When dining out, ask for fruit sorbet, sherbet, angel food cake, a fresh fruit cup, fruit compote, a low-fat frozen dessert, or cappuccino made with skim milk. For a happy ending to home-cooked meals, look for these same foods in the supermarket. Low-fat frozen yogurt, sorbet bars, and fudge bars are especially good. Today's dessert, Pear Sorbet (page 265), is fat-free and has just 87 calories per serving.

Southwest Chowder

Southwest Chowder

MAKES 8 SERVINGS

In this creamy, chunky, calcium-rich chowder, chipotle peppers lend the smoky flavor that usually comes from salt pork or bacon.

4	ears corn, husks and silks removed
2	dried chipotle peppers (wear plastic gloves when handling)
1	cup hot water
2	teaspoons olive oil
1½	cups chopped onions
1	cup sliced celery
2	cloves garlic, minced
1½	teaspoons ground cumin
5	cups defatted reduced-sodium chicken broth
8	ounces Yukon gold potatoes, cubed
1	bouquet garni (see hint)
2	cups peeled and cubed butternut squash
1	roasted sweet red pepper, chopped
¼	cup all-purpose flour
2	cups 1% low-fat milk

Cook the corn in a large pot of boiling water for 3 minutes, or until tender. Drain and set aside until cool enough to handle. Slice 2 cups kernels off the cobs; reserve the cobs.

Place the chipotle peppers in a small bowl. Add the water and let stand for 10 to 15 minutes, or until soft. Transfer the peppers to a cutting board. Remove and discard the stems and seeds. Mince the peppers; reserve the soaking liquid.

Warm the oil in a large saucepan over medium heat. Add the onions, celery, garlic, and cumin. Cook, stirring often, for 6 to 8 minutes, or until the vegetables are soft and tender. Stir in the broth, potatoes, bouquet garni, reserved corn cobs, chipotle soaking liquid, and minced chipotle peppers. Cook for 10 minutes. Add the squash and corn. Cook, stirring occasionally, for 15 minutes, or until the vegetables are tender. Remove and discard the bouquet garni and the corn cobs. Stir in the roasted red peppers.

Place the flour in a medium bowl. Slowly whisk in the milk until smooth. Stir into the soup and cook, stirring often, for 5 to 10 minutes, or until slightly thickened.

Nutrition Notes

Per serving

Calories 165
Fat 2.6 g.
% of calories from fat 13
Protein 6.7 g.
Carbohydrates 31.4 g.
Dietary fiber 3.7 g.
Cholesterol 2 mg.
Sodium 211 mg.

Kitchen Hints

◆ Bouquet garni is an herb bundle used to flavor soups and stews. To make it, place 1 bay leaf, 2 fresh parsley sprigs, ½ teaspoon dried thyme, and 6 peppercorns in a square of cheesecloth, a small coffee filter, or a tea infuser ball. If using cheesecloth or a coffee filter, tie the bundle shut with kitchen string.

◆ Chipotle peppers are smoke-dried jalapeño peppers. Most supermarkets carry them in the produce section. They can also be found canned in adobo sauce in the international aisle of larger supermarkets.

◆ This soup will keep refrigerated for up to 4 days or frozen for up to 1 month.

Nutrition Notes

Per serving

Calories 595
Fat 12.5 g.
% of calories from fat 19
Protein 55.4 g.
Carbohydrates 64.3 g.
Dietary fiber 7 g.
Cholesterol 97 mg.
Sodium 677 mg.

Kitchen Hint

◆ To jazz up commercial pasta sauces, try adding slivers of rehydrated sun-dried tomatoes, rehydrated dried wild mushrooms, roasted sweet red peppers, capers, roasted garlic paste, or anchovy paste.

Beef and Spinach Lasagna

MAKES 4 SERVINGS

In this easy yet elegant version of lasagna, several food groups combine for a nutrient-packed meal.

2	cups reduced-fat ricotta cheese
1	package (10 ounces) frozen chopped spinach, thawed and squeezed dry
$\frac{1}{2}$	teaspoon ground black pepper
$\frac{1}{2}$	teaspoon ground nutmeg
1	pound lean ground beef top round
1	teaspoon crushed red-pepper flakes
$\frac{1}{8}$	teaspoon salt
1	box (8 ounces) no-boil lasagna noodles
1	jar (26 ounces) fat-free tomato-basil sauce
5	leaves fresh sage, coarsely chopped
1	cup shredded fat-free mozzarella cheese
1	plum tomato, thinly sliced
5	large leaves fresh basil
$\frac{1}{4}$	cup grated Romano cheese

Preheat the oven to 375°F. Coat a 9" × 9" baking dish with no-stick spray.

In a medium bowl, combine the ricotta, spinach, black pepper, and nutmeg. Mix well.

Place a large no-stick skillet over medium heat until hot. Crumble the beef into the skillet. Cook, stirring to break up the meat, for 4 to 6 minutes, or until the meat is no longer pink. Drain off any accumulated fat. Add the red-pepper flakes and salt to the beef. Mix well.

Layer the bottom of the prepared baking dish with 3 of the lasagna noodles. Top with half of the tomato sauce and all of the beef. Sprinkle with half of the sage. Top with another layer of noodles. Spread the ricotta mixture over the noodles and sprinkle with $\frac{1}{2}$ cup of the mozzarella.

Top with a third layer of noodles and the remaining tomato sauce. Top with the tomatoes, basil, and the remaining sage. Sprinkle evenly with the Romano and the remaining $\frac{1}{2}$ cup mozzarella.

Cover with foil and bake for 20 to 25 minutes, or until bubbling and heated through.

Pear Sorbet

MAKES 8 SERVINGS

Light and refreshing, this low-calorie, nonfat sorbet is the perfect way to end a hearty fall meal. Make it in advance and puree the sorbet just before serving.

> 8 ripe pears, peeled and quartered
> ½ cup frozen apple juice concentrate
> 2 tablespoons lemon juice
> 2 cups sliced strawberries

In a food processor or blender, combine the pears, apple juice concentrate, and lemon juice. Process until smooth. Transfer to an airtight container and freeze for 2 hours, or until solid.

Just before serving, remove the sorbet from the freezer, break into chunks, and return to the food processor or blender. Process until smooth and light. Serve topped with the strawberries.

Vegetable Variations

The National Cancer Institute says that 5 servings of vegetables a day can help ward off some types of cancer and other illnesses. But how do you go about eating more? Here are 10 simple ways to reap the rewards of nature's nutritional gold mines.

- Add shredded carrots or zucchini to meat loaf, hamburgers, or lasagna. The vegetables will give the dish moisture, texture, and flavor.
- Put more vegetables on your sandwiches. Try lettuce and thinly sliced tomatoes, cucumbers, carrots, and zucchini.
- For a chunky soup, toss in some precut vegetables from the produce section of your supermarket.
- Get creative with pizza. Find out which vegetables your local pizzeria offers and order all your favorites.
- Add shredded carrots or zucchini to homemade breads and muffins.
- Add grated carrots to pasta sauce.
- Buy precut vegetables for quick-to-fix omelets, stir-fries, and pasta.
- Drink low-sodium vegetable juices like tomato juice.
- Roast some vegetables in your oven, then puree them to make a sauce for pasta or rice or to use as a dip for baked tortilla chips.
- Eat more salads. Get creative by combining carrots, broccoli, asparagus, cubed potatoes, or whatever else appeals to you. There's a lot more to a salad than just lettuce.

Nutrition Notes

Per serving

Calories 87
Fat 0.3 g.
% of calories from fat 3
Protein 0.7 g.
Carbohydrates 22.5 g.
Dietary fiber 3.8 g.
Cholesterol 0 mg.
Sodium 8 mg.

Kitchen Hints

◆ Apples can be substituted for the pears in this recipe. Add ¼ teaspoon ground cinnamon along with the apples and top with coarsely chopped plain or candied walnuts. To make candied walnuts, coat a baking dish with no-stick spray. Combine ¼ cup sugar and ½ teaspoon lemon juice in a small saucepan. Cook over medium-high heat, swirling the pan occasionally, for 2 to 3 minutes, or until the sugar is melted and light brown. Remove from the heat and stir in ¼ cup coarsely chopped walnuts. Transfer to the baking dish to cool.

◆ Store leftover sorbet in the freezer for up to 2 weeks.

Fall Menu Three

	1,500 CALORIES 33-43 G. FAT	2,000 CALORIES 44-56 G. FAT	2,500 CALORIES 57-69 G. FAT
Breakfast			
Pecan Cinnamon Rolls	1	1	2
kiwifruit	1	2	2
Lunch			
skim milk	1 cup	1½ cups	1½ cups
Eggless Egg Salad Sandwiches	1	1½	2
dill pickle spears	1	2	2
baby carrots	6	9	9
Dinner			
baked potato chips	12	18	24
pear	1	1	1
Cornish Hens with Wild Mushroom Dressing	1 serving	1½ servings	1½ servings
steamed green beans	¾ cup	1 cup	1 cup
Snack			
low-fat microwave popcorn with Cajun seasoning	3 cups popped 1½ teaspoons	3 cups popped 1½ teaspoons	3 cups popped 1½ teaspoons

DAILY TOTALS			
Calories	1,499	1,986	2,500
Fat (g.)	30	40	51
% of calories from fat	18	18	18
Protein (g.)	81	117	129
Carbohydrates (g.)	234	300	394
Dietary fiber (g.)	28	37	43
Cholesterol (mg.)	151	217	237
Sodium (mg.)	2,025	3,067	3,605

Pecan Cinnamon Rolls (page 268)

Nutrition Notes

Per roll

Calories 268
Fat 9.3 g.
% of calories from fat 30
Protein 6.3 g.
Carbohydrates 66.8 g.
Dietary fiber 2.4 g.
Cholesterol 21 mg.
Sodium 251 mg.

Kitchen Hints

◆ To boost the calcium in this dish, add 3 tablespoons skim milk powder to the dry ingredients before adding the yeast mixture.

◆ Unbaked rolls can be prepared 1 day in advance and refrigerated overnight. Or bake the cinnamon rolls, let cool completely in the baking dishes, then wrap the dishes tightly in foil. Freeze for up to 2 weeks. Leave the rolls covered and bake frozen at 375°F for 15 minutes, or until heated through.

◆ To save yourself some effort, use a heavy-duty standing mixer to prepare the dough. Combine the dry ingredients in a large mixer bowl using the paddle attachment. Beat in the yeast mixture, then the wet ingredients. Increase the
(continued)

Pecan Cinnamon Rolls

<u>MAKES 12</u>

You can't beat the flavor of this American breakfast classic. It's gooey, chewy, and full of cinnamon sweetness. With this version, you get less fat and more fiber.

Sweet Dough

 1 package quick-rising yeast
 ½ cup warm water (about 110°F)
 1 teaspoon + ¼ cup sugar
 3½ cups all-purpose flour
 ¼ cup whole-wheat flour
 1 teaspoon salt
 1 egg
 1 egg white
 ½ cup 1% low-fat milk, warmed (about 110°F)
 2 tablespoons canola oil
 1 teaspoon vanilla

Glaze

 1 cup reduced-calorie syrup
 ¾ cup packed light brown sugar
 1 tablespoon unsalted butter or margarine
 4 tablespoons chopped toasted pecans

Pecan Filling

 ½ cup chopped toasted pecans
 ½ cup raisins
 ½ cup packed light brown sugar
 2 teaspoons ground cinnamon

To make the sweet dough: In a small bowl, combine the yeast, water, and 1 teaspoon of the sugar. Set aside for 5 to 10 minutes, or until the mixture is foamy.

In a large bowl, combine the all-purpose flour, whole-wheat flour, salt, and the remaining ¼ cup sugar. Mix well. Add the yeast mixture and stir until combined.

In a small bowl, combine the egg, egg white, milk, oil, and vanilla. Mix well. Add to the flour mixture and stir until well-combined.

Using a wooden spoon, beat for 5 to 7 minutes, or until the dough is smooth and elastic. (The dough will be sticky.) Transfer to a floured surface and knead for 10 minutes.

Coat a large bowl with no-stick spray. Add the dough and turn to coat all sides. Cover with plastic wrap and let rise in a warm, draft-free place for 1 hour, or until doubled in size.

To make the glaze: Coat two 13" × 9" baking dishes with no-stick spray.

In a small saucepan, combine the syrup, brown sugar, and butter or margarine. Cook over medium heat for 1 to 2 minutes, or until the sugar is dissolved. Divide the glaze between the prepared baking dishes and spread to coat the bottom. Sprinkle each dish with 2 tablespoons of the pecans.

To make the pecan filling: In a small bowl, stir together the pecans, raisins, brown sugar, and cinnamon.

Punch down the dough and turn it out onto a lightly floured surface. Roll into an 18" × 12" rectangle. Sprinkle the filling evenly over the dough, leaving a ¼" border on all sides. Starting at the long side closest to you, tightly roll the dough to form a long cylinder. Pinch the seam together to seal. Cut into 12 equal-size rolls.

Arrange 6 rolls, cut side up and evenly spaced, in each of the baking dishes. Lightly press down on the rolls. Cover with plastic wrap and let rise in a warm, draft-free place for 50 minutes, or until almost doubled in size. Remove the plastic wrap.

Preheat the oven to 375°F. Line 2 baking sheets with parchment or foil.

Bake the rolls in the baking dishes for 20 minutes, or until the tops are golden brown and the glaze bubbles. Remove from the oven. Place a baking sheet over each baking dish. Carefully invert the rolls onto the sheets. Let cool for 5 minutes before serving.

speed to medium and beat for 5 to 7 minutes, or until the dough is smooth and elastic. Transfer to a floured work surface and knead by hand for 2 minutes.

♦ For very speedy preparation, replace the sweet dough with store-bought low-fat crescent-roll dough.

Nutrition Notes

Per serving

Calories 453
Fat 13.9 g.
% of calories from fat 28
Protein 48.6 g.
Carbohydrates 30.7 g.
Dietary fiber 5.7 g.
Cholesterol 126 mg.
Sodium 734 mg.

Kitchen Hint

◆ Mushroom duxelles are finely chopped and sautéed mushrooms that can be used to flavor savory dishes, such as omelets, stuffings, sandwiches, and pasta. They are a great way to use extra mushrooms. To make, finely chop 12 ounces mushrooms with a sharp knife or in a food processor. Transfer to a clean nonterry towel and ring out any liquid. Transfer to a no-stick skillet and sauté over medium heat with 1 teaspoon olive oil and 3 ta-blespoons minced shallots for 15 to 20 minutes, or until the mushrooms are browned and the liquid has evaporated. Season with salt and pepper. Use imme-diately or freeze for up to 2 months.

Cornish Hens with Wild Mushroom Dressing

MAKES 4 SERVINGS

These moist and tender Cornish hens are topped with a savory mushroom dressing. For an elegant presentation (and to reduce the saturated fat), remove the skin after roasting the hens.

Hens

- 1 lemon
- 2 Cornish hens (1½ pounds each), trimmed of excess fat and giblets discarded
  Salt and ground black pepper
- 4 sprigs fresh rosemary
- 2 bay leaves
- ½ cup sliced celery
- ½ cup chopped onions
- 1 cup defatted reduced-sodium chicken broth

Wild Mushroom Dressing

- 1 ounce dried porcini mushrooms
- 1 cup hot water
- 1 teaspoon olive oil
- ½ cup chopped onions
- 6 ounces button mushrooms, finely chopped
- ⅓ cup chopped celery
- 2 tablespoons chopped fresh Italian parsley
- ½ teaspoon dried rosemary, crushed
- ½ teaspoon dried thyme
- ¼ cup Madeira or nonalcoholic white wine
- 4 cups cubed day-old Italian bread, preferably semolina
- 1 egg white, lightly beaten
  Salt and ground black pepper

To make the hens: Preheat the oven to 400°F.

Grate 1 teaspoon rind from the lemon into a large bowl; set aside to use in the dressing. Slice the lemon.

Sprinkle the hen cavities with the salt and pepper and stuff each with half of the lemon slices, 2 rosemary sprigs, and 1 bay leaf. Set the hens in a roasting pan. Sprinkle the celery and onions around the hens and pour the broth into the pan.

Bake for 30 minutes. Reduce the oven temperature to 350°F and bake, basting occasionally, for 30 minutes, or until crispy and the internal temperature reads 165°F to 170°F on an instant-read thermometer.

To make the wild mushroom dressing: While the hens are roasting, place the dried mushrooms and water in a small bowl. Let soak for 20 minutes, or until softened. Remove the mushrooms and chop. Strain the water through a coffee filter to remove any grit. Reserve the liquid.

Warm the oil in a medium no-stick skillet over medium heat. Add the onions, button mushrooms, celery, parsley, rosemary, thyme, and the chopped mushrooms. Cook, stirring occasionally, for 6 to 8 minutes, or until the onions are soft. Add the wine and cook for 2 to 3 minutes, or until the liquid has evaporated. Transfer the vegetables to the bowl with the lemon rind. Add the bread and toss to combine. Stir in the reserved mushroom broth, $\frac{1}{3}$ cup at a time, until the stuffing is moist but not soggy. Stir in the egg white and season with the salt and pepper.

Spoon the dressing into a 1-quart baking dish and cover with foil. Place in the oven with the hens 30 minutes before the hens are due to be finished. Remove the foil for the last 5 minutes of baking time.

Cut each hen in half lengthwise and remove the skin. Serve topped with the dressing.

Nutrition Notes

Per sandwich

Calories 184
Fat 2.4 g.
% of calories from fat 12
Protein 9.4 g.
Carbohydrates 32.6 g.
Dietary fiber 3.9 g.
Cholesterol 0 mg.
Sodium 408 mg.

Kitchen Hints

◆ For the best flavor, make this salad ahead and refrigerate overnight to allow the flavors to develop.

◆ This recipe works well as an appetizer, too. Serve it as a dip for vegetables or spoon it on top of whole-grain crackers or toast rounds.

Eggless Egg Salad Sandwiches

MAKES 4

This no-egg mixture satisfies tried-and-true egg-salad fans. The texture of tofu is much like that of eggs, yet it's cholesterol-free.

1	box (10½ ounces) reduced-fat firm silken tofu, diced
¼	cup minced sweet red peppers
3	tablespoons nonfat mayonnaise
2	tablespoons sweet pickle relish
1	tablespoon chopped fresh Italian parsley
1	teaspoon yellow mustard
½	teaspoon reduced-sodium soy sauce
¼	teaspoon turmeric
¼	teaspoon garlic powder
4	whole-wheat pita breads
4	leaves lettuce
4	tomato slices

In a large bowl, combine the tofu, peppers, mayonnaise, relish, parsley, mustard, soy sauce, turmeric, and garlic powder. Mix well and refrigerate for at least 30 minutes, or until chilled.

Cut the very top off each pita. Open the pockets and line with the lettuce and tomatoes. Divide the filling among the pitas.

Tofu Tips

There are two basic types of tofu: regular and silken. Regular tofu comes in 1-pound blocks packed in plastic tubs with water. Most supermarkets carry soft, firm, and extra-firm varieties. It can be marinated and baked, sautéed, or added to simmered dishes like chili. Before using, drain and press out the excess water: Place a heavy object over the tofu; let stand for 20 minutes. For a quick snack, cube the tofu, sauté it in sesame oil and chopped garlic until browned, then toss with soy sauce.

For a firmer texture, regular tofu can be frozen: Wrap the drained block in plastic and freeze until solid. Thaw and squeeze out the excess liquid before using.

Silken tofu comes in 10½-ounce boxes. It's also available in soft, firm, and extra-firm varieties. When pureed, it resembles yogurt. Use pureed silken tofu for creamy dressings, sauces, and desserts.

Both types of tofu provide calcium and protein with little fat and no cholesterol. For the least fat, choose low-fat regular tofu and "lite" silken tofu.

Fall Menu Four

	1,500 CALORIES	2,000 CALORIES	2,500 CALORIES
	33-43 G. FAT	44-56 G. FAT	57-69 G. FAT

Breakfast

Texas Breakfast Burritos	1	1	2
calcium-fortified orange juice	½ cup	1 cup	1 cup

Lunch

Fish Sticks with Banana Chutney	1 serving	1 serving	1½ servings
baked frozen potato fries	12	12	12
steamed carrots	½ cup	½ cup	½ cup

Dinner

Harvest Shepherd's Pie	1 serving	2 servings	2 servings
mixed greens with	1 cup	1 cup	1 cup
nonfat dressing	1 tablespoon	1 tablespoon	1 tablespoon
sliced apple with	1	1	1
cinnamon sugar	1 teaspoon	1 teaspoon	1 teaspoon

Snack

diet root beer with	½ cup	½ cup	¾ cup
nonfat vanilla frozen yogurt	¾ cup	¾ cup	¾ cup

DAILY TOTALS

Calories	1,514	1,970	2,505
Fat (g.)	27	30	45
% of calories from fat	16	13	16
Protein (g.)	73	83	121
Carbohydrates (g.)	251	354	414
Dietary fiber (g.)	27	41	46
Cholesterol (mg.)	194	194	358
Sodium (mg.)	1,727	2,020	3,071

NUTRIENT BONUS

This menu (at 2,000 calories) exceeds the Daily Value for:

Dietary fiber	162%
Vitamin A	2,840%
Riboflavin	104%
Vitamin B$_6$	161%
Folate	115%
Vitamin C	665%
Calcium	139%
Potassium	148%

HEALTHY TIP OF THE DAY

Take steps to prevent heart disease. The Framingham Heart Study, which medically tracked thousands of adults for over 50 years, identified risk factors for developing coronary artery disease. They include smoking, lack of physical activity, obesity, high blood pressure, too much fat and cholesterol in the blood, diabetes, and a family history of heart disease. Most of these risk factors can be managed simply by leading a healthy lifestyle. Eating healthy foods, remaining physically active, reducing stress, and avoiding cigarettes can literally save your life.

Harvest Shepherd's Pie

Harvest Shepherd's Pie

MAKES 6 SERVINGS

Traditional shepherd's pie is made with ground lamb or beef. This vegetarian version uses fall vegetables. Mashed sweet potatoes make a colorful topping. Underneath all that flavor is a gold mine of fiber and antioxidants.

4	ounces medium mushrooms, quartered
3	carrots, cut into $\frac{1}{2}$" pieces
2	parsnips, cut into $\frac{1}{2}$" pieces
2	stalks celery, sliced
$\frac{1}{2}$	butternut squash, peeled, seeded, and cubed
1	sweet red pepper, cut into 1" pieces
3	large shallots, cut into wedges
2	teaspoons olive oil
$2\frac{1}{2}$	pounds sweet potatoes
	Salt and ground black pepper
1	tablespoon cornstarch
2	cups reduced-sodium vegetable broth
1	teaspoon reduced-sodium soy sauce
1	teaspoon dried Italian herb seasoning
$\frac{1}{4}$	cup chopped fresh Italian parsley

Preheat the oven to 400°F.

In a large bowl, combine the mushrooms, carrots, parsnips, celery, squash, red peppers, shallots, and oil. Mix well to coat with the oil. Transfer to 2 baking sheets and spread evenly. Add the sweet potatoes to 1 of the sheets.

Bake for 30 to 40 minutes, or until the cut vegetables are almost tender. Transfer them to a 2-quart baking dish. Return the sweet potatoes to the oven and bake for 20 minutes, or until soft and tender when tested with a fork. Cut the sweet potatoes in half and scoop the flesh into a small bowl; mash until smooth. Discard the sweet-potato skins. Season with the salt and black pepper.

Place the cornstarch in a small saucepan. Add about $\frac{1}{4}$ cup of the broth and stir until smooth. Stir in the soy sauce, herb seasoning, and the remaining $1\frac{3}{4}$ cups broth. Bring to a boil over medium heat, whisking often. Cook for 1 minute, or until slightly thickened. Stir in the parsley. Pour over the vegetables in the baking dish. Spread the mashed sweet potatoes over the vegetables.

Reduce the oven temperature to 375°F. Bake for 25 minutes. Increase the temperature to 500°F and bake for 3 to 5 minutes, or until the top is lightly browned.

Nutrition Notes

Per serving

Calories 357
Fat 2.2 g.
% of calories from fat 5
Protein 8.2 g.
Carbohydrates 80.4 g.
Dietary fiber 12.3 g.
Cholesterol 0 mg.
Sodium 244 mg.

Kitchen Hint

◆ If you are crunched for time, replace the fresh vegetables with thawed frozen vegetable assortments that are packaged for stews.

Nutrition Notes

Per burrito

Calories 317
Fat 11.6 g.
% of calories from fat 33
Protein 18.9 g.
Carbohydrates 33.2 g.
Dietary fiber 3.2 g.
Cholesterol 134 mg.
Sodium 809 mg.

Kitchen Hints

◆ Nonfat hash-brown potatoes can be found in the dairy or freezer section of most grocery stores. If using frozen ones, thaw them first.

◆ Try using English muffins instead of tortillas to make an open-faced breakfast dish. Or make sandwiches with two English muffin halves. To vary the flavors, experiment with different fillings like beans, fresh herbs, and additional vegetables.

Texas Breakfast Burritos

MAKES 4

Take a trip south of the border without leaving your breakfast table. This dish is loaded with enough calcium, protein, and flavor to make you say olé!

1	teaspoon olive oil
½	cup chopped onions
3½	ounces reduced-fat turkey sausage
2	cups nonfat hash-brown potatoes
1	can (4 ounces) chopped green chili peppers
¼	teaspoon ground black pepper
2	eggs
4	egg whites
2	tablespoons skim milk
¼	teaspoon ground red pepper
4	flour tortillas (8" diameter)
½	cup shredded reduced-fat Monterey Jack cheese
4	tablespoons fat-free salsa
2	tablespoons sliced black olives

Warm the oil in a large no-stick skillet over medium heat. Add the onions. Crumble the sausage into the pan. Cook, stirring occasionally, for 4 to 5 minutes, or until the onions are soft and the sausage is browned. Add the potatoes and cook, stirring occasionally, for 5 to 8 minutes, or until the potatoes begin to brown. Stir in the chili peppers and black pepper. Transfer to a large bowl.

In a small bowl, whisk together the eggs, egg whites, milk, and red pepper. Pour into the same skillet and place over medium heat. Cook, stirring occasionally, for 3 to 4 minutes, or until lightly scrambled. Do not overcook. Stir in the potato mixture.

Wrap the tortillas in plastic wrap. Microwave on high power for 1 minute.

Sprinkle each tortilla with 2 tablespoons of the Monterey Jack. Divide the egg mixture among the tortillas. Roll to enclose the filling. Serve topped with the salsa and olives.

Fish Sticks with Banana Chutney

These fish sticks can be put together in a snap. The zesty coating is made with baked barbecue potato chips.

Banana Chutney

2	limes
2	medium bananas, chopped
1	cup chopped sweet red and green peppers
¼	cup chopped scallions
1	jalapeño pepper, minced (wear plastic gloves when handling)
1½	tablespoons packed light brown sugar
1	teaspoon canola oil
	Salt and ground black pepper

Fish Sticks

⅓	cup all-purpose flour
1	teaspoon ground black pepper
¼	cup fat-free egg substitute
1½	cups crushed baked barbecue potato chips
¼	cup grated Parmesan cheese
¼	teaspoon ground red pepper
1	pound red snapper fillets, skin removed, cut into 16 strips

To make the banana chutney: Grate 1 tablespoon rind from the limes into a medium bowl; cut the limes in half and squeeze 3 tablespoons juice into the bowl. Discard the limes. Stir in the bananas, red and green peppers, scallions, jalapeño peppers, brown sugar, and oil. Season with the salt and black pepper. Cover and set aside for about 25 minutes to allow the flavors to develop.

To make the fish sticks: Preheat the oven to 500°F. Coat a baking sheet with no-stick spray.

On a large plate, mix the flour and black pepper. Pour the egg substitute into a shallow bowl. In another shallow bowl, mix the potato chips, Parmesan, and red pepper.

Dredge the fish strips in the flour mixture, shaking off the excess. Dip into the egg substitute, then roll in the potato-chip mixture to coat completely. Place on the prepared baking sheet in a single layer.

Bake for 8 to 10 minutes, or until golden brown. Serve with the chutney.

Nutrition Notes

Per serving

Calories 435
Fat 7.2 g.
% of calories from fat 15
Protein 38.3 g.
Carbohydrates 54 g.
Dietary fiber 4.7 g.
Cholesterol 58 mg.
Sodium 484 mg.

Kitchen Hints

◆ If red snapper isn't available, you can use grouper, halibut, orange roughy, or cod. Or replace the fish with 1 pound boneless, skinless chicken or turkey breast cut into strips.

◆ To make low-fat tartar sauce, combine 1 cup low-fat mayonnaise, 1 dill pickle spear (finely chopped), 2 tablespoons minced fresh parsley, 1 tablespoon lemon juice, and 2 teaspoons chopped capers in a small bowl.

Fall Menu Five

	1,500 CALORIES 33-43 G. FAT	2,000 CALORIES 44-56 G. FAT	2,500 CALORIES 57-69 G. FAT
Breakfast			
Orange Bran Muffins	2	2	3
skim milk	¾ cup	1 cup	1 cup
Lunch			
angel hair pasta with	2 ounces	3 ounces	3 ounces
marinara sauce	½ cup	¾ cup	¾ cup
romaine lettuce with	1 cup	2 cups	2 cups
nonfat Caesar dressing	1 tablespoon	2 tablespoons	2 tablespoons
French bread	1 slice	2 slices	2 slices
Dinner			
Lamb Racks with			
Rosemary-Mustard Crust	1 serving	1 serving	2 servings
Saffron-Scented Potato Gratin	1 serving	2 servings	2 servings
steamed broccoli	½ cup	½ cup	½ cup
Snack			
baby carrots with	6	6	6
nonfat sour-cream dip	¼ cup	¼ cup	¼ cup

DAILY TOTALS			
Calories	1,496	1,983	2,520
Fat (g.)	32	37	55
% of calories from fat	20	18	20
Protein (g.)	82	102	144
Carbohydrates (g.)	206	285	340
Dietary fiber (g.)	26	33	42
Cholesterol (mg.)	219	257	385
Sodium (mg.)	2,225	2,757	3,806

Lamb Racks with Rosemary-Mustard Crust (page 281) and Saffron-Scented Potato Gratin (page 282)

Nutrition Notes

Per muffin

Calories 233
Fat 7.1 g.
% of calories from fat 25
Protein 5.7 g.
Carbohydrates 43 g.
Dietary fiber 6.4 g.
Cholesterol 18 mg.
Sodium 486 mg.

Kitchen Hints

◆ If you don't have buttermilk, you can use soured milk instead. To make ¾ cup soured milk, pour a generous ⅔ cup 1% low-fat milk into a measuring cup. Add enough lemon juice to make ¾ cup. Let stand for 5 minutes.

◆ Most recipes for 12 muffins baked in a 12-cup muffin pan can also be baked in an 8" × 4" loaf pan. Bake at the specified temperature but add 10 to 12 minutes to the baking time.

◆ Store any leftover muffins in the freezer for a breakfast on the go.

Orange Bran Muffins

MAKES 12

For added moistness and flavor, these fiber-rich muffins get a last-minute drizzle of tangy orange syrup.

2	cups shredded all-bran cereal
¾	cup hot water
¼	cup canola oil
1	orange
¾	cup 1% low-fat buttermilk or soured milk (see hint)
2	tablespoons light molasses
2	tablespoons honey
1	egg
1	cup all-purpose flour
¼	cup whole-wheat flour
2	teaspoons baking soda
½	teaspoon salt
1	cup raisins
¼	cup chopped toasted walnuts (optional)
¼	cup sugar
¼	cup orange juice

Preheat the oven to 400°F. Coat a 12-cup muffin pan with no-stick spray.

In a medium bowl, combine the cereal, water, and oil. Stir together until the cereal is softened.

Grate 1 tablespoon rind from the orange into another medium bowl; cut the orange in half and squeeze ¼ cup juice into the bowl. Whisk in the buttermilk, molasses, honey, and egg until well-blended. Add to the cereal mixture and mix well.

In a large bowl, combine the all-purpose flour, whole-wheat flour, baking soda, and salt. Mix well. Add the cereal mixture and stir until just incorporated. Stir in the raisins. Do not overmix.

Divide the batter equally among the muffin cups, filling the cups about two-thirds full. Sprinkle with the walnuts (if using). Bake for 15 to 18 minutes, or until a toothpick inserted into the center of a muffin comes out almost clean. Place the pan on a wire rack.

Combine the sugar and orange juice in a small saucepan. Bring to a boil over medium heat and stir to dissolve the sugar. Use a toothpick or skewer to poke holes in the muffin tops. Brush with the orange syrup. Let the muffins stand for 5 minutes, then remove from the pan.

Lamb Racks with Rosemary-Mustard Crust

MAKES 4 SERVINGS

Easy to prepare, these juicy lamb racks are rolled in a refreshing herb-mustard crust. This simple, elegant dish is perfect for company or special occasions.

2	large cloves garlic, minced
2½	tablespoons Dijon mustard
2	tablespoons lemon juice
2	tablespoons nonfat mayonnaise
2	tablespoons chopped fresh rosemary
1	tablespoon reduced-sodium soy sauce
¼	teaspoon ground black pepper
2	lamb racks (1½ pounds each), trimmed of all visible fat
1	cup fresh bread crumbs

Preheat the oven to 500°F. Line a baking sheet with foil.

In a small bowl, combine the garlic, mustard, lemon juice, mayonnaise, rosemary, soy sauce, and pepper. Mix until smooth.

Fold a double strip of foil over the rib ends to prevent them from burning. Spread the mustard mixture over the tops and sides of the lamb. Coat with the bread crumbs. Place on the baking sheet.

Roast the lamb for 10 minutes. Reduce the oven temperature to 400°F and roast for 20 minutes, or until an instant-read thermometer inserted in the center of a rack registers 130°F for medium-rare. (If you prefer your lamb done medium-well, continue to roast, checking every 2 minutes, until the temperature registers 140°F.) Transfer to a cutting board and let stand for 5 minutes. Cut each rack into 6 chops.

Nutrition Notes

Per serving

Calories 304
Fat 11.2 g.
% of calories from fat 34
Protein 36.9 g.
Carbohydrates 12 g.
Dietary fiber 1.8 g.
Cholesterol 109 mg.
Sodium 564 mg.

Kitchen Hint

◆ Have your butcher remove the backbone from the ribs and "French" them for you. In this process, the fatty layer covering the ribs is removed. Exposing the bones creates a more dramatic presentation and has the added benefit of lowering the saturated fat content.

Nutrition Notes

Per serving

Calories 249
Fat 2.5 g.
% of calories from fat 9
Protein 9.8 g.
Carbohydrates 48.2 g.
Dietary fiber 4.9 g.
Cholesterol 5 mg.
Sodium 203 mg.

Kitchen Hint

◆ To get consistently thin potato slices, use a mandoline or a food processor fitted with a slicing blade. Uniform potato slices will result in more even cooking and a beautiful presentation.

Saffron-Scented Potato Gratin

<u>MAKES 6 SERVINGS</u>

Saffron lends a wonderful flavor and brilliant yellow color to this potassium-rich potato gratin. Look for saffron in your grocer's spice section.

1	clove garlic, halved
1	teaspoon olive oil
1½	pounds Spanish onions, thinly sliced
1¼	cups defatted reduced-sodium chicken broth
1	cup evaporated skim milk
½	teaspoon saffron threads, crushed
1½	pounds Yukon gold potatoes, very thinly sliced
½	teaspoon ground black pepper
¼	teaspoon salt
4	tablespoons grated Parmesan cheese

Preheat the oven to 375°F. Coat a 3-quart shallow baking dish with no-stick spray. Rub the bottom and sides with the cut sides of the garlic; discard the garlic.

Warm the oil in a large no-stick skillet over medium heat. Add the onions and cook, stirring occasionally, for 8 to 10 minutes, or until golden brown and softened.

In a small saucepan, combine the broth, evaporated milk, and saffron. Bring to a boil over medium heat.

Arrange half of the potato slices in the prepared baking dish. Sprinkle with ¼ teaspoon of the pepper and ⅛ teaspoon of the salt. Top with the onions and 2 tablespoons of the Parmesan. Decoratively arrange the remaining potatoes on top and sprinkle with the remaining ¼ teaspoon pepper, ⅛ teaspoon salt, and 2 tablespoons Parmesan. Pour the broth mixture over the potatoes.

Cover with foil and bake for 30 minutes. Remove the foil and bake for 30 to 35 minutes, or until almost all of the liquid has been absorbed and the potatoes are tender. Let stand for 5 minutes before serving.

Fall Menu Six

	1,500 CALORIES 33-43 G. FAT	2,000 CALORIES 44-56 G. FAT	2,500 CALORIES 57-69 G. FAT
Breakfast			
Fruit and Nut Cereal	1 serving	1½ servings	2 servings
skim milk	½ cup	1 cup	1½ cups
Lunch			
Old-Fashioned Macaroni and Cheese	1 serving	1 serving	1½ servings
apple	1	1	1
Dinner			
boneless, skinless chicken breast baked with	3 ounces	5 ounces	7 ounces
honey mustard	1½ teaspoons	1 tablespoon	1½ tablespoons
cooked rice pilaf	½ cup	1 cup	1¼ cups
steamed broccoflower	½ cup	¾ cup	1 cup
Banana Bread Pudding with Caramel Sauce	1 serving	1 serving	1 serving
Snack			
kiwifruit	1	2	2

DAILY TOTALS			
Calories	1,528	2,014	2,520
Fat (g.)	32	44	58
% of calories from fat	19	19	21
Protein (g.)	67	93	120
Carbohydrates (g.)	244	319	384
Dietary fiber (g.)	14	21	25
Cholesterol (mg.)	86	120	167
Sodium (mg.)	1,545	2,101	2,710

NUTRIENT BONUS

This menu (at 2,000 calories) exceeds the Daily Value for:

Thiamin	117%
Riboflavin	105%
Niacin	125%
Vitamin C	356%
Calcium	128%

HEALTHY TIP OF THE DAY

Rescue your favorite recipes. Whenever possible, transform a favorite recipe into a low-fat rendition. A typical 7-ounce serving of macaroni and cheese has about 478 calories and 19 grams of fat. Today's lunch item, Old-Fashioned Macaroni and Cheese (page 285), has just 358 calories and 10 grams of fat per serving. To cut the fat and calories but keep the flavor, we used reduced-fat cheese and low-fat milk.

For more fat-trimming tips, see "Tricks of the Trade" on page 18.

Old-Fashioned Macaroni and Cheese

Old-Fashioned Macaroni and Cheese

MAKES 6 SERVINGS

We've revamped this traditionally high-fat dish by using reduced-fat Cheddar and low-fat milk. This is comfort food at its best!

- 8 ounces elbow macaroni
- ½ cup all-purpose flour
- 3 cups 1% low-fat milk
- 5 ounces shredded reduced-fat extra-sharp Cheddar cheese
- ¼ teaspoon salt
- ¼ teaspoon ground black pepper
- ¼ teaspoon ground nutmeg
- ⅛ teaspoon ground red pepper
- ½ cup + 2 tablespoons grated Parmesan cheese
- 3 tablespoons unseasoned dry bread crumbs
- ¼ teaspoon paprika

Preheat the oven to 375°F. Coat a 9" × 9" baking dish with no-stick spray.

Cook the macaroni in a large pot of boiling water according to the package directions. Drain and return to the pot.

Place the flour in a medium saucepan. Slowly whisk in ½ cup of the milk until smooth. Whisk in the remaining 2½ cups milk. Cook over medium heat, whisking often, for 8 to 10 minutes, or until the sauce is thickened. Remove from the heat and add the Cheddar, salt, black pepper, nutmeg, red pepper, and ½ cup of the Parmesan. Stir until the Cheddar is melted and the sauce is smooth. Pour over the macaroni and mix well. Transfer to the prepared baking dish.

In a small bowl, combine the bread crumbs, paprika, and the remaining 2 tablespoons Parmesan. Sprinkle evenly over the macaroni and bake for 30 minutes, or until lightly browned and bubbling.

Nutrition Notes

Per serving

Calories 358
Fat 10.3 g.
% of calories from fat 27
Protein 20.3 g.
Carbohydrates 43.3 g.
Dietary fiber 1.4 g.
Cholesterol 30 mg.
Sodium 557 mg.

Kitchen Hint

◆ You can buy reduced-fat extra-sharp Cheddar cheese in white or orange varieties. In this recipe, we prefer orange Cheddar for its rich color.

Nutrition Notes

Per serving

Calories 459
Fat 2.9 g.
% of calories from fat 6
Protein 13.9 g.
Carbohydrates 92.6 g.
Dietary fiber 2 g.
Cholesterol 7 mg.
Sodium 387 mg.

Kitchen Hints

◆ The bread pudding will keep in the refrigerator for up to 4 days.

◆ The caramel sauce will keep in the refrigerator for up to 1 week. Try this sauce over nonfat frozen yogurt or apple slices, too.

Banana Bread Pudding with Caramel Sauce

MAKES 6 SERVINGS

Ripe bananas are combined with a hint of rum and crusty French bread in this soft and creamy dessert. Egg substitute and skim milk give the pudding a custardy texture without the fat of whole eggs and cream. Cinnamon-scented caramel sauce provides a final touch of sweet flavor.

Bread Pudding

3	ripe bananas, thinly sliced
1	tablespoon unsalted butter or margarine, melted
¼	cup + ⅔ cup packed light brown sugar
1½	cups skim milk
1	can (12 ounces) evaporated skim milk
1½	cups fat-free egg substitute
3	tablespoons rum or 2 teaspoons rum extract
1	tablespoon vanilla
6	cups cubed day-old French or Italian bread

Caramel Sauce

1	tablespoon cornstarch
1	cup skim milk
1½	cups sugar
2	teaspoons lemon juice
½	teaspoon vanilla
½	teaspoon ground cinnamon

To make the bread pudding: Preheat the oven to 350°F. Coat a 9" × 9" baking dish with no-stick spray.

In a medium bowl, combine the bananas, butter or margarine, and ¼ cup of the brown sugar. Transfer to the prepared baking dish.

In a large bowl, whisk together the milk, evaporated milk, egg substitute, rum or rum extract, vanilla, and the remaining ⅔ cup brown sugar. Add the bread and stir to coat evenly. Let stand for 10 minutes.

Pour over the banana mixture and cover with foil. Place the dish in a larger baking dish and add 1" of hot water to the outer dish. Bake for 30 minutes. Remove the foil. Bake for 30 minutes, or until puffed and golden brown.

To make the caramel sauce: Place the cornstarch in a small saucepan. Add the milk and stir until smooth. Cook over medium heat, whisking constantly, for 5 minutes, or until boiling and slightly thickened.

In a medium saucepan, combine the sugar and lemon juice. Cook over medium-high heat, stirring occasionally, for 2 minutes, or until the sugar is melted. Bring to a boil and cook, swirling the pan occasionally, for 3 to 5 minutes, or until thickened and light brown. Do not let the sugar burn. Remove from the heat and continue to swirl the pan for 2 minutes, or until slightly cooled.

Gradually stir in the milk mixture. Cook over medium heat, stirring, for 2 minutes, or until the mixture is melted. Remove from the heat and stir in the vanilla and cinnamon. Let cool slightly. (The caramel sauce will thicken as it cools.) Serve over the bread pudding.

Alcohol Alternatives

Sometimes you want the flavor of specialty liqueurs without all the alcohol (or calories). What's the answer? Try liqueur extracts. Rum extract is probably the most common. You can also find liqueur extracts for brandy, amaretto, Kahlúa, and Grand Marnier. These make good substitutes for the alcohol called for in your favorite desserts and sauces. For every 2 tablespoons alcohol called for in the recipe, use 1 teaspoon liqueur extract plus 1½ tablespoons water to replace the lost liquid. Look for liqueur extracts in the baking aisle of large supermarkets or in coffee shops and specialty food stores.

Nutrition Notes

Per serving (about ⅔ cup)

Calories 305
Fat 11.9 g.
% of calories from fat 34
Protein 7.5 g.
Carbohydrates 45.4 g.
Dietary fiber 5.8 g.
Cholesterol 0 mg.
Sodium 59 mg.

Kitchen Hints

◆ Store the cereal in an air-tight container in a cool, dry place for up to 2 weeks.

◆ If desired, use other dried fruits. Many stores now carry packages of mixed dried fruits in the produce section. Or make your own signature cereal by experimenting with different dried fruits, such as pineapple, mango, papaya, peaches, or pears. For contrasting texture, add your favorite puffed or shredded cereals.

Fruit and Nut Cereal

MAKES 9 SERVINGS; ABOUT 6 CUPS

Synergy's own crunchy-sweet granola is a powerhouse of fiber, potassium, and other vital nutrients. The complex carbohydrates will give you lots of energy for morning tasks. This cereal makes a great take-along snack, too.

> 2 cups rolled oats
> 1 cup wheat flakes
> 2 tablespoons sunflower seeds
> 1½ tablespoons sesame seeds
> ¼ cup frozen apple juice concentrate, thawed
> ¼ cup packed light brown sugar
> 2 tablespoons canola oil
> ½ teaspoon ground cinnamon
> ¼ cup chopped dried figs
> ¼ cup chopped dried apple rings
> ¼ cup chopped dried apricots
> ¼ cup slivered toasted almonds

Preheat the oven to 250°F. Coat a jelly-roll pan with no-stick spray.

In a medium bowl, combine the oats, wheat flakes, sunflower seeds, sesame seeds, apple juice concentrate, brown sugar, oil, and cinnamon. Mix well.

Spread the oat mixture in the prepared pan. Bake, stirring occasionally, for 45 to 60 minutes, or until golden brown. Let cool.

Stir in the figs, apples, apricots, and almonds.

Fall Menu Seven

	1,500 CALORIES 33-43 G. FAT	2,000 CALORIES 44-56 G. FAT	2,500 CALORIES 57-69 G. FAT

Breakfast

scrambled fat-free egg substitute	¼ cup	½ cup	½ cup
Homestyle Hash Browns	1 serving	1½ servings	2 servings
calcium-fortified orange juice	¾ cup	1 cup	1½ cups

Lunch

reduced-sodium turkey breast and	4 ounces	4 ounces	6 ounces
reduced-fat, reduced-sodium Swiss cheese on	2 ounces	2 ounces	3 ounces
whole-wheat bread with	2 slices	2 slices	2 slices
honey mustard	1 tablespoon	1 tablespoon	1 tablespoon
vegetable soup	¾ cup	1¼ cups	2 cups

Dinner

Asian Barbecued Pork Tenderloin	1 serving	1 serving	2 servings
Scallion Noodles	1 serving	2 servings	2 servings

Snack

dried figs	5	6	6

DAILY TOTALS

Calories	1,490	1,996	2,517
Fat (g.)	30	36	50
% of calories from fat	18	16	17
Protein (g.)	90	113	159
Carbohydrates (g.)	225	318	370
Dietary fiber (g.)	26	37	44
Cholesterol (mg.)	152	152	262
Sodium (mg.)	2,169	2,883	3,874

NUTRIENT BONUS

This menu (at 2,000 calories) exceeds the Daily Value for:

Dietary fiber	148%
Vitamin A	197%
Thiamin	148%
Vitamin C	378%
Calcium	136%
Potassium	101%

HEALTHY TIP OF THE DAY

Most Americans focus on weight loss, but some people have the opposite goal. If you're trying to put on pounds, don't simply fill up on fats—you'll miss out on key nutrients. For healthy weight gain, eat small, frequent meals and drink lots of beverages between meals. Make stir-fries, salads, and baked dishes with small amounts of fats such as olive, canola, or peanut oil. Avocados and olives also contribute calories, in the form of heart-healthy monounsaturated fat. Add calorie-dense nuts to your day, such as pistachios, almonds, cashews, or pecans. Or snack on dried fruits like figs for calories packed with nutrients.

Asian Barbecued Pork Tenderloin (page 291) and Scallion Noodles (page 292)

Asian Barbecued Pork Tenderloin

Makes 4 servings

After you've marinated the pork, this entrée comes together in a snap. The zesty ginger-soy marinade adds a wonderful smoky flavor. This dish is a good source of niacin and has a minimal amount of fat.

Pork and Marinade

- 2 tablespoons ketchup
- 2 tablespoons reduced-sodium soy sauce
- 2 tablespoons rice wine
- 1 tablespoon minced fresh ginger
- 2 cloves garlic, minced
- 1 tablespoon sugar
- ½ teaspoon five-spice powder (see hint)
- ¼ teaspoon salt
- 1¼ pounds pork tenderloin, trimmed of all visible fat

Basting Sauce

- 2 tablespoons hoisin sauce
- 1 tablespoon honey
- ⅛ teaspoon five-spice powder

To make the pork and marinade: In a medium bowl, combine the ketchup, soy sauce, rice wine, ginger, garlic, sugar, five-spice powder, and salt. Mix well. Add the pork and turn to coat. Cover and refrigerate for at least 2 hours or up to 8 hours; turn at least once while marinating.

Coat a grill rack or broiler pan with no-stick spray. Preheat the grill or broiler.

To make the basting sauce: In a small bowl, stir together the hoisin sauce, honey, and five-spice powder.

Cook the pork 4" from the heat for 4 to 5 minutes per side, or until no longer pink in the center when tested with a sharp knife. Brush occasionally with the basting sauce. Discard the remaining basting sauce.

Transfer the pork to a cutting board and let stand for 5 minutes before slicing.

Nutrition Notes

Per serving

Calories 205
Fat 4.2 g.
% of calories from fat 19
Protein 25.1 g.
Carbohydrates 14 g.
Dietary fiber 0.4 g.
Cholesterol 67 mg.
Sodium 527 mg.

Kitchen Hints

◆ Five-spice powder is a blend of ground star anise, peppercorns, fennel seeds, cinnamon, and cloves. It can be found in the spice section of most supermarkets.

◆ The pork tenderloin used in this recipe can be replaced with the same quantity of turkey tenders. Turkey tenders are the strips of meat attached to the turkey breast. They are often packaged and sold on their own in the meat department at the supermarket. Reduce the cooking time by 1 minute per side to account for the difference in size from the pork.

Nutrition Notes

Per serving

Calories 304
Fat 5.4 g.
% of calories from fat 16
Protein 12.5 g.
Carbohydrates 10.1 g.
Dietary fiber 1.2 g.
Cholesterol 98 mg.
Sodium 550 mg.

Kitchen Hint

◆ For a decorative garnish, make scallion brushes. For each brush, remove the root from a scallion. Remove the top two-thirds of the scallion, leaving a 3" piece. Starting at the root end, make several 2" slashes along the length of the scallion to create the strands for the brush; leave the opposite end intact. Place in a bowl of cold water and refrigerate for at least 30 minutes or up to 3 days. The scallion strands will curl and separate.

Scallion Noodles

Here's a simple, high-flavor side dish or light meal. Angel hair pasta gets a lift from ginger, oyster sauce, and a small amount of toasted sesame oil.

12	ounces angel hair pasta
1	teaspoon peanut oil
3	tablespoons minced fresh ginger
1½	cups sliced scallions
3	tablespoons oyster sauce
1	teaspoon toasted sesame oil
½	teaspoon ground black pepper
¼	teaspoon salt

Cook the angel hair in a large pot of boiling water according to the package directions. Drain.

Place a wok or large no-stick skillet over medium-high heat until hot. Add the peanut oil. Add the ginger; stir-fry for 10 seconds, or until fragrant. Add the scallions; stir-fry for 30 seconds, or until wilted. Remove from the heat. Add the angel hair, oyster sauce, sesame oil, pepper, and salt. Toss to coat. Serve warm or cold.

The Power of Potassium

Health experts say that eating potassium-rich foods can help prevent high blood pressure. It's no wonder, since potassium helps regulate blood pressure, transmit nerve impulses, and contract muscles. Both men and women should get about 3,500 milligrams of potassium a day. Go for fresh fruits, vegetables, and whole-grain foods to meet your daily needs. Here are some good choices.

Food	Potassium (mg.)
10 dried peach halves	1,295
1 cup cooked winter squash	1,043
1 cup cooked lima beans	955
1 cup cooked spinach	839
½ cantaloupe	826
1 cup cooked pinto beans	722
10 prunes	626
1 baked potato with skin	510
1 banana	451
1 cup cooked asparagus	366

Homestyle Hash Browns

MAKES 4 SERVINGS

Made with just a small amount of olive oil, these crispy potatoes and onions are a hearty companion to your morning eggs and toast.

1½	pounds Yukon gold potatoes, cut into ¾" cubes
1	cup thinly sliced onions
1	roasted sweet red pepper, coarsely chopped
2	teaspoons olive oil
2	teaspoons chopped fresh rosemary or thyme
¼	teaspoon salt
¼	teaspoon ground black pepper

Place the potatoes in a large saucepan. Cover with cold water and bring to a boil over high heat. Reduce the heat to medium and simmer for 15 minutes, or until just tender when tested with a sharp knife. Drain.

Coat a large no-stick skillet with no-stick spray and place over medium heat. Add the onions and cook, stirring occasionally, for 3 to 5 minutes, or until softened. Add the red peppers, oil, rosemary or thyme, salt, black pepper, and the cooked potatoes. Mix well, cover, and cook for 6 to 8 minutes, or until the underside is crispy and golden brown. Using a wide spatula, turn the potatoes over. Cover and cook for 6 to 8 minutes, or until the potatoes are golden brown. (For extra-crispy hash browns, cook for an additional 5 to 10 minutes, turning the potatoes occasionally.)

Nutrition Notes

Per serving

Calories 163
Fat 2.5 g.
% of calories from fat 14
Protein 3 g.
Carbohydrates 33.2 g.
Dietary fiber 2.8 g.
Cholesterol 0 mg.
Sodium 142 mg.

Kitchen Hint

◆ Hash browns are a great way to use up leftover cooked potatoes. Add a little shredded reduced-fat cheese and some Canadian bacon for a quick one-pan skillet breakfast or supper.

Fall Menu Eight

	1,500 CALORIES	2,000 CALORIES	2,500 CALORIES
	33-43 G. FAT	44-56 G. FAT	57-69 G. FAT

Breakfast

fruited cottage cheese	¾ cup	1¾ cups	1¾ cups
toasted English muffin with	1	1	2
jam	2 tablespoons	2 tablespoons	¼ cup

Lunch

Wild Mushroom Pizza	2 slices	3 slices	3 slices
mixed baby lettuce with	2 cups	3 cups	3 cups
nonfat dressing	2 tablespoons	3 tablespoons	3 tablespoons
seedless red grapes	½ cup	¾ cup	1 cup

Dinner

Bayou Shrimp Casserole	1 serving	1½ servings	2 servings
Key Lime Pie	1 slice	1 slice	1 slice

Snack

low-fat granola bar	1	1	2

DAILY TOTALS			
Calories	1,499	1,988	2,498
Fat (g.)	24	32	35
% of calories from fat	14	14	12
Protein (g.)	66	99	117
Carbohydrates (g.)	262	335	442
Dietary fiber (g.)	19	26	36
Cholesterol (mg.)	219	299	366
Sodium (mg.)	2,127	3,172	3,682

NUTRIENT BONUS

This menu (at 2,000 calories) exceeds the Daily Value for:

Dietary fiber	105%
Vitamin A	140%
Vitamin C	303%
Iron	106%

HEALTHY TIP OF THE DAY

Fend off fad diets. Magical foods, food combinations, and fad diets are often touted as the best way to lose weight. They usually capitalize on the initial water weight that you might lose, but most people gain all the weight back quickly—and sometimes they gain even more. Always remember: If it sounds too good to be true, it probably is. Scientific research has not yet proven that certain foods or food combinations will increase your metabolism. The only reliable strategy for controlling your weight is a plan that combines a healthy and balanced diet with regular exercise.

Key Lime Pie (page 298)

Nutrition Notes

Per slice

Calories 155
Fat 4.6 g.
% of calories from fat 27
Protein 7.1 g.
Carbohydrates 21.7 g.
Dietary fiber 1.8 g.
Cholesterol 7 mg.
Sodium 292 mg.

Kitchen Hint

◆ Try pizza toppings with a regional American flair. For Southern flavors, use barbecued chicken and sliced red onions. For Southwestern accents, try cooked ground beef, green chili peppers, onions, and tomatoes. Get flavors from the West with grilled vegetables, roasted garlic, sun-dried tomatoes, and mozzarella. For a taste of the Northwest, use smoked salmon and a low-fat dill–cream cheese spread. Visit the Midwest with turkey sausage, tomato sauce, and mozzarella. For East Coast flavors, try smoked shrimp, roasted peppers, and pesto.

Wild Mushroom Pizza

MAKES 8 SLICES

Portobello and shiitake mushrooms give this crispy pizza a meaty, earthy flavor. Goat cheese and shaved Parmesan curls lend their own distinctive tastes.

1 tablespoon cornmeal
1 tube (10 ounces) refrigerated pizza dough
1 cup thinly sliced red onions
4 ounces shiitake mushrooms, thinly sliced
4 ounces portobello mushrooms, thinly sliced
3 ounces goat cheese, crumbled
1 tablespoon chopped fresh rosemary
1 ounce Parmesan cheese

Preheat the oven to 475°F. Coat a baking sheet with no-stick spray. Sprinkle with the cornmeal.

Unroll the pizza dough and spread on the prepared baking sheet.

Coat a large no-stick skillet with no-stick spray and place over medium heat. Add the onions, shiitake mushrooms, and portobello mushrooms. Cook, stirring often, for 8 to 10 minutes, or until browned. Spread on top of the dough, leaving a ½" border around the edge. Sprinkle with the goat cheese and rosemary.

Bake for 12 to 15 minutes, or until the bottom is browned and crispy.

Hold the Parmesan over the pizza and, using a vegetable peeler, make curls to dot the surface.

Bayou Shrimp Casserole

This Creole-style shrimp dish uses brown rice for a nutty flavor and extra fiber. Don't be thrown off by the number of ingredients—they're mostly spices. The actual hands-on time for this dish is only about 15 minutes.

3	cups cooked long-grain brown rice
2	teaspoons olive oil
2	cups chopped onions
1½	cups chopped celery
1½	cups chopped sweet red and yellow peppers
2	teaspoons minced garlic
2	teaspoons dried thyme
1	teaspoon dried basil
1½	teaspoons ground black pepper
½	teaspoon ground red pepper
¼	teaspoon salt
1	bay leaf
1	cup defatted reduced-sodium chicken broth
1	can (28 ounces) no-salt-added chopped tomatoes (with juice)
1	can (8 ounces) no-salt-added tomato sauce
2	teaspoons sugar
1½	pounds large shrimp, peeled and deveined

Preheat the oven to 375°F.

Coat a 13" × 9" baking dish with no-stick spray. Spread the rice evenly in the dish.

Warm the oil in a large no-stick skillet over medium heat. Add the onions, celery, red and yellow peppers, and garlic. Cook, stirring often, for 6 to 8 minutes, or until lightly browned and softened. Add the thyme, basil, black pepper, red pepper, salt, and bay leaf. Cook for 1 minute.

Stir in the broth and increase the heat to medium-high. Cook, stirring occasionally, for 5 minutes, or until the liquid is reduced by one-half. Stir in the tomatoes (with juice), tomato sauce, and sugar. Stir in the shrimp and pour over the rice.

Bake for 25 to 30 minutes, or until hot and bubbly.

Nutrition Notes

Per serving

Calories 277
Fat 3.4 g.
% of calories from fat 11
Protein 20.3 g.
Carbohydrates 42.2 g.
Dietary fiber 6.7 g.
Cholesterol 135 mg.
Sodium 439 mg.

Kitchen Hint

◆ The easiest way to remove fat from canned broth is to place the opened can in the freezer for 5 to 10 minutes. The fat will congeal on the top so it can be easily removed with a spoon.

Nutrition Notes

Per slice

Calories 246
Fat 7.8 g.
% of calories from fat 28
Protein 7.5 g.
Carbohydrates 60.6 g.
Dietary fiber 0.5 g.
Cholesterol 65 mg.
Sodium 209 mg.

Kitchen Hints

◆ Adding a teaspoon of cornstarch to the sugar before beating it into the egg whites adds structure to the meringue and prevents it from separating as it is baking or when it starts to cool.

◆ You can substitute ½ cup bottled Key lime juice for the fresh lime juice. Key limes are grown on the Florida Keys and have a more intense lime flavor than regular limes. Look for Key lime juice in the international aisle of your supermarket.

◆ Experiment with different kinds of low-fat cookie crusts. Try using crushed low-fat vanilla or chocolate wafers or cinnamon graham crackers.

Key Lime Pie

MAKES 8 SLICES

This updated classic has a velvety filling and a gingersnap crust.

Crust

1	egg white
1½	cups crumbled gingersnap cookies (about 30)
1½	tablespoons unsalted butter or margarine, melted
1½	tablespoons canola oil

Filling

½	cup lime juice
1	tablespoon grated lime rind
1	can (14 ounces) nonfat sweetened condensed milk
2	egg yolks
½	cup sugar
1	teaspoon cornstarch
4	large egg whites
¼	teaspoon cream of tartar

To make the crust: Preheat the oven to 375°F. Coat a 9" pie plate with no-stick spray.

Place the egg white in a medium bowl and beat lightly with a fork. Add the gingersnaps, butter or margarine, and oil. Blend well. Pour into the prepared pie plate and press in an even layer on the bottom and up the sides. Bake for 8 to 10 minutes, or until lightly browned and firm. Cool on a wire rack.

To make the filling: In a large bowl, combine the lime juice and lime rind. Whisk in the condensed milk and egg yolks.

In a small bowl, combine the sugar and cornstarch. Mix well.

Place the egg whites and cream of tartar in a medium bowl. Using an electric mixer, beat on medium speed until foamy. Increase the speed to high and gradually beat in the sugar mixture. Continue to beat until the whites are firm and glossy.

Fold ¾ cup of the meringue into the lime mixture. Pour into the prepared crust and bake for 15 minutes. Remove from the oven.

Spoon the remaining meringue over the filling and spread to the edges of the crust. Using the spoon, make small peaks in the meringue. Bake for 10 minutes, or until the meringue is golden brown and set. (If the meringue browns too quickly, reduce the oven temperature to 350°F.) Cool completely on a wire rack. Refrigerate for 1 to 2 hours.

Fall Menu Nine

	1,500 CALORIES	2,000 CALORIES	2,500 CALORIES
	33-43 G. FAT	44-56 G. FAT	57-69 G. FAT

Breakfast

low-fat frozen waffles	1	2	3
reduced-calorie syrup	1 tablespoon	2 tablespoons	3 tablespoons
calcium-fortified orange juice	1 cup	1½ cups	1½ cups

Lunch

Ham and Cheese Melt Sandwiches	1	1	1½
baked potato chips	12	12	12
seedless red grapes	1 cup	1¼ cups	1 cup

Dinner

Rotini with Roasted Vegetable Sauce	1 serving	1½ servings	2 servings

Snack

Chewy Oatmeal Cookies	3	3	3
skim milk	1 cup	1½ cups	1½ cups

DAILY TOTALS			
Calories	1,512	1,988	2,507
Fat (g.)	29	37	51
% of calories from fat	17	16	18
Protein (g.)	60	76	99
Carbohydrates (g.)	263	354	434
Dietary fiber (g.)	24	33	43
Cholesterol (mg.)	100	130	182
Sodium (mg.)	1,896	2,306	3,137

NUTRIENT BONUS

This menu (at 2,000 calories) exceeds the Daily Value for:

Dietary fiber	132%
Vitamin A	344%
Thiamin	175%
Riboflavin	132%
Niacin	109%
Vitamin B$_6$	104%
Vitamin C	613%
Calcium	174%
Iron	101%
Potassium	108%

HEALTHY TIP OF THE DAY

Small amounts of cheese can really make the flavor difference in a low-fat dish. But don't get carried away. An ounce of Cheddar has 114 calories and 9.4 grams of fat; an ounce of brie has 95 calories and 7.9 grams of fat. The trick is to choose a strong-flavored cheese so you won't need to use as much. If you must use more, go with the low-fat or part-skim variety of any cheese. Most low-fat and part-skim varieties melt well and taste very similar to the original.

Rotini with Roasted Vegetable Sauce

Rotini with Roasted Vegetable Sauce

MAKES 4 SERVINGS

Roasted vegetables make a robust pasta sauce that's perfect for autumn. Plus, you get lots of vitamin A, vitamin C, and potassium in the bargain.

- 1 sweet red pepper, cut into 1" pieces
- 1 medium sweet potato, peeled and cut into ½" pieces
- ½ medium butternut squash, peeled and cut into ½" pieces
- ½ medium eggplant, cut into 1" pieces
- 3 portobello mushrooms, thickly sliced
  Salt and ground black pepper
- 1 whole bulb garlic
- 2 pounds plum tomatoes
- 1 can (15 ounces) reduced-sodium tomato sauce
- 8 ounces rotini
- ¼ cup shredded fresh basil
- 2 tablespoons toasted pine nuts

Preheat the oven to 400°F. Coat 2 baking sheets with no-stick spray.

Place the red peppers, sweet potatoes, squash, eggplant, and mushrooms on 1 of the baking sheets. Mist with no-stick spray. Sprinkle lightly with the salt and black pepper.

Slice ¼" off the top of the garlic bulb and discard. Set the bulb on a piece of foil and wrap loosely. Place on the second baking sheet. Cut the tomatoes in half lengthwise. Squeeze each half to remove the seeds and excess juice. Place the tomatoes, cut side up, on the sheet with the garlic. Mist with no-stick spray. Sprinkle lightly with the salt and black pepper.

Place both sheets in the oven. Bake for 25 minutes. Remove the tomatoes and garlic from the oven. Bake the vegetables for 10 to 15 minutes more, or until lightly browned and softened.

Transfer the tomatoes and other vegetables to a large saucepan. Stir in the tomato sauce. Squeeze the cloves of garlic from their skins into a small bowl. Mash into a paste and stir into the sauce. Simmer for 15 minutes.

Cook the rotini in a large pot of boiling water according to the package directions. Drain. Add to the saucepan and toss to coat. Serve sprinkled with the basil and pine nuts.

Nutrition Notes

Per serving

Calories 437
Fat 6.2 g.
% of calories from fat 12
Protein 15.9 g.
Carbohydrates 85.7 g.
Dietary fiber 12.8 g.
Cholesterol 0 mg.
Sodium 327 mg.

Kitchen Hints

◆ The sauce can be made up to 2 days in advance. To reheat, stir in about ¼ cup water and place over low heat for 10 minutes, or until hot.

◆ You can roast or steam the unused squash and eggplant to serve alongside any lean red meat, poultry, or fish.

Nutrition Notes

Per sandwich

Calories 340
Fat 11.1 g.
% of calories from fat 30
Protein 24.1 g.
Carbohydrates 33.6 g.
Dietary fiber 4.4 g.
Cholesterol 50 mg.
Sodium 971 mg.

Kitchen Hint

◆ To save time, buy prepackaged shredded cabbage from the produce section of your supermarket. The coleslaw can be made up to 2 days in advance and refrigerated.

Ham and Cheese Melt Sandwiches

MAKES 4 SANDWICHES

Looking for something different for lunch? Here, lean ham, smoked Cheddar, Granny Smith apples, and crunchy nonfat coleslaw combine to make an unusually delicious sandwich.

Coleslaw

1½	cups shredded green cabbage
2	tablespoons nonfat sour cream
1	teaspoon red-wine vinegar
1	teaspoon sugar
½	teaspoon poppy seeds
½	teaspoon dried dill

Sandwiches

8	ounces thinly sliced lean reduced-sodium ham
1	Granny Smith apple, thinly sliced
4	ounces thinly sliced smoked Cheddar cheese
8	slices rye bread

To make the coleslaw: In a medium bowl, combine the cabbage, sour cream, vinegar, sugar, poppy seeds, and dill. Mix well.

To make the sandwiches: Layer the ham, coleslaw, apples, and Cheddar on 4 slices of the bread. Top with the remaining bread.

Coat a large no-stick skillet with no-stick spray and place over medium heat. Working in batches if necessary, place the sandwiches in the skillet, cover, and cook for 3 to 4 minutes, or until golden brown and toasted. Coat the tops of the sandwiches with no-stick spray, turn, and cook for 2 to 3 minutes, or until the Cheddar is melted.

Chewy Oatmeal Cookies

MAKES 36

Loaded with rolled oats and plump juicy raisins, these chewy treats are high in soluble fiber and have just half the fat of traditional oatmeal cookies.

1½	cups all-purpose flour
1	teaspoon ground cinnamon
¾	teaspoon baking soda
¼	teaspoon salt
¼	cup margarine or unsalted butter, at room temperature
½	cup sugar
½	cup packed light brown sugar
1	egg
⅓	cup skim milk
1	tablespoon light corn syrup
1	teaspoon vanilla
1½	cups quick-cooking rolled oats
⅔	cup raisins

Preheat the oven to 375°F. Coat 2 baking sheets with no-stick spray.

In a medium bowl, combine the flour, cinnamon, baking soda, and salt. Mix well.

In a large bowl, combine the margarine or butter, sugar, and brown sugar. Using an electric mixer, beat on medium speed until blended. Add the egg and beat for 2 to 3 minutes, or until light and fluffy. Add the milk, corn syrup, and vanilla. Beat until blended.

Reduce the speed to low and gradually add the flour mixture, beating until just combined. Stir in the oats and raisins.

Drop the dough by level tablespoons onto the prepared baking sheets. Bake 1 sheet at a time for 8 to 10 minutes, or until lightly browned. Transfer the cookies to a wire rack to cool.

Nutrition Notes

Per cookie

Calories 76
Fat 1.7 g.
% of calories from fat 20
Protein 1.4 g.
Carbohydrates 14 g.
Dietary fiber 0.7 g.
Cholesterol 6 mg.
Sodium 46 mg.

Kitchen Hint

◆ If you like, substitute ⅓ cup miniature semisweet chocolate chips for ⅓ cup of the raisins. The calories and fat per cookie will increase slightly to 81 calories and 2.1 grams of fat.

Fall Menu Ten

HEALTHY TIP OF THE DAY

Burn fat, build muscle. Contrary to some headlines, fat cannot be "turned into" muscle. Fat must be burned through aerobic exercise. Even though some muscle tone is acquired through aerobic exercise, extensive muscle toning requires strength training, or weight lifting. The best way to burn fat and tone muscle is through aerobic, weight-bearing exercise such as walking, jogging, skiing, and aerobics. See a qualified exercise physiologist to develop an exercise plan that meets your individual goals.

	1,500 CALORIES 33-43 G. FAT	2,000 CALORIES 44-56 G. FAT	2,500 CALORIES 57-69 G. FAT
Breakfast			
Pear and Apple Sauce	½ cup	1 cup	1¼ cups
cooked oatmeal	½ cup	1 cup	1¼ cups
skim milk	1 cup	1¼ cups	1¼ cups
Lunch			
Santa Fe Salad	1 serving	1½ servings	2 servings
toasted whole-wheat pita bread	1	2	2
apple	1	1	1
Dinner			
Baked Chicken and Vegetable Couscous	1 serving	1 serving	1½ servings
mixed greens with	1 cup	2 cups	2 cups
nonfat dressing	1 tablespoon	2 tablespoons	2 tablespoons
Snack			
nonfat fruit yogurt	1 cup	1 cup	1 cup

DAILY TOTALS			
Calories	1,506	2,001	2,488
Fat (g.)	16	22	27
% of calories from fat	9	9	9
Protein (g.)	88	103	133
Carbohydrates (g.)	268	371	456
Dietary fiber (g.)	35	49	61
Cholesterol (mg.)	103	104	151
Sodium (mg.)	1,253	1,818	2,087

Baked Chicken and Vegetable Couscous (page 308)

Nutrition Notes

Per ¹/₂ cup

Calories 146
Fat 0.7 g.
% of calories from fat 4
Protein 0.5 g.
Carbohydrates 37.7 g.
Dietary fiber 4.4 g.
Cholesterol 0 mg.
Sodium 1 mg.

Kitchen Hints

◆ For a less chunky sauce, mash the fruit against the side of the pan with a wooden spoon during cooking. Or pass the sauce through a food mill.

◆ Serve this sauce warm over vanilla frozen yogurt, pancakes, or waffles. Or serve as a simple side dish.

Pear and Apple Sauce

MAKES 2 CUPS

Seasoned with a hint of cinnamon, this warm fruit sauce is rich in vitamin C. Enjoy it for breakfast, as a snack, or as a naturally sweet alternative to high-sugar spreads and toppings.

¼ cup water
2 tablespoons sugar
5 whole cloves
2 cinnamon sticks
4 small McIntosh apples, peeled and thinly sliced
2 pears, peeled and thinly sliced

In a medium saucepan, combine the water, sugar, cloves, and cinnamon sticks. Bring to a boil over medium heat. Add the apples and pears. Simmer for 20 to 30 minutes, or until a chunky sauce forms. Remove and discard the cloves and cinnamon sticks.

Label Lingo

Food labels make lots of claims about nutrition. Here's how to decipher the lingo and make sure you're getting the vitamins and minerals that you're looking for. Remember that each food label claim refers to 1 serving of the food, and percentages are based on a daily intake of 2,000 calories (the average daily calorie intake for adults).

Food Label Claim	Definition
Enriched	A food with added nutrients, particularly in processed cereals and breads where nutrients are added to make up for those lost in processing
Fortified	A food with added nutrients, particularly where vitamins or minerals exceed the amount originally found in the food
Excellent source of... High in... Rich in...	Contains 20% or more of the Daily Value per serving
Good source of... Contains... Provides...	Contains 10% to 19% of the Daily Value per serving
More... Added...	Contains at least 10% of the Daily Value per serving

Santa Fe Salad

Bursting with color and packed with fiber, this rice and bean salad can be assembled at a moment's notice. Serve it as a lunch entrée or as a side dish with roasted meat.

- 1 teaspoon + 1 tablespoon canola oil
- ½ cup long-grain white rice
- ¾ cup reduced-sodium vegetable broth
- ⅓ cup water
- 1 lime
- 2 small cloves garlic, minced
- ¼ cup reduced-sodium vegetable juice
- ¼ teaspoon ground cumin
- ¼ teaspoon ground red pepper
-   Dash of hot-pepper sauce
-   Salt and ground black pepper
- 1 can (19 ounces) chickpeas, rinsed and drained
- 5 ounces frozen corn kernels, thawed
- 5 ounces frozen peas, thawed
- 2 plum tomatoes, chopped
- ¼ cup chopped red onions
- 2 tablespoons chopped fresh cilantro (optional)

Warm 1 teaspoon of the oil in a medium saucepan over medium heat. Add the rice and stir to coat. Cook, stirring, for 2 minutes. Add the broth and water. Bring to a boil over high heat. Reduce the heat to medium-low, cover, and cook for 20 to 25 minutes, or until the liquid is absorbed and the rice is tender. Transfer to a large bowl.

Grate the rind of the lime into a small bowl. Cut the lime in half and squeeze the juice into the bowl. Discard the lime. Whisk in the garlic, vegetable juice, cumin, red pepper, hot-pepper sauce, and the remaining 1 tablespoon oil. Season with the salt and black pepper. Pour over the rice. Add the chickpeas, corn, peas, tomatoes, and onions. Toss to combine. Sprinkle with the cilantro (if using). Serve warm or cold.

Nutrition Notes

Per serving

Calories 241
Fat 5.3 g.
% of calories from fat 18
Protein 9.2 g.
Carbohydrates 45.5 g.
Dietary fiber 6.7 g.
Cholesterol 0 mg.
Sodium 167 mg.

Kitchen Hints

◆ This salad can be made up to 4 days in advance so it's ready to pack for a quick lunch.

◆ Don't eliminate a recipe from your repertoire simply because you don't like an ingredient or two. Experiment with recipes and substitute ingredients that you and your family prefer. For example, in this recipe, use Italian parsley in place of cilantro for a more mild flavor.

Nutrition Notes

Per serving

Calories 588
Fat 5.3 g.
% of calories from fat 8
Protein 48.9 g.
Carbohydrates 86.4 g.
Dietary fiber 12.8 g.
Cholesterol 95 mg.
Sodium 369 mg.

Kitchen Hints

◆ To peel and cube winter squash, cut it in half and remove the seeds. Cut the halves into 2" sections and, using a sharp knife, cut the flesh away from the skin.

◆ Clay pots are a wonderful way to bake almost any type of marinated poultry, meat, fish, or vegetables. A clay pot seals in the juices and imparts a richer flavor to the dish. Most dishes take less time to cook in a clay baking pot than in a conventional baking dish, so start checking for doneness 5 to 10 minutes earlier than the recipe suggests.

Baked Chicken and Vegetable Couscous

Makes 4 servings

Chicken breasts marinated in an Indian spice mixture complement a harvest of roasted vegetables. Couscous turns this into a complete meal.

Chicken and Marinade

1   lemon
1   cup nonfat plain yogurt
1   tablespoon grated fresh ginger
2   cloves garlic, minced
1½ teaspoons turmeric
1   teaspoon ground coriander
1   teaspoon paprika
1   teaspoon ground cardamom
½   teaspoon ground cumin
¼   teaspoon ground black pepper
⅛   teaspoon salt
4   bone-in, skinless chicken breast halves
    (about 8 ounces each)

Roasted Vegetables

4   carrots, cut into 1" pieces
4   parsnips, cut into 1" pieces
2   cups peeled and cubed butternut squash
1   red onion, cut into 1" pieces
    Salt and ground black pepper
1½ cups defatted reduced-sodium chicken broth

Couscous

2¼ cups water
1   box (10 ounces) couscous

To make the chicken and marinade: Grate the rind of the lemon into a shallow 3-quart baking dish. Cut the lemon in half and squeeze the juice into the baking dish. Discard the lemon. Stir in the yogurt, ginger, garlic, turmeric, coriander, paprika, cardamom, cumin, pepper, and salt. Mix well. Add the chicken and turn to coat. Cover and refrigerate for at least 4 hours or up to 12 hours; turn at least once while marinating.

To make the roasted vegetables: Preheat the oven to 400°F. Line 2 baking sheets with foil and coat with no-stick spray.

Arrange the carrots, parsnips, squash, and onions on the baking sheets; season with the salt and pepper. Bake for 30 to 35 minutes, or until almost tender. Remove from the oven. Reduce the temperature to 375°F.

Remove the chicken from the refrigerator. Uncover and add the broth to the baking dish. Cover the chicken loosely with foil and roast for 25 minutes, basting occasionally with the marinade. Remove the foil, turn the chicken pieces over, and add the vegetables. Bake for 10 to 15 minutes, or until the chicken is no longer pink in the center when tested with a sharp knife.

To make the couscous: Bring the water to a boil in a medium saucepan over high heat. Stir in the couscous. Remove from the heat. Cover and let stand for 5 minutes, or until the liquid is absorbed. Fluff with a fork. Serve with the chicken and vegetables.

9 Uses for Leftover Chicken

Cooked chicken has hundreds of uses. Here are a few ideas for cooked boneless, skinless chicken breasts (the leanest choice).

1. Add cooked chicken strips to a green salad or pasta salad.
2. Add chunks of cooked chicken to soups.
3. For a quick Southwestern-style sandwich, toss grilled chicken strips with corn and barbecue sauce, then wrap in a tortilla.
4. Make nachos with baked tortilla chips, nonfat refried beans, tomatoes, lettuce, nonfat sour cream, low-fat cheese, and shredded cooked chicken breast.
5. For tropical chicken salad, toss cooked chicken cubes with nonfat mayonnaise, fresh grapes, pineapple chunks, celery, and a few toasted walnuts.
6. Make a quick chicken pizza. Add diced cooked chicken to marinara sauce and place on top of a bagel or low-fat pizza crust. Add your favorite vegetables and top with low-fat cheese.
7. For chicken dumplings, mix together low-fat herbed cream cheese and shredded cooked chicken. Place 1 tablespoon of the mixture between 2 small wonton wrappers and seal the edges with water. Cook in simmering water. When the bundles rise to the top, drain and serve with your favorite sauce.
8. Make a chicken frittata. Combine fat-free egg substitute, cooked chicken, cooked vegetables, and Parmesan cheese. Cook in a skillet coated with no-stick spray. When the eggs are just set, place in a hot oven until the top is browned and the eggs are fully cooked.
9. Make savory crêpes. Thin low-fat condensed cream soup with a small amount of water and heat. Stir in the cooked chicken. Place $\frac{1}{2}$ cup of the mixture into the center of a crêpe and fold up the sides like a package. Serve seam side down. Look for premade crêpes in the produce aisle at supermarkets.

Fall Menu Eleven

	1,500 CALORIES	2,000 CALORIES	2,500 CALORIES
	33-43 G. FAT	44-56 G. FAT	57-69 G. FAT

Breakfast

bran flakes with raisins	1¼ cups	1½ cups	2 cups
skim milk	1 cup	1¼ cups	1½ cups
grapefruit	½	½	1

Lunch

Chicken Tacos with Charred Salsa	1 serving	1½ servings	2 servings
nonfat refried beans	½ cup	¾ cup	1 cup
plum	1	1	1

Dinner

Salmon with White Beans and Watercress	1 serving	1½ servings	2 servings
steamed sugar snap peas	½ cup	¾ cup	1 cup
cooked rotini with	1 cup	1¼ cups	1¼ cups
chopped fresh herbs	1½ teaspoons	2 teaspoons	2 teaspoons

Snack

Chocolate Mousse	1 serving	1 serving	1 serving

DAILY TOTALS

Calories	1,501	2,000	2,528
Fat (g.)	23	32	40
% of calories from fat	14	14	14
Protein (g.)	103	145	187
Carbohydrates (g.)	232	297	372
Dietary fiber (g.)	29	39	51
Cholesterol (mg.)	159	224	289
Sodium (mg.)	1,527	2,146	2,823

NUTRIENT BONUS

This menu (at 2,000 calories) exceeds the Daily Value for:

Dietary fiber	155%
Vitamin A	309%
Thiamin	280%
Riboflavin	293%
Niacin	368%
Vitamin B6	305%
Vitamin B12	343%
Folate	234%
Vitamin C	364%
Calcium	128%
Iron	269%
Potassium	120%

HEALTHY TIP OF THE DAY

Just beginning an exercise routine? The American College of Sports Medicine recommends starting slowly. Exercise 3 to 5 times a week for 20 to 30 minutes per session. Try moderate activities like jogging, walking, hiking, cycling, swimming, and aerobics. Once you are comfortable, intensify your program. Exercise 4 or 5 times a week and progress to 1-hour sessions. Most people burn 250 calories for every 30 minutes of walking—the perfect amount for steady weight loss and good fitness.

Chicken Tacos with Charred Salsa (page 312)

Nutrition Notes

Per serving

Calories 371
Fat 6.4 g.
% of calories from fat 16
Protein 31.7 g.
Carbohydrates 45.8 g.
Dietary fiber 2.7 g.
Cholesterol 63 mg.
Sodium 406 mg.

Kitchen Hint

◆ If you're in a hurry, use fat-free bottled salsa. Or prepare the charred salsa ahead and store it in the refrigerator for up to 2 days.

Chicken Tacos with Charred Salsa

MAKES 4 SERVINGS

These soft tacos are topped with a fresh salsa that's bursting with smoky flavor. You won't notice the absence of traditional high-fat taco toppings like guacamole and cheese.

Chicken and Marinade

  3 limes
¼ cup orange juice
¼ cup chopped fresh cilantro
  1 tablespoon minced garlic
½ teaspoon ground cumin
  4 boneless, skinless chicken breasts (4 ounces each)

Charred Salsa

  8 plum tomatoes
  2 jalapeño peppers (wear plastic gloves when handling)
⅓ cup chopped scallions
    Juice of 1 lime
  2 tablespoons chopped fresh cilantro
  1 teaspoon minced garlic
⅛ teaspoon salt
  1 large red onion, thinly sliced
  6 whole-wheat flour tortillas (8" diameter)
¾ cup nonfat sour cream
  2 cups finely shredded leaf lettuce

To make the chicken and marinade: Grate the rind from the limes into a large bowl; cut the limes in half and squeeze the juice into the bowl. Discard the limes. Stir in the orange juice, cilantro, garlic, and cumin.

Pound the chicken to an even thickness of ½". Add to the marinade and turn to coat. Cover and refrigerate for at least 1 hour or up to 4 hours; turn at least once while marinating.

To make the charred salsa: Set a large cast-iron skillet over high heat until hot. Add the tomatoes and peppers. Cover and cook, turning occasionally, for 8 to 10 minutes, or until charred on all sides. Remove the pan from the heat and let stand, covered, until the vegetables are cool enough to handle.

Remove and discard the skins and seeds from the peppers. Finely
mince the peppers and transfer to a medium bowl. Cut the
tomatoes in half crosswise; squeeze each half to remove the
seeds. Coarsely chop the tomatoes and add to the bowl. Stir in
the scallions, lime juice, cilantro, garlic, and salt.

To assemble the tacos: Coat the skillet with no-stick spray and place
over medium heat. Add the chicken and red onions. Cook for
about 3 minutes per side, or until the chicken is no longer pink
in the center when tested with a sharp knife and the onions are
softened. Cut the chicken into 1" slices.

Wrap the tortillas in plastic wrap and microwave on high power for 1
minute to soften. Divide the chicken mixture among the
tortillas. Top with the salsa, sour cream, and lettuce. Roll to
enclose the filling. Slice each taco in half.

Regular or Reduced-Fat?

Cutting back on fat doesn't necessarily mean eliminating butter
and regular mayonnaise. It means being aware of how much you
use and controlling the amounts. Studies show that when "light"
foods are chosen, people often eat a larger-than-normal portion and
actually consume more calories and fat than if they had an average-
size portion of the higher-fat food. The key is controlling portion
size and eating fats in moderation. Of course, reduced-fat cheeses
and low-fat milk can help achieve these goals. Here's a chart with
typical serving sizes to help you make smart choices when using
fats.

Food	Amount	Calories	Fat (g.)
Oil, canola or olive	1 teaspoon	40	4.5
Butter	1 teaspoon	34	3.8
Margarine	1 teaspoon	34	3.8
Peanut butter	2 tablespoons	188	16
Peanut butter, reduced-fat	2 tablespoons	190	12
Mayonnaise	1 tablespoon	99	11
Mayonnaise, reduced-fat	1 tablespoon	50	5
Mayonnaise, nonfat	1 tablespoon	10	0
Sour cream	2 tablespoons	62	6
Sour cream, light	2 tablespoons	40	2.5
Sour cream, nonfat	2 tablespoons	31	0
Cream cheese	2 tablespoons	101	10
Cream cheese, reduced-fat	2 tablespoons	70	6
Cream cheese, nonfat	2 tablespoons	30	0

Salmon with White Beans and Watercress

MAKES 4 SERVINGS

This full-bodied fish is a good source of omega-3 fatty acids. Here, the salmon is poached with white beans for a light-tasting dish that's high in fiber.

4	salmon fillets (4 ounces each)
	Salt and ground black pepper
2	tablespoons water
2	cloves garlic, minced
1	can (15 ounces) cannellini beans, rinsed and drained
4	plum tomatoes, diced
½	cup defatted reduced-sodium chicken broth
1	bunch watercress, rinsed and coarsely chopped
¼	cup chopped fresh Italian parsley

Coat a broiler pan with no-stick spray. Preheat the broiler.

Season the salmon fillets with the salt and pepper; place on a broiler pan. Broil 4" from the heat for 3 minutes per side, or until just opaque in the center when tested with a sharp knife.

Place the water in a large no-stick skillet. Bring to a boil over medium-high heat. Add the garlic and stir for 1 minute. Add the beans, tomatoes, and broth. Cook, stirring occasionally, for 3 to 4 minutes, or until heated through. Add the watercress and parsley. Cook for 30 seconds, or until the watercress begins to wilt. Season with the salt and pepper. Serve with the salmon.

Chocolate Mousse

MAKES 8 SERVINGS

It's a chocoholic's dream come true! This mousse can be eaten without remorse. We used 1% low-fat milk, cocoa powder, and egg whites to significantly reduce the fat and cholesterol without sacrificing the creamy texture.

¾	cup 1% low-fat milk
1	tablespoon instant coffee powder
⅔	cup unsweetened cocoa powder
¼	cup packed light brown sugar
1	egg, lightly beaten
2	tablespoons coffee liqueur or strong brewed coffee
1	teaspoon unflavored gelatin
2	ounces bittersweet chocolate, coarsely chopped
1	tablespoon vanilla
4	egg whites
½	cup sugar
½	teaspoon cream of tartar
1	cup fat-free nondairy whipped topping

In a medium saucepan, combine the milk and instant coffee powder. Cook over medium heat, stirring occasionally, for 2 to 3 minutes, or until steaming. Whisk in the cocoa and brown sugar until smooth. Remove from the heat and slowly whisk in the egg. Reduce the heat to low and whisk constantly for 5 minutes, or until thickened. Remove from the heat.

Place the coffee liqueur or coffee in a cup. Sprinkle with the gelatin. Let stand for 1 minute to soften. Stir into the cocoa mixture until dissolved. Add the chocolate and vanilla. Stir until the chocolate is melted. Transfer to a large bowl and set aside for 30 minutes, or until cooled to room temperature.

Pour about 2" water into another medium saucepan and bring to a simmer.

In a large heatproof bowl that will fit over the saucepan, combine the egg whites, sugar, and cream of tartar. Whisk well to combine. Set the bowl over the simmering water and gently whisk for 2 minutes, or until an instant-read thermometer registers 140°F (the mixture will be too hot to touch). Remove from the heat. Using an electric mixer, beat on medium-high speed for 5 minutes, or until cool.

Fold the egg-white mixture into the chocolate mixture. Fold in the whipped topping. Divide among dessert glasses and refrigerate for at least 2 hours or up to 24 hours.

Nutrition Notes

Per serving

Calories 164
Fat 4.6 g.
% of calories from fat 23
Protein 5.9 g.
Carbohydrates 27.8 g.
Dietary fiber 2.4 g.
Cholesterol 27 mg.
Sodium 53 mg.

Kitchen Hints

◆ Try using Dutch-process cocoa in this recipe. Dutch cocoa is darker, richer, and smoother than nonalkalized (or regular) cocoa.

◆ For a more festive presentation, make chocolate mousse parfaits. In parfait glasses, layer chocolate mousse, crushed low-fat chocolate wafers, and raspberries or mashed bananas. Top the parfaits with chocolate curls.

◆ This mousse also makes a wonderful filling for cakes and pies. One recipe is enough to fill a 9" layer cake (between the 2 cake layers). For a 9" pie shell, double the recipe. Prebake a graham cracker or chocolate crumb pie crust, fill with the mousse, and refrigerate for at least 2 hours before serving.

NUTRIENT BONUS

This menu (at 2,000 calories) exceeds the Daily Value for:

Dietary fiber	115%
Riboflavin	128%
Niacin	118%
Vitamin B6	109%
Vitamin C	620%
Calcium	128%
Potassium	108%

HEALTHY TIP OF THE DAY

Fewer than 2 percent of adults suffer from actual food allergies. Food intolerances, on the other hand, are much more common. The most common is lactose intolerance, or an inability to digest lactose (the sugar in milk). Symptoms include gas, bloating, or diarrhea after eating milk products. If you have these symptoms, look for lactose-free dairy products. You can also buy pills that can make digestion easier. With these products, you can enjoy the flavors of milk products without the discomfort.

	1,500 CALORIES	2,000 CALORIES	2,500 CALORIES
	33-43 G. FAT	44-56 G. FAT	57-69 G. FAT
Breakfast			
Chocolate Chip–Banana Muffins	1	2	2
skim milk	1 cup	1¼ cups	1½ cups
nonfat vanilla yogurt and	¾ cup	1 cup	1 cup
kiwifruit	2	2	2
Lunch			
water-packed tuna with	3 ounces	3 ounces	4 ounces
nonfat mayonnaise on	2 tablespoons	2 tablespoons	2 tablespoons
pumpernickel bagel	1	1	1
plum tomato	1	1	2
baked tortilla chips with	13	13	26
fat-free salsa	¼ cup	¼ cup	½ cup
orange	1	1	2
Dinner			
Cracked Peppercorn Veal Chops	1 serving	1 serving	2 servings
Braised Burgundy Cabbage	1 serving	2 servings	2 servings
steamed brussels sprouts	½ cup	½ cup	¾ cup
Snack			
low-sodium soda crackers with	5	10	10
reduced-fat peanut butter	1 tablespoon	2 tablespoons	2 tablespoons

DAILY TOTALS			
Calories	1,472	1,977	2,478
Fat (g.)	34	53	64
% of calories from fat	20	24	23
Protein (g.)	101	119	168
Carbohydrates (g.)	199	266	320
Dietary fiber (g.)	23	29	37
Cholesterol (mg.)	187	212	346
Sodium (mg.)	1,792	2,244	2,880

Cracked Peppercorn Veal Chops (page 319) and Braised Burgundy Cabbage (page 320)

Nutrition Notes

Per muffin

Calories 204
Fat 7.2 g.
% of calories from fat 31
Protein 3.9 g.
Carbohydrates 32.1 g.
Dietary fiber 1.5 g.
Cholesterol 18 mg.
Sodium 202 mg.

Kitchen Hints

◆ If you're fresh out of buttermilk, use soured milk instead. To make ⅓ cup soured milk, pour a generous ¼ cup 1% low-fat milk into a measuring cup. Add enough lemon juice to make ⅓ cup. Let stand for 5 minutes.

◆ To perk up day-old muffins, sprinkle with a few drops of water and loosely wrap in foil. Heat in a 350°F oven for 8 to 10 minutes, or until moist and warm. To store muffins, double-wrap them in plastic and freeze for up to 1 month.

Chocolate Chip–Banana Muffins

MAKES 12

These tender muffins are lower in fat and cholesterol than traditional ones, but you'd never know by tasting them. Apple butter stands in for some of the oil.

2 cups all-purpose flour
1 teaspoon baking powder
1 teaspoon ground cinnamon
½ teaspoon baking soda
½ teaspoon ground nutmeg
½ teaspoon salt
½ cup packed light brown sugar
¼ cup canola oil
¼ cup apple butter
⅓ cup 1% low-fat buttermilk or soured milk (see hint)
1 egg
1 egg white
1 teaspoon vanilla
1 cup mashed ripe bananas
⅓ cup mini semisweet chocolate chips
¼ cup chopped toasted walnuts
2 tablespoons shredded coconut (optional)

Preheat the oven to 350°F. Coat a 12-cup muffin pan with no-stick spray.

In a large bowl, combine the flour, baking powder, cinnamon, baking soda, nutmeg, and salt. Mix well.

In another large bowl, combine the brown sugar, oil, apple butter, buttermilk, egg, egg white, and vanilla. Using an electric mixer, beat on medium speed for 4 to 5 minutes, or until smooth and light. Reduce the speed to low and gradually add the flour mixture, beating until just combined. Fold in the bananas, chocolate chips, and walnuts.

Divide the batter equally among the muffin cups, filling them about two-thirds full. Sprinkle with the coconut (if using). Bake for 15 to 20 minutes, or until a toothpick inserted in the center of a muffin comes out clean. Let the muffins stand for 5 minutes, then remove from the pan.

Cracked Peppercorn Veal Chops

MAKES 4 SERVINGS

A savory coating of peppercorns seals in the lean veal juices in this entrée. Ready in a flash, these chops are perfect for any special occasion or Sunday dinner. For the most flavor, try a blend of pink, black, green, and white peppercorns.

4	bone-in veal loin chops (8 ounces each), trimmed of all visible fat
1½	tablespoons reduced-sodium teriyaki sauce
1	teaspoon grated lemon rind
1	teaspoon coarsely ground peppercorns
1	teaspoon dried oregano
½	teaspoon garlic powder

Coat a large no-stick skillet with no-stick spray and place over medium-high heat until hot.

Brush both sides of the chops with the teriyaki sauce.

In a small bowl, combine the lemon rind, peppercorns, oregano, and garlic powder. Press the coating into both sides of the chops.

Add the chops to the skillet and cook for 3 to 4 minutes per side, or until light pink in the center when tested with a sharp knife. Let stand for 2 minutes before serving.

Nutrition Notes

Per serving

Calories 229
Fat 9 g.
% of calories from fat 36
Protein 33.2 g.
Carbohydrates 2.1 g.
Dietary fiber 0.3 g.
Cholesterol 122 mg.
Sodium 202 mg.

Kitchen Hint

◆ Use this method of preparation with any lean cut of meat, such as flank steak, beef tenderloin, pork tenderloin, or leg of lamb.

Nutrition Notes

Per serving

Calories 93
Fat 4.6 g.
% of calories from fat 42
Protein 3.6 g.
Carbohydrates 10.7 g.
Dietary fiber 2.9 g.
Cholesterol 4 mg.
Sodium 65 mg.

Kitchen Hint

◆ To compensate for the reduced quantities of fat called for in low-fat recipes, try experimenting with flavorful oils, such as walnut, hazelnut, almond, toasted sesame, and peanut. Or try olive oils infused with basil, rosemary, roasted garlic, chili peppers, or other flavorings. The distinctive flavor of these oils allows you to use only a small amount and still get big taste from them.

Braised Burgundy Cabbage

MAKES 6 SERVINGS

The main component of this dish is the red cabbage, which many doctors revere for its potential cancer-preventing benefits.

2	teaspoons walnut oil
1	cup thinly sliced red onions
$\frac{1}{4}$	cup chopped walnuts
1	clove garlic, minced
4	cups shredded red cabbage
2	tablespoons balsamic vinegar
2	tablespoons chopped fresh oregano
	Salt and ground black pepper
1	red apple, cut into $\frac{1}{2}$" pieces
$2\frac{1}{2}$	ounces goat cheese, crumbled

Warm the oil in a large no-stick skillet over medium heat. Add the onions, walnuts, and garlic. Cook, stirring often, for 5 to 7 minutes, or until the onions are softened and the walnuts are toasted. Add the cabbage, vinegar, and oregano. Cover and cook, stirring occasionally, for 12 to 15 minutes, or until the cabbage is soft and tender. Season with the salt and pepper.

Remove from the heat and add the apples and goat cheese. Toss to combine.

Fall Menu Thirteen

	1,500 CALORIES	2,000 CALORIES	2,500 CALORIES
	33-43 G. FAT	44-56 G. FAT	57-69 G. FAT

Breakfast

mini shredded wheat cereal	1½ cups	2 cups	2 cups
skim milk	1 cup	1½ cups	1½ cups
blueberries	½ cup	¾ cup	¾ cup

Lunch

Wild Greens with Creamy Beet Dressing	1 serving	2 servings	2 servings
reduced-sodium split pea soup with nonfat croutons	1½ cups ½ cup	2 cups ½ cup	2 cups ½ cup
nonfat fruit yogurt	1 cup	1 cup	1 cup

Dinner

Turkey Meat Loaf	1 serving	1 serving	2 servings
Buttermilk-Herb Mashed Potatoes	1 serving	1 serving	2 servings
steamed mixed carrots, corn, and peas	½ cup	¾ cup	1 cup

Snack

fig cookies	3	4	5
skim milk	½ cup	1 cup	1¼ cups

Daily Totals

Calories	1,500	1,985	2,496
Fat (g.)	17	24	30
% of calories from fat	10	11	11
Protein (g.)	92	115	154
Carbohydrates (g.)	258	344	421
Dietary fiber (g.)	32	44	50
Cholesterol (mg.)	81	87	157
Sodium (mg.)	1,597	2,052	2,482

NUTRIENT BONUS

This menu (at 2,000 calories) exceeds the Daily Value for:

Dietary fiber	176%
Vitamin A	486%
Thiamin	121%
Riboflavin	174%
Niacin	149%
Vitamin B₆	143%
Vitamin B₁₂	106%
Folate	127%
Vitamin C	418%
Calcium	182%
Iron	140%
Potassium	167%

HEALTHY TIP OF THE DAY

Some women avoid weight training for fear of "bulking up." But women have lower levels of testosterone than men do, so their muscles tend to be less bulky. Weight training is essential to deter the loss of lean muscle mass that occurs naturally in women as they age. In addition, muscles burn more calories than fat, making weight training an essential component of any weight-loss exercise plan. To get started with weight training, consult your physician and meet with an exercise specialist.

Wild Greens with Creamy Beet Dressing

Wild Greens with Creamy Beet Dressing

MAKES 4 SERVINGS

In this harvest of flavors and colors, mixed baby lettuce (an excellent source of folate) is drizzled with a bright magenta dressing made of beets and topped with crisp apples and toasted walnuts.

6	ounces beets, peeled, halved, and thinly sliced
2	cups orange juice
1	tablespoon grated orange rind
2	teaspoons minced crystallized ginger (optional)
1	cup 1% low-fat buttermilk
3	cups mixed baby lettuce
2	cups torn red-leaf lettuce
1	tart apple, coarsely chopped
¼	cup chopped toasted walnuts

In a medium saucepan, combine the beets, orange juice, orange rind, and ginger. Cover and cook over medium-high heat for 7 to 10 minutes, or until the beets are tender when tested with a sharp knife. Transfer half of the beets to a large bowl. Cover and refrigerate.

Place the remaining beets in a food processor or blender. Add the buttermilk and process until smooth. Pour into a small bowl and refrigerate for 1 hour, or until chilled.

Add the baby lettuce, red leaf-lettuce, apples, and walnuts to the sliced beets. Pour the dressing over the salad and toss to coat.

Nutrition Notes

Per serving

Calories 180
Fat 5.6 g.
% of calories from fat 26
Protein 6.7 g.
Carbohydrates 28.7 g.
Dietary fiber 3.2 g.
Cholesterol 2 mg.
Sodium 116 mg.

Kitchen Hints

◆ Best loved for their sweetness and beautiful color, fresh beets are also a good source of folate. Beets are now available in different colors, such as yellow-orange and peppermint swirl of white and red. These varieties offer the same nutrients as their red counterparts, but they have the added advantage of not bleeding their color. Try shredding raw beets into salads, juicing them with carrots, or baking, steaming, or braising them for side dishes.

◆ For the best flavor, use freshly squeezed orange juice for this recipe.

Nutrition Notes

Per serving

Calories 186
Fat 4.1 g.
% of calories from fat 20
Protein 28 g.
Carbohydrates 9.9 g.
Dietary fiber 1.4 g.
Cholesterol 66 mg.
Sodium 194 mg.

Kitchen Hints

◆ To make meat loaf with gravy, form the mixture into a 4" × 8" oval and place in a 9" × 9" baking dish. In a small bowl, combine 1 cup chopped canned plum tomatoes (with juice), ½ cup defatted beef broth, 2 tablespoons minced onions, 2 tablespoons chopped Italian parsley, and 1½ teaspoons tomato paste. Pour around the meat; bake as directed. (If the liquid evaporates too quickly, add water or broth to make a thick gravy as the meat loaf cooks.)

◆ For a hidden surprise, press half of the meat-loaf mixture into the loaf pan. Top with a cooked long carrot, several cooked asparagus spears, and slices of hard-cooked egg whites. Press the remaining meat-loaf mixture on top. Bake as directed.

Turkey Meat Loaf

MAKES 6 SERVINGS

A favorite comfort food takes a healthy turn. By using skim milk and egg substitute and replacing some of the ground beef with ground turkey, we cut the fat but kept the hearty texture of this homestyle dish.

⅓	cup sun-dried tomatoes
½	teaspoon olive oil
⅓	cup chopped onions
½	cup chopped celery
½	cup chopped green peppers
2	cloves garlic, minced
½	teaspoon dried thyme
⅛	teaspoon ground black pepper
1	pound extra-lean ground beef top round
8	ounces ground turkey breast
⅓	cup reduced-sodium ketchup
¼	cup toasted bread crumbs
¼	cup skim milk
¼	cup fat-free egg substitute
2	teaspoons dried dill
2	teaspoons Worcestershire sauce

Preheat the oven to 350°F. Coat a 9" × 5" loaf pan with no-stick spray.

Place the tomatoes in a small bowl. Cover with boiling water and let stand for 10 minutes, or until the tomatoes are softened. Drain the tomatoes and chop. Set aside.

Warm the oil in a medium no-stick skillet over medium heat. Add the onions, celery, green peppers, garlic, thyme, and black pepper. Cook, stirring occasionally, for 8 to 10 minutes, or until the vegetables are softened.

In a large bowl, stir together the beef and turkey. Add the ketchup, bread crumbs, milk, egg substitute, dill, Worcestershire sauce, the reserved tomatoes, and cooked vegetables. Mix well.

Press the mixture into the prepared pan. Bake for 1 hour, or until golden brown and no longer pink in the center when tested with a sharp knife. Let stand for 10 minutes before slicing.

Buttermilk-Herb Mashed Potatoes

MAKES 6 SERVINGS

These creamy mashed potatoes are a good source of calcium and a perfect accompaniment to almost any meal. Low-fat buttermilk and nonfat sour cream bring the fat content down to healthy levels.

3	pounds Yukon gold potatoes, cut into 1" cubes
1½	cups 1% low-fat buttermilk
¾	cup nonfat sour cream
1	tablespoon chopped fresh Italian parsley
1	tablespoon chopped fresh chives
⅛	teaspoon salt
⅛	teaspoon ground black pepper

Place the potatoes in a large saucepan. Cover with cold water and bring to a boil over high heat. Reduce the heat to medium and cook for 15 to 20 minutes, or until the potatoes are tender when tested with a sharp knife. Drain and return to the saucepan. Off heat, mash with a potato masher until almost smooth.

In a medium saucepan, combine the buttermilk, sour cream, parsley, chives, salt, and pepper. Whisk until smooth. Whisk over medium heat for 3 to 4 minutes, or until hot. Pour over the potatoes and mash until the buttermilk mixture is thoroughly incorporated.

Nutrition Notes

Per serving

Calories 229
Fat 0.8 g.
% of calories from fat 3
Protein 7.3 g.
Carbohydrates 48.4 g.
Dietary fiber 2.6 g.
Cholesterol 2 mg.
Sodium 141 mg.

Kitchen Hint

◆ Make ordinary mashed potatoes extraordinary by adding steamed and mashed parsnips, celeriac, turnips, or roasted garlic.

Fall Menu Fourteen

	1,500 CALORIES	2,000 CALORIES	2,500 CALORIES
	33-43 G. FAT	44-56 G. FAT	57-69 G. FAT

Breakfast

Mediterranean Breakfast Bake	1 serving	1 serving	2 servings
mixed fresh fruit salad	½ cup	1 cup	1 cup

Lunch

baked potato topped with	1	1	2
black beans,	2 tablespoons	3 tablespoons	¼ cup
fat-free salsa, and	2 tablespoons	3 tablespoons	¼ cup
shredded low-fat cheese	1 ounce	1½ ounces	2 ounces
seedless red grapes	½ cup	1 cup	1 cup

Dinner

mixed greens with	1 cup	2 cups	2 cups
nonfat vinaigrette	1 tablespoon	2 tablespoons	2 tablespoons
Seaside Clams with Linguine	1 serving	2 servings	2 servings
English Trifle	1 serving	1 serving	1 serving

Snack

gingersnaps	6	8	8
skim milk	1 cup	1 cup	1 cup

DAILY TOTALS			
Calories	1,492	2,017	2,523
Fat (g.)	28	38	52
% of calories from fat	17	17	18
Protein (g.)	73	91	129
Carbohydrates (g.)	228	313	370
Dietary fiber (g.)	15	22	28
Cholesterol (mg.)	170	193	312
Sodium (mg.)	1,876	2,410	3,249

Mediterranean Breakfast Bake (page 328)

Mediterranean Breakfast Bake

MAKES 4 SERVINGS

This dish is tailor-made for weekend brunch. Sautéed vegetables and an egg-white omelet are layered between sheets of flaky phyllo dough. No time to make it in the morning? You can easily assemble this dish a day in advance and bake it just before serving.

1	container (15 ounces) nonfat ricotta cheese
1	teaspoon olive oil
1½	cups sliced scallions
1	clove garlic, minced
2	ounces feta cheese, crumbled
¼	teaspoon ground allspice or nutmeg
3	small yellow squash, thinly sliced
	Salt and ground black pepper
1	egg
4	egg whites
½	teaspoon dried Italian herb seasoning
5	sheets phyllo dough, thawed if frozen
1	cup shredded reduced-fat mozzarella cheese
2	sweet red peppers, roasted
1	tablespoon grated Parmesan cheese

Set a strainer over a small bowl. Pour in the ricotta and let drain for 10 minutes.

Warm the oil in a large no-stick skillet over medium heat. Add the scallions and garlic. Cook for 2 to 3 minutes, or until tender. Add the feta and cook for 1 minute, or until almost melted. Transfer to a large bowl. Stir in the ricotta and allspice or nutmeg.

Coat the same skillet with no-stick spray. Add the squash and cook, stirring occasionally, over medium heat, for 3 to 4 minutes, or until softened. Season with the salt and black pepper. Transfer to a medium bowl.

Coat the skillet with no-stick spray. Place over medium heat. In a small bowl, lightly beat the egg, egg whites, and Italian herb seasoning. Pour into the skillet, cover, and cook for 2 minutes, or until the eggs are almost set. Flip the omelet over and cook for 2 minutes, or until the eggs are set. Transfer to a plate.

Preheat the oven to 400°F.

Coat a 9" × 9" baking dish with no-stick spray. Drape 2 sheets of the phyllo across the baking dish; press into place along the bottom and over the sides. Mist with no-stick spray. Working in the opposite direction, drape 2 more sheets of the phyllo across the baking dish. Mist with no-stick spray. (The phyllo should overhang all sides of the baking dish.)

Sprinkle with ½ cup of the mozzarella. Top with the ricotta mixture. Layer with the omelet, roasted peppers, squash, and the remaining ½ cup mozzarella. Sprinkle with the Parmesan.

Cut the last sheet of phyllo in half and place on top of the dish. Fold the overhanging phyllo over the top to completely cover the mixture. Mist with no-stick spray.

Bake for 40 to 45 minutes, or until golden brown and hot throughout. Serve warm or at room temperature.

Nutrition Notes

Per serving

Calories 263
Fat 4.6 g.
% of calories from fat 16
Protein 11.3 g.
Carbohydrates 34.9 g.
Dietary fiber 2.2 g.
Cholesterol 14 mg.
Sodium 141 mg.

Kitchen Hints

◆ Clams should be scrubbed well before cooking. They can also be soaked in a mixture of salted water and cornmeal, which both whitens the clams and causes them to eject the black material in their stomachs.

◆ Cherrystone clams, which are small quahogs, are great steamed on their own or cooked in bouillabaisse. Chowder clams, which are large quahogs, are usually chopped into smaller pieces and added to soups and chowders. Use clams as soon as possible after purchasing.

Seaside Clams with Linguine

MAKES 4 SERVINGS

The tomato sauce for this dish takes no time at all. The steamed clams contribute lots of vitamin B$_{12}$ and iron, with barely any fat and not much cholesterol.

12	ounces linguine
1	tablespoon olive oil
$\frac{1}{2}$	cup chopped shallots
1	tablespoon minced garlic
1	cup chopped plum tomatoes
1	cup dry white wine or nonalcoholic wine
$1\frac{1}{2}$	cups defatted reduced-sodium chicken broth
$\frac{1}{4}$	cup + 2 tablespoons chopped fresh Italian parsley
3	dozen cherrystone or large littleneck clams, scrubbed
1	tablespoon cornstarch
$\frac{1}{4}$	cup bottled clam juice or water

Cook the linguine in a large pot of boiling water according to the package directions. Drain.

Warm the oil in a Dutch oven over medium-high heat. Add the shallots and garlic. Cook, stirring often, for 3 to 4 minutes, or until soft. Add the tomatoes and cook for 1 minute. Add the wine and bring to a boil. Cook for 2 minutes. Add the broth and $\frac{1}{4}$ cup of the parsley. Bring to a boil.

Add the clams, cover, and cook for 3 to 5 minutes, or until the clams open. (Discard any clams that remain closed after 5 minutes of cooking time.) Transfer the clams to a large bowl as they open. Remove 24 of the clams from their shells and mince; discard those shells. Keep the remaining 12 clams in their shells.

Place the cornstarch in a cup. Add the clam juice or water and stir until smooth. Add to the Dutch oven. Cook, stirring, for 1 minute, or until the sauce is slightly thickened and bubbling. Add the minced clams and pasta. Toss to combine. Add the clams in the shells. Cover and cook for 1 minute. Serve sprinkled with the remaining 2 tablespoons parsley.

English Trifle

MAKES 10 SERVINGS

This dessert is so low in fat that you can eat more than just a trifle! In our spin-off of the traditional English pudding, fat-free pound cake is spread with raspberry jam and layered with vanilla custard made with skim milk.

    1   egg
    1   egg white
  1/3   cup sugar
  1/3   cup cornstarch
    3   cups skim milk
    1   tablespoon vanilla
    1   fat-free pound cake (13 ounces), cut into 2" slices
  1/3   cup raspberry jam
    4   tablespoons dry sherry or orange juice
    2   cups sliced strawberries
    1   cup blueberries
    1   cup raspberries
    2   kiwifruit, sliced
    2   tablespoons sliced toasted almonds

In a small bowl, combine the egg, egg white, sugar, and cornstarch. Whisk well to combine. Whisk in 1/2 cup of the milk.

Place the remaining 2 1/2 cups milk in a medium saucepan. Place over medium heat until warm but not boiling. Remove from the heat and gradually whisk in the egg mixture. Cook, whisking constantly, for 5 to 7 minutes, or until the mixture comes to a boil and thickens. Strain through a sieve into a medium bowl. Stir in the vanilla. To prevent a skin from forming, place a piece of plastic wrap directly on the surface of the custard. Refrigerate for at least 30 minutes.

Spread 1 side of the cake slices with the jam. Cut the cake slices into thirds. Arrange half of the slices, jam side up, in the bottom of a 2 1/2-quart baking dish or decorative bowl. Sprinkle with 2 tablespoons of the sherry or orange juice. Top with one-third of the strawberries, one-third of the blueberries, one-third of the raspberries, and one-third of the kiwifruit. Spoon one-half of the custard over the fruit.

Repeat the layering. Decoratively arrange the remaining fruit over the top. Cover and refrigerate for at least 4 hours or up to 24 hours.

Just before serving, sprinkle the trifle with the almonds.

Nutrition Notes

Per serving

Calories 252
Fat 1.6 g.
% of calories from fat 6
Protein 6 g.
Carbohydrates 51.9 g.
Dietary fiber 1.9 g.
Cholesterol 23 mg.
Sodium 185 mg.

Kitchen Hint

◆ If you're in a time crunch, replace the custard mixture with instant fat-free vanilla pudding. Angel food cake also works well in place of the pound cake.

Nutrient Bonus

This menu (at 2,000 calories) exceeds the Daily Value for:

Dietary fiber	107%
Vitamin A	737%
Niacin	161%
Vitamin B$_6$	145%
Vitamin C	163%
Calcium	106%
Potassium	120%

Healthy Tip of the Day

Need a fast-food breakfast? Go for a homemade "breakfast on the go." You'll save loads of fat and calories and get a head start on your day. Try these easy breakfasts: ¾ cup scrambled egg substitute on a bagel or English muffin, 1 cup cooked oatmeal with 1 tablespoon raisins and 1 tablespoon brown sugar, 1 cup whole-grain cereal with 1 cup skim milk, 2 slices whole-grain toast with 1 tablespoon jelly and ½ cup orange juice, 1 cup mixed fresh fruit with 2 tablespoons low-fat granola, or 2 pancakes with 1 tablespoon maple syrup or ½ cup sliced fresh fruit.

	1,500 CALORIES 33-43 G. FAT	2,000 CALORIES 44-56 G. FAT	2,500 CALORIES 57-69 G. FAT
Breakfast			
Sunrise Smoothies	1 serving	1 serving	2 servings
Sausage Melt Sandwiches	1	1	1½
Lunch			
cooked cubed chicken breast mixed with	3 ounces	5 ounces	5 ounces
nonfat mayonnaise on	2 tablespoons	3 tablespoons	3 tablespoons
whole-wheat toast	2 slices	2 slices	2 slices
sourdough pretzels	1 ounce	2 ounces	2 ounces
apple slices	½ cup	¾ cup	1 cup
Dinner			
Butternut Squash Soup	1 serving	2 servings	2½ servings
grilled beef round steak	4 ounces	6 ounces	6 ounces
grilled zucchini and	½ cup	¾ cup	¾ cup
summer squash	½ cup	¾ cup	¾ cup
cooked basmati rice	¾ cup	1 cup	1 cup
Snack			
nonfat frozen fruit yogurt	½ cup	¾ cup	1¼ cups

Daily Totals			
Calories	1,477	2,030	2,506
Fat (g.)	14	19	22
% of calories from fat	8	8	8
Protein (g.)	100	134	159
Carbohydrates (g.)	239	330	420
Dietary fiber (g.)	19	27	33
Cholesterol (mg.)	163	223	249
Sodium (mg.)	2,069	2,746	3,348

Sunrise Smoothies (page 334) and Sausage Melt Sandwiches (page 335)

Nutrition Notes

Per serving

Calories 132
Fat 0.9 g.
% of calories from fat 6
Protein 3.2 g.
Carbohydrates 29.6 g.
Dietary fiber 1 g.
Cholesterol 3 mg.
Sodium 44 mg.

Kitchen Hint

◆ Fruit smoothies are quick to whip up and a great way to get your daily allotment of fruit. Keep a few ripe bananas in the refrigerator for this purpose; their skin will turn black, but their flavor will be fine. Experiment with whatever fruits and dairy products you have on hand, or simply blend fruit and fruit juice for a refreshing alternative.

Sunrise Smoothies

MAKES 4 SERVINGS

The beautiful color of creamy low-fat peach yogurt blended with apricot nectar is like an early-morning sunrise.

    1 banana
    1 cup apricot nectar, chilled
    1 container (8 ounces) low-fat peach yogurt
    1 tablespoon frozen lemonade concentrate
  ½ cup club soda, chilled

In a blender or food processor, combine the banana, apricot nectar, yogurt, and lemonade concentrate. Process for 30 seconds, or until smooth and creamy. Stir in the club soda and serve immediately.

Sausage Melt Sandwiches

MAKES 8

This satisfying breakfast sandwich sounds sinful, but it's not. Quick-to-fix homemade turkey sausage and fat-free American cheese keep the fat low.

1	teaspoon canola oil
1	cup finely chopped onions
1	tart apple (such as Granny Smith), shredded
8	ounces ground turkey breast
$\frac{1}{2}$	cup nonfat shredded hash-brown potatoes, thawed if frozen
1	egg white, lightly beaten
$\frac{1}{2}$	teaspoon dried thyme
$\frac{1}{4}$	teaspoon dried sage
$\frac{1}{4}$	teaspoon salt
$\frac{1}{4}$	teaspoon ground black pepper
	Pinch of ground nutmeg
2	cups fat-free egg substitute
8	ounces thinly sliced fat-free or reduced-fat American cheese
8	English muffins, split and toasted

In a large no-stick skillet, combine the oil and onions. Cook over medium heat, stirring occasionally, for 3 minutes, or until softened. Add the apples and cook for 3 to 5 minutes, or until the apples are very tender. Transfer to a large bowl and let cool for 10 minutes.

Add the turkey, hash browns, egg white, thyme, sage, salt, pepper, and nutmeg. Mix well. Form the mixture into 8 patties, making them about $\frac{3}{4}$" thick.

Wipe out the skillet and coat with no-stick spray. Place over medium heat until hot. Working in batches if necessary, add the patties and cook for 3 to 4 minutes per side, or until no longer pink in the center. Transfer to a plate and cover with foil to keep warm.

Coat the same skillet with no-stick spray. Add the egg substitute and cook, occasionally scraping the bottom of the skillet, for 4 to 6 minutes, or until lightly scrambled.

Preheat the broiler.

Divide the cheese among the bottom halves of the muffins. Place the muffins on a broiler pan or baking sheet. Broil 4" from the heat for 2 minutes, or until the cheese is melted. Top with the eggs, sausage patties, and the other muffin halves.

Nutrition Notes

Per sandwich

Calories 318
Fat 2.9 g.
% of calories from fat 8
Protein 30.3 g.
Carbohydrates 41 g.
Dietary fiber 3.2 g.
Cholesterol 43 mg.
Sodium 824 mg.

Kitchen Hints

◆ Nonfat shredded hash-brown potatoes can be found in the dairy or freezer sections of most supermarkets.

◆ The sausage patties will keep in the freezer for up to 3 months. Wrap them in a double layer of plastic wrap and foil. Reheat thawed patties in a no-stick skillet over medium heat for 3 minutes per side, or until heated through.

Nutrition Notes

Per serving

Calories 146
Fat 0.7 g.
% of calories from fat 4
Protein 4.1 g.
Carbohydrates 33.5 g.
Dietary fiber 5.5 g.
Cholesterol 1 mg.
Sodium 163 mg.

Kitchen Hints

◆ You can substitute frozen cubed or pureed butternut squash for the fresh squash. You can also use rinsed and drained canned sweet potatoes instead of fresh.

◆ This soup can be frozen for up to 3 months in an airtight container.

Butternut Squash Soup

<u>MAKES 8 SERVINGS</u>

Packed with vitamin A and fiber, this creamy soup blends the flavors of squash, sweet potatoes, and apples. Molasses and cinnamon add sweet and spicy overtones.

2	pounds butternut squash, peeled, seeded, and cut into 2" pieces
1	sweet potato, peeled and cut into 2" pieces
2	cans (13¾ ounces each) reduced-sodium chicken broth, defatted
2	tablespoons light molasses
2	tablespoons chopped fresh tarragon or sage
1	teaspoon ground cinnamon
¼	teaspoon ground nutmeg
1	large onion, chopped
1	tart apple, sliced
2	cloves garlic, sliced
	Salt and ground black pepper
1	cup 1% low-fat buttermilk
2	tablespoons chopped fresh Italian parsley

In a large saucepan, combine the squash and sweet potatoes. Cover with cold water and bring to a boil. Cook for 25 to 35 minutes, or until very soft when tested with a sharp knife. Drain and return the vegetables to the saucepan. Stir in the broth, molasses, tarragon or sage, cinnamon, and nutmeg. Remove from the heat.

Coat a medium no-stick skillet with no-stick spray and place over medium heat until hot. Add the onions, apples, and garlic. Cook, stirring occasionally, for 5 to 7 minutes, or until soft. Add to the squash mixture.

Working in batches, puree the squash mixture in a blender or food processor. Season with the salt and pepper. Return the mixture to the saucepan.

Cook over medium heat for 3 to 5 minutes, or until warm. Ladle into bowls. For each serving, swirl in 2 tablespoons of the buttermilk. Sprinkle with the parsley.

Fall Menu Sixteen

	1,500 CALORIES 33-43 G. FAT	2,000 CALORIES 44-56 G. FAT	2,500 CALORIES 57-69 G. FAT

Breakfast

cooked cream of wheat cereal with	½ cup	1 cup	1½ cups
raisins and	1 tablespoon	2 tablespoons	3 tablespoons
brown sugar	1 teaspoon	1½ teaspoons	1 tablespoon
grapefruit juice	½ cup	1 cup	1½ cups

Lunch

Seafood Salad Sandwiches	1	1½	1½
seedless green grapes	¼ cup	½ cup	1 cup
French roll	1	1	2

Dinner

Pasta Carbonara	1 serving	1 serving	1½ servings
spinach with	1 cup	2 cups	3 cups
nonfat dressing	1 tablespoon	2 tablespoons	3 tablespoons
Baked Apples	1	1	1

Snack

hot chocolate made with skim milk	½ cup	1 cup	1½ cups

DAILY TOTALS

Calories	1,477	1,992	2,478
Fat (g.)	24	32	36
% of calories from fat	14	14	13
Protein (g.)	78	101	129
Carbohydrates (g.)	247	341	427
Dietary fiber (g.)	18	25	29
Cholesterol (mg.)	326	371	491
Sodium (mg.)	2,244	2,888	3,759

NUTRIENT BONUS

This menu (at 2,000 calories) exceeds the Daily Value for:

Vitamin A	200%
Thiamin	134%
Riboflavin	119%
Vitamin C	369%
Calcium	117%
Iron	157%
Potassium	104%

HEALTHY TIP OF THE DAY

Magnesium plays an important role in your body's metabolism. It helps transmit nerve impulses and relaxes muscles after contraction. The recommended daily allowance for magnesium is 350 milligrams for men and 280 milligrams for women. Good sources include dark green vegetables, tofu, nuts, legumes, whole grains, and shellfish.

Baked Apples

Baked Apples

MAKES 4

These citrus-flavored apples are an effortless dessert. Plus, they're a good source of fiber and vitamin C.

4	Rome or Gala apples
1	lemon
½	cup raisins, coarsely chopped
¼	cup chopped toasted walnuts
¼	cup packed light brown sugar
1	tablespoon cognac (optional)
1	teaspoon ground cinnamon
¼	teaspoon ground cloves
1½	teaspoons cornstarch
1½	cups orange juice

Preheat the oven to 350°F.

Using a corer or paring knife, make a 1"-diameter hole through the core of each apple. Place the apples, right side up, in a 9" × 9" baking dish.

Grate the rind from the lemon into a medium bowl. Cut the lemon in half and squeeze the juice into the bowl. Discard the lemon. Stir in the raisins, walnuts, brown sugar, cognac (if using), cinnamon, and cloves. Spoon into the apples.

Place the cornstarch in a small bowl. Add the orange juice and stir until smooth. Pour around the apples.

Bake for 50 to 60 minutes, or until softened; occasionally baste the apples with the pan juices. Serve warm.

Nutrition Notes

Per apple

Calories 275
Fat 5.3 g.
% of calories from fat 16
Protein 3.6 g.
Carbohydrates 59.1 g.
Dietary fiber 4.4 g.
Cholesterol 0 mg.
Sodium 8 mg.

Kitchen Hint

◆ For superquick baked apples, fill the apples with store-bought mincemeat. Mincemeat can be found in the jelly or baking aisle of most supermarkets.

Nutrition Notes

Per serving

Calories 486
Fat 12.2 g.
% of calories from fat 22
Protein 27.3 g.
Carbohydrates 68.2 g.
Dietary fiber 6.1 g.
Cholesterol 87 mg.
Sodium 803 mg.

Kitchen Hints

◆ To make peeling garlic easier, gently mash the whole clove with the flat side of a chef's knife to loosen the skin.

◆ To remove garlic or other strong odors from your hands, rub your hands with parsley or a lemon wedge. Or try the nifty gadget available at many kitchen-supply stores: a stainless steel bar specifically designed to eliminate odors.

Pasta Carbonara

<u>MAKES 4 SERVINGS</u>

Traditionally made with cream, bacon, and egg yolks, this dish is notoriously high in fat and cholesterol. Here, turkey bacon and egg whites significantly reduce the fat, while Romano cheese keeps the flavor.

10	ounces spaghetti
4	ounces turkey bacon, cut into 1" pieces
2	cloves garlic, minced
3	egg whites
1	egg
1	cup 1% low-fat milk
½	teaspoon ground black pepper
⅛	teaspoon salt
¼	teaspoon ground nutmeg
1	cup frozen peas, thawed
½	cup grated Romano cheese
2	tablespoons chopped fresh Italian parsley

Cook the spaghetti in a large pot of boiling water according to the package directions. Drain. Transfer to a large bowl and keep warm.

Cook the bacon in a medium no-stick skillet over medium heat for 5 to 7 minutes, or until crisp. Add the garlic; cook and stir for 1 minute. Transfer to the bowl with the pasta.

In a medium saucepan, whisk together the egg whites and egg. Whisk in the milk, pepper, salt, and nutmeg. Whisk gently over medium heat for 5 to 7 minutes, or until thick and creamy.

Pour the sauce over the pasta mixture. Add the peas and Romano. Toss to combine. Sprinkle with the parsley.

Seafood Salad Sandwiches

MAKES 4

Nonfat mayonnaise and sour cream keep down the fat in this delicious indulgence. Imitation crab keeps down the cost.

- ⅓ cup nonfat sour cream
- 3 tablespoons mango chutney
- 2 tablespoons nonfat mayonnaise
- 1 pound peeled and deveined baby shrimp
- 8 ounces imitation crabmeat, squeezed dry and coarsely chopped
- ½ cup sliced celery
- ⅓ cup sliced scallions
- ⅓ cup currants
- 4 leaves lettuce, halved
- 4 whole-wheat pita breads, halved

In a medium bowl, combine the sour cream, chutney, and mayonnaise. Mix until well-blended. Add the shrimp, crabmeat, celery, scallions, and currants. Toss to mix well. Refrigerate for 15 minutes, or until chilled.

Divide the lettuce among the pita halves. Add the seafood mixture.

Nutrition Notes

Per sandwich

Calories 267
Fat 3.6 g.
% of calories from fat 12
Protein 32.7 g.
Carbohydrates 25.5 g.
Dietary fiber 1.7 g.
Cholesterol 234 mg.
Sodium 829 mg.

Kitchen Hint

◆ For a delicious twist on this seafood salad, add 2 teaspoons curry powder and ½ cup drained canned pineapple tidbits. Serve the salad buffet-style in a pineapple boat. To make the boat, halve a pineapple lengthwise and use a grapefruit knife to remove the flesh. Use the hollowed shell as a serving dish.

HEALTHY TIP OF THE DAY

When reading food labels, check the "% Daily Value" column to see how well specific foods meet your nutrient needs for the day. The percentages in this column are based on a daily intake of 2,000 calories—the average intake for moderately active adults. If you're eating 1,500 calories a day, your goal is to reach 75 percent of the values shown on the label. If you eat 2,500 calories a day, your goal is to reach 125 percent. Note that eating more or less than one serving will decrease or increase your nutrient intake automatically.

Fall Menu Seventeen

	1,500 CALORIES	2,000 CALORIES	2,500 CALORIES
	33-43 G. FAT	44-56 G. FAT	57-69 G. FAT

Breakfast

sunny-side-up egg	1	1	1
whole-wheat toast	2 slices	2 slices	2 slices
calcium-fortified orange juice	½ cup	1 cup	1¼ cups

Lunch

Turkey Sandwiches with Cranberry-Walnut Spread	1	1½	1½
shredded broccoli slaw with	¼ cup	½ cup	¾ cup
nonfat mayonnaise	1 teaspoon	2 teaspoons	1 tablespoon

Dinner

Gnocchi Florentine	1 serving	1 serving	2 servings
mixed greens with	1 cup	2 cups	3 cups
nonfat dressing	1 tablespoon	2 tablespoons	3 tablespoons
Peppermint Patty Cake	1 serving	1 serving	1½ servings

Snack

nonfat pudding	½ cup	1 cup	1 cup

DAILY TOTALS			
Calories	1,522	2,021	2,480
Fat (g.)	23	27	32
% of calories from fat	13	12	12
Protein (g.)	81	107	130
Carbohydrates (g.)	250	334	418
Dietary fiber (g.)	17	22	28
Cholesterol (mg.)	344	380	421
Sodium (mg.)	1,872	2,288	3,046

Peppermint Patty Cake (page 346)

Nutrition Notes

Per sandwich

Calories 532
Fat 8.2 g.
% of calories from fat 14
Protein 38.9 g.
Carbohydrates 78.7 g.
Dietary fiber 5.6 g.
Cholesterol 72 mg.
Sodium 582 mg.

Kitchen Hint

◆ To vary the sandwiches, use pita bread in place of the multigrain bread. Replace the lettuce with sprouts.

Turkey Sandwiches with Cranberry-Walnut Spread

MAKES 4

For a taste of Thanksgiving anytime, try these satisfying sandwiches piled high with sliced turkey breast and low-fat cranberry spread.

Cranberry-Walnut Spread

1	can (15 ounces) whole-berry cranberry sauce
2	ounces nonfat cream cheese, at room temperature
2	ounces reduced-fat cream cheese, at room temperature
1	tablespoon grated orange rind
1	tablespoon chopped toasted walnuts

Sandwiches

8	slices multigrain bread
14	ounces sliced reduced-sodium turkey breast
4	leaves lettuce
4	slices tomato
½	cup thinly sliced English cucumbers

To make the cranberry-walnut spread: Spoon the cranberry sauce into a strainer set over a medium bowl. Press on the sauce with the back of a spoon until most of the juice is extracted (you should be left with about ½ cup sauce). Discard the juice and spoon the sauce into the bowl. Stir in the nonfat cream cheese, reduced-fat cream cheese, orange rind, and walnuts. Mix well.

To make the sandwiches: Divide the cranberry-walnut spread among 4 slices of the bread. Top with the turkey, lettuce, tomatoes, and cucumbers. Top with the remaining 4 bread slices.

Gnocchi Florentine

MAKES 4 SERVINGS

These little Italian dumplings make a wonderful Sunday supper. Here, the gnocchi are made with spinach instead of potatoes.

1¼	cups all-purpose flour
8	ounces nonfat ricotta cheese
¼	cup grated Parmesan cheese
½	teaspoon salt
¼	teaspoon ground nutmeg
¼	cup thawed frozen spinach
½	cup fat-free egg substitute
2	cups fat-free tomato-basil sauce, heated

In a large bowl, combine the flour, ricotta, Parmesan, salt, and nutmeg.

Squeeze the liquid out of the spinach and discard. Chop the spinach finely; you should have 2 tablespoons. Place in a small bowl. Stir in the egg substitute. Add to the flour mixture. Using a wooden spoon, stir until a soft dough forms.

Transfer the dough to a lightly floured work surface. Flour your hands, then knead gently for 2 minutes, or until the dough is soft, pliable, and only slightly sticky. (Add more flour if the dough is too sticky to be rolled.) Divide the dough into 4 pieces.

Using your hands, roll each piece of dough into a ½"-thick rope. Cut each rope into ½" pieces.

Add the gnocchi to a large pot of boiling water and cook for 3 to 4 minutes, or until the pieces float and are cooked through when tested with a fork. Drain. Serve topped with the sauce.

Nutrition Notes

Per serving

Calories 264
Fat 2.5 g.
% of calories from fat 8
Protein 18.6 g.
Carbohydrates 42.4 g.
Dietary fiber 3.1 g.
Cholesterol 23 mg.
Sodium 509 mg.

Kitchen Hints

◆ The gnocchi can be stored, uncovered, in the refrigerator for up to 24 hours. Place the pieces in a single layer on a baking sheet lined with wax paper or parchment.

◆ To vary the flavor, add fresh herbs to the dough or replace the spinach with tomato paste.

Nutrition Notes

Per serving

Calories 254
Fat 4.4 g.
% of calories from fat 14
Protein 5.3 g.
Carbohydrates 53.3 g.
Dietary fiber 3.6 g.
Cholesterol 36 mg.
Sodium 250 mg.

Kitchen Hints

◆ To make ⅔ cup prune puree, combine 6 ounces pitted prunes and 1½ tablespoons corn syrup in a food processor or blender; process for 10 seconds. Add ¼ cup water and process until smooth, occasionally scraping down the sides of the bowl.

◆ If there's no time to make prune puree, use an equal amount of pureed baby-food prunes or prune butter. Prune butter (lekvar) can be found in the baking aisle of most supermarkets. You can also use a product called Lighter Bake.

◆ The cake will keep, covered, in the refrigerator for about 3 days.

◆ Top the cake with small peppermint candy canes for special occasions.

Peppermint Patty Cake

MAKES 12 SERVINGS

This minty chocolate cake is a surefire hit with kids and adults.

Cake

6	egg whites
1½	cups sugar
2	egg yolks
⅔	cup prune puree (see hint)
½	cup water
⅓	cup 1% low-fat buttermilk
2	tablespoons canola oil
2	teaspoons instant coffee powder
¼	teaspoon peppermint extract
1	cup all-purpose flour
¾	cup unsweetened cocoa powder
2	teaspoons baking powder
1	teaspoon baking soda
⅛	teaspoon salt

Icing

1	cup confectioners' sugar
2	tablespoons skim milk
⅛	teaspoon peppermint extract
2	cups fat-free nondairy whipped topping

To make the cake: Preheat the oven to 350°F. Coat a 13" × 9" baking dish with no-stick spray. Line with wax paper; coat with spray.

Place the egg whites in a large bowl. Using an electric mixer, beat on medium speed until soft peaks form. Gradually add ½ cup of the sugar and continue to beat until the whites are firm and glossy.

In a small bowl, combine the egg yolks, prune puree, water, buttermilk, oil, coffee powder, and peppermint extract. Whisk together until well-blended.

In a large bowl, combine the flour, cocoa, baking powder, baking soda, salt, and the remaining 1 cup sugar. Mix well. Add the prune mixture and stir until just moistened; do not overmix. Fold in the beaten egg whites.

Pour into the baking dish. Bake for 25 to 30 minutes, or until a toothpick inserted in the center comes out clean. Cool completely in the pan.

To make the icing: In a medium bowl, mix the confectioners' sugar, milk, and peppermint extract until smooth. Fold in the whipped topping. Spread over the cake. Refrigerate for 2 hours.

Fall Menu Eighteen

	1,500 CALORIES 33-43 G. FAT	2,000 CALORIES 44-56 G. FAT	2,500 CALORIES 57-69 G. FAT
Breakfast			
Cheesy Grits Casserole	1 serving	1½ servings	2 servings
apple cider	¾ cup	1 cup	1 cup
pear slices	½ cup	½ cup	1 cup
Lunch			
reduced-sodium black bean soup	1 cup	1½ cups	1½ cups
soda crackers	5	10	10
baby carrots and	¼ cup	¼ cup	¾ cup
sweet red pepper strips	¼ cup	½ cup	¾ cup
apple	1	1	1
Dinner			
Sole in Parchment	1 serving	1½ servings	2 servings
cooked orzo with	¼ cup	¾ cup	1¼ cups
chopped fresh basil	¾ teaspoon	1½ teaspoons	1 tablespoon
Plum Strudel	1 serving	1 serving	1 serving
Snack			
soft pretzel with	1	1	1
honey mustard	2 tablespoons	2 tablespoons	2 tablespoons

DAILY TOTALS			
Calories	1,473	1,984	2,472
Fat (g.)	16	22	27
% of calories from fat	10	10	10
Protein (g.)	84	123	155
Carbohydrates (g.)	252	325	401
Dietary fiber (g.)	32	43	50
Cholesterol (mg.)	154	231	308
Sodium (mg.)	1,468	1,992	2,409

NUTRIENT BONUS

This menu (at 2,000 calories) exceeds the Daily Value for:

Dietary fiber	171%
Vitamin A	314%
Thiamin	111%
Riboflavin	108%
Vitamin C	199%
Iron	104%

HEALTHY TIP OF THE DAY

Get out the kinks. Several factors may contribute to lower-back pain, including weak abdominal muscles; poor flexibility of the hamstrings and torso; poor posture while sitting, standing, or lying down; poor lifting habits; and increased stress levels. To relieve and prevent lower-back pain, stretch your back often, do some abdominal situps, and work back-strengthening exercises into your daily routine.

Sole in Parchment

Sole in Parchment

MAKES 4 SERVINGS

Baking in parchment paper (also called en papillote*) is the perfect no-fuss way to cook fish. It retains moisture and flavor, eliminating the need for added fats. In this elegant dish, fillet of sole and fresh vegetables are topped with mustard-herb sauce. Try this cooking method with poultry and other types of seafood. (See "Parchment Pointers" on page 350.)*

3	tablespoons nonfat mayonnaise
2	tablespoons minced shallots
1	tablespoon Dijon mustard
1	tablespoon lemon juice
1	teaspoon minced garlic
½	teaspoon dried tarragon
½	teaspoon dried dill
4	sole fillets (6 ounces each)
4	plum tomatoes, sliced lengthwise
1	zucchini, cut into matchsticks
1	yellow squash, cut into matchsticks
4	tablespoons white wine or nonalcoholic white wine
¼	teaspoon salt
¼	teaspoon ground black pepper

Preheat the oven to 450°F.

In a small bowl, combine the mayonnaise, shallots, mustard, lemon juice, garlic, tarragon, and dill. Mix well.

Cut 4 pieces of parchment paper, each 14" long. For each packet, lay 1 piece of parchment on a work surface with a long edge facing you, like an open book. Place a fillet on one half of the parchment.

Spread 1 tablespoon of the sauce over the fillet. Top with overlapping tomato slices, zucchini strips, and yellow squash strips. Pour 1 tablespoon of the wine over each fillet and season with the salt and pepper.

Fold the parchment over the fillet so that the short edges come together (as if you were closing the book). Seal the packages by tightly rolling up and crimping each of the 3 open edges. Place the packages on a baking sheet and lightly coat with no-stick spray.

Bake for 10 to 12 minutes, or until the packets are puffed and browned. Place on dinner plates and cut an X in the top of each package. Fold back the corners and serve.

Nutrition Notes

Per serving

Calories 238
Fat 3.2 g.
% of calories from fat 12
Protein 37.2 g.
Carbohydrates 12 g.
Dietary fiber 2.4 g.
Cholesterol 90 mg.
Sodium 464 mg.

Kitchen Hints

◆ To cut the zucchini and squash into matchsticks (also known as julienne), trim off the ends. Slice crosswise on an angle into thin 2"-long ovals. Stack the ovals and slice lengthwise into thin strips.

◆ The fish packets can be assembled and refrigerated for up to 8 hours before baking.

◆ You can remove the fish and vegetables from the parchment before serving, but the presentation will be less dramatic.

Nutrition Notes

Per serving

Calories 261
Fat 5.4 g.
% of calories from fat 19
Protein 18.1 g.
Carbohydrates 34.1 g.
Dietary fiber 1.1 g.
Cholesterol 64 mg.
Sodium 324 mg.

Kitchen Hints

◆ Garlic paste, which can be found in the international aisle of many supermarkets, is an easy substitute for minced fresh garlic. Substitute 2 teaspoons paste for each teaspoon of minced garlic.

◆ Grits are dried, hulled corn kernels that have been finely ground. They are available in the baking aisle of most supermarkets.

Cheesy Grits Casserole

MAKES 4 SERVINGS

This recipe sets the record straight: Grits are not tasteless or high-fat.

1   cup sliced scallions
1   teaspoon minced garlic
1½   cups defatted reduced-sodium chicken broth
1½   cups 1% low-fat milk
¾   cup quick-cooking white grits
1   egg yolk
¾   cup shredded reduced-fat Cheddar cheese
½   teaspoon hot-pepper sauce
¼   teaspoon ground black pepper
5   egg whites

Preheat oven to 375°F. Coat a 2-quart baking dish with no-stick spray.

Coat a medium no-stick skillet with no-stick spray and place over medium heat. Add the scallions and garlic. Cook and stir for 1 to 2 minutes, or until softened. Remove from the heat.

In a medium saucepan, combine the broth and milk. Bring to a boil over medium heat. Slowly stir in the grits. Cook, stirring often, for 8 to 12 minutes, or until thickened.

Place the egg yolk in a small bowl and whisk lightly. Gradually whisk in 1 cup of the grits, then whisk the mixture back into the saucepan. Stir in the Cheddar, hot-pepper sauce, black pepper, and scallions. Remove from the heat. Let cool for 10 minutes.

Place the egg whites in a medium bowl. Using an electric mixer, beat on medium speed until firm and glossy. Fold into the grits. Spoon into the prepared baking dish and bake for 40 to 45 minutes, or until golden and set.

Parchment Pointers

Parchment paper makes healthy cooking easier. It's a ready-made, no-stick surface that lets you cook with less fat. Plus, it makes cleanup a snap. If you don't have no-stick bakeware, line your baking sheets with parchment paper for the same effect. In most recipes, the paper eliminates the need for no-stick spray. To cook fish, chicken, or vegetables in parchment, place the food and seasonings on a piece of parchment, fold the parchment over the food, then roll up the edges to form a tight packet. Bake until the packet is puffed and lightly browned. Look for parchment paper near the wax paper at your supermarket. If you can't find it, foil and a bit of no-stick spray make a good substitute.

Plum Strudel

Juicy plums and crunchy toasted walnuts fill this low-fat homestyle dessert.

¼	cup chopped toasted walnuts
1	teaspoon ground cinnamon
¾	cup sugar
1⅓	pounds Italian purple plums or red-skinned plums, sliced
⅓	cup plum preserves
¼	cup all-purpose flour
2	teaspoons grated orange rind
8	sheets phyllo dough, thawed if frozen

Preheat the oven to 400°F. Line a baking sheet with foil and coat with no-stick spray.

In a food processor or blender, combine the walnuts, cinnamon, and ¼ cup of the sugar. Process until the walnuts are finely ground.

In a large bowl, combine the plums, plum preserves, flour, orange rind, and the remaining ½ cup sugar. Mix until the sugar is dissolved.

Place a double layer of phyllo on a counter with one of the long edges facing you. (Cover the remaining sheets with a lightly moistened dish towel to keep them from drying out.) Coat with no-stick spray; sprinkle with 2 tablespoons of the walnut mixture. Repeat 3 times to use all the phyllo and walnut mixture.

Spoon the plum mixture lengthwise down the center third of the phyllo, leaving a 2" border at the top and bottom (along the long sides). Pick up one of the short sides and fold the phyllo over the plum mixture. Fold the other short side over the phyllo. Starting from the end closest to you, tightly roll the phyllo away from you into a cylinder. Place the strudel, seam side down, on the prepared baking sheet. Coat with no-stick spray.

Bake for 45 to 50 minutes, or until golden brown and crispy.

Nutrition Notes

Per serving

Calories 246
Fat 4 g.
% of calories from fat 14
Protein 3.5 g.
Carbohydrates 51.6 g.
Dietary fiber 2.5 g.
Cholesterol 0 mg.
Sodium 98 mg.

Kitchen Hints

◆ Use butter-flavored no-stick spray to more closely approximate the rich, buttery flavor of the traditional version of this dessert.

◆ There are lots of ways to use phyllo dough. It makes a wonderful crust for quiches and savory tarts. Or make vegetable and cheese purses by cutting the phyllo sheets into squares and topping with a filling of your choice. Gather the ends together and twist to close. Bake at 400°F for about 15 minutes, or until golden brown.

Thanksgiving Menu

	1,500 CALORIES	2,000 CALORIES	2,500 CALORIES
	33-43 G. FAT	44-56 G. FAT	57-69 G. FAT

Breakfast

buttermilk pancakes	1	2	3
reduced-calorie syrup	1 tablespoon	2 tablespoons	3 tablespoons
turkey bacon	1 slice	2 slices	2 slices
calcium-fortified orange juice	¾ cup	1 cup	1¼ cups

Lunch

nonfat fruit yogurt	¾ cup	1 cup	1½ cups
whole-wheat bagel	1	1	1

Dinner

roasted turkey breast	5 ounces	8 ounces	8 ounces
Pear and Cranberry Sauce	1 serving	1 serving	2 servings
Baked Stuffed Acorn Squash	1 serving	1½ servings	2 servings
Mile-High Apple Pie	1 slice	1 slice	1 slice

Snack

caramel rice cakes	1	2	2

DAILY TOTALS

Calories	1,506	2,015	2,530
Fat (g.)	22	28	31
% of calories from fat	12	12	11
Protein (g.)	70	104	117
Carbohydrates (g.)	279	367	484
Dietary fiber (g.)	37	50	66
Cholesterol (mg.)	136	217	227
Sodium (mg.)	1,165	1,792	2,217

NUTRIENT BONUS

This menu (at 2,000 calories) exceeds the Daily Value for:

Dietary fiber	200%
Thiamin	151%
Niacin	146%
Vitamin B₆	158%
Vitamin C	415%
Calcium	118%
Potassium	144%

HEALTHY TIP OF THE DAY

There's nothing worse than feeling ill on an airplane—especially from the food. Before you fly, ask your travel agent about in-flight meals that meet your needs. Whether you're looking for a low-fat, low-cholesterol, gluten-free, lactose-free, or vegetarian meal, most airlines have several special meals available. What's more, you often get a better-tasting meal by making a special request. And if you don't care for the fatty peanuts offered as a snack, ask for pretzels or bring your own.

Pear and Cranberry Sauce (page 354), Baked Stuffed Acorn Squash (page 355), and Mile-High Apple Pie (page 356)

Nutrition Notes

Per serving

Calories 141
Fat 1.5 g.
% of calories from fat 9
Protein 1.1 g.
Carbohydrates 33.4 g.
Dietary fiber 3.6 g.
Cholesterol 0 mg.
Sodium 8 mg.

Kitchen Hint

◆ Cranberries are high in both fiber and potassium. Plus, ½ cup of cranberries has just 27 calories and supplies 13 percent of the daily recommendation for vitamin C. Cranberries will keep for up to 1 week in the refrigerator or up to 6 months in the freezer. You can freeze them right in their bag without sorting or washing them.

Pear and Cranberry Sauce

MAKES **8** SERVINGS

Trim your Thanksgiving turkey in style with this refreshing cranberry sauce. It requires minimal hands-on time.

1	navel orange
1	bag (12 ounces) cranberries
2	ripe Bartlett pears, chopped
1	cup orange juice
1	cup packed light brown sugar
½	cup currants
¼	cup brandy (optional)
2	tablespoons chopped toasted walnuts
1½	teaspoons minced crystallized ginger
1	teaspoon ground cinnamon
¼	teaspoon ground nutmeg
⅛	teaspoon ground cloves

Grate the rind from the orange into a medium saucepan. Peel the orange and separate it into sections; transfer the sections to the saucepan and discard the peel. Add the cranberries, pears, orange juice, brown sugar, currants, brandy (if using), walnuts, crystallized ginger, cinnamon, nutmeg, and cloves. Bring to a simmer over low heat. Cover and cook, stirring occasionally, for 35 to 40 minutes, or until thickened.

Serve at room temperature or chilled.

Baked Stuffed Acorn Squash

MAKES 6 SERVINGS

Here's a side dish that can double as an entrée for the vegetarians at the Thanksgiving table.

3 small acorn squash
1 cup chopped dried cherries
½ cup hot water
8 ounces shiitake mushrooms, sliced
¾ cup chopped onions
1½ tablespoons slivered almonds
½ teaspoon chopped fresh sage
1 cup fresh bread crumbs
Salt and ground black pepper

Preheat the oven to 425°F.

Cut the squash in half lengthwise. Scoop out and discard the seeds. Place the squash, cut side down, in a 13" × 9" baking dish. Cover with vented plastic wrap and microwave on high power for 12 to 15 minutes, or until almost tender. Uncover and turn the squash over.

Place the cherries and water in a small bowl. Let soak for 7 to 10 minutes, or until the cherries are softened.

Coat a large no-stick skillet with no-stick spray and place over medium heat. Add the mushrooms, onions, almonds, and sage. Cook, stirring occasionally, for 7 to 9 minutes, or until the onions are softened. Stir in the bread crumbs and cook for 3 minutes. Remove from the heat and stir in the cherries and their soaking liquid. Season with the salt and pepper.

Divide the mixture among the squash cavities. Mist with no-stick spray. Cover with foil and bake for 20 minutes. Remove the foil and bake for 10 to 12 minutes, or until the squash are very tender.

Nutrition Notes

Per serving

Calories 354
Fat 2.3 g.
% of calories from fat 5
Protein 7.4 g.
Carbohydrates 91.3 g.
Dietary fiber 22 g.
Cholesterol 0 mg.
Sodium 103 mg.

Kitchen Hint

◆ To make fresh bread crumbs, process soft bread cubes or slices in a food processor or blender until crumbs form.

Per slice

Calories 352
Fat 12.6 g.
% of calories from fat 31
Protein 4.5 g.
Carbohydrates 57.8 g.
Dietary fiber 3.8 g.
Cholesterol 12 mg.
Sodium 114 mg.

Kitchen Hints

◆ In autumn, farmers' markets are teeming with a great assortment of apples. Try as many as you can and remember that certain varieties are better for baking. Others are best eaten whole or used for applesauce or apple butter. Some favorite baking apples are Gala, Pippin, Golden Delicious, Cortland, Rhode Island Greening, and Wolf River.

◆ If you notice the pie crust beginning to brown too early, cover it with foil.

Mile-High Apple Pie

MAKES 10 SLICES

Take advantage of fall apples with a delicious double-crust pie.

Crust

2¼	cups all-purpose flour
1	tablespoon sugar
½	teaspoon salt
¼	cup cold unsalted butter or margarine, cut into small pieces
¼	cup canola oil
3–4	tablespoons ice water

Filling

1	lemon
10	Gala apples, cut into ½" pieces
⅓	cup apple juice
¼	cup chopped toasted walnuts
3	tablespoons all-purpose flour
2	tablespoons packed light brown sugar
1½	teaspoons ground cinnamon
½	cup + 1 teaspoon granulated sugar
2	tablespoons fat-free egg substitute

To make the crust: Coat a 9" pie plate with no-stick spray.

In a large bowl or food processor, combine the flour, sugar, and salt. Stir or process until mixed. Add the butter or margarine and drizzle with the oil. Cut in with a fork or process with on/off turns until the mixture resembles fine meal. Add the ice water, 1 tablespoon at a time; stir or process just until the dough comes together. Gather the dough into a ball and divide in half. Roll out each half between sheets of wax paper into a 12" circle. Line the prepared pie plate with one of the pie-crust circles; set the other circle aside. Refrigerate both pieces until needed.

To make the filling: Preheat the oven to 425°F. Grate the rind from the lemon into a large bowl; cut the lemon in half and squeeze the juice into the bowl. Discard the lemon. Add the apples, apple juice, walnuts, flour, brown sugar, cinnamon, and ½ cup of the granulated sugar. Mix well. Spoon into the prepared crust. Cover with the other pie-crust circle and crimp the edges. Brush with the egg substitute and sprinkle with the remaining 1 teaspoon granulated sugar. Cut 4 slashes in the top crust.

Bake for 20 minutes. Rotate the pie and reduce the temperature to 350°F. Bake for 50 minutes, or until the crust is golden brown and the fruit is bubbling. Cool on a wire rack.

Lora Brody's Menu

	1,500 CALORIES	2,000 CALORIES	2,500 CALORIES
	33-43 G. FAT	44-56 G. FAT	57-69 G. FAT

Breakfast

Oatmeal with Dried Cherries	1 serving	1 serving	2 servings
coffee with	6 ounces	8 ounces	8 ounces
skim milk	2 ounces	4 ounces	4 ounces
orange	1	1	2

Lunch

Hot and Cold Salad	1 serving	1½ servings	1½ servings
whole-wheat pita breads	1	1	2
dried figs	5	5	5

Dinner

steamed artichoke	1	1	1
Dijon mustard mixed with	1 tablespoon	1 tablespoon	1 tablespoon
lemon juice for dipping	1 tablespoon	1 tablespoon	1 tablespoon
Salsa Pizza	1 slice	2 slices	2 slices
pears	1	1	2

Snack

nonfat plain yogurt	¾ cup	¾ cup	1 cup
strawberries	¼ cup	¼ cup	½ cup

DAILY TOTALS

Calories	1,517	1,993	2,488
Fat (g.)	23	38	41
% of calories from fat	13	16	14
Protein (g.)	68	95	109
Carbohydrates (g.)	283	342	457
Dietary fiber (g.)	43	53	68
Cholesterol (mg.)	55	93	94
Sodium (mg.)	2,301	3,270	3,767

Lora Brody

Lora Brody has been dubbed "queen of the bread machine." Her best-selling cookbooks have taken the mystery out of making perfect breads, pizza doughs, and even desserts from a bread machine. Brody is also a featured chef on Julia Child's *Baking at Julia's* series of cooking shows on PBS. In this menu, the dough for the Salsa Pizza (page 359) can be made by hand, in a bread machine, in a food processor, or with an electric standing mixer. Whichever way you do it, the pizza makes a great dinner entrée for a fall day.

NUTRIENT BONUS

This menu (at 2,000 calories) exceeds the Daily Value for:

Dietary fiber	213%
Vitamin A	209%
Thiamin	117%
Riboflavin	109%
Vitamin B6	106%
Folate	147%
Vitamin C	483%
Calcium	152%
Potassium	153%

Salsa Pizza

Salsa Pizza

MAKES 10 SLICES

Here's a unique deep-dish pizza crust made with whole-wheat flour and nonfat refried beans. Topped with chunky salsa and reduced-fat cheese, this Mexican-style pizza is a one-stop shop for many of your daily nutrient requirements.

2	cups whole-wheat flour
1	cup nonfat refried beans
⅔	cup water
½	cup yellow cornmeal
¼	cup fat-free egg substitute
3	tablespoons nonfat dry milk powder
2	tablespoons canola oil
1	tablespoon honey
1	tablespoon active dry yeast
2	teaspoons chili powder
1½	teaspoons salt
2	packages (8 ounces each) nonfat cream cheese, at room temperature
2	cups chunky fat-free salsa, drained
1	cup shredded reduced-fat Cheddar cheese

In a large bowl, combine the flour, beans, water, cornmeal, egg substitute, milk powder, oil, honey, yeast, chili powder, and salt. Mix well with a wooden spoon. Turn out onto a lightly floured surface and knead until a soft, smooth ball forms. Transfer the dough to a clean large bowl. Cover and let rise in a warm place for about 45 minutes, or until doubled in volume. Punch down the dough and place on a floured surface. Let stand for 5 minutes.

Coat a 12" deep-dish pizza pan with no-stick spray.

Roll the dough into a 14" circle. Transfer to the prepared pan. Push the dough up the sides of the pan to form a rim.

Spread the bottom of the dough with the cream cheese. Top with the salsa and sprinkle with the Cheddar. Let rise in a warm place for 30 minutes, or until puffy.

Preheat the oven to 475°F.

Bake for 17 to 20 minutes, or until the crust is deep brown and the cheese is bubbling.

Nutrition Notes

Per slice

Calories 300
Fat 11.6 g.
% of calories from fat 35
Protein 15 g.
Carbohydrates 33.5 g.
Dietary fiber 6.2 g.
Cholesterol 25 mg.
Sodium 702 mg.

Kitchen Hints

◆ The dough can also be made in the bowl of an electric mixer fitted with a dough hook (knead with the hook for 7 to 9 minutes), in a food processor fitted with a plastic blade (knead for two 2-minute periods with a 2-minute rest between), or in a bread machine programmed for dough (knead until the light indicates the end of the dough cycle).

◆ Need to speed along the second rising of dough? Run an empty dishwasher on the rinse cycle. When it's done, open the door to allow a small amount of steam to escape, then quickly place the bowl of dough on the upper rack. Close the door. Make sure the machine doesn't restart. After 15 minutes, the dough should be puffy and ready to bake.

Nutrition Notes

Per serving

Calories 171
Fat 1.3 g.
% of calories from fat 6
Protein 3.5 g.
Carbohydrates 42.1 g.
Dietary fiber 2.9 g.
Cholesterol 0 mg.
Sodium 273 mg.

Kitchen Hint

◆ Irish, or steel-cut, oatmeal is simply oat groats that have been cut into 2 or 3 pieces and not rolled. Irish oatmeal takes longer to cook than regular rolled oats, but the delicious chewy texture is worth the wait. Look for tins of Irish oatmeal in health food stores, gourmet shops, or the baking aisle of large supermarkets. Note that instant Irish oatmeal is not a suitable substitute.

Oatmeal with Dried Cherries

MAKES 4 SERVINGS

Cook breakfast while you sleep. Start your day with this low-fat, high-carbohydrate breakfast, and you'll see that life really is a bowl of cherries.

4	cups water
1	cup Irish (steel-cut) oatmeal
$\frac{3}{4}$	cup dried cherries
$\frac{1}{2}$	cup packed dark brown sugar
$\frac{1}{2}$	teaspoon salt
$\frac{1}{4}$	cup maple syrup
4	teaspoons margarine or butter (optional)

In a 6-quart Crock-Pot or other slow cooker, combine the water, oatmeal, cherries, brown sugar, and salt. Cover and cook on low for at least 4 hours or overnight. Serve topped with the maple syrup and margarine or butter (if using).

Hot and Cold Salad

MAKES 4 SERVINGS

This easy-to-assemble salad is reminiscent of salade niçoise. It's an excellent source of vitamin A, niacin, vitamin C, potassium, and folate.

4	small Belgian endive, sliced
2	small heads radicchio, torn
2	small heads Boston lettuce, torn
2	small bunches watercress
4	hot baked potatoes, cut into bite-size pieces
2	cups sugar snap peas or snow peas
16	cherry tomatoes, halved
½	cup shredded reduced-fat Cheddar cheese
2	cans (4 ounces each) water-packed solid white tuna, drained and flaked
½	cup low-fat salad dressing

In a large bowl, combine the endive, radicchio, Boston lettuce, watercress, potatoes, sugar snap peas or snow peas, tomatoes, Cheddar, and tuna. Toss lightly. Drizzle with the dressing and toss to combine.

Nutrition Notes

Per serving

Calories 310
Fat 5.8 g.
% of calories from fat 17
Protein 21.1 g.
Carbohydrates 44.1 g.
Dietary fiber 7.2 g.
Cholesterol 25 mg.
Sodium 473 mg.

Kitchen Hint

◆ Many markets now carry a wide variety of leafy vegetables. You can customize your salads by choosing lettuces that are spicy, bitter, nutty, or mild. Spicy greens include radicchio, watercress, and arugula. For a bitter accent, choose frisée, Belgian endive, and curly endive (chicory). Greens with a nutty flavor include mâche (lamb's lettuce) and romaine. For a mild taste, choose leaf or Bibb lettuce. Since every green has a distinctive flavor and color, combine several for a lively salad.

Winter Menus

Old-Fashioned Beef Stew

(page 419)

Winter Menu One

	1,500 CALORIES	2,000 CALORIES	2,500 CALORIES
	33-43 G. FAT	44-56 G. FAT	57-69 G. FAT

HEALTHY TIP OF THE DAY

Not sure if you're at risk for disease? Go to your physician or local clinic for a few simple tests. These tests could detect and help prevent oncoming illness. The American Heart Association and the American Cancer Society recommend the following tests for adults.
- Blood pressure check
- Cholesterol check
- Lipid evaluation to assess triglyceride levels
- Weight assessment such as Body Mass Index and waist-to-hip ratio to determine diabetes risk
- Complete physical exam, including Pap test, pelvic exam, breast exam, and mammogram for women, and a prostate cancer test plus a prostate-specific antigen blood test for men

Breakfast

Citrus French Toast	2 slices	2 slices	3 slices
calcium-fortified orange juice	¾ cup	1¼ cups	1½ cups

Lunch

Southern Barbecue Pizza	1 slice	2 slices	3 slices
mixed green salad with	1 cup	2 cups	3 cups
nonfat dressing	1 tablespoon	2 tablespoons	3 tablespoons

Dinner

baked halibut with	5 ounces	6 ounces	6 ounces
couscous	½ cup	1 cup	1 cup
steamed snow peas and	¼ cup	½ cup	½ cup
steamed carrots	¼ cup	½ cup	½ cup
Chocolate-Cinnamon Flan	1 serving	1 serving	1 serving

Snack

gingersnaps	5	6	8
skim milk	¾ cup	1¼ cups	1¼ cups

DAILY TOTALS			
Calories	1,484	1,989	2,482
Fat (g.)	22	28	35
% of calories from fat	13	13	13
Protein (g.)	85	118	142
Carbohydrates (g.)	233	310	393
Dietary fiber (g.)	9	15	18
Cholesterol (mg.)	271	312	356
Sodium (g.)	1,582	2,191	3,011

Citrus French Toast (page 366)

Nutrition Notes

Per 2 slices

Calories 400
Fat 4 g.
% of calories from fat 9
Protein 12.9 g.
Carbohydrates 79.5 g.
Dietary fiber 1.6 g.
Cholesterol 33 mg.
Sodium 564 mg.

Kitchen Hint

◆ Try substituting cinnamon-raisin bread or nut bread for the challah in this recipe. Also, experiment with other spices and flavorings, such as ground cloves, nutmeg, almond extract, and orange extract.

Citrus French Toast

<u>MAKES **8** SLICES</u>

This low-fat breakfast treat brightens up the morning. Light and airy challah bread is soaked in a creamy custard, then topped with a light orange syrup.

Orange Syrup

  1 cup reduced-calorie syrup
  ¼ cup orange juice

French Toast

  ¾ cup fat-free egg substitute
  ½ cup nonfat plain or lemon yogurt
  ½ cup orange juice
  2 tablespoons honey
  1 teaspoon ground cinnamon
  1 loaf day-old challah bread
  2 teaspoons confectioners' sugar

To make the orange syrup: In a small saucepan, combine the syrup and orange juice. Cook over medium heat, stirring often, for 2 minutes, or until warm. Turn off the heat and cover to keep warm.

To make the French toast: In a large shallow bowl, whisk together the egg substitute, yogurt, orange juice, honey, and cinnamon until frothy.

Coat a large no-stick skillet or griddle with no-stick spray and place over medium heat until hot.

Cut the bread into eight ½"-thick slices. Dip each slice into the egg mixture and turn to soak thoroughly. Carefully transfer to the skillet or griddle and cook for 2 to 3 minutes per side, or until golden brown. Serve with the orange syrup and a dusting of confectioners' sugar.

Southern Barbecue Pizza

MAKES 8 SLICES

Here's a great Friday-night meal for the whole family. This crispy pizza comes together pretty quickly and is loaded with flavor.

- 1 teaspoon cornmeal
- 1 sweet red pepper, cut into strips
- 1 red onion, thinly sliced
- 12 ounces boneless, skinless chicken breasts
- ½ cup fat-free barbecue sauce
- 1 tube (10 ounces) refrigerated pizza dough
- ½ cup shredded reduced-fat mozzarella cheese
- ½ cup shredded reduced-fat sharp Cheddar cheese
- 2 tablespoons chopped fresh cilantro (optional)

Preheat the oven to 475°F. Coat a baking sheet with no-stick spray. Sprinkle with the cornmeal.

Coat a large no-stick skillet with no-stick spray and place over medium heat. Add the peppers and onions. Cook for 4 to 6 minutes, or until just softened. Transfer to a plate.

Coat the skillet with no-stick spray and add the chicken. Cook for 4 to 6 minutes per side, or until no longer pink in the center when tested with a sharp knife. Transfer to a medium bowl. Using a fork, shred the chicken into small pieces. Add ¼ cup of the barbecue sauce and toss to combine.

Roll out the pizza dough to a 10" circle. Transfer to the prepared baking sheet. Spread the remaining ¼ cup barbecue sauce over the dough. Top with the chicken, ¼ cup of the mozzarella, and ¼ cup of the Cheddar. Sprinkle with the vegetables, the remaining ¼ cup mozzarella, the remaining ¼ cup Cheddar, and the cilantro (if using).

Bake for 14 to 16 minutes, or until the bottom crust is browned and the cheese is melted.

Nutrition Notes

Per slice

Calories 185
Fat 4 g.
% of calories from fat 20
Protein 15.8 g.
Carbohydrates 20.7 g.
Dietary fiber 1.1 g.
Cholesterol 27 mg.
Sodium 380 mg.

Kitchen Hint

◆ Dusting the pan with cornmeal creates a more crispy crust.

Nutrition Notes

Per serving

Calories 258
Fat 5.6 g.
% of calories from fat 19
Protein 10.3 g.
Carbohydrates 43.8 g.
Dietary fiber 1.4 g.
Cholesterol 148 mg.
Sodium 125 mg.

Kitchen Hints

◆ The flans can be covered with plastic wrap and refrigerated for up to 2 days before serving.

◆ What's the difference between flan, crème caramel, and crème brûlée? Flan and crème caramel are simply two different names for a custard that's baked in a dish lined with caramel. Crème brûlée, on the other hand, is a chilled custard that is sprinkled with sugar and then placed under a broiler to create a hard glaze of caramelized sugar.

Chocolate-Cinnamon Flan

MAKES 6 SERVINGS

We took the flab out of chocolate flan by using unsweetened cocoa and low-fat milk. This dessert takes a little time to make, but the rich, creamy texture and chocolate-cinnamon flavor are well worth the effort.

- 4 cups 1% low-fat milk
- ¼ cup unsweetened cocoa powder
- 1 teaspoon ground cinnamon
- 1 cup sugar
- 3 tablespoons water
- 4 eggs
- 1 teaspoon vanilla

Preheat the oven to 350°F. Place six 4-ounce custard cups in a baking dish.

In a large saucepan, combine the milk, cocoa, cinnamon, and ¼ cup of the sugar. Bring to a boil over medium heat. Cook, stirring often, for 20 to 25 minutes, or until reduced to about 2 cups. Set aside to cool slightly.

In a medium saucepan, combine the water and the remaining ¾ cup sugar. Cook over medium-high heat, stirring, for 1 minute, or until the sugar is dissolved. Cover the pan, bring to a boil, and cook for 2 to 3 minutes, or until the bubbles are thick. Uncover, reduce the heat to medium, and cook, without stirring, for 2 minutes, or until the syrup darkens to a medium amber color. Immediately pour the syrup into the custard cups and swirl to coat the bottom and halfway up the sides.

Whisk the eggs in a large bowl. Slowly whisk in the milk mixture. Stir in the vanilla, then strain the mixture through a sieve and pour into the custard cups.

Fill the baking dish with ½" of warm water and cover with foil. Bake for 30 to 40 minutes, or until the custards are just set.

Remove the pan from the oven and carefully remove the cups from the pan. Let cool for 15 minutes, then refrigerate for 30 minutes, or until chilled. Just before serving, run a knife around the edge of each flan, and invert onto a plate.

Winter Menu Two

	1,500 CALORIES	2,000 CALORIES	2,500 CALORIES
	33-43 G. FAT	44-56 G. FAT	57-69 G. FAT

Breakfast

scrambled egg substitute	¼ cup	¼ cup	½ cup
toasted sourdough bread with	1 slice	2 slices	2 slices
jam	1 tablespoon	2 tablespoons	2 tablespoons

Lunch

tomato-rice soup	½ cup	¾ cup	1 cup
cooked cubed skinless chicken breast with	2 ounces	2 ounces	4 ounces
nonfat mayonnaise on	1 tablespoon	1 tablespoon	2 tablespoons
whole-wheat bread with	2 slices	2 slices	2 slices
low-sodium, low-fat Swiss cheese	1 ounce	2 ounces	2 ounces
clementine	1	1	2

Dinner

Chicken Paprikash	1 serving	1½ servings	2 servings
Spinach Spaetzle	1 serving	1½ servings	2 servings
steamed broccoli	½ cup	½ cup	½ cup
Pear and Cranberry Crisp	1 serving	1 serving	1 serving

Snack

graham crackers	2 whole sheets	2 whole sheets	3 whole sheets

DAILY TOTALS

Calories	1,479	1,997	2,502
Fat (g.)	26	38	46
% of calories from fat	15	17	16
Protein (g.)	82	114	152
Carbohydrates (g.)	239	309	378
Dietary fiber (g.)	20	24	28
Cholesterol (mg.)	131	196	263
Sodium (g.)	2,057	2,748	3,683

NUTRIENT BONUS

This menu (at 2,000 calories) exceeds the Daily Value for:

Vitamin A	129%
Thiamin	107%
Niacin	170%
Vitamin C	202%
Calcium	104%

HEALTHY TIP OF THE DAY

The key to a healthy diet is balance, variety, and moderation. To see if you're eating well, look at your diet as a whole rather than looking at individual foods. A variety of fresh foods and whole grains should make up the bulk of your meals, but that doesn't mean depriving yourself of occasional indulgences. The important thing is to balance high-fat foods with low-fat choices.

Chicken Paprikash (page 371) and Spinach Spaetzle (page 372)

Chicken Paprikash

MAKES 4 SERVINGS

Nonfat sour cream works wonders in this classic one-pot dish. The sauce is creamy, and the chicken is moist and tender.

1	teaspoon olive oil
2	cups chopped onions
1	teaspoon minced garlic
4	boneless, skinless chicken breast halves (5 ounces each)
	Salt and ground black pepper
1	tablespoon paprika
1	cup defatted reduced-sodium chicken broth
2	teaspoons tomato paste
½	cup nonfat sour cream
1	tablespoon all-purpose flour
1	tablespoon chopped fresh Italian parsley

Warm the oil in a large no-stick skillet over medium heat. Add the onions and garlic. Cook, stirring often, for 5 minutes, or until softened. Season the chicken with the salt and pepper. Add to the skillet and cook for 2 minutes per side, or until lightly golden. Sprinkle with the paprika and cook for 30 seconds. Flip the chicken and cook for 30 seconds.

In a small bowl, whisk together the broth and tomato paste until thoroughly combined. Pour into the skillet. Cover and cook for 20 minutes, or until the chicken is no longer pink in the center when tested with a sharp knife. Transfer the chicken to a plate and keep warm.

In the same small bowl, whisk together the sour cream and flour. Reduce the heat to low and whisk the mixture into the skillet. Cook, stirring constantly, for 3 to 4 minutes, or until thickened and bubbling. Season with the salt and pepper.

Serve the chicken topped with the sauce and sprinkled with the parsley.

Nutrition Notes

Per serving

Calories 254
Fat 4.9 g.
% of calories from fat 18
Protein 32.7 g.
Carbohydrates 18.4 g.
Dietary Fiber 2.5 g.
Cholesterol 78 mg.
Sodium 212 mg.

Kitchen Hint

◆ Tomato paste is available packaged in a tooth-pastelike tube with a resealable screw cap. This packaging makes it easy to use just a small amount and store the rest. Look for it in the canned goods aisle of your supermarket. You can also find pesto, garlic paste, and roasted garlic paste in these handy tubes.

Nutrition Notes

Per serving

Calories 310
Fat 4.1 g.
% of calories from fat 12
Protein 10.5 g.
Carbohydrates 56.7 g.
Dietary fiber 2.5 g.
Cholesterol 10 mg.
Sodium 442 mg.

Kitchen Hint

◆ Spaetzle are delicious in soups and stews. They also pair well with chicken, pork, and veal. To vary the flavor, use tomato paste instead of spinach. You can also flavor the dough with lemon rind and parsley or lime rind and cilantro. For sweet dishes like fruit soup, omit the spinach or tomato paste and add cinnamon and orange rind.

Spinach Spaetzle

MAKES 4 SERVINGS

Spaetzle is a cross between a dumpling and a noodle. This side dish can be mixed and shaped in the time it takes to boil a pot of water.

2¼	cups all-purpose flour
¾	teaspoon baking powder
½	teaspoon salt
¾	cup 1% low-fat milk
¼	cup fat-free egg substitute
1	tablespoon unsalted butter or margarine, melted
2	tablespoons thawed frozen chopped spinach, squeezed dry

Bring a large pot of water to a boil over high heat.

Place 2 cups of the flour in a medium bowl. Add the baking powder and salt. Mix well. Make a well in the center of the mixture.

In a small bowl, whisk together the milk, egg substitute, butter or margarine, and spinach. Pour into the flour mixture and stir until a soft, slightly sticky dough forms.

Sprinkle the remaining ¼ cup flour over a work surface. Pat or roll out the dough to a ¼"-thick rectangle. (Use more flour if the dough is sticking.) Cut the dough into ¼" × 1" pieces.

Drop the pieces, one at a time, into the boiling water. Cook until they rise to the surface. Stir and cook for 45 seconds more. Remove the pieces with a slotted spoon.

Paprika Quiz

What do paprika, chili powder, and cayenne pepper have in common? It's true that they're all red spices. What's more, they're all made from the ground pods of dried chili peppers. Paprika, the Hungarian favorite, is usually made exclusively from mild chili peppers. Chili powder, on the other hand, is made from medium-hot chili peppers and sometimes other ingredients like ground cumin, oregano, and salt. Cayenne pepper, the hottest spice, is made from fiery cayenne-type chili peppers. Now, here's the rub: You can also buy "hot paprika," made from chili peppers with a bit more heat. For the recipes in this book, use whatever type of paprika you have on hand—hot or mild. If you like a little extra zip, add a pinch of cayenne pepper (also known as ground red pepper).

Pear and Cranberry Crisp

MAKES 8 SERVINGS

Here's seasonal cooking at its best. This easy-to-make dessert warms up the kitchen on a cold winter day. The pears and cranberries give you lots of fiber and vitamin C.

Filling

1	lemon
8	ripe pears, cut into 1/2" slices
1	cup dried cranberries
2/3	cup sugar
2/3	cup pear nectar or apple juice
3	tablespoons all-purpose flour

Topping

2/3	cup quick-cooking rolled oats
1/3	cup packed light brown sugar
1/4	cup all-purpose flour
1	teaspoon ground cinnamon
2	tablespoons unsalted margarine or butter, melted

To make the filling: Preheat the oven to 375°F. Coat a 1 1/2-quart baking dish with no-stick spray.

Grate 1 teaspoon rind from the lemon into a large bowl. Cut the lemon in half and squeeze the juice into the bowl. Discard the lemon. Add the pears and toss to coat. Stir in the cranberries, sugar, pear nectar or apple juice, and flour. Mix well and spoon into the prepared baking dish.

To make the topping: In a small bowl, stir together the oats, brown sugar, flour, cinnamon, and margarine or butter. Sprinkle over the filling.

Bake for 40 to 50 minutes, or until the filling is bubbling and the top is browned. Serve warm or at room temperature.

Nutrition Notes

Per serving

Calories 255
Fat 3.5 g.
% of calories from fat 11
Protein 2.5 g.
Carbohydrates 59.3 g.
Dietary fiber 4.9 g.
Cholesterol 0 mg.
Sodium 31 mg.

Kitchen Hint

◆ To make a summer crisp, substitute fresh peaches for the pears, pitted Bing cherries or blueberries for the cranberries, and apricot nectar for the pear nectar.

Winter Menu Three

	1,500 CALORIES	2,000 CALORIES	2,500 CALORIES
	33-43 G. FAT	44-56 G. FAT	57-69 G. FAT

Breakfast

Morning Tea Cakes	1	2	3
kiwifruit chunks and	¼ cup	½ cup	¾ cup
mango chunks	¼ cup	½ cup	¾ cup
skim milk	1 cup	1 cup	1½ cups

Lunch

low-sodium turkey breast on	3 ounces	4 ounces	4 ounces
rye bread with	2 slices	2 slices	2 slices
Dijon mustard,	1 tablespoon	1 tablespoon	1 tablespoon
lettuce, and	1 leaf	1 leaf	1 leaf
tomato	2 slices	2 slices	2 slices
Broccoli-Cherry Salad	1 serving	2 servings	2 servings
plum	1	1	2

Dinner

Spaghetti and Meatballs with Garlic Bread	1 serving	1 serving	1½ servings
spinach leaves with	1 cup	2 cups	2 cups
nonfat vinaigrette	1 tablespoon	2 tablespoons	2 tablespoons

Snack

apple with	1	1	1
nonfat caramel sauce	2 tablespoons	2 tablespoons	2 tablespoons

DAILY TOTALS

Calories	1,488	1,982	2,506
Fat (g.)	20	28	36
% of calories from fat	11	12	12
Protein (g.)	85	109	139
Carbohydrates (g.)	255	342	434
Dietary fiber (g.)	24	36	43
Cholesterol (mg.)	125	160	187
Sodium (g.)	2,332	3,279	3,923

NUTRIENT BONUS

This menu (at 2,000 calories) exceeds the Daily Value for:

Dietary fiber	143%
Vitamin A	197%
Thiamin	102%
Riboflavin	125%
Folate	126%
Vitamin C	627%
Calcium	135%
Potassium	101%

HEALTHY TIP OF THE DAY

Don't be scared by all additives. Many are derived from natural sources and are considered safe by the Food and Drug Administration. These natural substances have the ability to swell and gel in water, creating a smooth, uniform consistency that enhances the body and texture of foods. They're usually used to stabilize, thicken, or texturize foods like dairy products, gravies, sauces, salad dressings, and puddings. Some common natural additives include vegetable gums (from trees), carrageenan (Irish moss and seaweed), flour, starch, pectin (a fruit source), and cellulose (a vegetable or fruit source).

Spaghetti and Meatballs with Garlic Bread (page 378)

Morning Tea Cakes

MAKES 12

Crystallized ginger and dates moisten and sweeten these light tea cakes. Try them for breakfast or as an afternoon pick-me-up.

1³⁄₄	cups all-purpose flour
¹⁄₄	cup finely chopped crystallized ginger
2	tablespoons cornstarch
2	teaspoons grated lemon rind
1	teaspoon baking powder
1	teaspoon baking soda
¹⁄₄	teaspoon salt
¹⁄₄	cup + 2 teaspoons sugar
3	tablespoons unsalted margarine or butter, cut into small pieces
¹⁄₂	cup pitted dates, coarsely chopped
2	egg whites
¹⁄₂	cup nonfat plain yogurt
1	tablespoon skim milk

Preheat the oven to 375°F. Line a baking sheet with foil and coat with no-stick spray.

In a large bowl, whisk together the flour, ginger, cornstarch, lemon rind, baking powder, baking soda, salt, and ¹⁄₄ cup of the sugar. Cut in the margarine or butter until the mixture resembles coarse meal. Add the dates and toss to coat.

In a small bowl, whisk together the egg whites and yogurt. Stir into the flour mixture until just blended. (The dough will be slightly sticky.)

Turn the dough out onto a floured work surface and pat to ¹⁄₂" thickness. Using a floured 3" round cutter, cut out the cakes and transfer to the prepared baking sheet. Reroll and cut the scraps to make a total of 12 cakes (handle the dough as little as possible to avoid toughening it).

Brush the tops of the cakes with the milk and sprinkle with the remaining 2 teaspoons sugar. Bake for 14 to 17 minutes, or until the tops are golden and firm to the touch.

Nutrition Notes

Per tea cake

Calories 151
Fat 3.2 g.
% of calories from fat 19
Protein 3.3 g.
Carbohydrates 27.9 g.
Dietary fiber 1.2 g.
Cholesterol 0 mg.
Sodium 209 mg.

Kitchen Hint

◆ Crystallized ginger is fresh ginger that has been sliced, cooked in a sugar syrup, and dried. Look for it in the spice aisle of your supermarket.

Broccoli-Cherry Salad

MAKES 6 SERVINGS

This colorful salad is brimming with interesting flavors and textures. It also has calcium for healthy bones.

6	cups broccoli florets
¼	cup water
¾	cup dried cherries, coarsely chopped
1	can (8 ounces) water chestnuts, rinsed and drained
4	ounces feta cheese, crumbled
1	cup nonfat mayonnaise
1	cup nonfat plain yogurt
¼	cup cider vinegar
2	tablespoons sugar

Place the broccoli and water in a large microwave-safe bowl. Cover with vented plastic wrap and microwave on high power for a total of 6 minutes, or until crisp-tender; stop and stir after 3 minutes. Plunge the broccoli into a bowl of cold water, drain, and pat dry. Return the broccoli to the large bowl.

Place the cherries in a small bowl and add hot water to cover. Let soak for about 10 minutes, or until softened. Drain and add to the broccoli.

Add the water chestnuts and feta. Toss lightly to combine.

In a small bowl, whisk together the mayonnaise, yogurt, vinegar, and sugar. Pour over the salad and toss to combine. Refrigerate for 15 minutes, or until chilled.

Nutrition Notes

Per serving

Calories 342
Fat 7.1 g.
% of calories from fat 17
Protein 16.5 g.
Carbohydrates 59.8 g.
Dietary fiber 9.4 g.
Cholesterol 27 mg.
Sodium 907 mg.

Kitchen Hint

◆ Try varying the type of vinegar used. A fruit vinegar, such as raspberry, for instance, will give a sweet-tart bite.

Nutrition Notes

Per serving

Calories 489
Fat 6.5 g.
% of calories from fat 12
Protein 32.2 g.
Carbohydrates 74.4 g.
Dietary fiber 5.2 g.
Cholesterol 50 mg.
Sodium 740 mg.

Kitchen Hints

◆ The meatballs can be shaped then double-wrapped in plastic and frozen for up to 3 months. Defrost in the refrigerator overnight before baking.

◆ If you're in a hurry, spread each bread half with 1½ teaspoons roasted garlic paste in place of the roasted garlic and oil.

Spaghetti and Meatballs with Garlic Bread

<u>MAKES 6 SERVINGS</u>

A combination of ground turkey breast and lean ground beef keeps this timeless dish from going to your waist. All you need is a spinach salad to round out the meal.

Meatballs

¼ cup finely chopped onions
2 cloves garlic, finely chopped
8 ounces lean ground beef round
8 ounces ground turkey breast
⅓ cup seasoned dry bread crumbs
1 egg white
½ teaspoon dried oregano
1 jar (26 ounces) fat-free tomato sauce

Garlic Bread

1 whole bulb garlic
1 tablespoon water
2 teaspoons olive oil
½ loaf French or Italian bread, halved lengthwise
1 tablespoon grated Parmesan cheese

Spaghetti

10 ounces spaghetti
¼ cup chopped fresh Italian parsley

To make the meatballs: Preheat the oven to 375°F. Coat a 9" × 9" baking dish with no-stick spray.

Coat a small no-stick skillet with no-stick spray and place over medium heat. Add the onions and cook for 3 to 4 minutes, or until lightly browned. Add the garlic and cook for 1 to 2 minutes. Remove from the heat.

In a large bowl, stir together the beef and turkey. Add the onion mixture, bread crumbs, egg white, oregano, and ½ cup of the tomato sauce. Mix well.

Form the mixture into 12 meatballs. Place in the prepared baking dish. Cover with foil. Place the dish in a larger pan and add about 1" of water to the outer pan. Bake for 25 to 30 minutes, or

until the meatballs are no longer pink in the center when tested with a sharp knife.

Pour the remaining tomato sauce into a medium saucepan and warm over low heat. Add the meatballs and stir to combine.

To make the garlic bread: Meanwhile, slice ¼" off the top of the garlic bulb and discard. Set the bulb on a piece of foil, sprinkle with the water, and wrap loosely. Place in the oven alongside the meatballs and roast for 25 to 30 minutes, or until very soft. Let cool for 5 minutes.

Preheat the broiler.

Squeeze the roasted garlic into a small bowl and discard the papery skin. Add the oil. Using a fork, mash the garlic and oil into a smooth paste. Spread the paste over the inside of the bread halves. Sprinkle with the Parmesan and place the halves on a baking sheet. Broil for 2 to 3 minutes, or until the Parmesan is slightly melted. Cut each half into 6 slices.

To make the spaghetti: Cook the spaghetti in a large pot of boiling water according to the package directions. Drain.

Serve the meatballs and sauce over the spaghetti. Sprinkle with the parsley. Serve with the garlic bread.

Pasta Swaps

Fresh out of bucatini? Don't worry—you can use fettuccine instead. In most pasta recipes, you can switch varieties even if a specific type is called for. Just keep it in the family by swapping shapes with shapes and strands with strands. Shapes like penne and shells work best with chunky sauces. Strands like spaghetti and linguine work best with smooth sauces. Bear in mind that cooking times and yields may vary. Here are some dried pasta varieties that are easily swapped, along with their approximate cooked equivalents.

This amount of dried pasta...	Equals this amount cooked...
4 oz. spaghetti, linguine, cappellini, or vermicelli	2 cups
4 oz. elbow macaroni, penne, rotini, ziti, rigatoni, or shells	2½ cups
4 oz. fettuccine, bucatini, tagliatelle, or wide egg noodles	3 cups

Winter Menu Four

	1,500 CALORIES 33-42 G. FAT	2,000 CALORIES 44-56 G. FAT	2,500 CALORIES 57-69 G. FAT
Breakfast			
cooked cream of rice cereal with	½ cup	¾ cup	1 cup
banana, sliced	1	1	1
skim milk	1 cup	1 cup	1¼ cups
Lunch			
Yellow Submarine Sandwiches	1	1½	2
nonfat fruit yogurt	½ cup	¾ cup	1 cup
Dinner			
Five-Star Vegetable Chili	1 serving	1 serving	1½ servings
Jalapeño Cornbread	1 piece	2 pieces	2 pieces
orange	1	1	1
Snack			
nonfat granola bar	1	1	1

DAILY TOTALS			
Calories	1,520	1,989	2,511
Fat (g.)	15	23	28
% of calories from fat	9	10	10
Protein (g.)	87	118	154
Carbohydrates (g.)	275	344	433
Dietary fiber (g.)	34	39	52
Cholesterol (mg.)	79	119	155
Sodium (g.)	1,726	2,631	3,268

NUTRIENT BONUS

This menu (at 2,000 calories) exceeds the Daily Value for:

Dietary fiber	157%
Thiamin	158%
Riboflavin	108%
Niacin	177%
Vitamin B₆	196%
Vitamin C	1,204%
Iron	101%
Calcium	126%
Potassium	128%

HEALTHY TIP OF THE DAY

Heart-healthy omega-3 fatty acids make seafood a top pick for lean meals. But don't fry your fish. Try baking, broiling, and pan-searing instead. Serve seafood with nonfat tartar sauce or nonfat mayonnaise mixed with mustard. Today's Yellow Submarine Sandwiches (page 382) beat fast-food fish by a mile. The typical fast-food fish sandwich has up to 20 grams of fat. Ours has just 7 grams.

Five-Star Vegetable Chili (page 383) and Jalapeño Cornbread (page 384)

Nutrition Notes

Per sandwich

Calories 568
Fat 7.1 g.
% of calories from fat 11
Protein 46.4 g.
Carbohydrates 80.2 g.
Dietary fiber 7 g.
Cholesterol 69 mg.
Sodium 984 mg.

Kitchen Hint

◆ What fish do Americans eat most? Tuna—usually from a can. Why not try fresh instead? The most common types are albacore, bluefin, and yellowfin. Albacore tuna has white flesh and less than 1 gram of fat per 3½ ounces, making it a very healthy choice. Yellowfin has a light red color and 1 gram of fat per 3½ ounces. Bluefin tuna has a deep red color and 6 grams of fat per 3½ ounces.

Yellow Submarine Sandwiches

MAKES 4

Made with moist yellowfin tuna and sweet yellow peppers, this deep-sea submarine is swimming in omega-3 fatty acids, vitamin C, and vitamin A.

1	whole bulb garlic
1	tablespoon water
4	sweet yellow peppers
⅔	cup nonfat mayonnaise
1	tablespoon lemon juice
¼	teaspoon crushed saffron threads
¼	teaspoon ground red pepper (optional)
	Salt and ground black pepper
1	pound yellowfin tuna, cut into 1"-thick steaks
4	leaves lettuce
1	loaf French or Italian bread, halved lengthwise

Preheat the oven to 400°F. Line a baking sheet with foil.

Slice ¼" off the top of the garlic bulb and discard. Set the bulb on a piece of foil, sprinkle with the water, and wrap loosely. Place on the baking sheet. Add the yellow peppers. Bake, turning the peppers every 10 minutes, for 25 to 30 minutes, or until the peppers are lightly charred and the garlic is soft. Set the garlic aside to cool. Transfer the peppers to a paper bag to steam for 5 minutes.

Remove the tops, charred skin, seeds, and ribs from the peppers and discard. Cut the peppers into wide strips.

Squeeze the roasted garlic into a small bowl and discard the papery skin. Using a fork, mash the garlic until a smooth paste forms. Add the mayonnaise, lemon juice, saffron, and red pepper (if using). Mix well. Season with the salt and black pepper.

Preheat the broiler. Line the baking sheet with new foil and coat with no-stick spray.

Coat the tuna with no-stick spray and place on the baking sheet. Broil 4" from the heat for 4 to 5 minutes per side, or until the fish is opaque and flakes easily when tested with a fork.

Layer the lettuce, pepper strips, and tuna on the bottom half of the bread. Spread the mayonnaise mixture on the top half and place on top of the tuna. Cut into 4 slices.

Five-Star Vegetable Chili

This thick chili is loaded with fiber, vitamin A, vitamin C, protein, and energy-giving complex carbohydrates.

1   teaspoon olive oil
1   onion, chopped
1   green pepper, chopped
2   cloves garlic, minced
1   jalapeño pepper, minced (wear plastic gloves when handling)
1   tablespoon dried oregano
2   teaspoons chili powder
1   teaspoon ground cumin
1   teaspoon ground coriander
¼   teaspoon ground red pepper
1   can (28 ounces) no-salt-added chopped tomatoes (with juice)
1   can (15 ounces) no-salt-added tomato sauce
2   cups water
2   teaspoons sugar
½   cup bulgur
1   can (14 ounces) cannellini beans, rinsed and drained
1   can (14 ounces) kidney beans, rinsed and drained

Warm the oil in a Dutch oven over medium heat. Add the onions and green peppers. Cook, stirring occasionally, for 5 minutes, or until softened. Add the garlic and jalapeño peppers. Cook for 2 minutes, or until the vegetables are tender.

Warm a small no-stick skillet over medium-high heat. Add the oregano, chili powder, cumin, coriander, and red pepper. Stir for 1 to 2 minutes, or until fragrant. Add to the vegetable mixture. Add the tomatoes (with juice), tomato sauce, water, and sugar.

Increase the heat to medium-high and cook, stirring occasionally, for 5 minutes. Stir in the bulgur, cannellini beans, and kidney beans. Reduce the heat to medium and cook for 15 minutes, or until thickened.

Nutrition Notes

Per serving

Calories 309
Fat 2.8 g.
% of calories from fat 7
Protein 15 g.
Carbohydrates 66.7 g.
Dietary fiber 17.2 g.
Cholesterol 0 mg.
Sodium 156 mg.

Kitchen Hints

◆ A great way to tone down the heat of your favorite chili is by pairing it with cooling condiments. Terrific low-fat chili toppers and add-ons include nonfat sour cream, nonfat plain yogurt, low-fat shredded cheese, lime wedges, chopped fresh cilantro, chopped fresh parsley, celery sticks, and carrot sticks.

◆ Bulgur is cracked wheat that has been hulled, steamed, and dried. When cooked, it has a slightly nutty flavor and soft texture. Bulgur comes in several different grain sizes. Traditionally, the coarsest grain is used for pilaf, the medium grain for cereal, and the finest grain for tabbouleh and salads.

Nutrition Notes

Per piece

Calories 123
Fat 3.9 g.
% of calories from fat 29
Protein 4.8 g.
Carbohydrates 17.1 g.
Dietary fiber 1.4 g.
Cholesterol 4 mg.
Sodium 377 mg.

Kitchen Hints

◆ To keep your flour fresh, store all-purpose flour in a dry, dark, moderately cool place. Keep whole-wheat and stone-ground flours in the refrigerator because the essential oils have not been processed out of the flour. Refrigeration retards rancidity.

◆ If you don't have buttermilk, use soured milk instead. To make 1 cup soured milk, pour a very generous ¾ cup 1% low-fat milk into a measuring cup. Add enough lemon juice to make 1 cup. Let stand for 5 minutes.

Jalapeño Cornbread

MAKES 12 PIECES

Low-fat buttermilk and nonfat sour cream add moistness to this crumbly cornbread. Jalapeño peppers and corn kernels contribute an extra layer of flavor.

1	cup yellow cornmeal
½	cup all-purpose flour
1	tablespoon sugar
1½	teaspoons baking powder
1	teaspoon baking soda
½	teaspoon salt
¼	teaspoon ground black pepper
1	cup 1% low-fat buttermilk or soured milk (see hint)
½	cup fat-free egg substitute
⅓	cup nonfat sour cream
2	tablespoons canola oil
1	jalapeño pepper, minced (wear plastic gloves when handling)
½	cup frozen corn kernels, thawed
2	ounces reduced-fat Cheddar cheese, diced

Preheat the oven to 400°F. Coat a 9" × 9" baking dish with no-stick spray.

In a large bowl, whisk together the cornmeal, flour, sugar, baking powder, baking soda, salt, and black pepper. Make a well in the center.

In a small bowl, whisk together the buttermilk, egg substitute, sour cream, oil, jalapeño peppers, corn, and Cheddar. Pour into the flour mixture and stir until just combined; do not overmix.

Pour the batter into the prepared baking dish. Bake for 25 to 30 minutes, or until a wooden toothpick inserted in the center of the cornbread comes out clean. Let cool slightly in the pan on a wire rack. Serve warm or at room temperature.

Winter Menu Five

	1,500 CALORIES	2,000 CALORIES	2,500 CALORIES
	33-43 G. FAT	44-56 G. FAT	57-69 G. FAT

Breakfast

Breakfast Bread Pudding	1 serving	1½ servings	2 servings
maple syrup	2 tablespoons	2 tablespoons	¼ cup
white grape juice	½ cup	1 cup	1 cup
banana	½	1	1

Lunch

lentil soup	¾ cup	1¼ cups	1½ cups
toasted rye bread with	2 slices	2 slices	2 slices
melted low-sodium, low-fat colby cheese	1 ounce	1 ounce	1 ounce
pear	1	1	1

Dinner

Chicken Osso Buco	1 serving	1½ servings	2 servings
Risotto Milanese	1 serving	1½ servings	2 servings

Snack

hot chocolate made with skim milk	1 cup	1 cup	1 cup

DAILY TOTALS

Calories	1,488	2,025	2,517
Fat (g.)	15	20	25
% of calories from fat	9	9	9
Protein (g.)	80	111	137
Carbohydrates (g.)	253	342	423
Dietary fiber (g.)	28	41	49
Cholesterol (mg.)	98	142	185
Sodium (g.)	1,663	2,163	2,651

NUTRIENT BONUS

This menu (at 2,000 calories) exceeds the Daily Value for:

Dietary fiber	165%
Vitamin A	415%
Riboflavin	118%
Vitamin C	233%
Iron	111%
Calcium	135%

HEALTHY TIP OF THE DAY

Gather 'round for the holidays. Plan to spend time with friends and family decorating, card writing, and shopping instead of just getting together for food and drinks. Also, plan ahead for the holiday season by marking your calendar with upcoming parties and social events. Keep track of the festivities so you can balance out total calories for party days and work in a little exercise to offset holiday noshing.

Chicken Osso Buco (page 387) and Risotto Milanese (page 388)

Chicken Osso Buco

MAKES 4 SERVINGS

By substituting chicken drumsticks for the veal shanks traditionally used in this recipe, we were able to cut the fat in half.

Osso Buco

¼	cup all-purpose flour
	salt and ground black pepper
8	skinless chicken drumsticks (about 1¾ pounds)
1	teaspoon olive oil
1	Spanish onion, coarsely chopped
2	carrots, sliced
2	stalks celery, sliced
2	cloves garlic, minced
1	cup dry white wine or nonalcoholic white wine
1	can (28 ounces) whole tomatoes (with juice)
2	cups defatted reduced-sodium beef broth
½	teaspoon dried basil
½	teaspoon dried oregano
1	bay leaf

Gremolata

¼	cup chopped fresh Italian parsley
1	teaspoon minced garlic
1	teaspoon grated lemon rind

To make the osso buco: Preheat the oven to 350°F. On a plate, combine the flour, salt, and pepper. Roll the chicken in the flour to coat.

Warm the oil in a Dutch oven over medium heat. Add the chicken and cook, turning occasionally, for 5 minutes, or until lightly browned on all sides. Transfer to a plate.

Coat the Dutch oven with no-stick spray. Add the onions, carrots, celery, and garlic. Cook over medium heat for 5 to 7 minutes, or until the onions are softened. Add the wine and, using a wooden spoon, scrape up any browned bits from the bottom and sides of the pan. Cook for 3 minutes, or until the wine is reduced by half.

Add the tomatoes (with juice), broth, basil, oregano, and bay leaf. Increase the heat to high and bring to a boil. Add the chicken. Cover and transfer to the oven. Bake, occasionally turning the chicken and basting it, for 1 hour, or until the chicken is very tender. Remove and discard the bay leaf.

To make the gremolata: In a small serving dish or bowl, combine the parsley, garlic, and lemon rind. Serve sprinkled over the chicken.

Nutrition Notes

Per serving

Calories 303
Fat 5.3 g.
% of calories from fat 16
Protein 29.5 g.
Carbohydrates 25.1 g.
Dietary fiber 5.1 g.
Cholesterol 82 mg.
Sodium 312 mg.

Kitchen Hints

◆ Turkey legs also work well in this recipe. Substitute 4 turkey legs for the chicken drumsticks and prepare the same way, but increase the baking time to 2 to 2½ hours.

◆ Gremolata is a classic topping for this hearty braised entrée.

Nutrition Notes

Per serving

Calories 220
Fat 3.4 g.
% of calories from fat 14
Protein 6.6 g.
Carbohydrates 35.2 g.
Dietary fiber 1 g.
Cholesterol 2 mg.
Sodium 374 mg.

Kitchen Hint

◆ Arborio, a medium- to short-grain rice of Northern Italy, is known for its oval shape and wonderful chewy texture. To vary the flavor of risotto, use broths made from chicken, seafood, wild mushrooms, lemons, tomatoes, or other vegetables.

Risotto Milanese

MAKES 4 SERVINGS

In this northern Italian classic, chewy Arborio rice grains are cooked in a fragrant broth for a naturally creamy but low-fat side dish. Risotto is a great accompaniment to any fish, poultry, or beef entrée.

6	cups defatted reduced-sodium beef broth
2	teaspoons olive oil
$\frac{1}{2}$	cup finely chopped onions
1	clove garlic, minced
1	cup Arborio rice
$\frac{1}{2}$	cup dry red wine or nonalcoholic red wine
$\frac{1}{4}$	teaspoon crushed saffron threads
$\frac{1}{4}$	teaspoon ground black pepper
$\frac{1}{4}$	cup chopped fresh Italian parsley
2	tablespoons grated Parmesan cheese

Place the broth in a medium saucepan and bring to a simmer over medium heat. Reduce the heat to low.

Warm the oil in a large saucepan over medium heat. Add the onions and garlic. Cook, stirring often, for 5 minutes, or until the onions are softened. Add the rice and cook, stirring constantly, for 2 minutes.

Add 1 cup of the broth. Stir constantly until most of the broth has been absorbed. Add the wine, saffron, pepper, and 1 cup of the remaining broth. Continue to stir until almost all of the liquid has been absorbed.

Continue to add broth in $\frac{1}{2}$-cup increments until the rice is tender yet firm. This should take about 25 to 30 minutes total cooking time; you might not need all the broth.

Serve sprinkled with the parsley and Parmesan.

Breakfast Bread Pudding

MAKES 8 SERVINGS

You'll never guess that this custardy pudding has less than a gram of fat per serving. Vary the pudding according to the dried fruit that you use. Apples, apricots, cherries, cranberries, figs, peaches, pears, and prunes are delicious options.

2	cups evaporated skim milk
1	cup fat-free egg substitute
²/₃	cup sugar
1	teaspoon vanilla
½	teaspoon ground cinnamon
½	cup chopped mixed dried fruit
⅓	cup currants
4	cups cubed multigrain bread, lightly toasted

Preheat the oven to 350°F. Coat a 1½-quart baking dish with no-stick spray.

In a large bowl, whisk together the evaporated milk, egg substitute, sugar, vanilla, cinnamon, dried fruit, and currants. Add the bread cubes and stir to coat. Transfer to the baking dish, making sure that the dried fruit is evenly distributed.

Bake for 1 hour, or until puffed and a knife inserted in the center of the pudding comes out clean. Serve warm.

Nutrient Notes

Per serving

Calories 189
Fat 0.3 g.
% of calories from fat 2
Protein 9.2 g.
Carbohydrates 39 g.
Dietary fiber 1.2 g.
Cholesterol 2 mg.
Sodium 168 mg.

Kitchen Hints

◆ The pudding can be covered with plastic and stored in the refrigerator for up to 3 days.

◆ You can use any slightly stale bread, bagels, or hamburger buns for bread pudding. Store your leftover bread in the freezer until needed.

Cream Substitutes

Heavy cream has a wonderfully rich texture and flavor. It also has more than 40 grams of fat and 400 calories per ½ cup. To get the creamy consistency without all the fat, try using evaporated skim milk instead. It has less than 1 gram of fat and 199 calories per ½ cup. Use evaporated skim milk in place of heavy cream for soups, sauces, casseroles, desserts, and even coffee. Most supermarkets carry evaporated skim milk in the baking aisle.

Winter Menu Six

	1,500 CALORIES	2,000 CALORIES	2,500 CALORIES
	33-43 G. FAT	44-56 G. FAT	57-69 G. FAT

HEALTHY TIP OF THE DAY

Treat seafood with respect. For optimum safety, buy seafood from a reputable marketplace. If fish has been frozen, avoid freezing it again. Store fresh fish in the refrigerator in an ice-filled colander placed over a pan; place where the temperature is between 34° and 37°F (the middle shelf toward the back is the best choice). Store for no more than 2 days; replenish the ice as needed. In the freezer, double-wrap fish in plastic and freeze at 0° to -15°F for no longer than 3 months. Cook all seafood thoroughly before eating.

Breakfast

Stewed Winter Fruits	1 serving	1 serving	2 servings
toasted cinnamon-raisin bagel	½	1	1
skim milk	1 cup	1¼ cups	2 cups

Lunch

low-sodium turkey breast and low-fat low-sodium	3 ounces	3 ounces	4 ounces
Swiss cheese in a	1 ounce	1 ounce	1½ ounces
whole-wheat pita bread with	1	1	1
lettuce and	1 leaf	1 leaf	1 leaf
tomato	2 slices	2 slices	2 slices
Cold Bean Salad	1½ servings	1½ servings	2 servings

Dinner

Neptune's Bounty Bouillabaisse	1 serving	2 servings	2 servings
crusty hard roll	1	1	2

Snack

low-fat granola bar	1	1	1

DAILY TOTALS

Calories	1,473	1,984	2,477
Fat (g.)	24	34	42
% of calories from fat	15	15	15
Protein (g.)	99	142	167
Carbohydrates (g.)	220	276	361
Dietary fiber (g.)	23	29	34
Cholesterol (mg.)	197	319	350
Sodium (g.)	1,399	2,085	2,409

Neptune's Bounty Bouillabaisse (page 394)

Nutrition Notes

Per serving

Calories 221
Fat 2.2 g.
% of calories from fat 8
Protein 2.6 g.
Carbohydrates 52.4 g.
Dietary fiber 2.6 g.
Cholesterol 0 mg.
Sodium 15 mg.

Kitchen Hint

◆ This flavorful compote works well with any assortment of dried fruit. For a change of pace, serve it as an accompaniment to lean savory meats, such as pork tenderloin, leg of lamb, or Cornish hens.

Stewed Winter Fruits

MAKES 5 SERVINGS

Stewing dried fruit in orange juice infused with a hint of cinnamon and vanilla gives you a perfect companion to a steaming bowl of oatmeal. As a dessert on its own, serve the compote warm, at room temperature, or cold.

2	cups mixed dried fruit, coarsely chopped
1½	cups orange juice
½	cup water
⅓	cup packed light brown sugar
2	cinnamon sticks
2	tablespoons chopped toasted walnuts
2	teaspoons vanilla

In a medium saucepan, combine the dried fruit, orange juice, water, brown sugar, and cinnamon sticks. Bring to a boil over medium-high heat, stirring constantly until the sugar is dissolved. Reduce the heat to medium and cook, stirring occasionally, for 15 minutes, or until the fruit is softened and the liquid is reduced to a thick syrup.

Remove and discard the cinnamon sticks. Stir in the walnuts and vanilla.

Toasting Nuts

To stretch the flavor of nuts, toast them. Toasting brings out their full flavor so you don't have to use as much. This technique lets you cut the amount of nuts in a recipe by up to a third. Almonds, walnuts, pecans, pine nuts, and peanuts work especially well. Use toasted nuts in cookies, quick breads, and even sauces such as pesto.

To toast nuts, place them in a dry skillet over medium heat. Cook, shaking the pan often, for 3 to 5 minutes, or until fragrant and golden. An alternative is to toast the nuts on a baking sheet in a 350°F oven for 5 minutes. Cool the nuts slightly, then chop them.

Cold Bean Salad

MAKES 6 SERVINGS

High in vitamin A as well as dietary fiber, this colorful bean salad is spiked with fresh basil and a hint of lemon juice. Serve alongside a sandwich or atop fresh greens for a colorful salad course. This recipe also makes a great packable lunch.

Dressing

¼	cup apple juice
3	tablespoons balsamic vinegar
2	tablespoons lemon juice
2	tablespoons chopped fresh basil
1½	teaspoons Dijon mustard
1	teaspoon olive oil
1	clove garlic, minced
	Salt and ground black pepper

Salad

2	cups green beans cut into 2" pieces
2	cups yellow wax beans cut into 2" pieces
¼	cup water
1	cup canned chickpeas, rinsed and drained
1	cup canned kidney beans, rinsed and drained
⅓	cup finely chopped onions
¼	cup chopped fresh Italian parsley

To make the dressing: In a medium bowl, whisk together the apple juice, vinegar, lemon juice, basil, mustard, oil, and garlic. Season with the salt and pepper.

To make the salad: Place the green beans, wax beans, and water in a large microwave-safe bowl. Cover with vented plastic wrap and microwave on high power for a total of 7 minutes, or until crisp-tender; stop and stir after 4 minutes. Plunge the beans into a bowl of cold water, drain, and lightly pat dry. Return the beans to the bowl. Add the chickpeas, kidney beans, onions, and parsley. Toss to combine. Add the dressing and toss to combine. Cover and refrigerate for at least 1 hour before serving.

Nutrition Notes

Per serving

Calories 85
Fat 1.2 g.
% of calories from fat 11
Protein 4.7 g.
Carbohydrates 17.8 g.
Dietary fiber 4.6 g.
Cholesterol 0 mg.
Sodium 90 mg.

Kitchen Hint

◆ This salad is best when prepared a day in advance so the flavors can blend. It can be stored in the refrigerator for up to 4 days.

Nutrition Notes

Per serving

Calories 393
Fat 8.5 g.
% of calories from fat 21
Protein 37.4 g.
Carbohydrates 33 g.
Dietary fiber 4.4 g.
Cholesterol 121 mg.
Sodium 540 mg.

Kitchen Hints

◆ Canned light coconut milk can be found in the international aisle of most supermarkets and at Asian grocery stores. It's lower in fat than regular coconut milk and coconut cream. To use, pour the milk into a bowl; the liquid and solids usually have separated and need to be whisked together before using.

◆ Mussels need to be cleaned thoroughly before cooking. Soak for about an hour in a mixture of salted water and cornmeal to rid them of any excess sand. Throw out any that are open before soaking and discard any that do not open after they have been cooked. Mussels often have dark threads, called beards, protruding from the shells. Pull them out or cut them off just before cooking.

Neptune's Bounty Bouillabaisse

MAKES 4 SERVINGS

Shrimp, scallops, halibut, and mussels provide a healthy dose of omega-3 fatty acids in this elegant yet easy seafood soup. The tomato-based broth is accented with tropical-tasting reduced-fat coconut milk.

1	teaspoon olive oil
1	medium bulb fennel (white part only), cut into 1/4"-thick slices
1	cup chopped onions
2	cloves garlic, minced
2	cups no-salt-added crushed tomatoes
1	cup clam juice
1	cup water
1	cup canned light coconut milk (see hint)
1/2	teaspoon crushed saffron threads
12	ounces small red potatoes, cut into 1/2" cubes
8	ounces halibut fillets, cut into 2" cubes
8	ounces bay scallops
8	ounces large shrimp, peeled and deveined
12	mussels, scrubbed and beards removed (see hint)
1/2	teaspoon hot-pepper sauce (optional)
	Salt and ground black pepper

Warm the oil in a Dutch oven over medium heat. Add the fennel, onions, and garlic. Cook, stirring often, for 7 to 10 minutes, or until the fennel is soft and tender. Add the tomatoes, clam juice, water, coconut milk, saffron, and potatoes. Cook for 15 minutes, or until the potatoes are just tender.

Add the halibut, scallops, shrimp, mussels, and hot-pepper sauce (if using). Reduce the heat to low, cover, and cook for 5 minutes, or until the mussels have opened and the halibut and shrimp are opaque in the center when tested with a sharp knife. (Discard any mussels that remain closed after 5 minutes of cooking time.) Season with the salt and pepper.

Winter Menu Seven

	1,500 CALORIES	2,000 CALORIES	2,500 CALORIES
	33-43 G. FAT	44-56 G. FAT	57-69 G. FAT

Breakfast

Bacon-Cheddar Muffins	2	2	2
pineapple chunks and	¼ cup	½ cup	¾ cup
cantaloupe cubes	¼ cup	¼ cup	¾ cup
skim milk	1 cup	1½ cups	1¾ cups

Lunch

canned salmon mixed with	3 ounces	4 ounces	4 ounces
nonfat mayonnaise on	2 tablespoons	2½ tablespoons	2½ tablespoons
rye bread	2 slices	2 slices	2 slices
baby carrots and	6	10	10
celery sticks	6	10	10
mixed dried fruit	¼ cup	½ cup	½ cup

Dinner

Italian Veal Torta	1 serving	1½ servings	2 servings
Goat Cheese Mashed Potatoes	1 serving	1½ servings	2 servings
steamed peas	½ cup	¾ cup	1¼ cups

Snack

apple	1	1	2

DAILY TOTALS

Calories	1,500	2,012	2,499
Fat (g.)	34	43	51
% of calories from fat	20	19	18
Protein (g.)	100	140	174
Carbohydrates (g.)	201	270	345
Dietary fiber (g.)	23	32	43
Cholesterol (mg.)	200	288	362
Sodium (g.)	1,961	2,369	2,631

NUTRIENT BONUS

This menu (at 2,000 calories) exceeds the Daily Value for:

Dietary fiber	128%
Vitamin A	315%
Thiamin	119%
Riboflavin	163%
Niacin	170%
Vitamin B₆	154%
Vitamin C	229%
Calcium	134%
Potassium	143%

HEALTHY TIP OF THE DAY

Eating less saturated fat can help keep your blood cholesterol levels down and possibly prevent heart disease and certain types of cancer. Meat and dairy products are often high in saturated fat, but even some vegetable foods contain it. Coconut oil, cocoa butter (in chocolate), and palm kernel oil (found in creamers, whipped dessert toppings, and baked goods) are prime examples. Be sure to read food labels for saturated fat content. Low-fat foods contain less than 3 grams of saturated fat per serving.

Italian Veal Torta (page 397) and Goat Cheese Mashed Potatoes (page 398)

Italian Veal Torta

MAKES 6 SERVINGS

Recreate a taste of Italy by combining aromatic vegetables and lean veal in this variation of cabbage rolls.

8	large leaves savoy cabbage
1/4	cup water
1	teaspoon olive oil
1	cup chopped onions
3/4	cup frozen peas, thawed
3/4	cup chopped carrots
1 1/2	teaspoons dried basil
1	teaspoon garlic powder
2	egg whites, lightly beaten
1/4	cup skim milk
1	can (15 ounces) no-salt-added diced tomatoes (with juice)
2	pounds lean ground veal
1/4	cup seasoned dry bread crumbs

Preheat the oven to 350°F. Coat a 9" round cake pan with no-stick spray.

Place the cabbage and water in a large microwave-safe bowl. Cover with vented plastic wrap and microwave on high power for a total of 4 minutes, or until tender; stop and turn after 2 minutes. Plunge the cabbage into a bowl of cold water, drain, and pat dry.

Warm the oil in a large no-stick skillet over medium heat. Add the onions and cook, stirring occasionally, for 5 minutes, or until softened. Add the peas, carrots, basil, and garlic powder. Cook for 5 minutes, or until the vegetables are tender. Set aside to cool.

In a large bowl, whisk together the egg whites and milk.

Drain the tomatoes, reserving 1/4 cup of the juice. Add the juice to the egg-white mixture. Stir in 1 cup of the tomatoes. Mix well. Add the veal, bread crumbs, and the cooled vegetables. Mix well. Shape the mixture into an 8" disk.

Line the prepared pan with 4 of the cabbage leaves, overlapping them. Set the veal loaf on top. Cover the loaf with the remaining 4 leaves and tuck them into the sides of the pan. Top with the remaining tomatoes.

Bake for 1 hour, or until the center of the loaf is cooked through; test with a sharp knife. Slice into wedges.

Nutrient Notes

Per serving

Calories 331
Fat 8.7 g.
% of calories from fat 24
Protein 45 g.
Carbohydrates 6.4 g.
Dietary fiber 3.8 g.
Cholesterol 134 mg.
Sodium 304 mg.

Kitchen Hint

◆ You can substitute other large-leaf greens for the savoy cabbage. Try Romaine lettuce, Swiss chard, collard greens, and red- and green-leaf lettuce. Lightly blanch these greens in hot water for 30 seconds to 1 minute and proceed with the recipe.

Nutrition Notes

Per serving

Calories 203
Fat 4.4 g.
% of calories from fat 19
Protein 7.1
Carbohydrates 34.6 g.
Dietary fiber 2.3 g.
Cholesterol 12 mg.
Sodium 141 mg.

Kitchen Hint

◆ There is no end to the number of ways you can prepare delicious low-fat mashed potatoes. Try adding any of the following ingredients to create your own special spuds: mashed roasted garlic, grated Parmesan or Romano cheese, nonfat sour cream, nonfat cream cheese or nonfat yogurt, low-fat buttermilk, chopped fresh herbs, or a dash of flavored olive oil, nutmeg, or ground red pepper.

Goat Cheese Mashed Potatoes

MAKES 6 SERVINGS

We've redefined one of the all-time greatest comfort foods and made it significantly lower in fat. There's no butter here, just creamy goat cheese and buttery-smooth Yukon gold potatoes.

2	pounds Yukon gold potatoes, peeled and cut into 1" cubes
¾	cup skim milk
3	ounces goat cheese, crumbled
2	tablespoons minced fresh basil
¼	teaspoon ground black pepper
⅛	teaspoon salt

Place the potatoes in a large saucepan and add cold water to cover. Bring to a boil over high heat. Reduce the heat to medium and cook for 10 to 15 minutes, or until the potatoes are tender when tested with a sharp knife. Drain and return to the pan. Mash the potatoes well.

Warm the milk in a small saucepan over medium heat. Gradually add to the potatoes and mix well. Add the goat cheese, basil, pepper, and salt. Mix well.

Bacon-Cheddar Muffins

MAKES 12

Perfect for a breakfast on the go, these whole-grain muffins are packed with flavor. Canadian bacon and just a small amount of Cheddar cheese enrich the muffins without sending their fat content off the charts.

- ²/₃ cup sliced scallions
- 3 ounces Canadian bacon, diced
- ½ teaspoon dried thyme
- 1½ cups all-purpose flour
- ½ cup yellow cornmeal
- 1 tablespoon sugar
- 1½ teaspoons baking powder
- ½ teaspoon baking soda
- ½ teaspoon salt
- 1 cup 1% low-fat buttermilk or soured milk (see hint)
- 2 egg whites
- 3 tablespoons canola oil
- 2 ounces reduced-fat Cheddar cheese, diced

Preheat the oven to 400°F. Coat a 12-cup muffin pan with no-stick spray.

Coat a large no-stick skillet with no-stick spray and place over medium heat. Add the scallions, bacon, and thyme. Cook for 2 to 3 minutes, or until the scallions are softened and the bacon has released some of its liquid.

In a large bowl, combine the flour, cornmeal, sugar, baking powder, baking soda, and salt. Mix well.

In a medium bowl, whisk together the buttermilk, egg whites, and oil. Stir into the flour mixture until just blended. Stir in the scallion mixture and the Cheddar.

Divide the batter among the prepared muffin cups, filling them two-thirds full. Bake for 10 to 12 minutes, or until a toothpick inserted in the center of a muffin comes out clean.

Cool on a wire rack for 5 minutes. Remove the muffins from the pan.

Nutrition Notes

Per muffin

Calories 149
Fat 5.2 g.
% of calories from fat 32
Protein 5.7 g.
Carbohydrates 19.2 g.
Dietary fiber 1.1 g.
Cholesterol 7 mg.
Sodium 344 mg.

Kitchen Hints

◆ If you don't have buttermilk, use soured milk instead. To make 1 cup soured milk, pour a very generous ¾ cup 1% low-fat milk into a measuring cup. Add enough lemon juice to make 1 cup. Let stand for 5 minutes.

◆ Double-wrap the muffins in plastic wrap and freeze for up to 2 months. Defrost the muffins in the plastic wrap. Remove from the wrap and warm in the oven or serve at room temperature.

◆ Experiment with different fillings, such as sautéed mushrooms, onions, broccoli, or sweet peppers, and fresh herbs, such as tarragon, basil, dill, cilantro, or parsley.

Winter Menu Eight

	1,500 CALORIES	2,000 CALORIES	2,500 CALORIES
	33-43 G. FAT	44-56 G. FAT	57-69 G. FAT

Breakfast

cooked oat bran cereal with	½ cup	¾ cup	1 cup
sliced banana and	½	½	1
raisins	2 tablespoons	3 tablespoons	3 tablespoons
grapefruit juice	¾ cup	1 cup	1 cup

Lunch

baked potato topped with	1	1	1
canned vegetarian chili and	½ cup	¾ cup	1 cup
nonfat sour cream	1 tablespoon	1½ tablespoons	2 tablespoons
mixed fresh fruit salad	½ cup	½ cup	1 cup
low-fat cornbread	1 square	1 square	1 square

Dinner

Chinese Pepper Steak	1 serving	1½ servings	2 servings
Oriental Spinach Salad	1 serving	1½ servings	2 servings

Snack

Peanut Butter Sandies	3	4	4
skim milk	½ cup	1 cup	1¼ cups

DAILY TOTALS			
Calories	1,495	2,021	2,504
Fat (g.)	30	42	51
% of calories from fat	18	18	18
Protein (g.)	67	97	125
Carbohydrates (g.)	250	329	406
Dietary fiber (g.)	17	21	27
Cholesterol (mg.)	113	155	192
Sodium (g.)	2,047	2,868	3,596

HEALTHY TIP OF THE DAY

Folate (folic acid or folacin) is a B vitamin that's essential for manufacturing new cells and regulating cell metabolism. For adults, the daily recommendation is 400 micrograms. Pregnant and nursing women should get more. Extra folate helps prevent neural tube defects, such as spina bifida. To boost your folate intake, look for these foods: ½ cup cooked spinach (130 mcg.); ½ cup cooked navy beans (125 mcg.); ¼ cup wheat germ (80 mcg.); ½ medium avocado (55 mcg.); 1 medium orange (45 mcg.); 1 slice whole-grain bread (15 mcg.); 8 ounces skim milk (15 mcg.).

Chinese Pepper Steak (page 402) and Oriental Spinach Salad (page 403)

Nutrition Notes

Per serving

Calories 449
Fat 7.2 g.
% of calories from fat 15
Protein 34.3 g.
Carbohydrates 59.8 g.
Dietary fiber 3.3 g.
Cholesterol 70 mg.
Sodium 629 mg.

Kitchen Hint

◆ When choosing fresh ginger, look for extremely hard roots that easily snap into pieces. Store fresh ginger in the refrigerator wrapped in a paper towel in a plastic bag for up to 3 weeks. Or peel and place in a small container of white wine; refrigerate for up to 3 months. Use the wine to flavor soups, stews, and stir-fries.

Chinese Pepper Steak

MAKES 4 SERVINGS

Pepper steak gets a flash of Asian flavors in this filling meal.

2	teaspoons olive oil
1	large onion, thinly sliced
1	green pepper, thinly sliced
1	sweet yellow pepper, thinly sliced
3	large plum tomatoes, thinly sliced
1	pound lean beef top round steak, trimmed of all visible fat and cut into ¼" × 2" strips
2	tablespoons cornstarch
1	teaspoon minced fresh ginger
1	clove garlic, minced
1	cup defatted reduced-sodium beef broth
1	cup water
¼	cup reduced-sodium soy sauce
3	cups hot cooked rice

Warm 1 teaspoon of the oil in a large no-stick skillet over medium heat. Add the onions, green peppers, and yellow peppers. Cook, stirring, for 5 to 7 minutes, or until softened. Add the tomatoes and cook, stirring, for 2 minutes. Transfer to a large bowl.

Add the remaining 1 teaspoon oil to the skillet and heat until warm.

Place the beef on a large plate and sprinkle with the cornstarch. Toss to coat. Add to the skillet and cook, stirring, for 2 minutes, or until lightly browned. Add the ginger and garlic. Stir for 1 minute, or until fragrant.

Add the broth, water, and soy sauce to the skillet. Using a wooden spoon, scrape up any browned bits from the bottom and sides of the skillet. Bring to a boil over medium-high heat.

Reduce the heat to medium-low, cover, and simmer for 25 minutes, or until the beef is tender. Stir in the onion mixture. Cook for 5 minutes, or until the vegetables are heated through. Add more water, if necessary, to thin the sauce.

Serve over the rice.

Oriental Spinach Salad

MAKES 4 SERVINGS

Ginger and sesame seeds flavor this salad. The spinach gives you a healthy helping of vitamins A and C plus folate.

Dressing

2	teaspoons cornstarch
1/3	cup defatted reduced-sodium chicken broth
3	tablespoons seasoned rice vinegar
1	tablespoon reduced-sodium soy sauce
1	tablespoon honey
1	teaspoon toasted sesame oil
1	teaspoon minced fresh ginger
1	clove garlic, minced
1	orange

Salad

5	cups lightly packed spinach leaves
1	cup thinly sliced mushrooms
1	cup mung bean sprouts
1	teaspoon toasted sesame seeds

To make the dressing: Place the cornstarch in a small saucepan. Whisk in the broth until smooth. Add the vinegar, soy sauce, honey, oil, ginger, and garlic. Mix well.

Grate 1 teaspoon rind from the orange into the saucepan; cut the orange in half and squeeze the juice into the pan. Discard the orange. Bring to a boil over medium heat. Cook, whisking often, for 3 to 5 minutes, or until thickened and translucent. Remove from the heat and let cool slightly.

To make the salad: In a large bowl, combine the spinach, mushrooms, sprouts, and sesame seeds. Add the dressing and toss to combine.

Nutrition Notes

Per serving

Calories 80
Fat 2 g.
% of calories from fat 20
Protein 4.1 g.
Carbohydrates 13.8 g.
Dietary fiber 2.8 g.
Cholesterol 0 mg.
Sodium 206 mg.

Kitchen Hint

◆ For this salad, choose small, tender spinach leaves. They will impart a more delicate flavor. For cooking, use larger, more mature leaves. Remember to wash spinach well in several changes of cold water to remove any sandy debris.

Nutrition Notes

Per cookie

Calories 68
Fat 2.4 g.
% of calories from fat 31
Protein 1.3 g.
Carbohydrates 10.7 g.
Dietary fiber 0.2 g.
Cholesterol 5 mg.
Sodium 61 mg.

Kitchen Hint

◆ Reduced-fat creamy peanut butter can also be used in this recipe. If using natural peanut butter, refrigerate the jar after opening; it will keep for up to 6 months.

Peanut Butter Sandies

MAKES 40

You'll be surprised by the richness of these low-fat peanut butter cookies. A glass of skim milk makes the perfect complement and adds bone-building calcium.

1¾	cups all-purpose flour
½	cup confectioners' sugar
2	tablespoons cornstarch
1½	teaspoons baking powder
½	teaspoon baking soda
¼	teaspoon salt
½	cup packed light brown sugar
⅓	cup reduced-fat chunky peanut butter
¼	cup canola oil
1	egg
2	tablespoons corn syrup
2	teaspoons vanilla
¼	cup sugar

Preheat the oven to 375°F. Coat 2 baking sheets with no-stick spray.

In a medium bowl, combine the flour, confectioners' sugar, cornstarch, baking powder, baking soda, and salt. Mix well.

In a large bowl, combine the brown sugar, peanut butter, and oil. Using an electric mixer, beat on medium speed until well-blended. Add the egg, corn syrup, and vanilla; beat until well-combined. Stir in the flour mixture (the dough will be crumbly).

Form the mixture into 1" balls. Roll each ball in the sugar and place on the prepared baking sheets, leaving 2" between balls. Flatten the balls with the bottom of a glass.

Bake one sheet at a time for 7 to 8 minutes, or until lightly browned. Remove from the oven and let stand on the baking sheet for 1 minute. Transfer to a wire rack to cool.

Winter Menu Nine

	1,500 CALORIES 33-43 G. FAT	2,000 CALORIES 44-56 G. FAT	2,500 CALORIES 57-69 G. FAT
Breakfast			
English muffin with	1	1	1
jam	2 tablespoons	2 tablespoons	2 tablespoons
grapefruit	½	1	1
Lunch			
Tuna-Pasta Bake	1 serving	1½ servings	2 servings
mixed greens with	1 cup	2 cups	3 cups
nonfat vinaigrette	1 tablespoon	2 tablespoons	3 tablespoons
plum	1	1	1
nonfat vanilla pudding	½ cup	¾ cup	1 cup
Dinner			
Apricot-Stuffed Pork Loin	1 serving	1½ servings	2 servings
baked sweet potato	1	1	1
steamed carrots and parsnips	½ cup	1 cup	1 cup
Snack			
Gold Rush Lemon Bars	2	2	2

DAILY TOTALS			
Calories	1,529	2,029	2,506
Fat (g.)	28	38	49
% of calories from fat	16	17	18
Protein (g.)	79	114	149
Carbohydrates (g.)	237	300	357
Dietary fiber (g.)	18	25	30
Cholesterol (mg.)	129	194	259
Sodium (g.)	1,162	1,607	2,031

NUTRIENT BONUS

This menu (at 2,000 calories) exceeds the Daily Value for:

Vitamin A	1,037%
Thiamin	171%
Riboflavin	111%
Niacin	124%
Vitamin B$_6$	120%
Vitamin B$_{12}$	119%
Vitamin C	325%
Potassium	112%

HEALTHY TIP OF THE DAY

Plan ahead. When food shopping, avoid fatty impulse purchases by using a list and by shopping after you have eaten. Focus on fresh fruits and vegetables as snack foods. When dining out, have the waiter remove the butter, margarine, or olive oil from the table. Ask for nonfat salad dressing or order the dressing on the side. Order calorie-free beverages or skim milk. Ask plenty of questions about how your food is prepared so you know what you're getting. And when ordering grilled or baked dishes, ask for them without added fats.

Gold Rush Lemon Bars

Gold Rush Lemon Bars

MAKES 36

These light, elegant bars are a snap to make. Fresh lemons create a bright sweet-tart flavor.

Crust

2	cups all-purpose flour
2/3	cup confectioners' sugar
8	tablespoons unsalted margarine or butter, cut into small pieces

Filling

3	lemons
1½	cups sugar
¼	cup all-purpose flour
1	cup fat-free egg substitute
2	tablespoons confectioners' sugar

To make the crust: Preheat the oven to 350°F. Coat a jelly-roll pan with no-stick spray.

In a medium bowl, stir together the flour and confectioners' sugar. Cut in the margarine or butter until the mixture resembles coarse meal. Press firmly and evenly into the bottom of the prepared pan.

Bake for 10 to 15 minutes, or until lightly browned. Transfer to a wire rack.

To make the filling: Grate the rind from 2 of the lemons into a medium bowl. Cut all the lemons in half and squeeze the juice into the bowl. Discard the 2 lemons. Whisk in the sugar, flour, and egg substitute until smooth. Pour over the prepared crust.

Bake for 18 to 20 minutes, or until the filling is set when lightly touched in the center and the edges are beginning to color.

Remove from the oven and let cool on a wire rack. When completely cooled, sift the confectioners' sugar over the top.

Nutrition Notes

Per bar

Calories 93
Fat 2.6 g.
% of calories from fat 24
Protein 1.5 g.
Carbohydrates 16.9 g.
Dietary fiber 0.3 g.
Cholesterol 0 mg.
Sodium 36 mg.

Kitchen Hints

◆ Lemon bars are best served within 48 hours of baking.

◆ For an interesting variation, replace the lemons with limes or oranges. Or use a combination of these citrus fruits for a tropical taste.

Nutrition Notes

Per serving

Calories 421
Fat 14 g.
% of calories from fat 30
Protein 41 g.
Carbohydrates 30.5 g.
Dietary fiber 2.6 g.
Cholesterol 102 mg.
Sodium 238 mg.

Kitchen Hint

◆ Wild rice is not a true rice. It is an aquatic grass seed that is rich in B vitamins. For three centuries, it has been harvested by Native Americans in upper Michigan, Minnesota, and Wisconsin. The labor involved in harvesting justifies wild rice's title of "the caviar of grains." Thanks to the creation of a hearty hybrid that can be picked by mechanical threshers, wild rice is now mass-marketed and more reasonable in price.

Apricot-Stuffed Pork Loin

MAKES 4 SERVINGS

Pork tenderloin makes a simple elegant entrée.

Pork Loin

¾	cup wild rice
1½	teaspoons olive oil
1	cup chopped onions
½	cup chopped fennel or celery
1	clove garlic, minced
1	teaspoon dried thyme
¼	cup Madeira or defatted reduced-sodium chicken broth
¼	cup chopped dried apricots
¼	cup chopped prunes
	Salt and ground black pepper
1	pork tenderloin (1½ pounds)

Sauce

1	cup defatted reduced-sodium chicken broth
⅓	cup apricot nectar or orange juice
2	teaspoons Dijon mustard
2	teaspoons cornstarch
2	tablespoons water

To make the pork loin: Cook the wild rice according to the package directions.

Warm the oil in a large no-stick skillet over medium heat. Add the onions, fennel or celery, garlic, and thyme. Cook, stirring often, for 6 to 8 minutes, or until the onions are soft. Add the Madeira or broth and increase the heat to high. Cook for 1 to 2 minutes, or until the liquid is evaporated. Remove from the heat and stir in the apricots, prunes, and wild rice. Season with the salt and pepper.

With a long slender knife, make a 1" slit from one end of the pork to the other, keeping the sides of the loin intact. Using your fingers, push the meat back from the slit to create a "tunnel." From both ends, stuff the cavity with the wild-rice mixture. Mist the pork with no-stick spray and sprinkle lightly with salt and pepper.

Preheat the oven to 350°F. Coat a large ovenproof skillet with no-stick spray and place over medium-high heat. Add the pork and cook for 3 to 5 minutes, or until browned on all sides. Transfer the skillet to the oven and cook for 25 minutes, or until the meat is only slightly pink on the inside. Transfer to a cutting board. Let stand for 5 minutes before slicing.

To make the sauce: In a small saucepan, whisk together the broth, apricot nectar or orange juice, and mustard. Bring to a boil over medium-high heat and cook for 2 minutes.

Place the cornstarch in a cup. Add the water and stir until smooth. Add to the saucepan and cook, whisking constantly, for 2 minutes, or until thickened. Serve over the pork.

Play It Safe

Food safety is important all year long. Bacteria are most often found in high-protein foods like dairy products, eggs, meats, poultry, and seafood. To avoid contamination, here's what experts advise.

Thaw foods in the refrigerator. Avoid thawing foods, especially meats, poultry, and seafood, at room temperature, where bacteria thrive.

Marinate in the refrigerator. Red meats and poultry should marinate in the refrigerator, not at room temperature. Discard the marinade after removing the meat. To use the marinade as a sauce or baste, boil it first to kill any bacteria that may have been picked up from the meat.

Use two plates. When grilling, avoid placing cooked meat, fish, or poultry back on the same platter that held the raw food. Use a separate platter for the cooked food.

Check for doneness. To ensure food safety, use an instant-read thermometer. Whole birds should reach an internal temperature of 180°F. Cook individual pieces until no longer pink at the thickest part and juices run clear when tested. Large pieces of red meat should reach an internal temperature of 165°F. For added safety, cook burgers, steaks, and chops until well-done. Avoid raw foods like steak tartare, carpaccio, sashimi (the fish in sushi), seviche, and other raw shellfish.

Keep foods cold. Avoid letting foods stand uncovered at room temperature for longer than 2 hours. If the room temperature is above 85°F, refrigerate foods after 1 hour. When eating outdoors, pack red meats, poultry, and fish on ice in a separate cooler.

Use two cutting boards. Designate one board for raw meats, poultry, and fish. Use the second board for all other foods. To sanitize cutting boards and sponges, wash them in a solution of 1 gallon warm water and 1 tablespoon bleach and then in hot soapy water.

Store toward the back. Keep eggs, red meat, poultry, seafood, lunchmeats, and leftover cooked meats in the coldest part of the refrigerator. The middle shelf toward the back is the best choice.

When in doubt, throw it out. If dairy or egg products, lunchmeats, and cooked meats look questionable—throw them out. Be especially cautious if the food has been in the refrigerator for more than a week. Use poultry, seafood, and ground beef within 2 days of purchase. Other raw red meats should be used within 3 to 4 days.

Be a clean cook. Remember to wash your hands with antibacterial soap after handling raw red meats, fish, and poultry.

Nutrition Notes

Per serving

Calories 291
Fat 6.5 g.
% of calories from fat 20
Protein 21.4 g.
Carbohydrates 36.5 g.
Dietary fiber 3 g.
Cholesterol 27 mg.
Sodium 459 mg.

Kitchen Hints

◆ Store leftover casserole, covered, in the refrigerator for up to 3 days.

◆ Low-fat, reduced-sodium condensed soups can be used in a number of ways to create quick and delicious dishes. Broccoli-cheddar, mushroom, and chicken soups are especially versatile. For a flavorful side dish, bring a 15-ounce can of soup to a simmer and stir in 2 cups cooked long-grain rice. For a quick main dish, buy a frozen vegetable-and-pasta mix and make a sauce using a can of soup, chopped fresh herbs, and about ¼ cup canned broth.

Tuna-Pasta Bake

MAKES 8 SERVINGS

The rich, creamy white sauce in this dish is surprisingly low in fat— thanks to evaporated skim milk. Fresh tuna and fusilli pasta update this classic casserole to today's health and taste standards.

8	ounces fusilli
1	tuna steak (10 ounces)
1	teaspoon olive oil
1	cup chopped onions
3½	ounces shiitake mushrooms, thickly sliced
½	cup chopped sweet red peppers
½	cup frozen peas, thawed
1	teaspoon minced garlic
1	can (15 ounces) low-fat, reduced-sodium condensed cream of mushroom soup
1	can (12 ounces) evaporated skim milk
2	teaspoons Dijon mustard
6	tablespoons grated Parmesan cheese
3	tablespoons unseasoned dry bread crumbs

Cook the fusilli in a large pot of boiling water according to the package directions. Drain and place in a large bowl.

Preheat the broiler. Coat a baking sheet with no-stick spray. Place the tuna on the sheet. Broil 4" from the heat for 3 to 4 minutes per side, or until the fish is opaque and flakes easily when tested with a fork. Cut into ½" cubes and add to the fusilli.

Preheat the oven to 350°F. Coat a 2-quart baking dish with no-stick spray.

Warm the oil in a large no-stick skillet over medium heat. Add the onions and cook for 2 to 3 minutes, or until just softened. Add the mushrooms, peppers, peas, and garlic. Cook, stirring often, for 3 to 4 minutes, or until the vegetables are tender. Add to the bowl with the fusilli. Toss lightly to mix.

In a medium bowl, whisk together the soup, milk, mustard, and 3 tablespoons of the Parmesan. Pour over the fusilli mixture. Toss to mix well. Transfer to the prepared baking dish.

In a small bowl, combine the bread crumbs and the remaining 3 tablespoons Parmesan. Sprinkle over the casserole. Cover with foil and bake for 20 minutes. Remove the foil and bake for 10 minutes, or until lightly browned and bubbling.

Winter Menu Ten

	1,500 CALORIES	2,000 CALORIES	2,500 CALORIES
	33-43 G. FAT	44-56 G. FAT	57-69 G. FAT

Breakfast

Apple Pancakes	1	2	3
maple syrup	1 tablespoon	2 tablespoons	3 tablespoons
skim milk	1 cup	1 cup	1¼ cups

Lunch

cooked turkey and	2 ounces	3 ounces	3 ounces
reduced-sodium tomato sauce over	½ cup	½ cup	½ cup
cooked rotini	1 cup	1 cup	1¼ cups
baby carrots	10	10	12
pear	1	1	1
whole-grain roll	1	1	1

Dinner

Blackened Snapper	1 serving	1½ servings	2 servings
Caribbean Rice	1 serving	1½ servings	2 servings
steamed spinach,	½ cup	1 cup	1 cup
green beans, and	¼ cup	¼ cup	½ cup
mushrooms	¼ cup	¼ cup	¼ cup

Snack

nonfat frozen yogurt with	1 cup	1 cup	1 cup
low-fat granola	3 tablespoons	3 tablespoons	3 tablespoons

DAILY TOTALS

Calories	1,523	1,987	2,505
Fat (g.)	16	23	29
% of calories from fat	9	10	10
Protein (g.)	77	100	121
Carbohydrates (g.)	275	356	452
Dietary fiber (g.)	23	26	31
Cholesterol (mg.)	90	142	183
Sodium (g.)	2,052	2,797	3,180

NUTRIENT BONUS

This menu (at 2,000 calories) exceeds the Daily Value for:

Dietary fiber	105%
Vitamin A	176%
Thiamin	121%
Riboflavin	117%
Vitamin B12	117%
Vitamin C	222%
Calcium	120%
Potassium	105%

HEALTHY TIP OF THE DAY

Give healthy gifts. Create an international food basket filled with grains, breads, beans, spices, and herbs; add a colorful tablecloth or rolled-up placemats. Fill a breakfast basket with homemade low-fat muffins, cakes, or breads (be sure to include the recipe); add marmalade, fresh fruit, low-fat hot chocolate mix, a selection of teas, cups, saucers, and a teapot. Give healthy-cooking gifts like a food processor or stove-top grill. Give a start-up membership to a health or racquet club. Or surprise someone with a tennis racquet, a pair of exercise shoes, or other outdoor activity gear.

Blackened Snapper (page 413) and Caribbean Rice (page 414)

Blackened Snapper

MAKES 4 SERVINGS

*Pan-searing this white-fleshed fish locks in flavor and moisture.
Instead of the traditional butter, we've used a small amount of olive oil to
reduce the saturated fat.*

1	teaspoon paprika
1/2	teaspoon dried oregano
1/4	teaspoon garlic powder
1/4	teaspoon onion powder
1/4	teaspoon salt
1/4	teaspoon ground black pepper
1/8	teaspoon ground red pepper
4	red snapper fillets (5 ounces each)
2	teaspoons olive oil

In a small bowl, combine the paprika, oregano, garlic powder, onion
powder, salt, black pepper, and red pepper.

Set a large cast-iron skillet over high heat until hot. Brush both sides
of the snapper with the oil and dust with the spice mixture. Mist
with no-stick spray and place in the skillet. Cook for 2 to 3
minutes per side, or until the fish flakes easily when tested with
a fork.

Nutrition Notes

Per serving

Calories 119
Fat 3.7 g.
% of calories from fat 29
Protein 19.8 g.
Carbohydrates 0.8 g.
Dietary fiber 0.2 g.
Cholesterol 35 mg.
Sodium 176 mg.

Kitchen Hint

◆ Almost any firm, white-
fleshed fish can be used in
this recipe—try grouper,
sea bass, redfish (red
drum), or pompano in place
of the snapper.

Nutrition Notes

Per serving

Calories 380
Fat 2.5 g.
% of calories from fat 6
Protein 4.2 g.
Carbohydrates 86.3 g.
Dietary fiber 1.9 g.
Cholesterol 0 mg.
Sodium 68 mg.

Kitchen Hints

◆ To toast the coconut, cook it in a dry skillet over medium heat, shaking the pan often, for 2 to 3 minutes, or until fragrant and golden.

◆ If you should happen to scorch rice while cooking it, you can still salvage it. First, transfer the rice to a clean pan, taking care not to scrape up any of the burned rice. Place a single layer of onion skins over the top of the rice, cover the pot, and let stand for about 15 minutes. The onion skins will absorb the scorched flavor. Discard the onion skins before serving.

Caribbean Rice

MAKES 4 SERVINGS

For a taste of the tropics, try this low-fat blend of rice, pineapple, and coconut. Pair this dish with chicken or fish for a good balance of complex carbohydrates and lean protein.

2¼	cups water
1	cup long-grain white rice
1	can (8 ounces) crushed pineapple packed in juice
2	limes
1	tablespoon packed light brown sugar
1	teaspoon minced fresh ginger
½	teaspoon minced garlic
½	cup chopped sweet red peppers
½	cup diagonally sliced scallions
¼	cup shredded coconut, toasted (see hint)
	Salt and ground black pepper

Bring the water to a boil in a medium saucepan over high heat. Stir in the rice. Reduce the heat to medium-low, cover, and cook for 20 to 25 minutes, or until the liquid is absorbed and the rice is tender.

Drain the pineapple and place ½ cup of the juice in a small saucepan. Transfer the pineapple to a large bowl. Discard the remaining pineapple juice.

Cut the limes in half and squeeze the juice into the saucepan with the pineapple juice. Discard the limes. Stir in the brown sugar, ginger, and garlic. Bring to a boil over high heat. Remove from the heat and let stand for 20 minutes.

Add the red peppers, scallions, and coconut to the pineapple. Fluff the rice with a fork and add to the bowl. Toss lightly to mix. Add the juice mixture. Toss to mix well. Season with the salt and black pepper.

Apple Pancakes

MAKES 10

A mixture of grains provides texture and color in these griddle cakes. Top them with your favorite preserves, fruit butter, or maple syrup for a satisfying start to your day.

$3/4$ cup all-purpose flour
$1/2$ cup whole-wheat flour
$1/2$ cup buckwheat flour
$1/4$ cup quick-cooking rolled oats
1 tablespoon sugar
1 teaspoon baking soda
$1/2$ teaspoon ground cinnamon
$1/4$ teaspoon salt
$1 1/4$ cups 1% low-fat buttermilk or soured milk (see hint)
$1/4$ cup apple juice
1 egg
1 tablespoon canola oil
1 cup shredded Granny Smith apples

In a large bowl, combine the all-purpose flour, whole-wheat flour, buckwheat flour, oats, sugar, baking soda, cinnamon, and salt. Mix well.

In a medium bowl, whisk together the buttermilk, apple juice, egg, oil, and apples. Pour into the flour mixture and stir until just combined.

Coat a large no-stick skillet with no-stick spray and place over medium heat until hot. For each pancake, pour $1/4$ cup of the batter into the skillet and spread to form a 5" pancake. Cook for 2 minutes, or until bubbling and slightly dry around the edges. Turn the pancakes over and cook for 1 minute, or until the center springs back when lightly pressed.

Nutrition Notes

Per pancake

Calories 126
Fat 2.8 g.
% of calories from fat 20
Protein 4.4 g.
Carbohydrates 21.5 g.
Dietary fiber 2 g.
Cholesterol 22 mg.
Sodium 219 mg.

Kitchen Hints

◆ If you don't have buttermilk, use soured milk instead. To make $1 1/4$ cups soured milk, pour a very generous $1 1/8$ cups 1% low-fat milk into a measuring cup. Add enough lemon juice to make $1 1/4$ cups. Let stand for 5 minutes.

◆ These pancakes are great made with almost any combination of fruit and fruit juice. Try substituting the same quantities of coarsely chopped bananas, strawberries, peaches, nectarines, or grated pears for the apples. Use a complementary juice or nectar in place of the apple juice.

HEALTHY TIP OF THE DAY

Use egg whites instead of whole eggs to cut dietary cholesterol. Two large eggs have 430 milligrams of cholesterol; 2 large egg whites contain none. Egg whites make splendid egg salad sandwiches, like the one on today's menu. You can also fashion delicious omelets, frittatas, and scrambled eggs from whites. Flavor them with fresh herbs and cooked vegetables.

Winter Menu Eleven

	1,500 CALORIES	2,000 CALORIES	2,500 CALORIES
	33-43 G. FAT	44-56 G. FAT	57-69 G. FAT
Breakfast			
Smoked Salmon Tart	1 serving	1½ servings	1½ servings
calcium-fortified orange juice	¾ cup	1½ cups	2 cups
rye toast	1 slice	2 slices	2 slices
Lunch			
cut-up cooked egg white with	3 large	3 large	4 large
nonfat mayonnaise on	2 tablespoons	2 tablespoons	3 tablespoons
multigrain bread with	2 slices	2 slices	2 slices
lettuce and	1 leaf	1 leaf	1 leaf
tomato	2 slices	2 slices	2 slices
baked tortilla chips with	13	13	26
fat-free salsa	¼ cup	¼ cup	½ cup
banana	1	1	2
Dinner			
Old-Fashioned Beef Stew	1½ servings	2 servings	2 servings
mixed greens with	1 cup	2 cups	3 cups
nonfat dressing	1 tablespoon	2 tablespoons	3 tablespoons
sourdough roll	1	2	2
Snack			
Apricot Kisses	2	2	4
DAILY TOTALS			
Calories	1,504	1,992	2,478
Fat (g.)	34	44	50
% of calories from fat	20	20	18
Protein (g.)	68	89	100
Carbohydrates (g.)	216	287	388
Dietary fiber (g.)	20	25	32
Cholesterol (mg.)	102	134	146
Sodium (g.)	2,165	2,860	3,542

Old-Fashioned Beef Stew (page 419)

Nutrition Notes

Per serving

Calories 111
Fat 3.6 g.
% of calories from fat 31
Protein 8.2 g.
Carbohydrates 10.4 g.
Dietary fiber 0.9 g.
Cholesterol 11 mg.
Sodium 429 mg.

Kitchen Hints

◆ Nonfat shredded hash-brown potatoes can be found in the dairy section and freezer section of most supermarkets. Thaw frozen ones before using.

◆ For smaller tarts, ladle ¼-cup amounts of the potato mixture into a hot skillet. Form thin 2" to 3" rounds. Top with the cream-cheese mixture and salmon.

Smoked Salmon Tart

MAKES 4 SERVINGS

It's easy to make a crispy crust from hash-brown potatoes. This tart is suitable for breakfast, lunch, or dinner.

2	cups nonfat shredded hash-brown potatoes (see hint)
1	egg white, lightly beaten
1	tablespoon all-purpose flour
¼	teaspoon salt
¼	teaspoon ground black pepper
2	teaspoons olive oil
2	ounces low-fat cream cheese, at room temperature
2	ounces nonfat cream cheese, at room temperature
¼	cup chopped scallions
2	teaspoons minced fresh dill
3	ounces thinly sliced smoked salmon

In a medium bowl, stir together the potatoes, egg white, flour, salt, and pepper.

Warm the oil in a large no-stick skillet over medium-high heat. Spoon the potato mixture into the skillet and flatten into an even 10" round. Cook for 2 to 3 minutes per side, or until golden and crispy. Transfer to a plate.

In a small bowl, stir together the low-fat cream cheese, nonfat cream cheese, scallions, and dill. Spread on top of the potato pancake and arrange the salmon on top. Cut into 4 wedges.

Old-Fashioned Beef Stew

MAKES 8 SERVINGS

With lots of chunky vegetables, this savory stew provides a kettleful of vitamin C and potassium.

- 1 tablespoon olive oil
- ¼ cup all-purpose flour
- ¼ teaspoon ground black pepper
  Pinch of salt
- 1½ pounds lean boneless beef round steak, trimmed of all visible fat and cut into 1" cubes
- 1 medium onion, coarsely chopped
- 2 cloves garlic, minced
- 1 teaspoon dried thyme
- 2 bay leaves
- 3 cups dry red wine or nonalcoholic red wine
- ¼ cup tomato paste
- 2 cans (14 ounces each) defatted reduced-sodium beef broth
- 1½ pounds baby red potatoes, quartered
- 20 baby carrots
- 16 baby pattypan squash, halved
- 1 pound shiitake mushrooms, thickly sliced
- ¼ cup chopped fresh Italian parsley

Warm 1½ teaspoons of the oil in a Dutch oven over medium-high heat. In a medium bowl, combine the flour, pepper, and salt. Working in batches, dredge the beef in the flour mixture, add to the Dutch oven, and cook for 3 to 4 minutes, or until browned on all sides; do not overcrowd the pan. Using a slotted spoon, transfer the beef to a plate.

Add the remaining 1½ teaspoons oil to the Dutch oven. Reduce the heat to medium and add the onions, garlic, thyme, and bay leaves. Cook, stirring often, for 6 to 7 minutes, or until the onions are tender. Stir in the wine and tomato paste. Using a wooden spoon, scrape up any browned bits from the bottom of the pan.

Add the broth and beef. Bring to a boil. Partially cover and simmer for 1½ hours, or until the beef is tender.

Add the potatoes and carrots. Simmer for 20 minutes. Add the squash, mushrooms, and parsley. Simmer for 10 minutes, or until the vegetables are tender. Season with salt and pepper.

Nutrition Notes

Per serving

Calories 384
Fat 13.7 g.
% of calories from fat 32
Protein 21.5 g.
Carbohydrates 30.3 g.
Dietary fiber 4.4 g.
Cholesterol 53 mg.
Sodium 180 mg.

Kitchen Hint

◆ This stew keeps well in the refrigerator for up to 4 days. It also freezes well; store for no longer than 3 months. If needed, thin the sauce with a little water when reheating.

Apricot Kisses

MAKES 36

Apricot preserves fill the center of these buttery tea cookies. Try using raspberry jam or orange marmalade.

6	tablespoons unsalted margarine or butter, at room temperature
$\frac{1}{2}$	cup sugar
$\frac{3}{4}$	cup apricot preserves
1	egg
1	teaspoon grated orange rind
$\frac{1}{4}$	teaspoon almond extract
$1\frac{3}{4}$	cups all-purpose flour
2	tablespoons cornstarch
$\frac{1}{2}$	teaspoon baking powder
$\frac{1}{4}$	teaspoon salt
$\frac{1}{4}$	cup confectioners' sugar

Preheat the oven to 375°F. Coat 2 baking sheets with no-stick spray.

Place the margarine or butter in a large bowl. Using an electric mixer, beat until light and fluffy. Add the sugar and $\frac{1}{4}$ cup of the preserves. Beat until well-blended. Add the egg, orange rind, and almond extract. Beat for 2 minutes.

In a medium bowl, whisk together the flour, cornstarch, baking powder, and salt. Gradually add to the apricot mixture and beat on low speed until just incorporated; do not overmix. Refrigerate the dough for 10 minutes, or until slightly firm.

Form the dough into 1" balls. Place on the prepared baking sheets, leaving $1\frac{1}{2}$" between balls. Dip the back of a $\frac{1}{4}$-teaspoon measuring spoon into the confectioners' sugar and press a deep indentation in the center of each ball. Fill the indentation with $\frac{1}{4}$ to $\frac{1}{2}$ teaspoon of the remaining preserves.

Bake one sheet at a time for 10 minutes, or until the cookies are just tinged with brown. Remove from the oven and let stand on the baking sheet for 1 minute. Transfer to a wire rack to cool.

Winter Menu Twelve

	1,500 CALORIES	2,000 CALORIES	2,500 CALORIES
	33-43 G. FAT	44-56 G. FAT	57-69 G. FAT

Breakfast

Cranberry Coffee Cake	1 serving	1 serving	1½ servings
skim milk	1 cup	1¼ cups	1½ cups

Lunch

Fennel and Bean Soup	1 serving	2 servings	2 servings
crusty hard roll	1	2	2
pear	1	1	1

Dinner

broiled flank steak	5 ounces	6 ounces	8 ounces
steamed Swiss chard	½ cup	¾ cup	1 cup
Sweet-Potato Gnocchi with Sage Sauce	1 serving	1½ servings	2 servings

Snack

nonfat vanilla pudding	½ cup	¾ cup	1 cup
banana	1	1	1

NUTRIENT BONUS

This menu (at 2,000 calories) exceeds the Daily Value for:

Dietary fiber	107%
Vitamin A	827%
Thiamin	113%
Riboflavin	119%
Vitamin C	178%
Calcium	113%

HEALTHY TIP OF THE DAY

Count on cranberries for fiber and vitamin C. Toss dried cranberries into salads or bake fresh cranberries in breads, pies, cobblers, muffins, or stuffings. Instead of using high-sugar canned cranberry sauce, make fresh cranberry relish at home. For a festive holiday beverage that's alcohol-free, mix cranberry juice cocktail with sparkling water.

DAILY TOTALS

Calories	1,496	2,010	2,503
Fat (g.)	27	34	44
% of calories from fat	16	15	16
Protein (g.)	71	97	122
Carbohydrates (g.)	239	325	395
Dietary fiber (g.)	19	27	30
Cholesterol (mg.)	108	127	173
Sodium (g.)	1,353	2,070	2,474

Cranberry Coffee Cake

Cranberry Coffee Cake

Makes 12 servings

Enjoy a slice of this moist coffee cake without a trace of guilt.

Topping

¾	cup packed light brown sugar
½	cup all-purpose flour
¼	cup chopped toasted walnuts
2	teaspoons ground cinnamon
2	tablespoons unsalted butter or margarine, at room temperature

Coffee Cake

¼	cup canola oil
1	cup sugar
1	egg
1	egg white
1	tablespoon grated orange rind
1	teaspoon vanilla
2	cups all-purpose flour
1	teaspoon baking powder
1	teaspoon baking soda
½	teaspoon salt
1	cup nonfat sour cream
2	cups fresh cranberries

To make the topping: In a small bowl, combine the brown sugar, flour, walnuts, cinnamon, and butter or margarine. Mix until crumbly.

To make the coffee cake: Preheat the oven to 350°F. Coat a 13" × 9" baking dish with no-stick spray.

In a large bowl, combine the oil, sugar, egg, and egg white. Using an electric mixer, beat on medium speed for 3 minutes, or until light in color. Beat in the orange rind and vanilla.

In a medium bowl, combine the flour, baking powder, baking soda, and salt. Mix well.

On low speed, beat one-third of the flour mixture into the sugar mixture. Beat in ½ cup of the sour cream. Repeat, beginning and ending with the flour. Beat for about 2 minutes, or until smooth and thick; do not overmix.

Spoon the batter into the prepared baking dish. Scatter the cranberries on top. Sprinkle with the topping. Bake for 40 to 45 minutes, or until a toothpick inserted in the center comes out clean.

Nutrition Notes

Per serving

Calories 305
Fat 8.7 g.
% of calories from fat 25
Protein 5.4 g.
Carbohydrates 51.8 g.
Dietary fiber 1.7 g.
Cholesterol 23 mg.
Sodium 264 mg.

Kitchen Hints

◆ This coffee cake is also perfect for a summer morning. Replace the cranberries with fresh blueberries.

◆ This cake can be covered and stored in the refrigerator for up to 4 days or double-wrapped in plastic and stored in the freezer for up to 2 months.

Nutrition Notes

Per serving

Calories 123
Fat 1.1 g.
% of calories from fat 7
Protein 6.1 g.
Carbohydrates 24.2 g.
Dietary fiber 4.1 g.
Cholesterol 0 mg.
Sodium 250 mg.

Kitchen Hints

◆ Ditalini are $1/4$"-long narrow tubes that resemble pieces of macaroni. Any other small pasta shape, such as orzo, may be substituted for the ditalini.

◆ Leftover soup can be stored in the refrigerator for up to 4 days or in the freezer for up to 3 months.

◆ If you should oversalt a soup, add a potato cut into large pieces to the pot. Cook the potatoes until tender; they will absorb excess salt as they cook. When the flavor is balanced again, discard the potato chunks.

Fennel and Bean Soup

Ditalini pasta adds complex carbohydrates to this hearty bean soup. Fresh herbs boost the flavor without added fat.

1	teaspoon olive oil
1	small red onion, sliced
1	medium bulb fennel (white part only), quartered and sliced
1	teaspoon minced garlic
1	teaspoon dried oregano
1	can (14 ounces) no-salt-added chopped tomatoes (with juice)
6	cups defatted reduced-sodium chicken broth
4	ounces ditalini pasta
1	can (15 ounces) cannellini beans, rinsed and drained
6	sprigs fresh thyme, chopped
1	cup coarsely chopped Swiss chard
	Salt and ground black pepper

Warm the oil in a Dutch oven over medium heat. Add the onions, fennel, garlic, and oregano. Cook, stirring occasionally, for 10 minutes, or until softened. Stir in the tomatoes (with juice) and broth. Cook for 10 minutes.

Cook the ditalini in a large pot of boiling water according to the package directions. Drain. Add to the Dutch oven.

Stir in the beans and thyme. Cook for 5 minutes, or until heated through. Stir in the Swiss chard. Season with the salt and pepper.

Sweet-Potato Gnocchi with Sage Sauce

MAKES 4 SERVINGS

Serve these low-fat dumplings with your favorite lean meat.

8	tablespoons semolina flour (see note)
1	pound sweet potatoes, peeled and cut into ½" cubes
¼	cup fat-free egg substitute
1	tablespoon chopped fresh thyme
¼	teaspoon salt
¼	teaspoon ground nutmeg
½	cup + 1 tablespoon all-purpose flour
¼	cup + 2 tablespoons grated Parmesan cheese
1	cup defatted reduced-sodium chicken broth
3	fresh leaves sage, chopped
⅔	cup nonfat nondairy creamer
	Ground black pepper

Evenly dust 2 baking sheets with 2 tablespoons of the semolina flour.

Place the sweet potatoes in a large saucepan. Cover with cold water and bring to a boil over high heat. Reduce the heat to medium and cook for 12 minutes, or until tender. Drain and place in a large bowl. Mash until smooth. Let cool for about 10 minutes.

Stir in the egg substitute, thyme, salt, and nutmeg. Add ½ cup of the all-purpose flour, ¼ cup of the Parmesan, and the remaining 6 tablespoons semolina flour. Mix well. Shape the dough into a ball and divide into 8 portions.

On a lightly floured surface, roll out 1 portion of the dough at a time into a ¼" × 16" rope. Cut into 1" pieces. Place the pieces on the prepared baking sheets as they are cut.

In a large saucepan over high heat, bring the broth and sage to a boil. Cook for 2 to 3 minutes, or until reduced by one-third. Reduce the heat to medium. In a small bowl, whisk together the creamer and the remaining 1 tablespoon all-purpose flour. Whisk into the broth. Whisk in the remaining 2 tablespoons Parmesan. Cook, stirring constantly, for 2 minutes, or until thickened. Season with the pepper. Keep warm over low heat.

Cook the gnocchi in a large pot of boiling water for 45 seconds to 1 minute, or until they float to the surface. Remove with a slotted spoon and transfer to the saucepan with the sauce. Stir into the sauce until well-coated.

Nutrition Notes

Per serving

Calories 308
Fat 3.4 g.
% of calories from fat 10
Protein 11.8 g.
Carbohydrates 57 g.
Dietary fiber 5.2 g.
Cholesterol 7 mg.
Sodium 407 mg.

Kitchen Hint

◆ Semolina flour is milled from the heart (or endosperm) of durum wheat. Also called pasta flour, it is favored for use in pasta, pizza, and gnocchi dough. Look for semolina flour in the baking section of large supermarkets and Italian grocery stores. If you can't find it, all-purpose flour can be substituted.

Winter Menu Thirteen

	1,500 CALORIES	2,000 CALORIES	2,500 CALORIES
	33-43 G. FAT	44-56 G. FAT	57-69 G. FAT

Breakfast

Lone Star Omelets	1	1	1
whole-wheat toast	1 slice	2 slices	2 slices
calcium-fortified orange juice	¾ cup	1¼ cups	1½ cups

Lunch

cooked pasta shells with	1 cup	2 cups	2 cups
reduced-sodium tomato sauce	¼ cup	¾ cup	¾ cup
mixed greens with	1 cup	2 cups	2 cups
nonfat dressing	1 tablespoon	2 tablespoons	2 tablespoons
apple	1	1	2

Dinner

Mardi Gras Jambalaya	1 serving	1½ servings	2½ servings
stewed okra and tomatoes	¾ cup	¾ cup	¾ cup
Carrot Cake	1 serving	1 serving	1 serving

Snack

whole-grain crackers with	6	6	9
reduced-fat peanut butter	1 tablespoon	1 tablespoon	1½ tablespoons

DAILY TOTALS			
Calories	1,497	2,007	2,483
Fat (g.)	39	46	58
% of calories from fat	23	20	21
Protein (g.)	65	87	111
Carbohydrates (g.)	228	320	391
Dietary fiber (g.)	21	30	37
Cholesterol (mg.)	313	346	384
Sodium (g.)	2,201	3,254	3,910

Lone Star Omelets (page 428)

Nutrition Notes

Per omelet

Calories 235
Fat 10.6 g.
% of calories from fat 42
Protein 20.7 g.
Carbohydrates 12.8 g.
Dietary fiber 3.1 g.
Cholesterol 228 mg.
Sodium 544 mg.

Kitchen Hint

◆ Tomatillos look like small green tomatoes with papery husks. After peeling off the husk, you can eat tomatillos raw or cooked. This staple ingredient of Mexican cooking tastes like a cross between a tomato and a tart strawberry. If tomatillos are not available, substitute seeded and drained fresh plum tomatoes.

Lone Star Omelets

MAKES 2

Round up chili peppers, corn, and tomatillos for this calcium-rich Tex-Mex omelet. Egg whites and reduced-fat Cheddar cheese help minimize the fat, making this a smart choice for any morning.

1/3	cup chopped scallions
1/4	cup chopped onions
1/4	cup canned chopped green chili peppers
1/4	cup frozen corn kernels, thawed
1/2	cup chopped tomatillos (see hint)
	Pinch of ground cumin
4	egg whites
2	eggs
2	tablespoons skim milk
1/4	teaspoon ground black pepper
	Pinch of salt
1 1/2	ounces reduced-fat Cheddar cheese, shredded
2	tablespoons medium-hot or hot salsa (optional)
2	tablespoons nonfat sour cream (optional)

Coat a medium no-stick skillet with no-stick spray and place over medium heat. Add the scallions, onions, chili peppers, and corn. Cook for 5 minutes, or until the onions are softened. Add the tomatillos and cumin. Cook for 3 to 4 minutes, or until the tomatillos are softened. Transfer to a small bowl.

Wipe out the skillet, coat with no-stick spray, and return to the heat.

In a medium bowl, whisk together the egg whites, eggs, milk, black pepper, and salt. Pour half of the egg mixture into the skillet and cook, occasionally scraping the bottom of the pan, for 2 to 3 minutes. Sprinkle half of the Cheddar and half of the vegetable mixture over the eggs. Cook, without stirring, for 3 to 4 minutes, or until the bottom is golden brown and the eggs are set. Using a spatula, flip the omelet in half and transfer to a plate.

Coat the pan with no-stick spray and repeat the procedure with the remaining egg mixture, Cheddar, and vegetable mixture.

Serve topped with the salsa (if using) and sour cream (if using).

Mardi Gras Jambalaya

MAKES 6 SERVINGS

Creole spices jazz up this healthful rendition of a Louisiana specialty. Smoked turkey sausage and lean chicken lend flavor without a lot of fat.

1	teaspoon olive oil
1½	cups chopped onions
1	large sweet red or green pepper, chopped
1	large stalk celery, sliced
1	clove garlic, minced
4	cups defatted reduced-sodium chicken broth
1	can (6 ounces) tomato paste
1	teaspoon herbes de provence (see hint)
1	bay leaf
¾	cup long-grain white rice
1	teaspoon hot-pepper sauce
8	ounces smoked turkey sausage, thinly sliced
8	ounces boneless, skinless chicken breast, cut into ¼" strips
½–1	cup water

Warm the oil in a large no-stick skillet over medium heat. Add the onions, red or green peppers, celery, and garlic. Cook, stirring often, for 10 minutes, or until softened. Stir in the broth, tomato paste, herbes de provence, and bay leaf. Bring to a boil over medium-high heat.

Stir in the rice and hot-pepper sauce. Bring to a boil. Reduce the heat to medium, cover, and simmer for 15 minutes. Add the sausage, chicken, and ½ cup of the water. Cover and cook for 10 minutes, or until the chicken and rice are cooked through. If necessary, thin with the remaining ½ cup water. Remove and discard the bay leaf.

Nutrition Notes

Per serving

Calories 268
Fat 7.5 g.
% of calories from fat 25
Protein 19.2 g.
Carbohydrates 31.3 g.
Dietary fiber 2.8 g.
Cholesterol 48 mg.
Sodium 712 mg.

Kitchen Hints

◆ Herbes de provence is a blend of dried herbs that includes thyme, savory, and fennel. Sometimes it also contains sage, lavender, rosemary, or bay leaf. It can be found in the spice aisle of most supermarkets.

◆ Serve the jambalaya with a side dish of stewed okra and tomatoes. To make 6 servings, coat a large no-stick skillet with no-stick spray. Add 15 ounces thawed frozen chopped okra and cook for 5 minutes, or until softened. Add 20 ounces canned reduced-sodium stewed tomatoes (with juice) and cook for 10 minutes, or until heated through.

Nutrition Notes

Per serving

Calories 343
Fat 7.6 g.
% of calories from fat 19
Protein 7 g.
Carbohydrates 63.6 g.
Dietary fiber 2.4 g.
Cholesterol 37 mg.
Sodium 356 mg.

Kitchen Hints

◆ A quick alternative to the cream-cheese frosting is a lemon or pineapple glaze. Stir together 2 cups confectioners' sugar and ¼ cup lemon juice or 6 tablespoons pineapple juice reserved from the drained canned pineapple. Spread over the cooled cake.

◆ For a more complex flavor, add 1 tablespoon brandy or 1 teaspoon brandy extract along with the pineapple and currants.

Carrot Cake

Each bite of this cake is rich, moist, and spicy.

Cake

1¾	cups all-purpose flour
1	cup whole-wheat flour
2	teaspoons baking powder
2	teaspoons baking soda
2	teaspoons ground cinnamon
1	teaspoon ground nutmeg
¾	teaspoon ground allspice
¼	teaspoon salt
2	eggs
4	egg whites
1	cup packed light brown sugar
1	cup nonfat plain or vanilla yogurt
¼	cup canola oil
2	cups grated carrots
1	cup drained canned crushed pineapple
⅔	cup currants

Frosting

1	package (8 ounces) reduced-fat cream cheese, at room temperature
1	box (16 ounces) confectioners' sugar
2	teaspoons vanilla

To make the cake: Preheat the oven to 325°F. Coat a 13" × 9" baking dish with no-stick spray.

In a medium bowl, combine the all-purpose flour, whole-wheat flour, baking powder, baking soda, cinnamon, nutmeg, allspice, and salt. Mix well.

In a large bowl, combine the eggs and egg whites. Using an electric mixer, beat on medium speed until foamy. Add the brown sugar. Beat for 3 minutes. Add the yogurt and oil. Beat until creamy.

On low speed, beat the flour mixture into the egg mixture until combined. Fold in the carrots, pineapple, and currants. Spoon into the prepared baking dish and bake for 40 to 50 minutes, or until a toothpick inserted in the center of the cake comes out clean. Let the cake cool completely in the pan on a wire rack.

To make the frosting: In a large bowl, combine the cream cheese, confectioners' sugar, and vanilla. Stir until smooth. Spread over the cooled cake.

Winter Menu Fourteen

	1,500 CALORIES	2,000 CALORIES	2,500 CALORIES
	33-43 G. FAT	44-56 G. FAT	57-69 G. FAT

Breakfast
Cherry-Oatmeal Bread	1 slice	1½ slices	2 slices
clementine	1	1	1
nonfat vanilla yogurt	1 cup	1 cup	1 cup

Lunch
Spaghetti Squash Gratin	1 serving	1½ servings	2 servings
mixed greens with	1 cup	2 cups	2 cups
nonfat vinaigrette and	1 tablespoon	2 tablespoons	2 tablespoons
low-fat croutons	¼ cup	¼ cup	¼ cup
whole-wheat pita bread	1	1	1
kiwifruit	½	1	1

Dinner
Poached Salmon with Creamy Spinach Fettuccine	1 serving	1½ servings	2 servings
steamed broccoli	½ cup	1 cup	1 cup
crusty French roll	1	1	2

Snack
mixed dried fruit	¼ cup	¼ cup	¼ cup

DAILY TOTALS
Calories	1,502	1,994	2,517
Fat (g.)	24	35	46
% of calories from fat	14	15	16
Protein (g.)	80	110	140
Carbohydrates (g.)	251	322	397
Dietary fiber (g.)	22	32	38
Cholesterol (mg.)	96	141	187
Sodium (g.)	1,827	2,427	3,146

NUTRIENT BONUS

This menu (at 2,000 calories) exceeds the Daily Value for:

Dietary fiber	125%
Vitamin A	209%
Thiamin	125%
Riboflavin	142%
Niacin	141%
Vitamin B$_6$	133%
Vitamin B$_{12}$	161%
Folate	121%
Vitamin C	535%
Calcium	153%
Potassium	144%

HEALTHY TIP OF THE DAY

Which is better for you, butter or margarine? Butter is high in saturated fat, which should be kept to a minimum to promote heart health. Likewise, margarine contains trans-fatty acids, which act like saturated fat in your body. Studies show that both of these fats can raise your blood cholesterol levels. The bottom line is that both butter and margarine are 100 percent fat and should be eaten in moderation. Instead, put the emphasis on mono-unsaturated fats found in oils like olive, canola, and peanut.

Poached Salmon with Creamy Spinach Fettuccine

Poached Salmon with Creamy Spinach Fettuccine

MAKES 4 SERVINGS

Serve this delicate dish for a heart-smart Valentine's Day dinner.

1½ teaspoons olive oil
2 cups sliced yellow squash
2 cups sliced zucchini
3 scallions, chopped
½ teaspoon dried oregano
4 salmon fillets (4 ounces each)
3 tablespoons lemon juice
3 tablespoons water
1 orange
1½ cups nonfat nondairy creamer
1½ tablespoons all-purpose flour
½ teaspoon orange extract (optional)
Salt and ground black pepper
8 ounces spinach fettuccine

Warm the oil in a large no-stick skillet over medium heat. Add the yellow squash, zucchini, scallions, and oregano. Cook, stirring, for 5 minutes, or until crisp-tender. Transfer to a large bowl and cover to keep warm.

Add the salmon, lemon juice, and water to the skillet. Cook over medium heat for 2 to 3 minutes per side, or until the salmon is bright pink and flakes easily when tested with a fork. Transfer the salmon to a plate and cover to keep warm. Discard the liquid in the skillet.

Finely grate 1 tablespoon rind from the orange and add to the skillet. Cut the orange in half and squeeze the juice into the skillet. Discard the orange. Whisk in the creamer, flour, and orange extract (if using). Bring to a boil over medium-high heat, whisking constantly. Reduce the heat to medium and cook, whisking often, for 5 minutes, or until thick and creamy. Season with the salt and pepper.

Cook the fettuccine in a large pot of boiling water according to the package directions. Drain and add to the bowl with the vegetables.

Pour the sauce over the pasta and toss gently to coat. Serve topped with the salmon.

Nutrition Notes

Per serving

Calories 418
Fat 11.2 g.
% of calories from fat 25
Protein 36.1 g.
Carbohydrates 40.3 g.
Dietary fiber 4.4 g.
Cholesterol 83 mg.
Sodium 103 mg.

Kitchen Hint

◆ When buying zucchini and yellow squash, look for small squash—about 7" long and an inch or less in diameter, with firm, unbroken skin. Generally, the smaller the squash, the more flavor it has.

Nutrition Notes

Per slice

Calories 156
Fat 3.7 g.
% of calories from fat 21
Protein 4.5 g.
Carbohydrates 27.6 g.
Dietary fiber 1.1 g.
Cholesterol 1 mg.
Sodium 242 mg.

Kitchen Hints

◆ Take advantage of the wide variety of dried fruit available year-round. Try substituting dried cranberries, blueberries, apricots, peaches, dates, apples, or pineapple for the dried cherries.

◆ If you don't have buttermilk, use soured milk instead. To make ¾ cup soured milk, pour a generous ⅔ cup 1% low-fat milk into a measuring cup. Add enough lemon juice to make ¾ cup. Let stand for 5 minutes.

Cherry-Oatmeal Bread

MAKES 16 SLICES

Warm up with a slice of this fragrant bread studded with chewy red cherries.

¾	cup dried cherries
¾	cup 1% low-fat buttermilk or soured milk (see hint)
1½	cups all-purpose flour
¾	cup rolled oats
2	teaspoons baking powder
1	teaspoon baking soda
½	teaspoon salt
1	cup nonfat vanilla yogurt
2	tablespoons canola oil
⅔	cup sugar
½	cup fat-free egg substitute
2	teaspoons vanilla
⅓	cup chopped toasted walnuts

In a small bowl, combine the cherries and buttermilk. Let soak for 25 minutes, or until softened.

Preheat the oven to 350°F. Coat a 9" × 5" loaf pan with no-stick spray.

In a large bowl, combine the flour, oats, baking powder, baking soda, and salt. Mix well.

In a medium bowl, whisk together the yogurt, oil, sugar, egg substitute, and vanilla. Add the buttermilk mixture and mix well. Pour into the bowl with the flour. Stir together until just combined; do not overmix. Stir in the walnuts.

Pour the batter into the prepared pan and bake for 40 to 45 minutes, or until a wooden toothpick inserted in the center of the loaf comes out clean. Let stand in the pan on a wire rack for 5 minutes. Turn out onto the rack to finish cooling.

Spaghetti Squash Gratin

MAKES 4 SERVINGS

This creamy dish is comfort food without the calories. The flavors of spaghetti squash and Parmesan cheese make it delicious.

- 1 spaghetti squash (2½–3 pounds)
- 1 teaspoon olive oil
- 1 cup chopped onions
- ¼ cup chopped fresh basil
- 1 teaspoon minced garlic
- 1 cup evaporated skim milk
- ¼ teaspoon salt
- ¼ teaspoon ground black pepper
- 5 plum tomatoes, thinly sliced
- ¼ cup seasoned dry bread crumbs
- ¼ cup grated Parmesan cheese
- ½ teaspoon paprika

Preheat the oven to 400°F. Line a baking sheet with foil.

Cut the squash in half lengthwise; scoop out and discard the seeds. Place the squash, cut side down, on the baking sheet. Bake for 1 hour, or until soft and tender. Set aside for 10 minutes. Use a fork to separate the squash strands. Transfer them to a large bowl. Discard the squash shells.

Warm the oil in a large no-stick skillet over medium heat. Add the onions and cook for 5 minutes, or until softened. Add the basil and garlic; cook for 2 minutes. Add to the bowl with the squash. Stir in the milk, salt, and pepper.

Coat a 2-quart baking dish with no-stick spray. Add the squash mixture. Arrange the tomatoes on top.

In a small bowl, stir together the bread crumbs, Parmesan, and paprika. Sprinkle over the tomatoes. Bake for 30 to 40 minutes, or until golden brown and bubbling.

Nutrition Notes

Per serving

Calories 222
Fat 4.5 g.
% of calories from fat 17
Protein 11.4 g.
Carbohydrates 36.2 g.
Dietary fiber 5 g.
Cholesterol 7 mg.
Sodium 574 mg.

Kitchen Hint

◆ A gratin is a dish that has a characteristic crisp, golden brown crust made by browning the dish in the oven or under a broiler. The crust usually consists of seasoned bread crumbs, grated cheese, or a white sauce. It is the crust itself that characterizes a gratin, not what lies beneath it.

Winter Menu Fifteen

	1,500 CALORIES	2,000 CALORIES	2,500 CALORIES
	33-43 G. FAT	44-56 G. FAT	57-69 G. FAT

Breakfast

poached egg with	1	1	1
Potatoes Peperonata	1 serving	1½ servings	2 servings
calcium-fortified orange juice	¾ cup	1 cup	1 cup

Lunch

Black and White Bean Soup	1 serving	2 servings	3 servings
toasted whole-grain bread with	2 slices	2 slices	2 slices
melted low-fat American cheese	2 ounces	2 ounces	2 ounces
plum	1	1	2

Dinner

Wrap and Roll Cabbage	2 bundles	3 bundles	4 bundles
boiled acorn-squash cubes	¾ cup	1 cup	1 cup
crusty hard roll	1	1	2

Snack

low-fat popcorn	3 cups popped	3 cups popped	3 cups popped

DAILY TOTALS

Calories	1,518	1,974	2,495
Fat (g.)	33	40	48
% of calories from fat	19	17	17
Protein (g.)	77	100	126
Carbohydrates (g.)	239	323	417
Dietary fiber (g.)	30	42	53
Cholesterol (mg.)	314	344	375
Sodium (g.)	1,641	2,022	2,550

Black and White Bean Soup (page 439)

Nutrition Notes

Per serving

Calories 165
Fat 2.9 g.
% of calories from fat 15
Protein 5.2 g.
Carbohydrates 31 g.
Dietary fiber 6.2 g.
Cholesterol 0 mg.
Sodium 228 mg.

Kitchen Hint

◆ To save time, roast the potatoes 1 day in advance and store, covered, in the refrigerator.

Potatoes Peperonata

<u>MAKES 6 SERVINGS</u>

Add zip, zest, and color to your breakfast spuds by spiking them with peppers, onions, and seasonings. For the best taste, make this dish the night before so that the flavors have a chance to blend.

1½	pounds small red potatoes, cut into ½" cubes
1	tablespoon olive oil
1¼	cups thinly sliced onions
1½	teaspoons minced garlic
3	cups cubed sweet red and green peppers
1	can (28 ounces) chopped tomatoes, drained
½	cup thinly sliced scallions
¼	cup slivered Kalamata olives
¼	cup chopped fresh basil
¼	cup balsamic vinegar
2	tablespoons minced fresh Italian parsley
1	teaspoon ground black pepper
¼	teaspoon salt

Preheat the oven to 400°F. Line a baking sheet with foil.

Place the potatoes on the baking sheet and drizzle with 1½ teaspoons of the oil. Toss to coat. Roast for 40 to 45 minutes, or until browned. Transfer to a large bowl.

Warm the remaining 1½ teaspoons oil in a large no-stick skillet over medium heat. Add the onions and garlic. Cook, stirring often, for 5 minutes. Add the red and green peppers. Cook, stirring often, for 3 minutes, or until the vegetables are softened. Add the tomatoes and cook for 1 to 2 minutes, or until heated through.

Transfer to the bowl with the potatoes. Add the scallions, olives, basil, vinegar, parsley, black pepper, and salt. Toss to combine.

Cover and refrigerate for at least 3 hours before serving.

Black and White Bean Soup

MAKES 9 SERVINGS

Canned beans make this a quick soup to assemble.

    1   tablespoon olive oil
    1   cup chopped onions
    1   cup chopped sweet red and green peppers
    ½   cup sliced carrots
    1½ teaspoons chopped garlic
    4   cups reduced-sodium vegetable broth
    1   cup canned black beans, rinsed and drained
    1   cup canned cannellini beans, rinsed and drained
    1   cup frozen corn kernels
    1   teaspoon ground cumin
    1   teaspoon ground coriander
    1   tablespoon chopped fresh Italian parsley

Warm the oil in a large saucepan over medium heat. Add the onions
and cook for 5 minutes, or until soft. Add the red and green peppers, carrots, garlic, and ½ cup of the broth. Cook, stirring often,
for 10 minutes. Add the black beans, cannellini beans, corn,
cumin, coriander, and the remaining 3½ cups broth. Simmer for
15 to 20 minutes, or until the vegetables are tender. Stir in the
parsley.

Nutrition Notes

Per serving

Calories 88
Fat 1.9 g.
% of calories from fat 17
Protein 4.7 g.
Carbohydrates 16.5 g.
Dietary fiber 3.5 g.
Cholesterol 0 mg.
Sodium 144 mg.

Kitchen Hints

◆ This soup can be stored
in the refrigerator for up to
5 days or in the freezer for
up to 3 months.

◆ For a little Southwestern
fire, try adding minced
jalapeño peppers or re-
constituted dried chipotle
peppers.

Nutrition Notes

Per 2 bundles

Calories 436
Fat 5.4 g.
% of calories from fat 11
Protein 29.7 g.
Carbohydrates 72.4 g.
Dietary fiber 3.9 g.
Cholesterol 61 mg.
Sodium 207 mg.

Kitchen Hint

◆ For a quicker variation of this recipe, replace the raw rice with 1 cup cooked rice. Form the filling into 1½" meatballs. Place in the baking dish and bake for 30 minutes at 350°F. Coarsely chop the raw cabbage and cook until wilted in a medium skillet that has been coated with no-stick spray. Add the sauce ingredients and cook over medium-low heat for 25 minutes. Add the cooked meatballs.

Wrap and Roll Cabbage

MAKES 8 BUNDLES

Ginger ale is the surprise ingredient in these sweet-and-sour rolls.

2	small onions, thinly sliced
8	large leaves savoy cabbage
¼	cup water
1	pound lean ground beef top round
½	cup instant white rice
¼	cup unseasoned dry bread crumbs
2	tablespoons fat-free egg substitute
1½	teaspoons chopped fresh Italian parsley
¼	teaspoon garlic powder
¼	teaspoon onion powder
¼	teaspoon ground black pepper
⅛	teaspoon salt
2	cups ginger ale
1½	cups reduced-sodium ketchup
¼	cup packed light brown sugar
¼	cup golden raisins

Preheat the oven to 350°F. Coat a 9" × 9" baking dish with no-stick spray. Scatter the onions in the dish.

Place the cabbage and water in a large microwave-safe bowl. Cover with vented plastic wrap and microwave on high power for a total of 4 minutes, or until tender; stop and turn after 2 minutes. Plunge the leaves into a bowl of cold water, drain, and pat dry.

In a large bowl, combine the beef, rice, bread crumbs, egg substitute, parsley, garlic powder, onion powder, pepper, and salt. Mix well and divide into 8 portions.

Place the cabbage leaves on a work surface, with the inside of each leaf facing upward (to form a cup). Place a portion of the beef mixture in the center of each leaf. Fold in the sides and then roll each leaf to enclose the filling.

Place the bundles, seam side down, on the onions in the dish.

In a medium bowl, whisk together the ginger ale, ketchup, and brown sugar. Pour the sauce over the cabbage bundles. Sprinkle with the raisins. Cover with foil.

Bake for 2 hours, basting the rolls every 30 minutes with the liquid.

Winter Menu Sixteen

	1,500 CALORIES	2,000 CALORIES	2,500 CALORIES
	33-43 G. FAT	44-56 G. FAT	57-69 G. FAT

Breakfast

shredded wheat cereal with	1 cup	1¼ cups	1½ cups
skim milk	¾ cup	1 cup	1½ cups
calcium-fortified orange juice	1 cup	1¼ cups	1½ cups

Lunch

Ballpark Club Sandwiches	1	1	1½
pear	1	1	1

Dinner

Chicken Mirabella	1 serving	1½ servings	2 servings
steamed carrots	½ cup	1 cup	1 cup
cooked long-grain white rice	½ cup	1 cup	1¼ cups
mixed greens with	1 cup	2 cups	2 cups
nonfat dressing	1 tablespoon	2 tablespoons	2 tablespoons
Apricot Soufflé	1 serving	1 serving	1 serving

Snack

low-sodium, low-fat fruited cottage cheese	¾ cup	1½ cups	1½ cups

DAILY TOTALS

Calories	1,522	2,002	2,506
Fat (g.)	21	25	33
% of calories from fat	12	11	12
Protein (g.)	95	124	161
Carbohydrates (g.)	243	325	392
Dietary fiber (g.)	17	22	25
Cholesterol (mg.)	148	188	260
Sodium (g.)	2,025	2,401	3,324

NUTRIENT BONUS

This menu (at 2,000 calories) exceeds the Daily Value for:

Vitamin A	891%
Thiamin	107%
Riboflavin	229%
Niacin	162%
Vitamin B$_6$	124%
Vitamin C	369%
Calcium	137%

HEALTHY TIP OF THE DAY

Many people have hunger pangs around 3:00 P.M. Conquer your snack attacks with foods from the base of the Food Guide Pyramid. Here are a few options: mini pita bread stuffed with 2 ounces sliced turkey; a handful of dried fruit with 1 tablespoon almonds; sweet red and green pepper strips with nonfat sour-cream dip; toasted sesame seed bagel with a slice of low-fat cheese; bowl of whole-grain cereal with skim milk; or a blended fruit smoothie made with low-fat milk, yogurt, and fresh fruit.

Chicken Mirabella

Chicken Mirabella

MAKES 4 SERVINGS

These marinated chicken breasts bake up moist and tender. Serve them over rice, bulgur, or couscous to sop up the flavorful marinade.

½ cup prunes, halved
¼ cup pimento-stuffed green olives, halved
6 tablespoons red-wine vinegar
6 tablespoons defatted reduced-sodium chicken broth
2 tablespoons dried oregano
2 tablespoons capers, rinsed and drained
1 tablespoon minced garlic
3 bay leaves
¼ teaspoon salt
¼ teaspoon ground black pepper
4 bone-in skinless chicken breast halves (about 8 ounces each)
½ cup packed light brown sugar
½ cup dry white wine or vermouth (see hint)
¼ cup chopped fresh Italian parsley

In a 13" × 9" baking dish, stir together the prunes, olives, vinegar, broth, oregano, capers, garlic, bay leaves, salt, and pepper. Add the chicken in a single layer and turn to coat. Cover and refrigerate for at least 4 hours or up to 12 hours; turn at least once while marinating.

Preheat the oven to 350°F.

Sprinkle the chicken with the brown sugar and pour the wine or vermouth around the chicken. Spoon some of the marinade on top.

Bake, basting occasionally with the pan juices, for 50 to 60 minutes, or until no longer pink in the center when tested with a sharp knife. Sprinkle with the parsley.

Nutrition Notes

Per serving

Calories 237
Fat 4.1 g.
% of calories from fat 16
Protein 27.3 g.
Carbohydrates 19.5 g.
Dietary fiber 0.9 g.
Cholesterol 73 mg.
Sodium 409 mg.

Kitchen Hint

◆ To make this dish without alcohol, replace the wine or vermouth with a combination of ¼ cup non-alcoholic wine and ¼ cup chicken broth.

Nutrition Notes

Per sandwich

Calories 422
Fat 12.6 g.
% of calories from fat 27
Protein 32.8 g.
Carbohydrates 44.2 g.
Dietary fiber 1.8 g.
Cholesterol 67 mg.
Sodium 1,308 mg.

Kitchen Hint

◆ Try substituting nonfat Russian dressing for the yellow mustard or replace the sauerkraut with nonfat coleslaw. To boost your fiber intake, replace the white bread with whole-grain, pumpernickel, or rye bread.

Ballpark Club Sandwiches

MAKES 4

In this home-run sandwich, sliced chicken breast, hot dogs, and sauerkraut are piled high on toasted bread. You'll enjoy this lunch even if spring training hasn't started yet.

4	low-fat hot dogs, halved lengthwise
8	ounces boneless, skinless chicken breasts
12	slices white bread
4	slices reduced-fat Monterey Jack cheese
4	leaves romaine lettuce
8	tomato slices
1⅓	cups low-sodium sauerkraut, rinsed and drained
4	teaspoons yellow mustard

Preheat the broiler.

Line a baking sheet with foil. Arrange the hot dogs, cut side down, on the sheet. Coat both sides of the chicken with no-stick spray and place on the sheet. Broil 4" from the heat for 3 to 4 minutes per side, or until the chicken is no longer pink in the center when tested with a sharp knife. Remove from the sheet and cut each hot-dog half on the diagonal into 4 pieces. Thinly slice the chicken.

Discard the foil. Place the bread slices in a single layer on the same baking sheet. Lightly broil on both sides. Remove 8 of the slices. Divide the Monterey Jack among the remaining 4 slices. Broil for 30 to 60 seconds, or until the cheese is melted.

Top with the chicken, lettuce, and tomatoes. Add another slice of bread to each sandwich and top with the hot dogs and sauerkraut. Spread the mustard on the remaining bread slices and top each sandwich with one of the slices. Cut in half on the diagonal.

Apricot Soufflé

Beaten egg whites make this elegant dessert very light. The apricots contribute a nice helping of beta-carotene.

  4 ounces dried apricots
 ½ cup water
 ½ cup orange juice
  8 tablespoons sugar
  2 teaspoons fresh lemon juice
 ½ teaspoon vanilla
  4 egg whites
 ¼ teaspoon cream of tartar
     Pinch of salt
  1 tablespoon confectioners' sugar

In a medium saucepan, combine the apricots, water, orange juice, and 3 tablespoons of the sugar. Cover and bring to a boil over medium heat. Simmer for 15 to 20 minutes, or until the apricots are soft. Let cool for 5 minutes. Transfer to a food processor or blender and puree. Transfer to a bowl and stir in the lemon juice and vanilla. Let cool to room temperature.

Preheat the oven to 350°F. Coat four 6-ounce ramekins or custard cups with no-stick spray. Use 2 tablespoons of the remaining sugar to coat the ramekins; tap out the excess. Place the ramekins on a baking sheet.

Place the egg whites, cream of tartar, and salt in a large bowl. Using an electric mixer, beat on medium speed until foamy. Gradually beat in the remaining 3 tablespoons sugar. Increase the speed to high and continue to beat until the whites are firm and glossy.

Stir one-third of the egg-white mixture into the apricot puree. Gently fold in the remaining egg-white mixture until thoroughly incorporated. Spoon the mixture into the prepared ramekins or custard cups and smooth the tops.

Bake for 20 to 25 minutes, or until puffed, golden brown, and just set in the center. Remove from the oven and sift the confectioners' sugar on top. Serve immediately.

Nutrition Notes

Per serving

Calories 143
Fat 0.2 g.
% of calories from fat 1
Protein 3.3 g.
Carbohydrates 33.7 g.
Dietary fiber 1.7 g.
Cholesterol 0 mg.
Sodium 62 mg.

Kitchen Hints

◆ The apricots can be cooked and pureed up to 4 days in advance and stored in the refrigerator in an air-tight container. Bring the puree to room temperature before folding in the beaten egg whites.

◆ This dish can also be made in a 1-quart soufflé dish. Increase the baking time to 30 to 35 minutes.

Winter Menu Seventeen

	1,500 CALORIES	2,000 CALORIES	2,500 CALORIES
	33-43 G. FAT	44-56 G. FAT	57-69 G. FAT

Breakfast

Cheese Blintzes	2	2	3
calcium-fortified orange juice	¾ cup	1¼ cups	1½ cups

Lunch

black bean soup	¾ cup	1½ cups	1½ cups
whole-grain muffin	1	1	1
papaya	1	1	1

Dinner

Pasta with Shrimp and Sun-Dried Tomato Pesto	1 serving	1½ servings	2 servings
mixed greens with	1 cup	2 cups	2 cups
nonfat low-sodium salad dressing	1 tablespoon	2 tablespoons	2 tablespoons
Fruitti Biscotti	1	2	2

Snack

nonfat vanilla pudding	½ cup	¾ cup	1 cup

DAILY TOTALS			
Calories	1,483	2,005	2,518
Fat (g.)	22	27	36
% of calories from fat	13	12	13
Protein (g.)	69	94	122
Carbohydrates (g.)	250	341	419
Dietary fiber (g.)	29	42	47
Cholesterol (mg.)	208	288	387
Sodium (g.)	1,605	2,215	2,720

NUTRIENT BONUS

This menu (at 2,000 calories) exceeds the Daily Value for:

Dietary fiber	170%
Vitamin A	308%
Thiamin	152%
Folate	167%
Vitamin C	765%
Calcium	136%
Iron	141%
Potassium	116%

HEALTHY TIP OF THE DAY

About 99 percent of your body's calcium is in your bones. To strengthen them and help prevent osteoporosis, eat calcium-rich foods and do weight-bearing exercises like walking, weight training, or aerobics. Adults under age 65 should get 1,000 milligrams a day. Adults over 65 should get 1,500 milligrams a day. Pregnant or breastfeeding women need between 1,200 and 1,500 milligrams. Most postmenopausal women need about 1,500 milligrams. The following foods contain 300 milligrams of calcium: 1 cup yogurt or skim milk, 1 cup calcium-fortified orange juice, 1 cup cottage cheese, and 1½ ounces low-fat cheese.

Fruitti Biscotti (page 450)

Nutrition Notes

Per blintz

Calories 175
Fat 3.6 g.
% of calories from fat 19
Protein 10.8 g.
Carbohydrates 24 g.
Dietary fiber 0.6 g.
Cholesterol 30 mg.
Sodium 257 mg.

Kitchen Hints

◆ For a decorative presentation, place the blintzes with the browner side down before filling them so that the brown side shows when the blintzes are rolled.

◆ To make a quick and delicious sauce for these blintzes, in a small saucepan, heat ½ cup orange marmalade, 3 tablespoons orange juice, and 3 tablespoons lemon juice until the marmalade is melted and the sauce is hot.

◆ These blintzes can be made ahead and frozen for up to 2 months.

Cheese Blintzes

MAKES 8

These thin pancakes are filled and rolled up with a creamy low-fat filling.

Filling

1⅔	cups	1% low-fat cottage cheese
⅓	cup	nonfat sour cream
¼	cup	fat-free egg substitute
2	tablespoons	1% low-fat buttermilk
¼	cup	sugar
1	teaspoon	grated orange rind
½	teaspoon	ground cinnamon
⅛	teaspoon	ground nutmeg

Blintzes

1	cup + 2 tablespoons	1% low-fat milk
1		egg
1	tablespoon	canola oil
1	teaspoon	vanilla
1	cup	all-purpose flour
1	teaspoon	sugar
		Pinch of salt

To make the filling: Place the cottage cheese in a blender or food processor and process until smooth. Transfer to a medium bowl. Add the sour cream, egg substitute, buttermilk, sugar, orange rind, cinnamon, and nutmeg. Mix well.

To make the blintzes: Rinse out the blender. Add the milk, egg, oil, and vanilla. Process to combine. Add the flour, sugar, and salt. Process until thoroughly combined.

Coat a medium no-stick skillet with no-stick spray and place over medium-high heat. Pour ¼ cup of the batter into the skillet and quickly swirl the skillet in all directions to make a thin, round blintz. Cook for about 1 minute per side, or until lightly browned. Remove to a plate and cover with a kitchen towel to keep warm. Repeat with the remaining batter to make a total of 8 blintzes.

Preheat the oven to 350°F. Coat a 13" × 9" baking dish with spray.

Spoon 3 tablespoons of the filling into the center of each blintz. Fold in each side to enclose the filling. Place the blintzes, seam side down, in the baking dish. Mist the tops with no-stick spray and cover with foil. Bake for 15 minutes. Remove the foil and bake for 10 minutes, or until the filling is hot.

Pasta with Shrimp and Sun-Dried Tomato Pesto

MAKES 4 SERVINGS

Bold flavored pesto makes the perfect sauce for shrimp.

Sun-Dried Tomato Pesto

- 1/2 cup sun-dried tomatoes
- 2 tablespoons chopped toasted walnuts
- 2 cloves garlic
- 1 can (14 1/2 ounces) no-salt-added whole tomatoes, drained
- 1/2 cup chopped fresh Italian parsley
- 1/4 cup chopped fresh oregano or basil
- 1 1/2 tablespoons grated Parmesan cheese
- 2 teaspoons olive oil

Pasta

- 1 teaspoon olive oil
- 1 cup sliced onions
- 1 cup sliced sweet red and green peppers
- 1 pound large shrimp, peeled and deveined
- 1/2 teaspoon ground black pepper
- 1/4 teaspoon salt
- 10 ounces angel hair pasta

To make the sun-dried tomato pesto: Place the sun-dried tomatoes in a small bowl. Cover with boiling water and let soak for about 20 minutes, or until softened. Drain and reserve the liquid.

Transfer the sun-dried tomatoes to a food processor or blender. Add the walnuts and garlic. Process briefly to combine. Add the whole tomatoes, parsley, oregano or basil, Parmesan, and oil. Process until smooth. Add just enough of the reserved liquid to form a paste; process until smooth.

To make the pasta: Warm the oil in a large no-stick skillet over medium heat. Add the onions and cook, stirring often, for 5 minutes, or until softened. Add the red and green peppers and cook, stirring often, for 5 to 8 minutes, or until softened. Add the shrimp and cook, stirring often, for 2 to 4 minutes, or until pink. Sprinkle with the black pepper and salt.

Cook the angel hair in a large pot of boiling water according to the package directions. Drain. Place in a large bowl. Top with the shrimp mixture and the pesto. Toss well to combine.

Nutrition Notes

Per serving

Calories 480
Fat 9.1 g.
% of calories from fat 17
Protein 28.9 g.
Carbohydrates 71.5 g.
Dietary fiber 7.3 g.
Cholesterol 136 mg.
Sodium 495 mg.

Kitchen Hint

◆ The pesto can be tightly covered and stored for up to 2 weeks in the refrigerator or up to 4 months in the freezer.

Nutrition Notes

Per biscotti

Calories 74
Fat 0.8 g.
% of calories from fat 10
Protein 1.7 g.
Carbohydrates 14.9 g.
Dietary fiber 0.5 g.
Cholesterol 12 mg.
Sodium 52 mg.

Kitchen Hint

◆ To vary the flavor, replace the raisins and almonds with dried cherries and hazelnuts or chocolate chips and walnuts. For slightly softer biscotti, bake them for 15 minutes after slicing. For a crunchier texture, replace ⅓ cup of the flour with cornmeal.

Fruitti Biscotti

MAKES 36

These fruit and nut cookies make a great midday snack or after-dinner treat. Try dunking them in coffee, tea, or milk.

⅓	cup golden raisins
2	tablespoons dry Marsala or apple juice
2¾	cups all-purpose flour
1	cup sugar
⅓	cup toasted sliced almonds
2	tablespoons chopped crystallized ginger
1	teaspoon baking powder
½	teaspoon baking soda
½	teaspoon ground cinnamon
¼	teaspoon salt
2	eggs
1	egg white
1	teaspoon vanilla
	Grated rind of 1 orange
	Grated rind of 1 lemon
1	tablespoon frozen orange juice concentrate, thawed

Preheat the oven to 325°F. Coat a baking sheet with no-stick spray.

Place the raisins and Marsala or apple juice in a small bowl. Let soak for 10 minutes, or until the raisins are softened.

In a large bowl, combine the flour, sugar, almonds, ginger, baking powder, baking soda, cinnamon, and salt. Mix well.

In a medium bowl, combine the eggs, egg white, vanilla, orange rind, lemon rind, and orange juice concentrate; mix well. Stir in the raisins and their soaking liquid. Pour into the flour mixture and mix well.

Divide the dough in half. Shape each half into a 13"-long log; flatten to a 1"-thickness. Transfer the logs to the prepared baking sheet and space them 2" apart. Bake for 25 minutes, or until firm to the touch. Remove the logs from the baking sheet and let cool on a wire rack for 10 minutes.

Reduce the oven temperature to 300°F.

Cut each roll diagonally into eighteen ½" slices. Place the slices, cut side down, on the baking sheet. Bake for 20 minutes. Transfer to a wire rack and cool completely.

Winter Menu Eighteen

	1,500 CALORIES 33-43 G. FAT	2,000 CALORIES 44-56 G. FAT	2,500 CALORIES 57-69 G. FAT
Breakfast			
shredded wheat cereal	¾ cup	1½ cups	1¾ cups
skim milk	½ cup	1 cup	1¼ cups
cran-raspberry juice	¾ cup	1 cup	1¼ cups
Lunch			
Eggplant Parmesan Sandwiches	1	1	1½
mixed greens with	1 cup	2½ cups	2½ cups
nonfat dressing	1 tablespoon	2½ tablespoons	2½ tablespoons
Dinner			
Baked Halibut Curry with Basmati Rice	1 serving	1½ servings	1½ servings
Indian Cauliflower Sauté	1 serving	1½ servings	2 servings
Snack			
orange	1	1	2

DAILY TOTALS			
Calories	1,527	2,026	2,528
Fat (g.)	24	31	38
% of calories from fat	14	14	13
Protein (g.)	83	113	135
Carbohydrates (g.)	247	329	419
Dietary fiber (g.)	23	30	40
Cholesterol (mg.)	76	106	116
Sodium (g.)	2,254	2,653	3,552

NUTRIENT BONUS

This menu (at 2,000 calories) exceeds the Daily Value for:

Dietary fiber	120%
Vitamin A	119%
Thiamin	113%
Riboflavin	116%
Niacin	141%
Folate	105%
Vitamin C	459%
Calcium	155%
Potassium	110%

HEALTHY TIP OF THE DAY

To help prevent dehydration, drink at least 8 cups of water a day. Go for water instead of soda to avoid caffeine and excess calories. Distilled water is pure water without added chemicals, minerals, or sugars. Natural soft water has a low mineral content. Mineral water is often flavored with citrus or berries and sweetened with juices, sugar, or corn syrup; read labels carefully. Sparkling water has bubbles that can be natural or added through carbon dioxide; the water may be sweetened. Still water is purified water used where tap-water purity is a problem.

Baked Halibut Curry with Basmati Rice (page 453) and Indian Cauliflower Sauté (page 454)

Baked Halibut Curry with Basmati Rice

MAKES 4 SERVINGS

Served over fragrant basmati rice with a low-fat curry sauce, this ocean catch is a good source of lean protein.

- 2 cups 1% low-fat milk
- ½ teaspoon chili powder
- ¼ teaspoon turmeric
- ¼ teaspoon salt
- ¼ teaspoon ground black pepper
- 4 skinless halibut fillets (5 ounces each)
- ⅓ cup unseasoned dry bread crumbs
- 1 tablespoon unsalted margarine or butter
- 2 tablespoons curry powder
- 2 tablespoons all-purpose flour
- 2 tablespoons chopped fresh cilantro
- 1 tablespoon lemon juice
- 3 cups hot cooked basmati rice

Preheat the oven to 425°F. Line a baking sheet with foil and coat with no-stick spray.

In a shallow dish, whisk together the milk, chili powder, turmeric, salt, and pepper. Add the halibut and let soak for 20 minutes.

Place the bread crumbs on a plate. Remove 1 fillet at a time from the milk mixture and dredge both sides in the crumbs. Place on the prepared baking sheet. Bake for 15 to 20 minutes, or until opaque in the center when tested with a sharp knife.

Transfer the milk mixture to a small saucepan and bring to a boil over medium-high heat. Reduce the heat to low and keep warm.

Melt the margarine or butter in a medium saucepan over low heat. Add the curry powder; cook and stir for 1 minute. Add the flour; cook and stir for 1 minute. Remove from the heat and whisk in the milk mixture. Return to the heat and increase the heat medium-high. Whisk for 5 minutes, or until the sauce is thickened and comes to a boil. Strain through a fine sieve and stir in the cilantro and lemon juice.

Serve the halibut over the rice. Top with the sauce.

Nutrition Notes

Per serving

Calories 484
Fat 9.6 g.
% of calories from fat 18
Protein 37.5 g.
Carbohydrates 58 g.
Dietary fiber 2.1 g.
Cholesterol 56 mg.
Sodium 382 mg.

Kitchen Hints

◆ Curry can be found in both a powder and a paste form. It's a blend of ground spices that can range in strength from mild to fiercely hot. The term *Madras* denotes a hot curry. The most common spices used are coriander, turmeric, red pepper, ginger, cumin, fenugreek, cardamom, and mustard seeds.

Nutrition Notes

Per serving

Calories 53
Fat 1.4 g.
% of calories from fat 21
Protein 3.3 g.
Carbohydrates 9.2 g.
Dietary fiber 3.3 g.
Cholesterol 0 mg.
Sodium 73 mg.

Kitchen Hint

◆ You can easily substitute broccoflower (a cross between broccoli and cauliflower) for the cauliflower in this dish.

Indian Cauliflower Sauté

<u>MAKES 4 SERVINGS</u>

Tired of steamed vegetables? Try this spicy side dish featuring cauliflower, a member of the cabbage family that is very high in dietary fiber.

1	medium head cauliflower
6	tablespoons water
1½	teaspoons yellow mustard seeds
1½	teaspoons ground coriander
1½	teaspoons curry powder
1½	cups chopped tomatoes
½	cup defatted reduced-sodium chicken broth
	Salt and ground black pepper
2	tablespoons chopped fresh cilantro or Italian parsley

Trim any leaves from the cauliflower and remove the thick core with a sharp knife. Place the cauliflower and 3 tablespoons of the water in a large microwave-safe bowl. Cover with vented plastic wrap and microwave on high power for a total of 9 minutes, or until tender; stop and rotate the bowl every 3 minutes. Let stand for 2 minutes. Cut into 2" florets.

Coat a large no-stick skillet with no-stick spray and place over medium heat. Add the mustard seeds, cover, and cook for 2 minutes, or until they pop. Remove from the heat.

In a small bowl, whisk together the coriander, curry powder, and the remaining 3 tablespoons water. Add to the skillet. Stir in the tomatoes, broth, and cauliflower. Cover and cook over medium heat for 6 to 8 minutes, or until the cauliflower is tender and the liquid is reduced by half. Season with the salt and pepper and sprinkle with the cilantro or parsley.

Eggplant Parmesan Sandwiches

MAKES 6

To avoid the fat but maintain the texture of fried eggplant, we dredged the eggplant in seasoned crumbs and baked it.

2	egg whites
2	tablespoons skim milk
½	cup seasoned dry bread crumbs
¼	cup wheat germ
2	tablespoons grated Parmesan cheese
1½	teaspoons crushed dried rosemary
1	teaspoon dried oregano
¼	teaspoon ground black pepper
1	pound eggplant, cut crosswise on the diagonal into ¼"-thick slices
1	loaf French bread, halved lengthwise
1	jar (26 ounces) fat-free tomato sauce
1½	cups shredded reduced-fat mozzarella cheese

Preheat the oven to 400°F. Line a baking sheet with foil and coat with no-stick spray.

In a small bowl, whisk together the egg whites and milk.

In a medium bowl, combine the bread crumbs, wheat germ, Parmesan, rosemary, oregano, and pepper.

Dip both sides of the eggplant slices into the egg mixture and then into the crumb mixture. Set the slices on the baking sheet. Bake for 20 to 25 minutes, or until the eggplant is tender and the outside is golden brown. Transfer the slices to a plate.

Preheat the broiler.

Scoop out the soft inner crumbs from each half of the bread; reserve for another use. Place the bread halves, cut side up, on the prepared baking sheet and broil 4" from the heat for 2 minutes, or until lightly toasted.

Spread one-fourth of the tomato sauce over each bread half. Top with the eggplant slices and the remaining tomato sauce. Sprinkle with the mozzarella.

Broil for 5 minutes, or until the mozzarella is melted. Slice each half into thirds.

Nutrition Notes

Per sandwich

Calories 388
Fat 7.2 g.
% of calories from fat 17
Protein 20.6 g.
Carbohydrates 59.4 g.
Dietary fiber 6.6 g.
Cholesterol 12 mg.
Sodium 984 mg.

Kitchen Hint

◆ Researchers have found that an average serving of deep-fried eggplant absorbs 83 grams of fat in just 70 seconds. That's four times as much fat as potatoes absorb. And it adds up to more than 700 calories. Our technique of baking the eggplant instead of frying it saves about 75 grams of fat.

Christmas Menu

	1,500 CALORIES	2,000 CALORIES	2,500 CALORIES
	33-43 G. FAT	44-56 G. FAT	57-69 G. FAT

Breakfast

Gingerbread Pancakes	2	2	3
nonfat vanilla yogurt	2 tablespoons	2 tablespoons	3 tablespoons
mixed fresh fruit salad	1 cup	1¾ cups	2 cups
skim milk	1 cup	1¼ cups	1½ cups

Lunch

minestrone soup	1 cup	1¾ cups	2 cups
whole-wheat toast	2 slices	2 slices	2 slices
baby carrots and	6	9	12
low-fat dip	¼ cup	6 tablespoons	½ cup

Dinner

Golden Potato Soufflé	1 serving	1½ servings	2 servings
Roasted Winter Vegetables	1 serving	2 servings	2 servings
broiled beef tenderloin	6 ounces	7 ounces	8 ounces

Snack

orange	1	1	2

DAILY TOTALS

Calories	1,501	2,006	2,483
Fat (g.)	34	45	54
% of calories from fat	20	19	19
Protein (g.)	84	107	129
Carbohydrates (g.)	220	299	378
Dietary fiber (g.)	30	45	54
Cholesterol (mg.)	145	180	216
Sodium (g.)	2,126	2,897	3,581

Golden Potato Soufflé (page 459) and Roasted Winter Vegetables (page 460) with broiled beef tenderloin

Nutrition Notes

Per pancake

Calories 124
Fat 2 g.
% of calories from fat 14
Protein 4 g.
Carbohydrates 22.8 g.
Dietary fiber 1.2 g.
Cholesterol 1 mg.
Sodium 200 mg.

Kitchen Hints

◆ To jazz up pancake syrup, try infusing it with fruit-flavored syrups, such as those used for specialty coffees. Add 2 tablespoons flavored syrup to every $^1/_3$ cup maple or reduced-calorie syrup.

◆ Extra pancakes can be double-wrapped in plastic and frozen for up to 3 months. To reheat, thaw the pancakes and warm them in a no-stick skillet over medium-low heat for 3 minutes per side.

Gingerbread Pancakes

MAKES 10

These spice-infused breakfast cakes are classic winter fare. Kids love the taste. We cut back on fat by using low-fat buttermilk, egg substitute, and just a touch of oil. Top the pancakes with low-fat vanilla yogurt for a boost of calcium.

1	cup all-purpose flour
$^1/_2$	cup whole-wheat flour
1	tablespoon sugar
$^3/_4$	teaspoon baking soda
$^1/_2$	teaspoon ground cinnamon
$^1/_2$	teaspoon ground ginger
$^1/_4$	teaspoon ground cloves
$^1/_4$	teaspoon salt
$1^1/_2$	cups 1% low-fat buttermilk
$^1/_4$	cup fat-free egg substitute
$^1/_4$	cup light molasses
1	tablespoon canola oil

In a large bowl, combine the all-purpose flour, whole-wheat flour, sugar, baking soda, cinnamon, ginger, cloves, and salt. Mix well.

In a medium bowl, combine the buttermilk, egg substitute, molasses, and oil. Mix well. Add to the flour mixture and mix well.

Coat a large no-stick skillet with no-stick spray and place over medium heat. Pour $^1/_4$ cup of the batter into the skillet and spread to form a 5" pancake. Cook for 1 to 2 minutes, or until the edges are slightly dry and bubbles appear on top. Turn the pancake and cook for 1 to 2 minutes, or until golden brown. Repeat with the remaining batter to make a total of 10 pancakes.

Golden Potato Soufflé

MAKES 8 SERVINGS

This light and fluffy soufflé is made with buttermilk and butter-flavored sprinkles, which lend a rich flavor to the dish without much fat. The golden hue provided by the Yukon gold potatoes is a warming accent to any holiday table.

2	tablespoons fresh bread crumbs
2	tablespoons grated Parmesan cheese
2½	pounds Yukon gold potatoes, peeled and cut into 1" cubes
1¼	cups 1% low-fat buttermilk or soured milk (see hint)
3	ounces reduced-fat cream cheese, cubed
2	tablespoons butter-flavored sprinkles
2	cloves garlic, halved
½	teaspoon baking soda
3	tablespoons chopped fresh chives
	Salt and ground black pepper
3	egg whites
⅛	teaspoon cream of tartar

Preheat the oven to 400°F. Coat a 2½-quart soufflé dish with no-stick spray.

In a small bowl, combine the bread crumbs and Parmesan. Coat the soufflé dish with half of the mixture.

Place the potatoes in a large saucepan. Cover with cold water and bring to a boil over high heat. Reduce the heat to medium and cook for 15 to 20 minutes, or until the potatoes are soft when tested with a sharp knife. Drain, transfer to a large bowl, and mash.

In a medium saucepan, combine the buttermilk, cream cheese, butter-flavored sprinkles, and garlic. Whisk over medium-high heat for 2 to 3 minutes, or until the mixture is smooth. Remove from the heat and let cool for 5 minutes. Remove and discard the garlic. Stir in the baking soda and pour over the potatoes. Mix well. Stir in the chives and season with the salt and pepper.

Place the egg whites and cream of tartar in a medium bowl. Using an electric mixer, beat on medium speed until soft peaks form. Fold into the potato mixture.

Transfer the mixture to the soufflé dish and sprinkle with the remaining bread-crumb mixture. Bake for 40 to 50 minutes, or until puffed and golden brown. Serve immediately.

Nutrition Notes

Per serving

Calories 188
Fat 3.4 g.
% of calories from fat 16
Protein 7.2 g.
Carbohydrates 32.7 g.
Dietary fiber 2.6 g.
Cholesterol 10 mg.
Sodium 255 mg.

Kitchen Hints

◆ To make fresh bread crumbs, process or blend soft bread cubes or slices in a food processor or blender until crumbs form.

◆ If you don't have buttermilk, use soured milk instead. To make 1¼ cups soured milk, pour a generous 1⅓ cups 1% low-fat milk into a measuring cup. Add enough lemon juice to make 1¼ cups. Let stand for 5 minutes.

◆ Butter-flavored sprinkles are butter substitutes, such as Butter Buds and Molly McButter. Most supermarkets carry them.

Nutrition Notes

Per serving

Calories 174
Fat 2.8 g.
% of calories from fat 13
Protein 3.4 g.
Carbohydrates 32.2 g.
Dietary fiber 6.7 g.
Cholesterol 0 mg.
Sodium 144 mg.

Kitchen Hints

◆ Experiment with roasting your favorite vegetables. Roasting brings out the natural sweetness in the vegetables by caramelizing their sugars. Try roasting celery root, beets, fennel, winter squash, celery, asparagus, mushrooms, eggplant, zucchini, or yellow squash.

◆ If desired, replace the Marsala with more chicken broth.

Roasted Winter Vegetables

MAKES 4 SERVINGS

In this simple side dish, butternut squash, parsnips, and carrots are roasted, then coated with a tasty mustard glaze.

1¾	cups butternut squash cut into 1½" pieces
1½	cups parsnips sliced into 1½" pieces
1½	cups carrots sliced into 1½" pieces
1½	cups small shallots
2	teaspoons olive oil
½	cup dry Marsala or apple cider
½	cup defatted reduced-sodium chicken broth
1	teaspoon whole-grain mustard
	Salt and ground black pepper

Preheat the oven to 375°F. Line a 13" × 9" baking dish with foil and coat with no-stick spray.

In a large bowl, combine the squash, parsnips, carrots, and shallots. Drizzle with the oil. Toss well to coat. Transfer to the prepared baking dish.

Bake, turning the vegetables every 10 minutes, for 20 to 25 minutes, or until soft and tender.

In a large no-stick skillet, combine the Marsala or apple cider, broth, and mustard. Mix well. Add the vegetables. Cook over medium heat for 5 minutes, or until the liquid is syrupy. Season with the salt and pepper.

Wolfgang Puck's Menu

	1,500 CALORIES	2,000 CALORIES	2,500 CALORIES
	33-43 G. FAT	44-56 G. FAT	57-69 G. FAT

Breakfast
shredded wheat cereal	¾ cup	1 cup	1¼ cups
skim milk	½ cup	¾ cup	1 cup
grapefruit	½	½	½

Lunch
Thai Shrimp	1 serving	1½ servings	2 servings
crusty French roll	1	2	2
blood orange	1	1	1

Dinner
Roasted Leg of Lamb	1 serving	1 serving	1½ servings
Black-Bean Ragoût	1 serving	1½ servings	2 servings
steamed asparagus	½ cup	½ cup	¾ cup
baked potato with	1	1	1
nonfat sour cream	2 tablespoons	2 tablespoons	2 tablespoons

Snack
nonfat vanilla pudding with	½ cup	¾ cup	¾ cup
low-fat granola and	2 tablespoons	3 tablespoons	3 tablespoons
chopped strawberries	2 tablespoons	3 tablespoons	3 tablespoons

DAILY TOTALS
Calories	1,509	2,003	2,471
Fat (g.)	32	41	55
% of calories from fat	19	18	20
Protein (g.)	109	138	184
Carbohydrates (g.)	197	272	312
Dietary fiber (g.)	28	38	47
Cholesterol (mg.)	352	456	632
Sodium (g.)	1,842	2,671	3,448

Wolfgang Puck

Wolfgang Puck is one of the world's best-known chefs. His Spago restaurants in Los Angeles, Chicago, Las Vegas, Mexico, and Japan have made gourmet pizzas and California-inspired cooking popular around the globe. By focusing on fresh ingredients and spectacular combinations, Puck is able to fuse great taste with good nutrition. He chose this menu for its fantastic international flavors and low-fat profile.

NUTRIENT BONUS

This menu (at 2,000 calories) exceeds the Daily Value for:

Dietary fiber	151%
Vitamin A	113%
Thiamin	135%
Riboflavin	111%
Niacin	142%
Vitamin B$_6$	104%
Vitamin B$_{12}$	136%
Folate	177%
Vitamin C	273%
Iron	126%
Potassium	112%

Thai Shrimp

Thai Shrimp

MAKES 4 SERVINGS

Flavors abound in this perfectly balanced combination of Asian seasonings, sweet shrimp, and mixed baby lettuce. Try it as a light lunch or a first course for an evening meal.

1½ pounds extra-large shrimp, peeled and deveined
Salt and ground black pepper
4 teaspoons peanut oil
2 tablespoons minced shallots
1 tablespoon minced fresh ginger
1 tablespoon minced garlic
2 cups diced tomatoes
2 teaspoons water
1 teaspoon Chinese mustard
¼ cup rice-wine vinegar
2 tablespoons honey
3 cups mixed baby lettuce
2 tablespoons diagonally sliced scallions

Place the shrimp in a shallow dish and sprinkle lightly with the salt and pepper. Drizzle with 2 teaspoons of the oil and toss to mix.

Warm the remaining 2 teaspoons oil in a medium saucepan over medium-high heat. Add the shallots and ginger. Cook for 5 minutes, or until soft. Add the garlic and cook for 1 minute. Stir in the tomatoes and cook for 2 to 3 minutes, or until softened.

In a cup, stir together the water and mustard. Add to the saucepan. Stir in the vinegar and honey. Cook for 1 to 2 minutes, or until the sauce is reduced and thickened.

Add the shrimp. Cook for 2 to 3 minutes, or until the shrimp are opaque.

Serve over the lettuce. Sprinkle with the scallions.

Nutrition Notes

Per serving

Calories 212
Fat 6.1 g.
% of calories from fat 25
Protein 23.6 g.
Carbohydrates 16.6 g.
Dietary fiber 1.9 g.
Cholesterol 202 mg.
Sodium 320 mg.

Kitchen Hint

◆ Chinese mustard is hot and can be found in the Asian section of most supermarkets.

Nutrition Notes

Per serving

Calories 336
Fat 15.7 g.
% of calories from fat 44
Protein 45.1 g.
Carbohydrates 0.4 g.
Dietary fiber 0 g.
Cholesterol 142 mg.
Sodium 375 mg.

Kitchen Hint

◆ Baby lamb is very tender. You may also use a regular leg of lamb. Roast at 450°F for 15 minutes per pound.

Roasted Leg of Lamb

MAKES 4 SERVINGS

Tender and succulent, this garlic-scented dish requires minimum effort and has spectacular results. Lean leg of lamb is a great source of B vitamins, iron, and zinc.

1 leg baby lamb (3 pounds), trimmed of all visible fat
1 clove garlic, slivered
1 tablespoon olive oil
2 tablespoons chopped fresh thyme
¼ teaspoon ground black pepper
½ teaspoon salt

Place the lamb in a 13" × 9" baking dish. With a sharp knife, cut 4 evenly spaced thin slits in the lamb and insert the garlic into the slits. Brush with the oil and sprinkle with the thyme and pepper. Cover and refrigerate for at least 8 hours or up to 24 hours.

Preheat the oven to 450°F.

Sprinkle the lamb with the salt and set in a roasting pan. Roast for 40 minutes, or until an instant-read thermometer inserted in the thickest part of the roast registers 130°F for medium-rare. If you prefer your lamb done medium-well, continue to roast for about 10 minutes until the temperature registers 140°F.

Cut the lamb into thin slices.

Black-Bean Ragoût

MAKES 6 SERVINGS

This fiber-filled accompaniment turns any meat entrée into a nutrition-packed meal.

4	teaspoons olive oil
1	onion, minced
1	clove garlic, minced
2	tablespoons chopped fresh thyme
2	cups dried black beans, soaked overnight
6	cups defatted reduced-sodium chicken broth
1½	teaspoons salt
¼	teaspoon ground black pepper
½	cup chopped tomatoes
8	large leaves fresh basil, chopped

Place the beans in a large bowl. Add cold water to cover and let soak overnight. Drain.

Warm 2 teaspoons of the oil in a Dutch oven over medium heat. Add the onions, garlic, and thyme. Cook for 5 minutes, or until the onions are soft. Drain the beans and add to the pot. Add the broth. Bring to a boil over high heat.

Reduce the heat to medium and simmer, stirring often, for 2 hours, or until the beans are tender and most of the liquid is absorbed. Stir in the salt and pepper.

Transfer 1 cup of the beans to a blender or food processor and puree. Return to the pan and stir in the tomatoes, basil, and the remaining 2 teaspoons oil.

Nutrition Notes

Per serving

Calories 253
Fat 6.2 g.
% of calories from fat 20
Protein 16.2 g.
Carbohydrates 37.7 g.
Dietary fiber 13 g.
Cholesterol 6 mg.
Sodium 787 mg.

Kitchen Hint

◆ Pinto, cannellini, or kidney beans can be substituted for the black beans.

Index

Underscored page references indicate sidebars and boxed text. **Boldface** references indicate photographs.

C

International Conversion Chart

These equivalents have been slightly rounded to make measuring easier.

VOLUME MEASUREMENTS

U.S.	Imperial	Metric
¼ tsp.	–	1.25 ml.
½ tsp.	–	2.5 ml.
1 tsp.	–	5 ml.
1 Tbsp.	–	15 ml.
2 Tbsp. (1 oz.)	1 fl. oz.	30 ml.
¼ cup (2 oz.)	2 fl. oz.	60 ml.
⅓ cup (3 oz.)	3 fl. oz.	80 ml.
½ cup (4 oz.)	4 fl. oz.	120 ml.
⅔ cup (5 oz.)	5 fl. oz.	160 ml.
¾ cup (6 oz.)	6 fl. oz.	180 ml.
1 cup (8 oz.)	8 fl. oz.	240 ml.

WEIGHT MEASUREMENTS

U.S.	Metric
1 oz.	30 g.
2 oz.	60 g.
4 oz. (¼ lb.)	115 g.
5 oz. (⅓ lb.)	145 g.
6 oz.	170 g.
7 oz.	200 g.
8 oz. (½ lb.)	230 g.
10 oz.	285 g.
12 oz. (¾ lb.)	340 g.
14 oz.	400 g.
16 oz. (1 lb.)	455 g.
2.2 lb.	1 kg.

LENGTH MEASUREMENTS

U.S.	Metric
¼"	0.6 cm.
½"	1.25 cm.
1"	2.5 cm.
2"	5 cm.
4"	11 cm.
6"	15 cm.
8"	20 cm.
10"	25 cm.
12" (1')	30 cm.

PAN SIZES

U.S.	Metric
8" cake pan	20 x 4-cm. sandwich or cake tin
9" cake pan	23 x 3.5-cm. sandwich or cake tin
11" x 7" baking pan	28 x 18-cm. baking pan
13" x 9" baking pan	32.5 x 23-cm. baking pan
2-qt. rectangular baking dish	30 x 19-cm. baking pan
15" x 10" baking pan	38 x 25.5-cm. baking pan (Swiss roll tin)
9" pie plate	22 x 4 or 23 x 4-cm. pie plate
7" or 8" springform pan	18 or 20-cm. springform or loose-bottom cake tin
9" x 5" loaf pan	23 x 13-cm. or 2-lb. narrow loaf pan or paté tin
1½-qt. casserole	1.5-liter casserole
2-qt. casserole	2-liter casserole

TEMPERATURES

Farenheit	Centigrade	Gas
140°	60°	–
160°	70°	–
180°	80°	–
225°	110°	–
250°	120°	½
300°	150°	2
325°	160°	3
350°	180°	4
375°	190°	5
400°	200°	6
450°	230°	8
500°	260°	–